To George I. Klein —
my adopted Doctor-Vater /
with deep gratitude a
affection. Bernie Blatt pr

This pioneering study documents the extent and diversity of the impact of the Nietzschean ideas on Soviet literature and culture. It shows for the first time how these ideas, unacknowledged and reworked, entered and shaped that culture and stimulated the imagination of both supporters and detractors of the regime. It addresses key peculiarities of the Soviet reception of Nietzsche – the role of the prerevolutionary interest in the occult, the way revolution figured as an allegorical subject, the intertwining of art and ideology in the obsession with creating a new culture, the continuing Russian interest in Nietzsche as a religious thinker, and the manner in which censorship affected the dynamic of reception and influence. The book offers a fresh perspective on the origins, formative years, and subsequent development of Soviet literature and culture, and raises new issues for research and discussion.

CAMBRIDGE STUDIES IN RUSSIAN LITERATURE

NIETZSCHE AND SOVIET CULTURE

NIETZSCHE AND SOVIET CULTURE

Ally and adversary

EDITED BY

BERNICE GLATZER ROSENTHAL

Professor of History, Fordham University

Published by the Press Syndicate of the University of Cambridge
The Pitt Building, Trumpington Street, Cambridge CB2 1RP
40 West 20th Street, New York, NY 10011–4211, USA
10 Stamford Road, Oakleigh, Melbourne 3166, Australia

© Cambridge University Press, 1994

First published 1994

Printed in Great Britain at the University Press, Cambridge

A catalogue record for this book is available from the British Library

Library of Congress cataloguing in publication data

Nietzsche and Soviet culture: ally and adversary / edited by Bernice Glatzer
Rosenthal.
p.   cm. – (Cambridge studies in Russian literature)
Includes index.
ISBN 0 521 45281 3
1. Soviet Union – Intellectual life – 1917–1970. 2. Nietzsche, Friedrich Wilhelm,
1844–1900 – Influence. I. Rosenthal, Bernice Glatzer, II. Series.
DK266.4.N54   1994
947.084 – dc20   93–29255   CIP

ISBN 0 521 45281 3 hardback

Contents

vii

Illustrations

Contributors

Mikhail Agursky (d. 1991), Associate, Soviet and East European Research Center, Hebrew University of Jerusalem

Henryk Baran, Professor, Slavic Department, State University of New York at Albany

Milka Bliznakov, Professor, College of Architecture, Virginia Polytechnical Institute

Menahem Brinker, Professor, Department of Philosophy, Hebrew University of Jerusalem

Maria Carlson, Associate Professor, Slavic Languages and Literatures Department, University of Kansas

Clare Cavanagh, Associate Professor, Slavic Department, University of Wisconsin

Edith Clowes, Associate Professor, Foreign Language Department, Purdue University

Gregory Freidin, Associate Professor, Slavic Languages and Literature Department, Stanford University

Boris Groys, Independent Scholar, Cologne, Germany

Bengt Jangfeldt, *Artes* (Quarterly Review of Swedish Academy)

Irina Paperno, Associate Professor, Department of Slavic Languages and Literature, University of California at Berkeley

Bernice Glatzer Rosenthal, Professor, History Department, Fordham University

Elaine Rusinko, Associate Professor, Modern Languages and Literatures, University of Maryland

Isabel A. Tirado, Associate Professor, History Department, William Paterson College

Margarita Tupitsyn, Independent Curator, New York City
James von Geldern, Associate Professor, Department of
German and Russian, Macalester College

Acknowledgements

This book grows out of a research conference on Nietzsche and Soviet Culture, held at Fordham University, June 1–3, 1988. Grateful acknowledgement is made to the National Endowment for the Humanities, Division of Research Programs (an independent federal agency), Fordham University, IREX, and the Institute for Modern Russian Culture, for support of the conference. The editor also expresses appreciation to the University Seminars at Columbia University for assistance in preparation of this manuscript for publication. Material drawn from the work was presented to the University Seminar on Slavic History and Culture and to the University Seminar on the History of Legal and Political thought.

Grateful acknowledgement is also made to Sona Aronian, Joachim Baer, Kenneth Brostrom, Yuri Davydov, Maria Deppermann, Luigi Magarotto, Patricia Mueller-Vollmer, and Maxim Tarnowsky for their presentations at the Conference; and to Caryl Emerson, Edith Clowes, John Burt Foster, Malcolm Jones, George L. Kline, Nina Melechen, Susan Ray, Anna Tavis, Victor Terras, and Carol Ueland, for their help at various stages of this project; and to Maria Deppermann for her suggestion of the title.

Abbreviations

Nietzsche's works are cited parenthetically in the text. Numbers in parentheses refer to page numbers, not sections. Unless otherwise specified, the following English translations have been used.

AC	*The Antichrist*, trans. R. J. Hollingdale (Harmondsworth and Baltimore, 1969)
BGE	*Beyond Good and Evil*, trans. W. Kaufmann (New York, 1966)
BT	*The Birth of Tragedy*, trans. W. Kaufmann (New York, 1967)
CW	*The Case of Wagner*, trans. W. Kaufmann (New York, 1967)
D	*Daybreak*, trans. R. J. Hollingdale (Cambridge, 1982)
EH	*Ecce Homo*, trans. W. Kaufmann (New York, 1967)
GM	*Genealogy of Morals*, trans. W. Kaufmann (New York, 1967)
GS	*The Gay Science*, trans. W. Kaufmann (New York, 1974)
H	*On the Advantage and Disadvantage of History for Life*, trans. Peter Preuss (Indianapolis, 1980)
HH	*Human, All Too Human*, trans. Marion Faber and Stephen Lehmann (Lincoln, 1984)
TI	*Twilight of the Idols*, trans. W. Kaufmann and R. J. Hollingdale (Harmondsworth and Baltimore, 1969)
UT	*Untimely Meditations*, trans. R. J. Hollingdale (Cambridge, 1983)
WP	*The Will to Power*, trans. W. Kaufmann and R. J. Hollingdale (New York, 1968)

$\mathcal{Z}$ *Thus Spoke Zarathustra*, trans. R. J. Hollingdale
      (Harmondsworth, 1961)

The following abbreviations are also used in parenthetical citations and in the notes:

LN   *Literaturnoe nasledstvo*
SS   *Sobranie sochinenii* [Collected Works]

Note on transliteration:
Transliteration follows the Library of Congress system, except that y has been substituted for ii in the endings of names in the text, that is Dostoevsky, rather than Dostoevskii, Gorky rather than Gorkii, and names of well-known persons, e.g. Meyerhold, are given as usually spelled in English.

Introduction

Bernice Glatzer Rosenthal

> Every author is surprised anew when a book, as soon as it
> has separated from him, begins to take on a life of its own.
>
> (*HH*, p. 125)

Nietzsche and Soviet Culture? Their very juxtaposition is
shocking. To Americans accustomed to associating the philosopher with individualism, self-fulfillment, artistic creativity,
and post-structuralist literary theories, Nietzsche seems the
polar opposite of Soviet culture, which subjugates the individual to the collective and art to politics. The juxtaposition is
equally shocking to Soviets raised on an image of Nietzsche as
prophet of Nazism; that he was a major influence on their own
culture was unthinkable until very recently. Reinforcing
neglect of the issue was the tendency of scholars, Soviet and
Western alike, to treat the Bolshevik Revolution as a sharp
dividing line in terms of politics and culture and to focus almost
exclusively on politics. Interest in Soviet culture *per se* is relatively new. Cultural historians, however, more interested in
social trends, institutional structure, or popular culture, than
in ideas, have ignored Nietzsche or merely mentioned him in
passing.[1] The same can be said for classic works of literary
scholarship such as Robert Maguire's *Red Virgin Soil* and Rufus
Mathewson's *The Positive Hero in Russian Literature*.[2] Katerina
Clark asserts that "God-building" formed the "subtext of high
Stalinist culture" and notes Nietzsche's importance to Zamiatin, Tynianov, and Kaverin,[3] but does not go into detail. The
few scholars who offer more extensive discussions of Nietzsche's
influence limit themselves to a particular author and ignore the
larger cultural context.[4] Thus, although American scholar-

ship[5] amply documented Nietzsche's towering presence in pre-revolutionary culture, Nietzsche's overall importance directly and by proxy for Soviet culture was unacknowledged. That Nietzsche might have crucial explanatory significance on the sources, nature, and evolution of Soviet culture as a whole, was not even considered.

This volume restores the hitherto buried Nietzschean elements of Soviet culture, reveals the channels by which they flowed into and helped shape that culture, and documents the diversity and importance of their impact. It was not so much the direct influence of Nietzsche's ideas, though that was certainly found, that accounts for his continued presence in the culture, but the persistence, in transmuted form, of ideas and images that had become embedded in the culture before the Bolshevik Revolution. Without knowledge of Nietzsche's own writings and of previous Russian adaptations and interpretations of his ideas, the subsequent process of transmutation is virtually invisible. The first phase of Nietzsche's Russian reception provides the key to this process.[6]

Russians learned about Nietzsche in the 1890s. His popularizers were artists and writers, who hailed Nietzsche as the prophet of a new culture of art and beauty, and of a new kind of human being – courageous, creative, and free. His ideas served as a battering ram to smash "the old tables of values" (Z, pp. 51, 52); his call for a "revaluation of all values" provided intellectuals with a philosophical rationale for self-assertion, artistic creativity, and enjoyment of life, and sparked a search for a new "ruling idea" by which to live. Dmitri S. Merezhkovsky, the initiator of Russian Symbolism, melded Nietzsche and French estheticism with ideas taken from Russian writers, Dostoevsky and Soloviev especially, into a virtual religion of art. Worship of beauty was its first commandment. The esthetes of the World of Art movement, including Sergei Diaghilev, future impresario of Ballet Russe, were devotees of Nietzsche and Wagner. Nietzsche justified Maksim Gorky's break with Populism. Gorky's early short stories featured Nietzschean hobo heroes – amoral, asocial, hard. Contemptuous of weakness and cowardice, Gorky frequently quoted Nietzsche's dictum: "Man is something that must be overcome" (*Z*, pp. 65, 83). Ultimately, Nietzsche provided him with a new ideal – a Russian Superman, a warrior leader devoted to the people, but using the whip on them as well. Nietzsche's Russian admirers stressed what they called "the inner man," – artistic, cultural, and psychological issues.

Around the turn of the century, a new movement emerged – "God-seeking." Once again, Merezhkovsky was the initiator. Having "turned to Christ," but also responding to Nietzsche's critique of Christianity, Merezhkovsky maintained that a new Revelation was imminent, a positive Christianity which sanctioned the passions, human creativity, and will. Together with his wife, Zinaida Hippius, and their associate, Dmitri Filosofov, he founded the Religious-Philosophic Society of St. Petersburg. The Society featured debates between intellectuals and high Church officials on such issues as Christian attitudes to sex, and the excommunication of Tolstoi. The meetings attracted capacity audiences and became the fountainhead of a religious renaissance. A diverse movement, "God-seeking" encompassed Symbolist writers, Idealist philosophers, and others. The Symbolist writers Viacheslav Ivanov, Andrei Bely, and Alexander Blok, developed an archetype of the Dionysian Christ and invested art with redemptive significance. V. V. Rozanov railed against the Christian apotheosis of celibacy and virginity. Philosophers such as Nikolai Berdiaev, Simeon Frank, and Lev Shestov, challenged traditional conceptions of good and evil and emphasized non-rational factors in the human psyche, each in his own way. Most "God-seekers" (Sergei Bulgakov is a notable exception) regarded Nietzsche as a mystic and a prophet, unintentionally pointing the way to a renovated Christianity. Pavel Florensky's Orthodox theology is in part his response to "God-seeking" and to Nietzsche.

Around 1904, some hitherto apolitical "God-seekers" began to turn their attention to social problems. Viacheslav Ivanov urged the Symbolists to progress from symbol to myth, to create new myths (or reformulate old ones) around which intelligentsia and people could unite. During the Revolution of

1905, he supported Georgy Chulkov's doctrine of Mystical Anarchism, a politicized Dionysianism which combined unlimited personal freedom with belongingness in a loving community. Not government or law, but love (Eros), sacrifice, and myth would cement it.

"God-building," another response to the Revolution of 1905, was a Marxist surrogate religion, a new myth to inspire the workers to fight and die for socialism. Gorky and Anatole Lunacharsky, future Bolshevik Commissar of Enlightenment, were its main formulators. Nietzsche provided Lunacharsky with a means to reconcile estheticism and Marxism, to argue that art can change consciousness, and is thus a powerful weapon in the revolutionary struggle. He was interested in religion and myth before he read Nietzsche, but Nietzsche reinforced his interest. Unlike most Marxists, Lunacharsky viewed religion positively as a vehicle for humankind's highest aspirations. He called Socialism the Religion of Labor. "God-building" reflects a collectivist application of *The Birth of Tragedy*. Its formulators championed both liberation of the instincts and transcendence of self in the cultic ecstasy (or enthusiasm) of a modern equivalent of the Dionysian rites.[7] Superior individuals, they claimed, achieve true self-fulfillment by going beyond themselves in artistic and social creativity and in performing heroic deeds. They developed a myth of the rebellious (Promethean) masses as a source of life-giving energy and urged intellectuals to renounce egotism and think in terms of "we," rather than "I". Gorky maintained that the people are the source of all creativity, that it is the people who create God and not vice versa. The People, the spirit of collective humanity, not God, is the proper object of worship. He also believed, however, that strong aggressive leaders must channel popular energy and enthusiasm. This belief underlay his admiration for Lenin and his later cooperation with Stalin.

Strictly speaking, their ally Aleksandr Bogdanov (Lunacharsky's brother-in-law), was not a "God-builder," but the doctrine was based on his epistemology, and his novels *Red Star* (1908) and *Engineer Menni* (1912) represent his version of myth-creation. Intended to inspire the workers to continue their struggle, they present a vision of a future Communist society on Mars. Lenin vehemently opposed "God-building," for he detested religion in any form, and because Bogdanov's anti-authoritarian collectivist ethos contradicted his own idea of a centralized hierarchical organization. In 1909, he had Bogdanov expelled from the Party. Cut off from political activity, Bogdanov ruminated on cultural issues. His conclusion that workers must develop their own culture in order to liberate themselves psychologically and spiritually from the bourgeoisie, became the basis of the Proletkult (proletarian culture) movement after the Revolution.

"God-seekers" and "God-builders" alike conflated Nietzsche's views on myth and cult with Richard Wagner's ideal of the *Gesamtkunstwerk* (total art work)[8] and with Viacheslav Ivanov's ideal of a cultic theater; the result was a Nietzsche/Wagner/Ivanov syndrome (Lars Kleberg's term) that exerted a wide influence on the art and thought of the era. Constantly polemicizing with and cross-fertilizing one another, both groups recognized the impact of art on the human psyche and envisioned a refurbished cultic theater as the progenitor of a new communal consciousness. They believed that artists and intellectuals could deliberately create a new culture. Expecting the Revolution to engender a new man: strong, creative, beautiful, and loving, they interpreted Nietzsche's "will to power" as cultural creativity rather than coercive political power. The very point of developing a new communal consciousness was to obviate the need for coercion. Psychic unity, resting on the passions and the instincts and evoked by art, would displace the rational self-interest of classic liberalism. Phrases such as the "unity of art and life," the "estheticization of life," and the "theatricalization of life," dot the writings of both groups, as does Nietzsche's phrase, "man is a bridge and not a goal" (*Z*, p. 215).

Apocalyptically oriented, both groups fused in various ways the eschatology of Russian sectarians, Soloviev, Merezhkovsky, Wagner, Bakunin, and Ibsen; to this brew the "God-builders" added revolutionary Marxism. Also important was the Slavophile ideal of *sobornost'*, unity in love and freedom, which they politicized to mean anarchism or syndicalism. Conflating *sobornost'* with visions of a cultic society that derived largely from Nietzsche and Wagner, the "God-seekers" emphasized an organic society whose members retain their individuality. The "God-building" version, "revolutionary *sobornost'*," to use Richard Stites's term, demanded almost total fusion of the individual with the collective.

Meanwhile, a kind of vulgar Nietzscheanism, a popular cult of the Superman which sanctioned immorality, abuse of power, promiscuity, self-will, anarchic individualism, and hedonism was percolating through Russian society. Nietzsche was widely interpreted to stand for sexual liberation and the return of the repressed rather than for sublimation, even though he often does argue for the latter. As early as 1904 Nietzsche was a household name; by 1911 all of his major works were available in Russian translation. Familiarity with his basic ideas, directly and as popularized by Russian and Western artists and writers, was simply assumed.

Symbolism, "God-seeking," and "God-building" served as points of departure for subsequent artists, thinkers, and political activists, and helped define the central issues of debates on art, literature, culture, and society which continued on through the twenties and were officially resolved in the early thirties. Symbolism entered a period of crisis around 1909–10; individual Symbolists remained creative, but went their separate ways. Two new literary/artistic movements, Futurism and Acmeism, arose to challenge it. These movements appropriated aspects of the Symbolist legacy, but read Nietzsche their own way, highlighting a different set of images and ideas, typically without acknowledging their source(s), for recognition was taken for granted. Indeed, differences between them were in many respects an argument over Nietzsche. The ideas of Bergson or Husserl, by contrast, were explicated precisely because they were new and as such unfamiliar to most readers. During the war, Nietzsche was associated with German militarism and Wagner's operas were banned from the Imperial Theaters, but around 1916, the "Nietzsche/Wagner/Ivanov" syndrome reemerged, to be adapted by the Bolsheviks to the new educational and propaganda tasks of the Soviet era. In the 1920s and 1930s, advocates of competing esthetic 'isms and cultural policies justified their respective positions with arguments taken from Nietzsche and/or his prerevolutionary Russian interpreters.

Despite Krupskaia's (Lenin's widow's) removal of Nietzsche's works (along with those of other "Idealists" such as Plato, Kant, and Soloviev), from the People's Libraries in 1923, his ideas continued to circulate. Early Soviet intellectuals and artists retained the cultural baggage of the Silver Age (roughly 1890–1914); privately owned works by and about Nietzsche passed from hand to hand, and young people heard about his ideas from older friends and colleagues. Symbolists found employment in early Soviet educational and cultural institutions, as teachers in the Proletkult schools, for example. New books on Nietzsche and reprints of earlier works on his ideas were brought out by newly legalized private publishers during the NEP (New Economic Policy – partial restoration of capitalism to provide incentives for productivity) years, 1921–27. State presses published Jack London, Upton Sinclair, and H. G. Wells, all admirers of Nietzsche, in hundreds of thousands of copies. Also translated were works by Romain Rolland, a French socialist interested in Nietzsche and Wagner. Soviet artists, intellectuals, and diplomats visited the West (ties were particularly close with Weimar Germany and, surprisingly, with Fascist Italy) and learned of the latest trends in art and thought there: new applications of Nietzsche by German Modernists, for example. Even in the Stalin era, two new books on Nietzsche were issued, and by state publishing houses at that: M. G. Leiteizen's *Nietzsche and Finance Capital*, with an Introduction by Anatole Lunacharsky (1928) and B. M. Bernadiner's *Nietzsche: Philosopher of Fascism* (1934). Between 1932 and 1934, Socialist Realism was established as the only permissible mode of artistic and literary expression. From then on it is important to distinguish between an official culture, Stalinism, and a non-official, often suppressed culture that began to surface after his death; Nietzschean ideas informed both of them. Continuously reformulated and re-adapted, they form a major link between prerevolutionary and Soviet culture, while at the same time illustrating the distinctive aspects of his Russian/Soviet reception and the concrete historical circumstances that shaped it. No serious studies of Nietzsche appeared in the Soviet period; the subject was too politicized.

Because Nietzsche was *persona non grata* for much of the Soviet era, his influence was exerted indirectly. Soviet readers received Nietzsche second-hand through the writings of Gorky, Lunacharsky, Mayakovsky, the Proletkult theorist Pavel Kerzhentsev, the theater and film critic Adrian Piotrovsky, the classical scholar Tadeusz Zielinski (one of the few academic admirers of Nietzsche), and Bogdanov. The latter's ideas, taken up, often crudely, by Proletkult activists, were propagated in countless pamphlets and periodicals; *Red Star* was reprinted in 1918, 1922, 1928, and a stage version was produced by the Proletkult theater in 1920. Oswald Spengler's *The Decline of the West* was still another conduit for Nietzsche (and Goethe), whose influence Spengler explicitly acknowledged. Translated into Russian as *Zakat Evropa* (*The Decline of Europe*), the book was banned in the Soviet Union, but its main ideas were discussed in Soviet journals and reinforced Bolshevik convictions of their superiority over the "rotting West." In many cases, it is virtually impossible to tell whether or not a particular Soviet writer or political activist read Nietzsche and/or one or more of the authors listed above, or simply picked up ideas which were "in the air." In this volume, the adjectival term Nietzschean will be used for ideas and images derived from him directly and indirectly.

Successive generations of writers, artists, and political activists extracted what they deemed relevant to their current concerns from the general stock of Nietzschean ideas and images. Reading Nietzsche is a very different experience than reading Marx. Rather than doctrine or ideology, Nietzsche created striking slogans, alluring images, and provocative ideas that often stuck with people long after their initial impression. People read their own meaning into the "Superman," the "revaluation of values," the "new values on new tablets." Nietzsche's memorable phrases and emotionally charged images became detached from their context and took on a life of their own. They exemplify that ineluctable process whereby ideas seize the imagination of an entire generation. Nietzsche keeps appearing, directly and by proxy, in discussions of art, literature, and cultural policy – rarely as an exclusive factor but, time and again, as a contributing factor. These contributions cumulatively shaped Soviet attempts at "culture-building," a dominant issue in Nietzsche's works and one which permeates our study. This does not imply that any Soviet intellectual who rejected or ignored Nietzsche was in the grips of a philistine state ideology.

This volume will avoid terms such as "deformed" or "distorted," for it is not intended to answer the question of what Nietzsche really meant, nor to promote one particular interpretation of his ideas. Rather, it will focus on which of his ideas were used, what the Soviet writer, artist, or political activist did with them, and why. Although most of the chapters treat literature, our focus is not so much on the text *per se*, but on the larger cultural context in which it was written and understood as part of a continuous, often covert, dialogue. Reaction to Nietzsche stimulated new and creative responses to his ideas on the part of writers, artists, and political activists. For this reason, even rejection of Nietzsche often denotes his influence.

If Nietzsche is not mentioned by name, how does one recognize his influence, what was the nature of that influence at different stages of Russian and Soviet history, and what accounts for its amazing durability? One cannot really expect artists, writers, and political activists to make statements such as "I read Nietzsche and then decided to paint the Superman." In some cases, we know for a fact that the writer read Nietzsche. In other cases, his influence can be deduced by the presence of parallel texts, ideas clearly associated with Nietzsche, or a "Nietzschean" vocabulary – the latter signifying one important way in which the philosopher's ideas were absorbed into the culture. Assessing his influence is a subtle process; it entails dealing with intangibles, digging up the "buried Nietzsche" (John Burt Foster's term), discovering ideas and assumptions taken for granted and hence undefended and unexplained by their advocates. Foster's seminal work *Heirs to Dionysus* focuses on the appropriation of Nietzsche by great writers of the West.[9] Edith Clowes's *The Transformation of Moral Consciousness* details how Nietzsche's influence led to reformulation of key intelligentsia myths before the Bolshevik Revolution. Our task is even more complex and elusive, for it goes beyond the issue of what individual writers took from Nietzsche to his influence on an entire culture. Complicating the issue even further, the transfer of ideas from one national culture to another entails shifts of meaning and emphasis. Nuances are lost in translation; the translator ascribes his/her own meanings, especially if there are no exact equivalents for certain words or concepts. Other mutations and transformations occur in the intrinsic and subtle process by which the original idea is adapted to the dominant ideas, values, and beliefs of the host culture.[10] On the other hand, as Graham Parkes notes, the responses of foreign interpreters who read their own cultural assumptions into the text are not necessarily distortions, but "may serve to open us to hitherto concealed aspects of the corpus."[11]

The contributors to this volume employ a variety of methodologies, including textual analysis. Where it is possible to establish a writer's specific dependence on Nietzsche, the authors have done so. Their chapters are also informed, in a general sort of way, by methodologies which go beyond the text, not so much to explain what the writer really meant, but to recapture the context in which the text was written, the unstated assumptions that permeate it, the ways it was interpreted by different people at different times. Here the insights of a new field, cultural studies, are relevant.[12] Not a discipline, but an area where different disciplines intersect, its practitioners move beyond the traditional view of culture as the product of a small creative elite to a more comprehensive view of the broad spectrum of practices through which a society constructs and transmits the meanings and values that inform its everyday life and which cumulatively comprise its culture.

Scholars concerned with such issues cross conventional disciplinary boundaries in order to rethink the nature and scope of the workings of culture in a given era. For example, the social analyses of Jürgen Habermas, Clifford Geertz, and Claude Lévi-Strauss draw on linguistics and literary theory. Historians use anthropology and literary theory to reconceptualize their subjects; they study mentalities, read historical events and narratives as cultural constructions, texts, and performances. Intellectual history is being reformulated as cultural history in order to treat ideas and their diffusion as part of a broader socio-cultural matrix which includes popular as well as high culture and no longer assumes a one-way trickle-down process and an intellectually passive public.[13] Literary scholars and theorists such as Hans Robert Jauss, Wolfgang Iser, Mikhail Bakhtin, Yuri Lotman, and Boris Uspensky have expanded, sometimes radically, on the sociological approach to literary criticism and have situated literary and artistic texts in their historical context in order to explicate their hidden meaning(s) and the way they changed over time. The ideas of Michel Foucault, a psychopathologist turned historian and philosopher, and himself indebted to Nietzsche, were taken up by literary scholars, and more recently, by historians. These approaches can help establish a particular writer's or movement's link to Nietzsche.

Each generation reacts to a different set of experiences which condition its world-view, including its interpretation and use of ideas received from the past.[14] Reception theory enables scholars to reconstitute the psychological and social factors that conditioned a particular generation's "horizons of expectations," "horizons of experiences," and "systems of references," by elucidating the assumptions, connections, and inferences made by different generations of readers.[15] According to Hans Robert Jauss, arguably the principal architect of reception theory, a literary work is not a monument that monologically reveals its timeless essence, but is much more like an orchestration that strikes ever new resonances among its readers in a continuous dialogue between a work and its audience. Wolfgang Iser speaks of an "implied reader" who fills in "indeterminacies" and "gaps" by means of shared associations and codes.

If Jauss stresses historical continuity, Foucaldian theory stresses ruptures, fissures, discontinuity, gaps, voids, absences, limits, divisions, erasures (forgetting). It is also true that he wants to examine long-term trends to see changes in economic and political processes. According to Foucault, particular discursive practices isolate each epoch; each discursive formation has its own "language," its own "rules" on what can and cannot be said, and its own mechanism for enforcing them. A particular discourse implies a play of prescriptions that designates its principles of exclusion and choice, things registered in the interstices of the text, its gaps and absences. To Foucault, an "author" is an "initiator of discursive practices," the originator of a theory, a tradition, or a discipline "within which new books and authors can proliferate." Marx and Engels, he states, "not only made possible a certain number of analogies that could be adopted by future texts, but, as importantly . . . cleared a space for the introduction of elements not their own . . . made possible a certain number of differences with respect to [their] books, concepts, and hypotheses."[16] Nietzsche certainly fits that definition of an (influential) author and Foucault used him in exactly that way. "For myself, I prefer to utilize [rather than comment on] the writers I like. The only valid tribute to thought such as Nietzsche's is precisely to use it, to reform it, to make it groan and protest. And if the commentator says that I am unfaithful to Nietzsche, that is of absolutely no interest."[17] Foucault adapted Nietzsche's ideas to his own theories of language, knowledge, and power, especially on the "rules" that govern the relations basic to discourse.

"Discourse" or "dialogue" is a central theme of Mikhail Bakhtin's work. For the problematic of this volume the differences in his and the above-noted conceptions of these terms is less important than what they have in common – an emphasis on the political and social (including genealogical) aspects of the text. Bakhtin was arguing against the Russian Formalists on the one hand and the Marxists on the other. He insisted that study of literature must overcome both the abstract Formalist approach to literature, briefly, reduction of literary art to technique, device, or style, and the equally abstract ideological approach of the Marxists, who reduced literature to class content. Bakhtin insisted that verbal discourse is a social phenomenon, that meaning is not contained in the text alone, but is inherent in the text's relation to a wider system of meaning, to other texts, codes, and norms in literature and in society as a whole. He treated canonization, reification, and reaccentuation (new readings) as constants of the socio-literary process.[18] The Soviet semioticians Yuri Lotman and Boris Uspensky similarly stress the social aspects of literature; they view the text as part of the larger culture, a dynamic system connected to past experience.

These literary theorists pay special attention to the historical and sociopolitical aspects of language, as do many intellectual and cultural historians. They note that words change their meaning over time, that entirely new words are coined and other words go out of use as the underlying values and beliefs of a society, its ruling myths, change. Each generation has its own vocabulary, its own tone, texture, and style. Even within the same age-cohort, different "fellowships of discourse" exist, each with its own "verbal clusters," to use Foucault's terms. Bakhtin spoke of "dialects" peculiar to social, ideological, professional, and generational groups, which intersect with one another, for there are many "dialects" spoken at the same time. In this context, Bakhtin alluded to the distinctive language of the Nietzscheans.[19]

Such insights enable scholars to follow the trail of ideas known to be influenced by Nietzsche from the pre-1909 period to Stalin and to disclose the hidden messages or codes in signs, words, or phrases that express one thing, but intimate another, the latter often more powerfully. Words, phrases, and images that fairly shouted "Nietzsche" to contemporaries include "fullness of life" (*polnota zhizni* – Nietzsche's *Lebensfülle*), "affirmation of life," "estheticization of life," "union of life and art," "theatricalization of life." Gorky's allusions to "Man" (with a capital M), "the will to [some goal]," are Nietzsche-specific, directly traceable to him or his early twentieth-century Russian popularizers. Other terms such as Promethean or Titanic (Prometheus was a Titan) took on a Nietzschean coloration, for they were used to describe the Nietzschean traits of rebelliousness, daring, defiance of the gods. Indeed Nietzsche himself used "Promethean" that way (*BT*, pp. 69–71). Titanic also connotes energy, a particularly desired attribute of the New Soviet Man. Copious use of words such as exuberance, energy, joyousness, passion (*pafos*), tragic, tragedy, value, valuation, selfhood, ecstasy, and enthusiasm (*entuziazm*, a foreign borrowing) – typically in distinctive "verbal clusters," signal the association with Nietzsche. The rhetoric of Marxists influenced by him conveys a spirit entirely different from that of Plekhanov or Lenin.[20]

In his essay "Kafka and His Precursors," Jorge Luis Borges claimed that Kafka's work somehow influenced writers who preceded him because they begin to look Kafkaesque once one has read Kafka himself. "Each writer," Borges states, "creates his precursors. His work modifies our conception of the past, as it will modify the future."[21] Nietzsche's striking impact led his admirers and detractors alike to perceive other writers as precursors, heirs, or kindred spirits and to frame them metonymically with Nietzsche, as links in a literary series. Western writers associated with Nietzsche include Goethe, Byron, Ibsen, Walt Whitman, and Max Stirner (1806–56, German anarchist and author of *The Ego and Its Own*, 1845), Georges Sorel (1847–1922, author of *Reflections on Violence*, translated into Russian in 1906, and "The Decomposition of Marxism," 1908), and Henri Bergson. The latter two wrote during the height of Nietzsche's and Wagner's popularity in France. Russian writers and thinkers so treated included such "Nietzscheans before Nietzsche" (Victor Terras's phrase) as Leontiev, Lermontov, and (for different reasons), Tiutchev, Dostoevsky,[22] and Pushkin. Political radicals conflated Nietzsche's views with Bakunin's anarchism and atheism, with Herzen's attacks on philistinism (*meshchanstvo*), which Nietzsche knew,[23] and with Darwin, despite Nietzsche's critique of the latter. These chains of associations intensified the impact of Nietzschean ideas. As Nietzsche's name became unmentionable except in a pejorative sense, these authors provided cover for discussing his ideas; their names became code words. In the 1920s, popular Futuristic literature commingled science fiction (including Jules Verne and H. G. Wells) with notions of Communist supermen and Nikolai Fedorov's (1828–1903)[24] visions of the conquest of nature, including death. Nietzschean themes are also evident in early Soviet historical novels.[25] Russians often read Nietzsche as the culmination of German Romanticism and Idealism, which had entered the mainstream of Russian culture in the course of the nineteenth century by way of the Slavophiles and Westernizers, including Marxists. Radicals of the 1860s helped prepare the ground for Nietzsche by their total rejection of existing social arrangements and conventional morality.[26] Bakhtin listed the "trial of the Nietzschean man"[27] as one of the organizing ideas of nineteenth- and early twentieth-century literature. The occult doctrines of Rudolf Steiner and P. D. Uspensky incorporated ideas taken from Nietzsche.

More than any other single work, *The Birth of Tragedy from the Spirit of Music* (1871) shaped the Russian reception of Nietzsche. Russian readers focused on its anti-rationalist, vitalist, and esthetic aspects. Myths are essential to the health of a culture, Nietzsche maintained, but the scientific spirit is undermining belief in myth. Excessive rationalism is sapping the vital sources of creativity itself. He asserted that life can be justified only in esthetic terms and that art is the metaphysical activity of humankind. Nietzsche considered Greek tragic drama, which affirms life despite its cruelty and suffering, the summit of human culture, a perfect balance of Apollo and Dionysus. According to Nietzsche, Apollonian (Olympian) culture rests on a hidden substratum of suffering and knowledge. The Apollonian image gives form to the boundless energy of Dionysus, covers the Dionysian reality with a veil of beauty. Nietzsche prophesied the collapse of contemporary illusions, the rebirth of tragedy from the spirit of music. As he used the terms, Apollo symbolizes clarity, harmony, measure, the form-giving power which engenders illusions, images, and visions. Dionysus is wild intoxication, ceaseless striving, boundless energy; his artistic expression is music and dance (even though Apollo was the Greek god of music). Apollo also signifies light, structure, individuation, reason, cosmos, ethics, while Dionysus signifies darkness, dissolution, loss of self, instinct, chaos, the overcoming of limits and norms. Like male and female, the two impulses unite and come apart, giving birth to new and more powerful forms of art, as in lyric poetry and Attic tragedy, the latter growing out of the cult of Dionysus and involving the entire community. Nietzsche's interpretation of the Dionysian rites was esthetic, or esthetic–psychological, but his Russian admirers, especially Viacheslav Ivanov, emphasized their religious and social aspects. Ivanov, moreover, invested the chorus with political significance, which Nietzsche did not.

Mingling idiosyncratically with these ideas were other Nietzschean images and slogans – the Superman, the will to power, Christianity as a slave morality, a new morality beyond good and evil, the death of God, and eternal recurrence. Not professional philosophers (who, in any case, do not agree on what Nietzsche really meant), Nietzsche's Russian and Soviet popularizers misunderstood or simplified some of these ideas. Nietzsche implied that the Superman would emerge only in the distant future, but some Russians expected his advent much sooner. The image of the Superman that emerges in Nietzsche's writings is vague. It can be understood as a new being who pursues lofty visions, dares to reach into the unknown, creates ever new goals, unimpeded by traditions, conventions, or other people, but it can also be vulgarized, and was, to denote sheer physical strength, gigantic stature, crude hedonism, pitilessness on principle. Nietzsche's "eternal recurrence" is a cosmic phenomenon, endless repetition of the same, as distinct from and opposed to theories of progress which assume an ultimately perfected higher state. Russians interpreted the concept in a variety of ways. To occult philosophers, it meant reincarnation; to Symbolists and Acmeists, historical cycles and the rebirth of Hellenic civilization in their own time. To the Futurists, "eternal recurrence" meant the end of history, of linear time, and even of death. Whether Nietzsche's "will to power" is an esthetic or a political concept is a matter of continuing dispute. In English, as in German, the verb "machen" (to make) can mean "to compel" or it can mean "to produce." The same ambiguity exists in the German phrase, the "Wille zur Macht." After the Bolshevik Revolution, new practical considerations, the need to reach a mass audience, virtually mandated simplification and even vulgarization. In the mass press, Nietzsche's name became a synonym for -isms or attitudes (especially individualism) hated by the Soviet regime, even as it covertly appropriated aspects of his thought.

Nietzsche's influence touched a deep chord in the Russian psyche that continued to reverberate long after his initial reception. The pictorial aspects of his images possessed multiple layers of meaning which resonated through the unconscious and also had the advantage in Soviet society, once they had become fully absorbed into the culture, of being readily accessible to illiterate or semi-literate people. There were no "pure" Nietzscheans in the sense of disciples. Ideas and images derived from his writings were fused, in various ways, with compatible elements in the Russian religious, intellectual, and cultural heritage, and with Marxism, as we will see. A similar process went on among the nationalities of the Russian Empire and the Soviet Union. Political activists took what was useful to them; artists and writers reworked images and ideas which struck their imagination and seemed relevant to their particular situation.

Why Nietzsche? Precisely because he did not offer a coherent philosophical system, his aphorisms were suited to selective adaptation on behalf of a wide range of artistic, literary, and political positions. His striking images and aphorisms could easily be detached from their text and grafted on to a wide variety of ideas, programs, and goals. Nietzsche could be read as an iconoclastic critic of old myths ("theoretical man," "idealism," "Christianity," "Populism") or as the proponent of new, though only vaguely described myths (Dionysus, the Superman, "eternal recurrence," "new values on new tablets"). Augmenting Nietzsche's continued relevance was the polaristic nature of his thought, for it accommodated diametrically opposed opinions and changed conditions. Apollo/Dionysus, order/chaos, ascent/descent, male/female, apocalypse/eternal recurrence, the moment/eternity, disintegration/reintegration, individuation/loss of self, poverty/plenitude, Christ/anti-Christ, sickness/health, slave/master – either could be stressed, depending upon the situation. Different aspects of his thought could appeal to unmaskers and simulators, sensualists and ascetics, egalitarians and elitists, liberators and tyrants. The Dionysian side of the polarity inspired revolt against old forms and structures in every area of life: the Apollonian side signaled the restoration of order, reintegration around a new myth. Either way, Nietzsche was relevant; his ideas were infinitely adaptable.

Any explanation of why Nietzsche's ideas took root and sprouted in all sorts of different ways must take into account the particular situation of late Imperial and early Soviet Russia. Russian intellectuals learned about him at the very time that their own "ruling ideas" or "myths" were collapsing. Rapid industrialization was reshaping the social structure, disestablishing traditional elites, undermining long-held beliefs and values. The transformations were exhilarating and anxiety-provoking at the same time. They provided new opportunities for self-fulfillment, fostered confidence in human powers, but also uprooted people psychologically and spiritually and, in some circles, aroused fear of the new "mass-men" of the burgeoning cities. Nietzsche's emphasis on myth, on destroying outmoded values and creating new life-affirming ones, spoke directly to Russians' most pressing concerns. His ideas particularly appealed to those who did not consider the *fin-de-siècle* West a model to be emulated. By the 1890s, moreover, the Enlightenment ideal was also fading in the West. Nietzsche's soaring popularity all over Europe reflected and reinforced the beginnings of a continent-wide cultural crisis.

In Russia, the cultural crisis was intertwined with political, social, economic, religious, and national conflicts of great intensity. They exploded in the Revolution of 1905 and again in February and October 1917. Nietzschean ideas helped explain the collapse of the old order and furnished persons living through it with a new vocabulary, new personal and cultural ideals. They became components of numerous utopian visions whose formulators wished to shape the future their own way, unimpeded by the laws of history, or (in some cases), by the laws of nature. Nietzschean Prometheanism blended with Fedorovian visions of the conquest of nature, including death, and with the Hegelian/Marxist conception of the leap from necessity to freedom.

Nietzschean categories described the bloody and cruel realities of the Civil War and highlighted the importance of naked power in a way that rationalist liberalism and Marxism could not. Intellectuals attributed the "collapse of humanism" to the "spirit of music," the triumph of culture over civilization; they considered the masses the "new barbarians" destined to revitalize a decadent civilization. Nietzschean paradigms, typically in combination with other 'isms, explained the earthquake that had shattered their world, but also offered hope for a future utopia. Nietzschean ideas permeated early Soviet debates on "proletarian" vs. "bourgeois" culture and the proper definition of each, the new educational tasks of art, the needs of mass audiences, and the role of artists, writers, and political activists in addressing them.

After the Bolshevik Revolution explicitly political considerations guided Soviet appropriations of Nietzsche. Censorship had been reinstated during the Civil War and relaxed, but not eliminated, in the NEP years. Aspects of Nietzsche that were compatible with the Bolshevik culture-building agenda were adapted to political theater, workers' clubs, mass festivals, literature, film, and art. Alternate readings of Nietzschean ideas were discouraged by removing some of their carriers from the scene and harassing others. In 1921, the Acmeist poet Nikolai Gumilev was executed. In 1922/23, Berdiaev, Frank, and other Nietzsche-influenced philosophers were forced into exile. Nietzschean ideas, typically not identified as such, infused Soviet theorizing on a wide variety of artistic and cultural issues. Political control of culture tightened after 1925;

its ultimate consequence was the establishment of a new official culture in the mid '30s, the institution of one, and only one, correct reading of Marx, Engels, and Lenin, and the proscription of non-Marxist thinkers, including Nietzsche. The stages by which this occurred cannot be detailed here.[28] Our concern is the culmination of this process: on the one hand, a new myth, new rituals, and a new god, Stalin as Superman – on the other, a non-official culture, that was also indebted to Nietzsche. Some of its spokesmen are included in this volume: Nikolai Gumilev, Osip Mandelstam, Boris Pasternak, Evgeny Zamiatin, Mikhail Bulgakov, Gustav Shpet, A. A. Meier, and Mikhail Bakhtin. In Stalin's time, Bakhtin was known only to a small circle.[29]

Bakhtin's writings perpetuate, in drastically changed conditions, key themes of early twentieth-century Russian literature and culture. His debt to Nietzsche by way of Ivanov and Zelinski, and perhaps directly, is clear.[30] Bakhtin's single most important concept – dialogue or discourse – ratifies Nietzsche's view that "Dialogue is the perfect conversation" (*HH*, pp. 191–92). It also carries on Modernist poets' apotheosis of the spoken word.[31] Bakhtin's insistence on the pluralistic structure of works and the interplay of their heterogeneous elements is an application to literature of the interaction of Apollo and Dionysus. The carnival consciousness Bakhtin exalts in his famous book on Rabelais (1965; English translation, *Rabelais and His World*, 1968) is a form of Dionysian revelry. His celebration of carnival inversion of hierarchies recalls Nietzsche's belief that "under the charm of the Dionysian" the union between man and man and between man and nature is reaffirmed. "Now the slave is a free man, now all the rigid hostile barriers that necessity, caprice, or 'impudent convention' have fixed between man and man are broken" (*BT*, p. 37). Bakhtin's bitter mocking carnival laughter is a variant of Nietzsche's dictum "learn to laugh!" (*Z*, p. 306). Nietzsche's physiologism and his earthiness ("Be true to the earth," *Z*, p. 13) also appear in *Rabelais and His World*. Bakhtin, however, disapproved of Nietzsche's "estheticized philosophy" and of his amoralism. Whether or not Bakhtin is a religious thinker is disputed, but the existential/vitalist aspects of Nietzsche's world-view are alien to Bakhtin's more spiritual/cosmic approach, as is the Superman.

DeStalinization, the discrediting of an established myth, fostered an interest in early twentieth-century artists and writers, including those influenced by Nietzsche, and eventually, in Nietzsche himself. New scholarly studies of the World of Art movement began to appear in the 1970s. Symbolist poetry was read for its spiritual content, not because Bely and Blok "accepted" the Bolshevik Revolution. The "God-seekers" were rediscovered; typewritten copies of their works circulated illegally since the 1970s. Evgeny Yevtushenko found a role model in the rebellious Futurist poet, Mayakovsky. Rehabilitation of banned writers began.

Under Gorbachev (1985–91), the unofficial culture surfaced and became a torrent. In 1988, plans were announced to publish a series of forty volumes on Russian Philosophy as a supplement to the journal *Problems of Philosophy* (*Voprosy filosofii*); included in this series were Berdiaev, Frank, Rozanov, and Florensky. Other previously banned works were published under official auspices and/or by newly legalized publishing cooperatives. Conferences were held on Merezhkovsky, Gumilev, Viach, Ivanov, Mandelstam, Akhmatova, Bakhtin, and others. Western scholars attended these conferences and Soviet scholars attended conferences in the West. Attacks on Stalin escalated and expanded to include Lenin himself. Bukharin was rehabilitated; Bogdanov's works were reprinted, and even Trotsky was published. Attempts to fill in the "blank spaces" of Russian and Soviet history caused so much confusion that in 1988 High School history texts were recalled and final examinations in history were canceled. Anti-totalitarian classics such as Zamiatin's *We* and George Orwell's *1984* appeared in Russian legally for the first time. The collapse of the Soviet Union, followed by the collapse of Communism itself after the failed coup of August, 1991, intensified Russians' desire to reconnect with their lost roots. Some previously banned writers, e.g. Berdiaev, Bulgakov, and Florensky, became virtual cult figures.

A by-product of this process of rediscovery and revaluation was the return of Nietzsche. Excerpts from his works were published in *Problems of Philosophy* and other official journals of philosophy and literature. *Antichrist* was included in a compendium, *Twilight of the Gods* (*Sumerki bogov*, 1988), along with works of other "bourgeois atheists," Camus, Sartre, and Erich Fromm. In 1990, *Mysl'* brought out a two-volume edition of Nietzsche's basic works in a print run of 100,000 copies which sold out immediately. The editor, K. A. Sviasian, challenged Nazi readings of Nietzsche and explicitly dissociated him from pan-Germanism, anti-semitism, and slavophobia. Once again, Sviasian stated, Russians can read Nietzsche for themselves; he is no longer "doomed to a piratical existence between the closed stacks [*spetskhram*] and the black market."[32] By 1991, reprints of prerevolutionary translations of *Zarathustra*, some of dubious quality, were also widely available, as were the occult treatises of Steiner and Uspensky, and Russian translations of Derrida, Foucault, and Heidegger.

Serious scholarship on Nietzsche is well underway. The Moscow State University for the Humanities has begun a study-group on his thought. Valery Podoroga of the Institute of Philosophy (Moscow) has three books in progress; their titles indicate his familiarity with recent Western interpretations of Nietzsche: *The Metaphysics of the Landscape in Kierkegaard, Nietzsche, and Heidegger; The Problem of the Body in Nietzsche,* and *Nietzsche and Marginal Philosophy*. Russians are also researching Nietzsche's influence on their own culture. R. Iu. Danilevsky's lengthy review of *Nietzsche in Russia* (*Russkaia literatura*, 1988), helped legitimize the subject.[33] Progress Publishers is bringing out a collection of early twentieth-century Russian essays on Nietzsche, edited by Viacheslav Shestakov. Sergei Averintsev considers Nietzsche a major component of late Imperial and early Soviet Utopianism.[34]

Like all other areas of contemporary Russian life, Nietzsche studies are very much in a state of transition, but to what is not clear. Some scholars view Nietzsche as a liberator, a truth-seeker, a deconstructor of outworn myths, and an advocate of pluralism. Others, however, regard Nietzsche as a harmful influence, the antipode of the Russian Idea, which they insist is a Christian idea, and as the very incarnation of Western decadence and self-will. Current arguments over Nietzsche encapsulate larger issues of cultural identity and national destiny. Their eventual resolution will shape Russian readings of Nietzsche and vice versa.

Space limitations do not allow me to chronicle the reception of Nietzsche by artists and writers of the non-Russian nationalities, nor the intellectual interchange between them, but some broad generalizations can be made. Nietzsche's initial impact on them occurred, as in Russia, around the turn of the century, except for Georgia, where it was a bit later. The "regressive-progressive"[35] impact of Nietzsche's thinking (use of the past to discredit the present and posit "new" models for the future) deepened the nationalities' search for their own cultural roots and ultimately impacted on the national independence movements of the revolutionary period. Like their turn-of-the-century Russian counterparts, these intellectuals also read Nietzsche as a liberator; their concept of liberation, however, conjoined personal and national liberation, which they saw as complementary, not conflicting. Their appropriations of Nietzsche were shaped by elements in their own national heritage and by their reactions to Russian (and often German) culture as well.

Compartmentalizing discussion of the nationalities must not blur the creative interaction between them and the Russians, nor give the misleading impression that the national cultures were hermetically sealed. They contributed to Russian culture and vice versa. Viacheslav Ivanov reshaped literal translations of Hayyim Bialik's Hebrew poetry into Russian poetic forms. In the 1930s, Pasternak did the same with poems of the Georgian modernist, T. T'abidze. Leading Futurists came from the provinces, especially Ukraine. Russian writers visited Georgia, Armenia, Poland, and Lithuania and exchanged ideas with local artists and intellectuals. The Polish Modernist Stanislaw Przybyszewski had a Russian following and his plays were staged in St. Petersburg.[36] Poland and Lithuania achieved independence in 1919, but intellectual exchange with Russia continued. In the 1920s, Party policy emphasized the repudiation of "Great Russian chauvinism" and encouraged the nationalities to find their own cultural voice. Nietzsche continued to be a presence in postrevolutionary Ukraine,[37] Georgia,[38] and among Jewish writers and intellectuals. In the 1930s, however, that policy was abrogated; the new slogan was "struggle against national deviations and against Great Russian chauvinism." The national literatures turned into mirror images of the Russian. DeStalinization led to new attempts to define their own political and cultural identities and to rediscovery of long-suppressed artists and writers, including those influenced by Nietzsche. The process continues in independent Ukraine, Georgia, and the Baltic nations, and among the Jewish population of the former Soviet Union.

Nietzsche's role as both ally and adversary of Soviet culture offers a case study of his still controversial legacy. At one extreme is Crane Brinton's *Nietzsche* (1941), blighted by the then-current view of Nietzsche as prophet of Nazism. At the other extreme is Walter Kaufmann, until his death the leading American translator and interpreter of Nietzsche, who interpreted Nietzsche almost solely in esthetic, cultural, and psychological terms. Just as the Nazis extracted the brutal, racist, dictatorial aspects of Nietzsche's *œuvre*, Kaufmann presented a domesticated, depoliticized Nietzsche. He interpreted the "will to power" as self-mastery and as the artist's power over materials. This volume illustrates the variety of possible appropriations of Nietzsche, some of them esthetically and philosophically productive, others dangerous. Rather than single out one particular appropriation or theme, its purpose is to establish the diversity and breadth of his impact across the board. In Russia, as elsewhere, Nietzsche's ideas challenged outmoded orthodoxies, inspired innovation and experimentation in all fields of art and thought, and spurred movements of personal and social liberation. But as in Fascist Italy and Nazi Germany, other concepts and slogans associated with Nietzsche – the will to power, beyond good and evil, Superman and herd, master morality, and his invocation of cruelty and hardness – served to undermine "bourgeois humanism" and rationalism. They helped establish new oppressive mythologies of an official, state-sponsored culture, centered on cults of personality, on the one hand,[39] and an unofficial culture of spiritual resistance on the other. Official and unofficial culture, incidentally, are not hard and fast: allies of the regime in one period could be adversaries or victims in the next.

This book offers a broad view of Soviet culture that is limited neither to Communist-sponsored initiatives, nor to Russians, nor to the years after 1917. Nietzsche's wide-ranging importance in the early Soviet period is documented, as is the intertwining of art and ideology in the early Soviet obsession with creating a new culture. Highlighting the neglected issue of "buried influence," the chapters that follow demonstrate the persistence of Nietzsche's ideas, images, and slogans, unacknowledged and reworked, in a largely hostile cultural environment. Also indicated are key peculiarities in the early Soviet reception of Nietzsche: the role of prerevolutionary interest in the occult, the way revolution figured as an allegorical subject of literature, the manner in which censorship changed the normal Western dynamic of reception and influence, and the continuing Russian interest in Nietzsche as a religious thinker.

The organization of the book into five parts corresponds to the major areas of Nietzsche's influence on Soviet culture. Part I, "Nietzsche and the Prerevolutionary Roots of Soviet Culture," is devoted to ideas and -isms that spanned the late Imperial and early Soviet periods. Elaine Rusinko discusses Acmeism – one of the two major successor schools to Symbolism – with particular emphasis on Gumilev's and Mandelstam's rejection of Symbolist Dionysianism for Apollonian readings of Nietzsche and a joyous (i.e. non-tragic) Christianity. Acmeism informed the unofficial Soviet culture that arose in the 1920s; the works of its leading representatives are very popular in contemporary Russia. Maria Carlson shows how idiosyncratic readings of Nietzsche infused the occult doctrines of Theosophy and Anthroposophy, popular in the late Imperial and early Soviet periods. Futurism, the other major successor school to Symbolism, enjoyed quasi-official status in the early Soviet period but was then suppressed. Mayakovsky, however, safely dead, was canonized in 1935. In the 1950s and '60s, his work attracted young Soviet rebels and led some of them away from Socialist Realism. Futurism's debt to Nietzsche is treated in Henryk Baran's chapter on Khlebnikov and in Bengt Jangfeldt's chapter on the poetry of the young Mayakovsky.

Part II, "Nietzsche and Soviet Initiatives in the Arts," illustrates the pervasive, often contradictory, nature of his influence. Early Bolshevism placed particular emphasis on theater and mass festivals as agitational tools; James von Geldern shows how Nietzschean arguments were used by opposing sides in discussions of theatrical issues. Gregory Freidin analyzes the responses of Nietzscheanized critics to the underlying Nietzscheanism of Isaac Babel's masterpiece *Red Cavalry*.[40] In the 1920s, architecture, rather than literature, was the paradigmatic art, for it suited the emphasis on building socialism; Milka Bliznakov shows how Nietzschean assumptions, including an unexpected individualism, shaped certain architectural theories during the first Five Year Plan. Irina Paperno traces the origins and development of "Pushkin" as a code-word for "Nietzsche" from Merezhkovsky's 1896 essay to the Soviet Pushkin Celebration of 1937.

Part III depicts "Adaptations of Nietzsche in Soviet Ideology" – simplified, even vulgarized, but effective as propaganda. Isabel Tirado reveals the Nietzschean motifs in the Komsomol's (Communist Youth League's) vanguardism. The late Mikhail Agursky discloses the roots of Stalinist Nietzscheanism in the Nietzscheanism of certain Bolsheviks, Soviet "Fellow Travellers," and Western writers influenced by Nietzsche. Margarita Tupitsyn provides striking pictorial applications of Superman (and Superwoman) imagery, including Stalin as Superman, in Soviet photomontage.

Part IV explores "Nietzsche Among Disaffected Writers and Thinkers." Edith Clowes reveals new formulations of the "God-building" and "God-seeking" myths in Zamiatin's *We* and Pasternak's *Doctor Zhivago*. Clare Cavanagh examines the great poet Mandelstam's creative adaptation of Nietzsche's views on the conscious creation of history. Boris Groys reveals Nietzsche's influence on the non-official culture of the 1930s, with special reference to the philosophers Gustav Shpett and A. A. Meier, the writer Mikhail Bulgakov, and, briefly, Bakhtin.

Though comprising only one chapter, Part V, "Nietzsche and the Nationalities: A Case Study," underscores the importance of different national heritages, socio-cultural agendas, and specific political and economic circumstances in shaping Nietzsche's reception. Menahem Brinker documents Nietzsche's impact on Hebrew writers' visions of a new Jewish culture and a new Jewish person.[41]

To recapitulate: this volume restores a major but up to now invisible component of Soviet culture, charts the focal points of Nietzsche's impact, and provides a basis for further research and discussion.[42] For the first time since the Bolshevik Revolution, Russians and non-Russians are engaged in a fruitful dialogue about essentials, and debates on leading writers of the period have become a prominent feature of Russian intellectual life. Hopefully, this volume will contribute to the reexamination of early twentieth-century Russian culture that is now going on in both the former Soviet Union and the West, and encourage a reappraisal of the roots, nature, and evolution of Soviet culture as a whole, now that it has passed into history. The writers and thinkers treated herein, especially those suppressed by the official culture, are now enjoying a wide popularity. Surely they will continue to speak to Russians, as will Nietzsche, but his ideas will be interpreted in new ways, which cannot yet be foreseen.

NOTES

1 Richard Stites, *Revolutionary Dreams* (Oxford, 1989); Christopher Read, *Culture and Power in Revolutionary Russia* (NY and London, 1990); A. Gleason, P. Kenez and R. Stites, *Bolshevik Culture* (Bloomington, 1985); Sheila Fitzpatrick, ed., *Cultural Revolution in Russia* (Bloomington, 1978) and *The Culture Front* (Ithaca, 1992);

Lynn Malley, Culture of the Future: The Proletkult Movement in Revolutionary Russia (Berkeley, 1990); Hans Gunther, ed., *The Culture of the Stalin Period* (New York, 1990); but see Günther's *Der sozialistische Übermensch. Gor'kij und der totalitare Heldenmythos* (Stuttgart, 1993).

2 Robert Maguire, *Red Virgin Soil* (Princeton, 1968); Rufus Mathewson, *The Positive Hero in Soviet Literature* (Stanford, 1975).

3 Katerina Clark, *The Soviet Novel: History as Ritual* (Chicago, 1981), pp. 152–54, 192, 196.

4 Lawrence Stahlberger, *The Symbolic System of Mayakovsky* (The Hague, 1964); Alex M. Shane, *The Life and Works of Evgenij Zamyatin* (California, 1968); James Falen, *Isaac Babel, Master of the Short Story* (Knoxville, 1974).

5 Bernice Glatzer Rosenthal, ed., *Nietzsche in Russia* (Princeton, 1986); Edith Clowes, *The Revolution of Moral Consciousness* (De Kalb, 1988); Anne Lane, "Nietzsche in Russian Thought," Ph.D. diss.: University of Wisconsin, 1976; George Kline, "Nietzschean Marxism in Russia," *The Boston College Studies in Philosophy*, 2 (1968), pp. 166–83; "The God-builders, Gorky and Lunacharsky," *Religious and Anti-Religious Thought in Russia* (Chicago, 1968), pp. 103–26; "The Nietzschean Marxism of Stanislav Volsky," *Western Philosophical Systems in Russian Litterature*, ed. Anthony M. Mlikotin (Los Angeles, 1979), pp. 177–95. There is also a growing literature in Germany. See, for example, Raimund Sesterhenn, "Nietzsche als Gotterbauer," *Das Bogostroitel'stvo bei Gorkij und Lunačarskij bis 1909* (Munich, 1982); Aage A. Hansen-Love, *Der russische Symbolismus* (Vienna, 1990), and Günther *Der sozialistische Übermensch.*

6 The following is a summary of the relevant chapters of *Nietzsche in Russia.*

7 Other sources of "God-building" were Feuerbach's humanistic anthropology, Comte's "religion of humanity," and Georges Sorel's mystique of violence, the latter influenced by Nietzsche.

8 For Wagner's influence, see Bernice Glatzer Rosenthal, "Wagner and Wagnerian Ideas in Russia," *Wagnerism in European Culture and Politics*, ed. David Large and William Weber (Ithaca, 1984); A. Gozenpud, *Rikhard Vagner i russkaia kultura* (Moscow, 1989); R. A. Bartlett, "Wagner in Russia: The Influence of the Music and Ideas of Richard Wagner on the Artistic and Cultural Life of Russia and the Soviet Union, 1841–1941," Ph.D. diss.: Oxford University, 1990.

9 John Burt Foster, *Heirs to Dionysus* (Princeton, 1981); comments at conference on Nietzsche and Soviet culture, June 1988.

10 Gunter Grimm, *Rezeptionsgeschichte, Grundlegung einer Theorie* (Munich, 1977), pp. 153–56; Bernard Zimmermann, *Literaturrezeption im historischen Prozess* (Munich, 1977), p. 13.

11 Graham Parkes, *Nietzsche and Asian Thought* (Chicago, 1991), p. 8.

12 Cultural studies began at the University of Birmingham, England, and is now spreading in the United States. The particular complex of disciplines involved and the approaches adopted vary from place to place.

13 See Lynn Hunt, ed., *The New Cultural History* (Berkeley, 1990). On historians' use of literary theory, see Lloyd S. Kramer, "Literature, Criticism, and Historical Imagination: The Literary Challenge of Hayden White and Dominick LaCapra," ibid., pp. 97–130.

14 For a generational interpretation of history see Robert Wohl, *The Generation of 1914* (Cambridge, 1979) and Peter Loewenberg, "The Nazi Psycho-Social Youth Cohort," *American Historical Review* 76 (1971), pp. 1457–1502. The latter depicts the trauma of defeat in World War I for German youths and the consequences of loss or delegitimation of the father. For a general consideration of the issue and additional bibliography, see Alan B. Spitzer, "The Historical Problem of Generations," *American Historical Review* 78 (1973), pp. 1353–85.

15 See especially Hans Robert Jauss, "Literaturgeschichte als Provokation der Literaturwissenschaft," *Literaturgeschichte als Provokation* (Frankfurt, 1970), pp. 175–85 and Wolfgang Iser, *The Implied Reader* (Baltimore, 1972), and his *The Act of Reading* (Baltimore, 1978). For a discussion of Jauss as applied to Russian literature, see Clowes, *Revolution of Moral Consciousness*, pp. 3, 5.

16 "What is an Author," *Foucault. Language, Counter-Memory, Practice*, ed. Donald F. Bouchard (Ithaca, 1977), pp. 131–32.

17 Quoted by Patricia O'Brien, "Michel Foucault's History of Culture," in Hunt, *The New Cultural History*, p. 25. See also, Foucault, "Nietzsche, Genealogy, History," *The Foucault Reader*, ed. Paul Rabinow (New York, 1984), pp. 76–100; "The Discourse on Language," *Critical Theory Since 1965*, ed. Hazard Adams and Leroy Searle (Tallahasee, FL, 1989), pp. 148–62; *The Archaeology of Knowledge*, trans. A. M. Sheridan (New York, 1972); and *The Order of Things* (New York, 1970).

18 Mikhail Bakhtin, "Discourse in the Novel," *The Dialogic Imagination* (Austin, 1981), pp. 259, 419–20.

19 "Discourse in the Novel," pp. 290–93; quote is on p. 291. See also pp. 262, 272.

20 Kline, "Volsky," p. 180.

21 Quoted by Morris Dickstein, "The Ever Changing Literary Past," *The New York Times*, October 26, 1991, p. 19.

22 For Dostoevsky's importance in shaping the Russian reception of Nietzsche, see Rosenthal, *Nietzsche in Russia* and Clowes, *Revolution of Moral Consciousness*, both passim.

23 Kline, *Nietzsche in Russia*, xv–xvi.

24 On Fedorov and his disciples, see Michael Hagemeister, *Nikolai Fedorov. Studien zu Leben, Werk und Wirkung* (Munich, 1989); Svetlana Semenova, *Nikolai Fedorov, Tvorchestvo zhizni* (Moscow, 1990); Irene Masing-Delic, *Overcoming Death* (Stanford, 1992).

25 Irina Gutkin, "The Novel of Socialist Realism as a Phenomenon of Literary Evolution," Ph.D. diss.: University of California, Berkeley (draft, Fall 1989).

26 For a discussion of the philosophical similarities between the Russian nihilists and Nietzsche, see Arthur Danto, *Nietzsche as Philosopher* (New York, 1965), pp. 29–33.

27 "Discourse in the Novel," p. 390.

28 This will be treated in my *From the Silver Age to Stalin's Time: The Nietzsche Connection*, in preparation.

29 *Problems of Dostoevsky's Art*, published in 1929, caused Bakhtin to be exiled to a provincial town for six years. A second edition appeared in 1963. His dissertation on Rabelais was written in the 1930s, accepted in 1946, and published (in a revised version) in 1965. Other major works appeared in the 1970s, some of them after his death in 1975. Discovery by Western scholars in the 1970s and '80s helped legitimize Bakhtin studies in the Soviet Union.

30 See Boris Groys's chapter in this volume; James Curtis, "Mikhail Bakhtin, Nietzsche, and Russian Prerevolutionary Thought," *Nietzsche in Russia*, pp. 331–54; Lena Szilard, "Karnaval'noe soznanie, karnavalizatsiia," *Russian Literature* 18 (1986), pp. 151–75; Hans Günther, "M. Bakhtin i 'Rozhdenie Tragedii' F. Nitsshe," *Dialog, karnaval khronotop*, 1992, no. 1, pp. 27–34.

31 On this, see Bernice Glatzer Rosenthal, "A New Word for a New Myth: Nietzsche and Russian Futurism," *The European Foundations of Russian Modernism*, ed. Peter I. Barta (Lewiston, NY, 1991), pp. 219–50.

32 *Nitsshe; Sochineniia*, 2 vols. (Moscow, 1990), i, p. 45. The translation of *Beyond Good and Evil* is by S. L. Frank.

33 "K istorii vospriiatiia F. Nitsshe v Rossii," *Russkaia literatura*, 1988, no. 4, pp. 232–39. See also R. Iu. Danilevskii, "Russkii obraz Fridrikha Nitsshe," *Na rubezhe xix i xx vekov* (Moscow,

1991), pp. 5–43 and M. Iu.Koreneva, "D. S. Merezhkovskii i nemetskaia kul′tura," ibid., pp. 44–76.

34 "'Sud′ba i vest' Osipa Mandelstama," *Osip Mandelstam: sochineniia v dvukh tomakh* (Moscow, 1990), pp. 23–26.

35 The phrase is Ophelia Schutte's, *Nietzsche Without Masks* (Chicago, 1984), p. 8.

36 On Nietzsche in Poland, see Joachim Baer, "Nietzsche and Polish Modernism," paper presented to conference on Nietzsche and Soviet Culture, June 1988; Peter Drews, *Die Slawische Avantgarde und der Westen* (Munich, 1983), mentions Nietzsche in passing. For the Polish Nietzschean Marxist, Stanislaw Brzozowski, see Andrzej Walicki, *Stanislaw Brzozowski and the Polish Beginnings of "Western Marxism"* (Oxford, 1989).

37 Maxim Tarnawsky, "Reflections of Nietzsche in Ukrainian Literature of the 1920s," paper presented to conference on Nietzsche and Soviet Culture, concentrates on the writers Volodymyr Vynnychenko and Valerian Pidmohylny. The impact of Nietzsche on turn of the century Ukrainian intellectuals and artists, including the feminist Ol′ha Kobylianska, still awaits its historian.

38 For Nietzsche in Georgia, see Luigi Magorotto, "Nietzsche, Robakidze, and the Georgian Avant-garde," paper presented to conference on Nietzsche and Soviet Culture, June 1988; and *L'avanguardia a Tiflis*, ed. L. Magarotto (Venice, 1982), published as "Nietzsche's Influence on the Early Works of Guigol Robakidze," *Annali di ca' Foscari* xxviii, 3, 1989, pp. 97–109 and "Vlianie Nitsshe na rannee tvorchestvo Grigola Robakidze," *Literaturnaia Gruziia*, 1989, 9, pp. 148–60.

39 The common Nietzschean elements in the cults of personality of Stalin, Hitler, and Mussolini will be discussed in *From the Silver Age to Stalin's Time*, for the subject is too complex to be treated adequately here.

40 For a discussion of Nietzsche's influence on Babel's style and a reading which stresses Babel's humaneness see Maria Deppermann's paper, "Reception as Creative Interpretation, Nietzsche and Babel," presented to the conference on Nietzsche and Soviet Culture.

41 This by no means exhausts the topic of Nietzsche's influence on the Jews of Imperial and Soviet Russia. David Roskies has noted the influence of Symbolism and Nietzsche on the famous Yiddish writer, I. L. Peretz. Nietzsche's possible impact on Soviet Yiddish writers such as Moishe Kulbak (emigrated 1920, returned 1928,

disappeared 1937), on Evsektsiia activists (Jewish Section of the Communist Party), and on Soviet Hebraists of the 1920s, has not been explored at all. The latter, a younger generation of writers were pro-Soviet and tried to undo the ban on Hebrew, but in vain. Only in 1988 was the ban lifted; Russian translations of Bialik's poetry were published the same year. Nietzsche's influence on political Zionism has been treated by Abram Yassour, "Philosophy-Religion-Politics: Borochov, Bogdanov, and Lunacharsky," *Studies in Soviet Thought* 31 (1986), pp. 199–230. Nietzschean ideas are obvious in the writings of Vladimir Jabotinsky, founder of Zionist Revisionism; like many Jewish writers, he wrote in several languages. The late Mikhail Agursky told me that Jabotinsky's Russian writings, rediscovered in the Brezhnev era, were a major factor in the Jewish revival of the 1970s. Russian Jewish thinkers are among those treated in *De Sils-Maria à Jérusalem: Nietzsche et la Judaïsme*, ed. D. Bouvel and J. LeRider (Paris, 1991).

42 Some research has been done on Tsvetaeva's debt to Nietzsche, but the full picture has yet to emerge. See Catherine Ciepiela, "The Category of the 'Tragic Poet' in Tsvetaeva's Literary Criticism," unpublished paper presented to AATSEEL, December 1987; Tomas Venclova, "On Russian Mythological Tragedy, Vjacheslav Ivanov and Marina Cvetaeva," *NYU Slavic Papers*, vol. V, *Mythic Literature* (New York, 1985), pp. 89–109. Also requiring further study is Nietzsche's influence on Olesha (discussed briefly by Agursky in this volume and by Anthony Vanchu, in his "Olyesha and Utopian Mythologies of the '20s," Ph.D. diss.: University of California, 1990) and on Zabolotsky, the Oberiu group, Zoshchenko, Ilf and Petrov, and on the Formalists.

PART I

Nietzsche and the Prerevolutionary Roots of Soviet Culture

CHAPTER I

Nietzsche and the young Mayakovsky

Bengt Jangfeldt

[Mayakovsky] will either perish, like Nietzsche, or shout "Hosanna", like Dostoevsky – this inspiredly tongue-tied poet of the Russian revolution, its prophet and clown, [...] together with it untiringly creating its road to Calvary.

Nikolai Ustrialov, 1920

Despite all the books written about Vladimir Mayakovsky, the general view of the poet and his work is, unfortunately, to a great extent a distorted one. After Stalin in 1935 proclaimed Mayakovsky "the best, most talented poet of our Soviet epoch" – and, subsequently, the "Father of Socialist Realism" in poetry – innumerable articles and books about his life and work have been published in the Soviet Union. Almost all of them have been of a teleological nature, i.e. their purpose has been to substantiate these very postulates. Many Western scholars have also, unwittingly, been led astray by this tendentious rendering of the poet's biography. The situation for Velimir Khlebnikov or Osip Mandelstam is in this respect more favorable, since every scholar, Soviet or Western, has been forced to begin – or, rather, has had the benefit of beginning – more or less from scratch.

One of the myths in connection with Mayakovsky is that he is first and foremost a "Soviet" writer, a poet who matured only after October, 1917, and whose main works, therefore, fall into the "Soviet" period of Russian literature. While it is indisputable that many important works were indeed written in the twenties – e.g. the long poems "150,000,000" (1921) and "About This" ("Pro eto," 1923), quite a few shorter poems,

and the plays "The Bedbug" ("Klop," 1929) and "The Bath-
house" ("Bania," 1930) – it is equally true that Mayakovsky
was a full-fledged master well before the Bolshevik takeover,
and that much of his best poetry was in fact written before the
Soviet period; his crowning achievement, the long poem
"Man" ("Chelovek") was completed in the interval between
February and October, 1917, and published at the very beginning of 1918, at the threshold of the New Order.

It is imperative to emphasize this perspective before
approaching the question of Nietzsche's influence on Mayakovsky. Whereas the traces of Nietzsche in Mayakovsky's later
work are more or less postrevolutionary common coin – the
socialist superman, faith in the future, antireligious sentiment,
etc. – the influence of Nietzsche on the early Mayakovsky can
not only be detected but also substantiated: contemporary
criticism, testimonies of contemporaries, and textual analysis
help us to establish the quality and quantity of this influence.
The present article, therefore, will concentrate on the prerevolutionary period of the poet's work.

Were it not for the above – and other – false conceptions
surrounding Mayakovsky's biography, we would no doubt
long ago have managed to reach a deeper understanding of the
poet's poetic universe and ascertain two of the main influences
behind the poet's work, namely Dostoevsky and – Nietzsche.

Describing the spiritual atmosphere in Russia by the turn of
the century, D. S. Mirsky remarks that "the influence of
Nietzsche and of French and English estheticism amalgamated
with that of Dostoevsky and Soloviev."[1] In such an abundant
cultural climate, of course, the question of influences becomes
rather complicated. Yet, when Mayakovsky and Nietzsche –
and especially *Zarathustra* – are mentioned, Dostoevsky's name
is never far away. This genealogical line was obvious to the
critic and religious thinker Nikolai Ustrialov, who said that
Mayakovsky "no doubt can say of himself, with the words of
Dostoevsky's famous hero: 'God has tormented me my whole
life.' [. . .] He is a typical Dostoevsky hero."[2]

As we know, Nietzsche, in his turn, was a staunch admirer of

Dostoevsky. What we are dealing with, then, are three writers of a similar spiritual makeup: they are all "religious natures," in Ustrialov's words, and they all raise and try to solve the "cursed" questions of Man, Being, God, Time. As far as Mayakovsky's relationship to Nietzsche and Dostoevsky is concerned, we are dealing with a fascination, and even identification, with ideas characteristic of these two metaphysical writers and the characters who express them: Ivan Karamazov, Kirillov, and Zarathustra. Fully endorsing Ustrialov's definition of Mayakovsky as a "typical Dostoevsky hero," it would be appropriate to add that he is also very much a "Nietzsche hero" and a "Zarathustra type."[3] "For Nietzsche there existed only one question," says Lev Shestov: "Lord, why has Thou forsaken me?"[4] If, by the same token, we wished to reduce the essence of Mayakovsky's spiritual quest to a single formula, this would no doubt be a proper one.

It is true that Nietzsche's name was very much "in the air" in the 1910s, and therefore used and abused by both critics and writers; but apart from this, Futurism in general, and Mayakovsky in particular, were often regarded by contemporary criticism as "Nietzschean" phenomena.[5] The Futurists are heirs to and continuers of Nietzsche," wrote the critic A. Zakrzhevsky,[6] and Genrikh Tasteven noted that "the antihistorical attitude of Futurism [...] was in fact formulated by Nietzsche in his study 'On the Use and Abuse of History for Life,' wherein one can see the embryo of some of the ideas of Futurism."[7] And the Futurist poet and theoretician, Aleksei Kruchenykh, in his book *Mayakovsky's Verse (Stikhi V. Mayakovskogo)*, stated that "[...] madness doesn't afflict us at all, although as imitators of madness, we outsnob both Dostoevsky and Nietzsche."[8] Casual as it may be, the reference to Nietzsche is still there.

The tendency to associate Mayakovsky with Nietzsche was particularly evident in the turbulent 1917–20 period, and especially on the part of philosophically inclined critics like Ivanov-Razumnik, Nikolai Ustrialov, and Nikolai Chuzhak. "Mayakovsky is today's 'shriek-lipped Zarathustra,' but gone so mad with pain that mad Nietzsche himself seems balanced

and 'literary' compared to him," N. Chuzhak wrote in an
article titled "The Thirteenth Apostle."[9] Referring to the same
lines from "A Cloud in Trousers," Ustrialov, in his article
"The Religion of the Revolution," notes that the poet "in
many ways resembles the bard of the superman with his eagle
and serpent who also extolled the sun and smashed the old
law-tables. Like Nietzsche, Mayakovsky is a *religious nature who
has killed God* [Ustrialov's italics]."[10] Ivanov-Razumnik, the
theorist of "Scythianism," referring to Mayakovsky's long
poem "Man" (1918), states that "[...] behind the revolution
the poet sees – 'Man.' [...] But what does he see in *this Man?
Who* is he? Herder's Angel? Nietzsche's Superman? Or simply
the 'blonda bestia' of vulgar Nietzscheanism?," and concludes
that "Futurism from the very beginning was easily enraptured
by the ideals of 'blondae bestiae,' and delighted in itself as its
precursor, herald, apostle."[11] Lev Sillov (later a *Lef* critic) in
1921 published an article named "The Revolution of the
Spirit," with the subtitle "Nietzsche and Mayakovsky," where
he claims that Mayakovsky is "an executer of Nietzsche's
sermon."[12] And when Mayakovsky visited the USA in 1925, he
was described by *The New York Times* as a "supporter of
Nietzsche's philosophy."[13]

One may in fact speak of a spiritual affinity, or congeniality
of mind, between the German philosopher and the Russian
poet. Nietzsche's influence on Mayakovsky was manifold. First
and foremost, Mayakovsky identified with Zarathustra as a
representative of what Andrei Bely in an article on Nietzsche
called "tragic individualism,"[14] and with his role as a prophet
and rebel. "Theoretical philosophy," writes Bely, "defines the
'I' in terms of its opposition to the 'not-I,'" and in Nietzsche's
œuvre "the 'I' becomes the subject, and the 'not-I' the object."[15]

In his analysis of the binary character of Mayakovsky's
poetical world, Roman Jakobson, echoing almost literally
Bely's words about Nietzsche, notes that "the exact equivalent
for this enmity would be the antinomy 'I' versus 'not-I'."[16]
Developing his thought, Jakobson in another article speaks
about Mayakovsky as a "metaphoric poet" (in contrast to the
"metonymic" Pasternak): "The lyrical impulse is [...] pro-

vided by the poet's own self. Images of the external world in the metaphoric lyric are made to harmonize with this impulse [...]. Metaphor works through creative association by similarity and contrast. The hero is confronted by the antithetical image of what is mortally inimical to him, protean like all the ingredients of a primarily metaphorical lyric poetry [...]."[17] This "I" assumes various embodiments or disguises: the poet is a Prophet, he is the Thirteenth Apostle, abandoned by a punishing God, the scapegoat, a martyr and a redeemer, but he is also a rebel, a herald of new truths, and an outcast; and he is a Zarathustra, staging his Tragedy in the market square of the Modern City.

"Mayakovsky's 'I' not only symbolizes the poet," says Lawrence Stahlberger, "but also the martyr-scapegoat who [...] sacrifices himself for all men. [...] Man [...] is the created who is also the creator, the finite being who is potentially infinite, the animal who is partly divine."[18] For someone who is aware of this paradox and the fact that suffering is a part of the Creation, there are various ways of reacting, and Stahlberger suggests that Mayakovsky's attitude, like Nietzsche's, was one of "heroic defiance" – which, "while it may begin with nihilism, pushes beyond it in an attempt to create 'new values' and a new myth or belief."[19] In other words: "Man is something that should be overcome" (Z, p. 41) or "My Ego is something that should be overcome, my Ego is to me the great contempt of man" (Z, p. 65) – a phrase echoed almost literally by Mayakovsky in "A Cloud in Trousers": "My 'I' is too small for me." (In Russian, the textual likeness between Nietzsche and Mayakovsky is more obvious: "Moe *ia* est' nechto, chto dolzhno prevozmoch': moe *ia* dlya menia [...]" (Nietzsche, Izrastsov's transl.); "'ia' dlia menia malo [...]" (Mayakovsky). Both Nietzsche and Mayakovsky underline the word "I" by putting it in italics and within quotation marks, respectively.) There is thus an apparent affinity between Mayakovsky's poetical "I" and Zarathustra; the same goes for many of the targets of Mayakovsky's struggle, the symbols or incarnations of the "not-I."

Mayakovsky's *Weltanschauung* and *œuvre* are essentially

tragic, something that Boris Pasternak, speaking about Mayakovsky's tragedy "Vladimir Mayakovsky," a play which bore
the poet's own name, aptly pointed out: "Art was called
tragedy – the right name for it.[20] And the tragedy was called
'Vladimir Mayakovsky.' The title concealed a simple discovery
of genius – that the poet is not the author, but the subject of a
lyricism addressing itself to the world in the first person. The
title was not the name of the author, but the surname of the
contents."[21]

Answering, some time before the première of "Vladimir
Mayakovsky" in December 1913, the question why the play
bears his own name, Mayakovsky said: "That will be the name
of the poet in the play who is destined to suffer for all."[22] The
image of the poet as scapegoat and redeemer is one of the most
powerful and persistent in Mayakovsky's poetical work. The
poet, alone, often rejected by the crowd, must suffer for all, and
takes on the burden of others precisely because he is a poet (cf.
the words of "The Elder with one Hairless Cat" in the play:
"Only you can sing" ["Ty odin umeesh' pet'"]).

Lev Shestov, in his essay on Dostoevsky and Nietzsche,
writes about "the people of tragedy, 'the abandoned,'" that
they "must wage a twofold war: both with 'necessity' and with
their neighbors, who can still adapt themselves, and therefore,
not knowing what they are doing, side with humanity's worst
enemy."[23] Here we have Mayakovsky in a nutshell: the lonely
"I" struggling against man's enemy, whose names are legion –
"necessity," philistinism, *byt* (mundane existence) – "my invincible foe," "the Ruler of All," as Mayakovsky calls him. And
Mayakovsky's feeling of loneliness was indeed of a cosmic
dimension: "I'm as alone as the last eye of someone who is
going blind!" ("Some Words About My Self," 1913).

The play "Vladimir Mayakovsky," however, is not the only
"Tragedy" in Mayakovsky's work: the poem "A Cloud in
Trousers" was originally titled "The Thirteenth Apostle" and
subtitled "Tragedy." When the poet twice published excerpts
from the poem before the book version came out, he called
them "fragments of a tragedy" and "Mayakovsky's second
tragedy," respectively, thereby establishing a direct genealogi-

cal connection with the play. Both titles were thus metaphors or embodiments of the poet's "I": Vladimir Mayakovsky and the Thirteenth Apostle. These two "tragedies" are also the most "Nietzschean" of Mayakovsky's works.

Owing to the canonical nature of Mayakovsky's position in Soviet literature, the names of Dostoevsky and Nietzsche have been more or less banned in connection with the poet. In 1966, Lili Brik, the woman Mayakovsky lived with from 1915 to 1930 and the main heroine of his poetry, in an article pointed to obvious echoes of Dostoevsky in Mayakovsky's work, but unfortunately this line of research has not been followed.[24] Yet Dostoevsky is the Russian writer who influenced Mayakovsky most.

With Nietzsche the situation is even worse. Viktor Pertsov, in his study of Mayakovsky's life and work,[25] does mention Nietzsche, but endows him with epithets like "the philosopher of misanthropy," "the apostle of decadence," "the ideologue of philistinism," and "the philosophic lackey of capitalism."[26] While juxtaposing quotations that bear unmistakable evidence of Nietzsche's influence on Mayakovsky, Pertsov nevertheless chooses to call Mayakovsky an "anti-Nietzschean."[27] On the other hand, the prominent Mayakovsky scholar Nikolai Khardzhiev suggests that "the question of Nietzsche's influence (as a poet) on the early Mayakovsky could become the subject of special research."[28]

However, Viktor Pertsov, for all his blinders, furnishes us with one priceless piece of information: "[Mayakovsky] knew Nietzsche's book [*Zarathustra*] well. It has been preserved by his older sister [. . .] among the books that once belonged to the poet."[29] We don't know if there are any traces (underlinings, commentaries, etc.) of the reading in Mayakovsky's copy, or whether Pertsov simply means that the fact that *Zarathustra* was preserved among Mayakovsky's books also means that he must have read it; but the fact that Pertsov specifically states that Mayakovsky knew *Zarathustra* "well" ("khorosho znal") points to the first alternative.[30]

Even without Pertsov's assurance that Mayakovsky did

indeed read *Zarathustra*, there are simply too many references to Nietzsche in his works to allow us to doubt that he did. Besides a general identification with the hero of Nietzsche's book, as well as thematic and textual parallels (see below), Mayakovsky identifies himself with Nietzsche's hero twice – in his poem "A Cloud in Trousers" (1915):

> It is today's shriek-lipped (*krikogubyi*) Zarathustra
> who preaches,
> dashing about and groaning!
>
> (trans. B. J.)

and in his article "About different Mayakovskys" (also 1915), where, referring to this very poem, he exclaims: "Isn't it only in order for the words extolling Man to be more unflinching that [the poet] allows himself to call himself Zarathustra?" (*PSS*, I, p. 346[31]). We know from Lili Brik[32] that Nietzsche was among the writers she and her husband read, but by the time Mayakovsky first met her (in July, 1915), he had already finished "A Cloud in Trousers." Discussions with the Briks about Nietzsche may have had some bearing on "The Backbone Flute" (Fleitapozvonochnik), the long poem written in the autumn of 1915 and published in February, 1916. This poem contains several very "Nietzschean" passages (see below), which shows that Mayakovsky was familiar with *Zarathustra* at the time, but there are clear indications that he had read the book before he met the Briks. If there is a connection to Lili Brik in "The Backbone Flute," it is of another nature; it was the passionate but tormenting love for Lili that triggered the notes of Nietzschean tragedy in this poem.

We do not know when Mayakovsky first read *Zarathustra* (or which translation, Antonovsky's or Izrastsov's[33]), but we can assume that it was no later than 1913, when the first traces of Nietzsche are to be found in his poetry. Nor do we know whether Mayakovsky read anything else by Nietzsche, although the ideas put forth in *The Birth of Tragedy* may have been familiar to him. It is also possible that Mayakovsky first learned about Nietzsche through a secondary source like Andrei Bely's essay "Friedrich Nietzsche" in his book *Ara-*

besques (*Arabeski*, Moscow, 1911; quoted above), which contains ideas and wordings that must have appealed to Mayakovsky.

"Vladimir Mayakovsky" was written and staged in 1913, and other possible traces of Nietzsche in Mayakovsky's poetry are also to be found in a poem from 1913, "Some Words About Myself" ("Neskol'ko slov obo mne samom"), where the poet for the first time speaks to the Sun, which is here identified with God the Father. A similar conversation is repeated in the poem "The Fop's Blouse" ("Kofta fata", 1914) and in later works. Although the Sun may be just an archetypal metaphor for Nature, something unchanging and unchangeable, a symbol of Creation itself, a "regulator of [...] the orderly succession of days,"[34] I would suggest that the poet's numerous appeals to the Sun were in fact influenced by Zarathustra's appeal to the same star in the very first lines of the book.

The fact that we know that Mayakovsky actually did read *Zarathustra* indeed simplifies our task. When discussing influences, however, we must also consider the question of what kind of reader Mayakovsky was. As opposed to the Symbolists or Acmeists, he was not a "learned poet," and he doesn't seem to have read a lot, especially not much prose. He had an exceptional capacity for memorizing poetry,[35] but depended a great deal on other people for his reading: "Burliuk made me a poet. Read the Frenchmen and the Germans to me. Kept shoving me books" (*PSS*, I, p. 20). Later, this role was taken over by Osip Brik, with whom he shared his library and who used to read poetry aloud to him and Lili.[36]

An incident recalled by Roman Jakobson illustrates how Mayakovsky made use of other sources: in the spring of 1920, upon Jakobson's return to Moscow from Reval, Mayakovsky made him "repeat several times my somewhat confused remarks on the general theory of relativity [...]. The idea of the liberation of energy, the problem of the time dimension, and the idea that movement at the speed of light may actually be a reverse movement in time – all these things fascinated Mayakovsky. I'd seldom seen him so interested and attentive. [...] He told me later that he was writing a poem called 'The

Fourth International' (he afterward changed it to 'The Fifth International') that would deal with such things."³⁷ Mayakovsky was not a systematic reader, and like all poets he used what he read or heard very much for his own poetic purposes (cf. "Sometimes the book helps me, sometimes I help the book" [*PSS*, XIII, p. 195]). Therefore, one should not expect a well-reasoned, coherent position *vis-à-vis* – or even polemics with – Nietzsche's philosophical thought, but rather influences of a more general order, as well as parallels in imagery and vocabulary. Moreover, when Mayakovsky first read Nietzsche, he was only about twenty years old, had written poetry for only two years, and had published his first poems only the year before; he was thus more readily open to immediate reading experiences than older, more erudite poets with an already developed world view.

I dwell at some length on the question of tragedy in Mayakovsky's work not only because Nietzsche is the author of *The Birth of Tragedy* (which Mayakovsky may never have read), but mainly because the main "Nietzschean" themes in Mayakovsky's *œuvre* are drafted in the tragedy *Vladimir Mayakovsky* for the first time.

For a poet preoccupied with the fundamental existential questions, many of these themes are obvious requisites. But the treatment of them, as well as the purely textual similarities, suggest direct influences from Nietzsche, and especially *Zarathustra*.

Zarathustra calls upon men to love their "children's land" (*Z*, p. 221): "The present and the past upon the earth – alas! my friends – that is *my* most intolerable burden; I should not know how to live, if I were not a seer of that which must come. [...] I will walk among men as among the fragments of the future: of the future which I scan" (*Z*, pp. 160, 161); "The creator seeks companions, not corpses or herds of believers. The creator seeks fellow-creators, those who inscribe new values on new tables" (*Z*, p. 52). And anticipating the coming of a new man, Zarathustra asks, "Who is it that must come one day?" (*Z*, p. 180).

The theme of the future is inherent in the very word Futurism; and in Mayakovsky's case this is not a mere slogan but the very essence of his work: only the future can free man from the fetters of *byt*, of *poshlost'* (banality, triviality), of the daily grind. The character "V. Mayakovsky" in the play carries his soul on a dish "to the dinner of coming years," and in "A Cloud in Trousers" the poet exclaims:

> I,
> mocked by my contemporaries,
> like a prolonged
> dirty joke,
> I see whom no one sees,
> crossing the mountain of time.
>
> (trans. George Reavey, p. 83)[38]

This quotation is from the end of the second, most "Nietzschean" part of "A Cloud in Trousers," where the theme of the future is intertwined with that of contempt for and struggle with the values of the present and the past. It is here that the poet speaks of himself as the "shriek-lipped Zarathustra" and that we find the famous statement:

> Glorify me!
> For me the great are no match.
> Upon every achievement
> I stamp *nihil*.
>
> (trans. George Reavey, p. 75)

– lines that echo several passages in Zarathustra. "I have unlearned [...] belief in words and values and great names" (*Z*, p. 285), says Zarathustra's shadow, and concludes: "A change in values – that means a change in the creators of values. He who has to be a creator always has to destroy" (*Z*, p. 85). It is also in this second part of the poem that the poet identifies himself with St. John Chrysostom (Zlatoust):

> I,
> the most golden-mouthed,
> whose every word
> gives new birth to [novoródit] the soul,
> gives a name to [imenínit] the body [...]
>
> (trans. B. J.)

This may, of course, simply be a tribute to the Russian Orthodox tradition, but it may also be an echo of Zarathustra's words: "I love him who throws golden words in advance of his deeds [...]" (*Z*, p. 44).

The struggle with God (intimately connected with the theme of blasphemy) is another major theme. "Zarathustra's message that God is dead is deeply embedded in the early work of Mayakovsky," concludes Edward J. Brown.[39] The question of Mayakovsky's struggle with God has been discussed at length by others,[40] and shall not be dwelt upon here. However, this was perhaps the most important of Nietzsche's "messages" to be absorbed by Mayakovsky. Just as in Mayakovsky's work, Zarathustra's God is severe, unjust, punishing: "this snorter of wrath." And it is, in fact, the blasphemous poet/rebel who is the real believer: "O Zarathustra, you are more pious than you believe, with such an unbelief. [...] Is it not your piety itself that no longer allows you to believe in God?" (*Z*, p. 274). The same way, Mayakovsky turns against a God who is unfailingly associated with "cruel retribution," "punishment," "thunder," "judgment," "inquisition." Mayakovsky's early work is in fact one long monologue with God: he speaks to Him, chases Him, visits Him in Heaven, threatens Him: "I'll rip you, reeking of incense, / wide open from here to Alaska!" ("A Cloud in Trousers"). Sometimes, the similarities between Nietzsche's text and Mayakovsky's are striking. The Sorcerer, in his lament, speaks to God in extremely derogatory terms, calling Him, among other things, "a thief" (*Z*, p. 266). This accusation has a direct parallel in the epilogue of the "Tragedy," where "V. Mayakovsky," doubting like St. Thomas, exclaims: "It was I / who stuck my finger into heaven / and proved: / he's a thief!"

At the same time, Mayakovsky is mocked at by his contemporaries, just like another prophet: "Don't you see! They spit / on the man of Golgotha again, / preferring Barabbas" ("A Cloud in Trousers"). Mayakovsky is Christ, the Thirteenth Apostle, a prophet of new truths, with God representing the old belief. In *Zarathustra*, as well as in Mayakovsky's longer poems, the theme of crucifixion is introduced as a logical continuation of the metaphor. "The good[41] *have* to be Pharisees," says Zarathustra, and they "*have* to crucify him who devises his own virtue [...] who breaks the law-tables and the old values [...] who writes new values on new law-tables, [...] they sacrifice the whole human future!" (*Z*, pp. 229, 230). In "A Cloud in Trousers," the passage at the beginning of which Mayakovsky speaks of himself as "the shriek-lipped Zarathustra" develops into an image where the prophet (Mayakovsky = today's Zarathustra) is crucified:

> This led to my Golgotha in the halls
> of Petrograd, Moscow, Odessa, and Kiev,
> where not a man
> but
> shouted:
> "Crucify,
> crucify him!"
> [...]
> I am where pain is – everywhere;
> on each drop of the tear-flow
> I have nailed myself on the cross.
>
> (trans. George Reavey, pp. 83, 85)

One of the most obvious textual parallels is to be found between the "Sorcerer's Lament", mentioned above, and the poet's monologues in "The Backbone Flute," "A Cloud in Trousers," and "Man." The sorcerer turns to a God who is "malicious, unknown," "jealous," "shameless," a "robber" and a "thief" [*grabitel'*] – an "invincible foe" [*neoborimy vrag*] who "torments" [*muchaet*] the sorcerer, who describes himself as a "prisoner" [*plennik*]. In order to illustrate the degree of Mayakovsky's borrowing from this monologue, I will have to quote extensively in Russian. God is the tormenter:

> Itak lezhu ia, izvivaias',
> sognuvshis', muchaias', postignutyi vsemi
> *mucheniami, chto na menia naslal ty,*
> bezzhalostnyi okhotnik,
> *nevedomyi mne bog!*
>
> [...] thus I lie,
> Bend myself, twist myself, tortured,
> By every eternal torment,

Smitten
By you, cruel huntsman,
You unknown – God!

(*Z*, p. 265)

[...] esli zvezd kover toboiu vytkan,
esli etoi boli,
ezhednevno mnozhimoi,
toboi nisposlana, gospodi, pytka,
sudeiskuiu tsep' naden'.

If the stars' carpet is your weave,
if, of this daily
multiplied pain,
you have have imposed the ordeal, o lord;
then wear the chain of a judge.
("The Backbone Flute," trans. George Reavey, p. 115)

In *Zarathustra*, God doesn't want to kill but only to torment man, to strike his heart:

Razi zhe glubzhe,
eshche raz popadi v menia i serdtse
razbei i prokoli!
[...] Da, ubivat' ne khochesh' ty,
a tol'ko muchit', muchit' khochesh'!

Strike deeper!
Strike once again!
Sting and sting, shatter this heart!
[...] Will you not kill,
Only torment, torment?

(*Z*, p. 265)

The first part of this quotation Mayakovsky answers in the last part of "A Cloud in Trousers," by going to attack himself:

Vidish', ya nagibaius',
iz-za golenishcha
dostaiu sapozhnyi nozhik. [...]
Ia tebia, propakhshego ladanom, raskroiu
otsiuda do Aliaski!

Watch me stoop
and reach for a shoemaker's knife
in my boot. [...]

I'll rip you, reeking of incense,
wide open from here to Alaska!
                    (trans. George Reavey, pp. 107, 109)

And the second has its counterpart in these lines:

> Vsemogushchii, ty vydumal paru ruk,
> sdelal,
> chto u kazhdogo est' golova, –
> otchego ty ne vydumal,
> chtob bylo bez muk
> tselovat', tselovat', tselovat'?!

Almighty, you concocted a pair of hands,
arranged
for everyone to have a head;
but why didn't you see to it
that one could without torture
kiss, and kiss and kiss?!
                    (trans. George Reavey, p. 107)

In the fourth stanza, Nietzsche's sorcerer talks about himself as a prisoner:

> *Ia plennik gordyi tvoj,*
> *za oblakami skryvshiisia razboinik!*
> Skazhi zhe, nakonets, chego,
> chego, grabitel', ot menya ty khochesh'?
>
> Kak? *Vykupa?*

I am [...] your proudest prisoner,
You robber behind the clouds!
For the last time, speak!
What do you want, waylayer, from me?
[...]
What? Ransom?
                    (*Z*, p. 266)

Compare the monologue in Mayakovsky's "Man":

> *Ia v plenu.*
> Net mne *vykupa!*
> [...] glavnyi tantsmeister zemnogo kankana
> To v vide idei,
> *to cherta vrode,*
> to bogom siiaet, *za oblako kanuv.*

I'm a prisoner.
For me there is no ransom!
[. . .] the dancing master of the earthly can-can.
Now in the form of an idea,
now like the devil,
then shining like a god who's vanished behind a cloud.[42]

A possible influence from Nietzsche in connection with the theme of God, is the theme of "dancing," which in Mayakovsky's poetry often accompanies religious images. "I should believe only in a God who understood how to dance," says Zarathustra, whose very name means "Star Dancer" (Z, p. 68). In "A Cloud in Trousers," Salome dances, the poet's "quantity of years" will "finish its dance," and "even frowning Apostle Peter will want to step out in a ki-ka-poo." In "Man," "the same old bald / unknown one leads [the people], / the main dancing master of the earthly can-can [. . .], / shining like a god vanished behind a cloud."

In his formula "a god gone mad," who shouts about "cruel retribution," Mayakovsky combines the theme of an unjust and punishing God with that of madness. "Mad" and "madness" ("bezumnyi" / "bezumie," "obezumevshii"; "sumasshedshii" / "sumasshestvie") are frequent and important attributes in Mayakovsky's early poetry. "Madness" is also one of the main characteristics of the Superman, "conscious of his folly" (Z, p. 284). Speaking to the people in the market square, Zarathustra even claims that he *is* madness: "Where is the lightning to lick you with its tongue? Where is the madness, with which you should be cleansed? Behold, I teach you the Superman: he is this lightning, he is this madness" (Z, p. 43). "Madness" is thus inherent in the prophet, a synonym of youth, love, free will ("The imprisoned will [. . .] liberates itself in a foolish way" [Z, p. 161]), of creativity – and an antonym of god: "Better no god, better to produce destiny on one's own account, better to be a fool, better to be a God oneself!" (Z, p. 274). "Madness" is also necessary in order to overcome Man and the abominable present: "'Things are ordered morally according to justice and punishment. Oh, where is the redemption from the stream of things and from the punishment "existence"?' Thus madness preached" (*Z*, p. 161).

These words could just as well have been pronounced by Mayakovsky, living in a world "conquered" by "things," where "madness" is an attribute of the poet and the rebel. Mayakovsky the Futurist is "mad," "sumasshedshii" ("They don't understand anything," 1914), the "V. Mayakovsky" of the play is "crowned in his madness," and the hero of "A Cloud in Trousers" is haunted by "the thought about mad-houses," whereupon the theme of "madness" in the first part of the poem is unleashed: "Already madness" – a theme which is repeated in many of Mayakovsky's works and returns in the last part of the poem "Man," where the poet once again goes mad with love, in an obvious reference to the earlier poem: "Welcome – again! – my madness!" Many other examples could be given.

The theme of "eternal recurrence" has been discussed by some scholars[43] in connection with the poem "Man," where the last two chapters ("The Return of Mayakovsky" and "Mayakovsky to the Ages") sees the poet returning to earth after a longer sojourn in heaven, only to find life totally unchanged, with *byt* and *poshlost'* reigning as before. But since Nietzsche's idea of an eternal recurrence aimed at the repetition of *the same events*, and was in fact an expression of "life-affirmation," as R. J. Hollingdale puts it,[44] Nietzsche's doctrine would be unacceptable to Mayakovsky. Nevertheless, Stahlberger concludes that in "this myth of the return with the repetition of past experiences it is tempting to see a poetic modification of Nietzsche's concept of the 'eternal recurrence.'"[45]

Indeed, the philosophical divergences are obvious: Mayakovsky's return or resurrection was supposed to take place in a transformed universe, not in a replica of the old one. But Mayakovsky may have been attracted by the device of letting the hero return back to earth after so and so many years to find out what has happened to man in his absence; just like Zarathustra, who came down from his mountain because he "wanted to learn what had been happening *to men* while he had been away: whether they had become bigger or smaller" (*Z*, p. 187). As in *Zarathustra*, where the houses (the living-rooms and bed-rooms) are symbols of the never-changing reality, Mayakovsky visits the house where his beloved used to live. But in the bed-room he finds a strange couple, the engineer Nikolaiev and his naked wife. The abode, where formerly love (eros) and poetry had reigned, is now debased by mediocrity and ordinary carnal love (libido) – the stressing of the profession "engineer" and the fact that the wife is described as naked are certainly not accidental. We are not far from Zarathustra's answer to the question at the beginning of the chapter: "*Everything* has become smaller." And while Zarathustra sighs and gazes into the distance, Mayakovsky, gone mad with love and pain, runs away to burn at the stake of his "unthinkable love," "to the Ages."

I would like to conclude this short introduction to the question of Nietzsche's influence on the early Mayakovsky by pointing to some striking parallels in atmosphere and imagery. The very setting of the play, a city square [*ploshchad'*], clearly resembles "the market place" [*bazarnaia ploshchad'*] in *Zarathustra*. The first act is described as "The Feast of the Poor." The theme of the crowd and the rebellion of the poor which is so important in *Zarathustra* ("Of Redemption"; "The Voluntary Beggar") resounds in both *Vladimir Mayakovsky* and "A Cloud in Trousers" – like *Zarathustra*, the play is based on an opposition between the poet/prophet and the crowd. The antipode of the crowd and hero of the play, the poet "V. Mayakovsky," talks about himself as "the last poet" (cf. Zarathustra's words about "the last man)" and speaks in "words, simple as mooing" [*slovami, prostymi*, kak mychanie] (Zarathustra: "[...] my words are poor, despised, halting [sic] words" [*Z*, p. 146], [...] moi slova – *slova* grubye, prezritel'nye i *prostye*).

Closely connected with the theme of the poor is the theme of the "cripple." The grotesque figures in the "Tragedy" – the men without ears, heads, legs, eyes, the man "with two kisses," the "enormous belly," etc. – are borrowed from the chapter "Of Redemption": "[...] this one lacks an eye and that one an

ear and a third one lacks a leg, and there are others who have
lost their tongue or their nose or their head. [. . .] men who lack
everything except one thing, of which they have too much –
men who are no more than a great eye or a great mouth or a
great belly or something else great – I call such men inverse
cripples" (*Z*, pp. 159–60).[46] By developing the theme of
"spittle" and "spitting" ("Of Passing By") and crossing it with
the "cripple theme," Mayakovsky produces a climax of grotesque imagery: "the spittles grow into enormous cripples."

Aside from these themes, there are several images in Mayakovsky's poetry which leave no doubt as to their origin. The
first one goes back to the passage where Zarathustra talks
about man as a tight-rope walker:

Chelovek – eto kanat, natianutyi mezhdu zhivotnym i sverkhchelovekom,
– kanat nad propast'iu

Man is a rope, fastened between animal and Superman – a rope over
the abyss (*Z*, p. 43)

[. . .] *kanatnyi pliasun* [. . .] poshel po *kanatu*, protianutomu mezhdu
dvumia bashniami i *visevshemu nad bazarnoi ploshchad'iu* i narodom

[. . .] the tight-rope walker [. . .] was proceeding across the rope,
which was stretched between two towers and thus hung over the
people and the market square (*Z*, p. 47)

Mayakovsky has the following image:

Ia dushu nad propast'iu natianul kanatom,
zhongliruia slovami, zakachalsia nad nei.

Over the abyss I've stretched my soul in a tightrope
and, juggling with words, totter above it.
("The Backbone Flute," trans. George Reavey, p. 125)

The other example is connected with the theme of death and
suicide.

Pust' [. . .] pridet buria i striakhnet s dereva vse *gniloe* i chervivoe! O,
esli by prishli propovedniki *skoroi smerti*!

I wish a storm would come and shake all this rottenness and worm-
eatenness from the tree! I wish preachers of *speedy* death would come!
(*Z*, p. 98)

Both words, "skoraia" and "smert," are spaced out in the
Russian translation (as opposed to the English one, where only
the attribute is italicized), and must have caught the eye even
of an unattentive reader. In "A Cloud in Trousers," Zarathustra's "gniloe" ("rotten") becomes "zaplesnevshii"
("moldly"), but otherwise the image is kept intact:

> Dai im,
> *zaplesnevshim* v radosti,
> *skoroi smerti* vremeni [...]

> Give them,
> who are moldly with joy,
> the quick death of time [...]

In this chapter, I have pointed to some of the most conspicuous
similarities between Nietzsche and Mayakovsky. Nietzsche's
influence on the early Mayakovsky is a question of the utmost
importance to the study of the poet's literary genealogy; nevertheless, my own reading of the Russian translation of *Zarathustra* with respect to Mayakovsky's poetry is the first modest
attempt at such a scrutiny. A more detailed stylistic analysis,
will, I am sure, only substantiate my thesis – namely that
Nietzsche in general and *Zarathustra* in particular served as
vital stimuli for Mayakovsky during his first, formative years as
a poet. In fact, no other writer beside Dostoevsky seems to
have had such a marked and thorough impact on Mayakovsky
as Nietzsche.

NOTES

1 D. S. Mirsky, *Russia: A Short Cultural History* (London, 1942),
  p. 273.
2 N. Ustrialov, "Religiia Revoliutsii," in his book of essays *Pod
  znakom revoliutsii* (Harbin, 1925), p. 282. Reprinted from the
  journal *Okno* no. 2 (Harbin, 1920).
3 This is why two of the most penetrating books on Dostoevsky,
  Nikolai Berdiaev's *Mirosozertsanie Dostoevskogo* (Moscow, 1921),
  with its analyses of the conception of the "Revolution of the
  Spirit," and Lev Shestov's *Dostoevskii i Nitshe* (St. Petersburg,

1903), where the author very acutely dissects the nature of tragedy, are also excellent introductions to the study of Mayakovsky's spiritual quest.

4 Shestov, *Dostoevskii i Nitshe*, p. 194.

5 Thus, for example, the Futurist exclamation "We look at their nothingness from the height of skyscrapers!" (from the manifesto in "A Slap in the Face of Public Taste," 1912) was no doubt perceived by this Nietzsche-oriented generation as a variation on the "mountain theme" in *Zarathustra*. Nietzsche's influence on Mayakovsky and Russian Futurism was recognized by Krystyna Pomorska: "Even a superficial glance at the Futurist ideology immediately shows the influence of or convergence with Nietzsche, especially his persistent and renowned concept of a superman in *Also sprach Zarathustra*. Majakovskij's poetry in particular reflects this myth in numerous variations" (Krystyna Pomorska, "Majakovskij's Cosmic Myth," *Myth in Literature*, ed. Andrej Kodjak, Krystyna Pomorska, and Stephen Rudy (Columbus, OH, 1985). See also Bernice Glatzer Rosenthal, "A New Word for a New Myth: Nietzsche and Russian Futurism," *The European Foundations of Russian Modernism*, ed. Peter Barta (Lewiston, NY 1991).

6 *Rytsari Bezumiia* (Kiev, 1914), p. 37.

7 G. Tasteven, *Futurizm* (Moscow, 1914), p. 53.

8 A. Kruchenykh, *Stikhi V. Mayakovskogo* (Petrograd, 1914), p. 13. Cf. Christa Baumgarth's commentary: "Im Grunde wollten die Futuristen nur konsequenter als Nietzsche sein [...]" (Christa Baumgarth, *Geschichte des Futurismus* [Reinbeck bei Hamburg, 1966], p. 128).

9 N. Chuzhak, "Trinadtsatyi apostol," *K dialektike iskusstva* (Chita, 1921), p. 64.

10 First printed in the journal *Okno* no. 2 (Harbin, 1920); quoted from the author's collection of essays, *Pod znakom revoliutsii*, p. 283.

11 "'Futurizm' i 'Veshch,'" *Kniga i Revoliutsiia* 8/9 (1921), pp. 26, 27. Ivanov-Razumnik's italics.

12 The article was published in the journal *Yun'* No 1 (Vladivostok, 1921).

13 *New York Times*, October 11, 1925; quoted from Viktor Pertsov, *Mayakovskii, Zhizn' i tvorchestvo*, (Moscow, 1972), III pp. 53–54.

14 Andrei Bely, "Fridrich Nitsshe," *Arabeski* (Moscow, 1911), p. 68.

15 Andrei Bely, "Fridrich Nitsshe," p. 74.

16 Roman Jakobson, "On a Generation that Squandered its Poets" (1931), in Roman Jakobson, *Language in Literature* (Cambridge, MA, 1987), pp. 278–79 (trans. Edward J. Brown).

17 Roman Jakobson, "Marginal Notes on the Prose of the Poet Pasternak," in *ibid.*, pp. 306–7 (trans. Angela Livingstone).
18 Lawrence L. Stahlberger, *The Symbolic System of Majakovskij* (The Hague, 1964), p. 67.
19 Stahlberger, *Symbolic System*, p. 67.
20 Cf. Schopenhauer, "Tragedy must be regarded [. . .] as the height of poetry" (*Welt as Wille und Vorstellung*, quoted from L. Vygotsky, *Psikhologiia iskusstva* [Moscow, 1987], p. 255).
21 Boris Pasternak, "Safe Conduct," *The Voice of Prose*, ed. Christopher Barnes (Edinburgh, 1986), p. 88.
22 Quoted from Vasilii Kamenskii, *Zhizn's Mayakovskim* (Moscow, 1940), p. 54.
23 Lev Shestov, *Dostoevskii i Nitsshe*, p. 229.
24 "Predlozhenie issledovateliam," *Voprosy Literatury* 9 (1966), pp. 203–8. See also Irina Shapiro Corten, "The Influence of Dostoevskij on Majakovskij's Poem 'Pro eto,'" *Studies Presented to Professor Roman Jakobson by His Students*, ed. Charles E. Gribble (Cambridge, MA, 1968), pp. 76–83.
25 V. Pertsov, *Mayakovskii: Zhizn' i tvorchestvo*, 3 vols. (Moscow, 1969–1972).
26 Pertsov, *Mayakovskii*, I, pp. 248, 249.
27 Pertsov, *Mayakovskii*, I, p. 249.
28 N. Khardzhiev, "Zametki o Mayakovskom," *Poeticheskaya kul'tura Mayakovskogo* (Moscow, 1970), p. 207.
29 V. Pertsov, *Mayakovskii*, I, p. 248.
30 Unfortunately, I have not been able to locate this copy to establish which edition/translation Mayakovsky read.
31 All references to Mayakovsky's works are cited parenthetically in the text as *PSS* (*Polnoe sobranie sochinenii*, 13 vols., Moscow, 1955–61).
32 Lili Brik, "Iz vospominanii," *S Mayakovskim* (Moscow, 1934), pp. 62–63.
33 This question is of little consequence when discussing the general influence of the book on Mayakovsky's work, but it becomes crucial for the analysis of textual parallels. I have used the 1913 edition of Antonovsky's translation, since this is the one Pertsov quotes from, and it may very well be the edition Pertsov refers to as having been preserved in Mayakovsky's library, although we cannot take it for granted. This creates an obvious textological problem. However, both translators have retained A. Bobrishchev-Pushkin's poetic rendering of "The Sorcerer's Lament," which, as we shall see, had a direct impact on Mayakovsky's monologues with God.

34 Stahlberger, *Symbolic System*, p. 117.
35 See L. Brik, "Mayakovskii i chuzhie stikhi," *Vladimir Mayakovskii v vospominaniiakh sovremennikov* (Moscow, 1963), pp. 328–54.
36 L. Brik, "Mayakovskii i chuzhie stikhi," p. 331.
37 Jakobson, "On a Generation that Squandered its Poets," p. 285.
38 Trans. George Reavey, *The Bedbug and Selected Poetry*, ed. Patricia Blake, Bloomington and London, 1975), p. 81. Henceforth cited parenthetically in the text.
39 Edward J. Brown, *Mayakovsky: Poet in The Revolution* (Princeton, 1973), p. 178.
40 See, for example, Stahlberger, *Symbolic System*.
41 In Nietzsche's vocabulary, a synonym for the feeble, the impotent. See Shestov, *Dostoevskii i Nitshe*, p. 218.
42 Trans. Gary Wiggins, *Russian Literature Triquarterly* 12 (1975), pp. 42, 56.
43 Stahlberger, *Symbolic System*, p. 141, and, referring to him, Brown, *Mayakovskii*, p. 162.
44 R. J. Hollingdale, "Introduction" to *Thus Spoke Zarathustra*, p. 27.
45 Stahlberger, *Symbolic System*, p. 141.
46 This parallel has been pointed out by N. Khardzhiev (*Poeticheskaia kul' tura mayakovskogo*, p. 207). V. V. Ivanov has suggested that Mayakovsky may have been influenced by Gogol as well ("Ob odnoi paralleli k gogolevskomu Viiu," *Trudy po znakovym sisteman* 5 (Tartu, 1971), pp. 138–41. Given the whole Nietzschean ambience of the play, however, this influence must be considered secondary in this particular case.

CHAPTER 2

Khlebnikov and Nietzsche: pieces of an incomplete mosaic

Henryk Baran

Velimir (Viktor Vladimirovich) Khlebnikov (1885–1922) was a leading figure in Russian Futurism during the 1910s and early 1920s. A poet, a theorist of language, and a utopian visionary, he inspired much of the poetic and cultural platform of Hylaea, the principal Futurist group. His ideas and literary practice, particularly his radical experimentation with language, influenced not only the young Vladimir Mayakovsky, a fellow Hylaean, but also, years later, such poetic innovators as Nikolai Zabolotsky and the Leningrad *oberiuty* Daniil Kharms and Aleksandr Vvedensky (Oberiu: Association for Real Art [Ob″edinenie Real′nogo Iskusstva]). In the past, Khlebnikov was little studied, a situation which enhanced his reputation as one of the most difficult modern Russian poets, the complexity of whose writings is akin to the challenges facing a reader of T. S. Eliot, Ezra Pound, or James Joyce. Since the mid-1960s, both readers and critics have paid increasing attention to Khlebnikov. As a result, his work is interpreted at a much deeper level than before, while our understanding of Khlebnikov's biography has advanced far beyond the widely-circulated misconceptions through the prism of which it was once seen.[1]

Hylaea came to the notice of the Russian public during the years 1912–13, though individual works by its members, as well as the important collection *A Trap for Judges* (*Sadok sudei*, 1910), had appeared earlier. Khlebnikov played a crucial role in developing the group's core myths, expressed both in a number of his own works, as well as texts by others. In this myth-making, which involved a rejection of many current

58

cultural norms, and an aggressive promulgation of a carefully constructed heroic model for both the individual and the social collective, lies the most important area of Nietzsche's influence on Khlebnikov. In particular, Nietzsche's conception of *self-definition*, his notion that one may *will* the shape and meaning of one's life, are an important source for Khlebnikov's assertion of his own role as a new man, both poet and heroic warrior. Of course, the idea of self-definition was not unique to Futurism: it formed an essential part of the reception and appropriation of Nietzsche's philosophy by turn-of-the-century Russian literature.[2] Khlebnikov's response to the German thinker and poet may be seen as part of a broader literary-cultural pattern.

Any discussion of Khlebnikov inevitably touches upon two topics: his ideas about and experimentation with language, and his theories of time and history. These preoccupations, particularly the second, parallel some of Nietzsche's concerns and may tempt one to see an influence. Yet in the realm of poetic language Khlebnikov was far more radical than Nietzsche.[3] His emphasis on "the word" (*slovo*) was partly based on the view that a poet may draw on earlier stages of a language, using elements that are potential but unrealized. He himself borrowed words and expressions from other Slavic languages; included in his texts forms from regional dialects; and, most important, coined new words. But early on he also started working with individual sounds (sometimes Khlebnikov uses the term letters), particularly in word-initial position. In his eyes, such a segment may contain the meaning of the entire lexeme. Though linguistically erroneous, this theory led him to a matchless wealth of creative explorations and poetic orchestration. Subsequently, Khlebnikov became even bolder, developing an "alphabet of the intellect" (*azbuka uma*), a "language of the stars" (*zvezdnyi iazyk*). Analyzing sets of words beginning with the same letter allowed him to isolate what he saw as its invariant meaning, which involved spatial parameters and transcended the differences of individual languages. As Khlebnikov notes in "Artists of the World!," "The alphabet common to a multitude of peoples is in fact a short lexicon of the spatial world that is of such concern to your art, painters, and to your paintbrushes" (Kh. *CW* I, p. 367). At the same time, the promise of the "language of the stars" lay in its being able to recreate the original unity of mankind: like his discoveries in the realm of time, it could serve as a tool and a weapon in the hands of the Futurist.

Khlebnikov himself asserted that his preoccupation with time was prompted by a desire to find an order within the flow of history, and that it was triggered by the Russian fleet's 1905 defeat at the battle of Tsushima. By 1911, he had developed a theory of cycles according to which both favorable and unfavorable historical events are a result of temporal repetitions. This theory, refined and extended during the years of war and revolution, ultimately became a sweeping mathematical conception (the "Futurian scale," *gamma Budetlianina*), which seemed to the poet to explain the chaos and destruction of the period. His claim was that the occurrence of historical events revolves around the numbers 2 and 3. As he wrote in "Excerpt from The Tables of Destiny":

I understood then that time was structured in powers of two and three, the lowest possible even and odd numbers.

I understood that the true nature of time consists in the recurrent multiplication of itself by twos and threes, and when I recalled the old Slavic belief in the powers of "odd and even" I decided that wisdom was indeed a tree that grows from a seed. The superstition is all in the quotation marks.

Once I had uncovered the significance for time of odd and even, I had the sensation of holding in my hands a mousetrap in which aboriginal Fate quivered like a terrified little animal. (Kh. *CW* I, p. 420)

According to the poet, a period of 2^m days separates analogous historical events, while 3^n days separate an event from its antithesis or "counter-event." In one of his many statements of these principles, he explains:

With the colors of blood, iron, and death we can adorn the phantasmal outlines of the time-clamp of 3^x days.

Behavior and punishment, act and retribution.

Say the victim dies at the initial point.

The killer will die after 3^5.

(Kh. *CW* I, p. 422).

Khlebnikov's ideas about temporal cycles are part of a broad concern with the category of time in twentieth-century culture.[4] To the extent that Nietzsche's conception of the "eternal recurrence" helped fan this widespread cultural and intellectual phenomenon, one may speak of it influencing, at some remove, Khlebnikov's theories. However, far more important for Khlebnikov in this regard were his own abiding scientific and mathematical interests and insights – areas where there are numerous striking points of contact and parallels between his ideas and those of various scientists and mathematicians.[5] Furthermore, his notion of temporal cyclicity affirms that history has a predictable *structure*, and does not imply, in Nietzsche's fashion, the eternal repetition of existence down to the minutest detail.

Clearly, Khlebnikov was a theorist as well as a poet, and his conception of the world was both organized and far-reaching. The sources of his vision were multiple: literary, artistic, philosophical, historical, mathematical, and scientific.[6] Disentangling Nietzschean strains from among them is a difficult matter, both on overall methodological grounds and for reasons that specifically relate to Khlebnikov, who was perhaps the most anti-archival, anti-self-documenting of modern Russian literary figures. The vicissitudes of the Civil War, during which Khlebnikov, a confirmed wanderer during much of his life, alternately found himself in zones controlled by the Reds and by the Whites, and the lack of a reliable place where, like Blok or Sologub, he would have been able to store and organize his personal papers, has left us with only limited information concerning his readings: a list of books he owned at the end of his life, an occasional title mentioned in an article, a citation or an author's name in a literary or polemical text. When seeking to trace the genesis of a particular strand of Khlebnikov's thematics, including the Nietzschean, the scholar is repeatedly forced into conjecture and reconstruction. The same is true in the present case.[7]

One can, of course, investigate conceptual parallels – coincidences and similarities between elements of Khlebnikov's world on the one hand, and themes and images found in

Nietzsche's writings on the other. This is a potentially fruitful approach, yet by itself questionable as a means of asserting the presence of an actual influence, given the diversity of Khlebnikov's readings, and the presence of similar ideas in some of them. Moreover, multiplicity of meanings was a cardinal principle of Khlebnikov's poetics (as it was for Nietzsche) and the presence of several sources and/or internal motivations for the appearance of an image or motif in one of his works is a common occurrence. Claims of reception and appropriation gain from proof of contact – proof that goes beyond such models as "A probably read the works of B because everyone at the time was reading them." Fortunately, there are traces in Khlebnikov's writings of some degree of direct reading of Nietzsche: several instances in which Nietzsche or his work is mentioned explicitly. A closer look at these prompts us to investigate further: as a result, certain suggestive parallels between some of Nietzsche's ideas and elements of Khlebnikov's world-view are uncovered, and the likelihood of an influence of the German thinker on the Russian poet – particularly in the realm of mythopoetic self-definition – may be legitimately considered as having been demonstrated.

Nietzschean themes could have entered Khlebnikov's purview by one or more of several paths. He could have read some of the numerous Russian translations of Nietzsche's texts or any number of scholarly or popular expositions of his views. He also could have assimilated Nietzschean elements indirectly, particularly through the writings and oral comments of the Symbolist poet and theoretician Viacheslav Ivanov, whose circle Khlebnikov belonged to for a brief time, and with whom he maintained close contacts in spite of his overall break with Symbolism. It is possible, as has been suggested recently, that Ivanov's interpretation and reformulation of Nietzsche's concept of the Dionysian principle provides the key to a successful reading of Khlebnikov's early play *The Virgins' God* ("Devii bog") and dramatic sketch "The Mystery of the Distant Ones" ("Tainstvo dal'nikh," 1908).[8] The roots of such possible sources and influences may become clearer in the future, if and when a full record of Khlebnikov's intellectual development is established; in this article, the main focus is on texts where the Nietzschean connection is explicit. The first instance of a reference to Nietzsche is found in the prose poem "Garden of Animals" ("Zverinets"), often regarded as having been written in broad imitation of Walt Whitman, and under the influence of Ivanov, to whom the work is dedicated.[9] The text is based on a visit to the St. Petersburg zoo. In it, capsule portraits of various animals are coupled with wide-ranging similes and metaphors, in which the world of Khlebnikov's cultural and political concerns is diversely reflected. One of these involves a walrus:

Where the massive gleaming walrus, like some languid beauty, fans itself with its slippery black flipper and falls into the water, and when it heaves itself back onto its platform, its great lubbering body sports the bristly whiskered, smooth-browed head of Nietzsche. (Kh. *CW* III, forthcoming)

The image of Nietzsche is the familiar one, and by itself would not imply much more than a superficial acquaintance with cultural iconography. Significantly, however, it is part of a category of images whereby the nature of the animals is explained by reference to culture and history. Most of these images are drawn from the Russian tradition, and are arrayed to convey a strongly nationalistic, anti-Western message. As a counterpoint to the noble world of the animals, Khlebnikov sets the mediocre world of human beings, particularly the Germans:

Where iron bars seem like a father who stops a bloody fight to remind his sons they are brothers. Where the Germans go to drink beer. And easy women sell their bodies. (Kh. *CW* III, forthcoming)

What is Nietzsche doing here, in a company with, among others, Gogol, *The Igor Tale*, and Ivan the Terrible? The answer lies in the second of the passages referred to above. This one comes from a 1913 article, "A Friend in the West" ("Zapadnyi drug"), which Khlebnikov contributed to *Slavianin*, a short-lived Slavophile newspaper:

The Russians are more than mere Slavs. Besides, there are signs to indicate that the German century is ending and the Slavic century is beginning. More and more great men of the West have Slavic connections: Ostwald, Nietzsche, Bismarck. Both Nietzsche and Bismarck are notably non-German. One of them even said "Praise the Lord" on that account. (Kh. *CW* I, p. 245)

There is some justification to Khlebnikov's assertion. Indeed, Nietzsche increasingly identified with the Slavs, claiming for himself Polish ancestry, as well as an affinity for what he termed "Russian fatalism."[10] At the same time, it is important to note that Khlebnikov's myth-making sometimes involved a rather disingenuous effort at turning cultural figures he approved of, whatever their national background, into Slavs – and Russians where possible. One example of this was Khlebnikov's transformation of a legend that the Byzantine emperor Justinian was of Slavic origin into an artistic-historical fact: a Slavicized Justinian appears in several of his works. Thus, the inclusion of Nietzsche in the category of "honorary Russians" is more than an amusing idiosyncrasy, but an expression of a marked status for the name and its referent in Khlebnikov's model of the world, and a signal of a likely interest in the philosopher's heritage.

The third of the passages in question occurs in an August 21, 1915 letter from Khlebnikov to his family. It comes up in a comment on his life in the literary-artistic colony of Kuokkala, on the Finnish coast:

I find a feeling of freedom here, and I have enough room to spread my wings like a Caspian osprey, and I scoop up my prey from the sea of numbers. Behold how the whitetail falcon flies, from the Volga over Beloostrov. Thus spake Zarathustra. (Kh. *CW* I, p. 104)

It may be that the last sentence is simply a rhetorical flourish, a casual mention of Nietzsche's best known work. Yet it is more likely, given the emphasis on polysemy and intertextuality in Khlebnikov's poetics, that the quotation is a signal of a deeper link to Nietzsche's *œuvre*. More specifically, the bird simile Khlebnikov uses to characterize himself may derive from, among other sources, a notable passage at the end of Part Three in *Thus Spoke Zarathustra*:

If ever I spread out a still sky above myself and flew
with my own wings into my own sky:
if, playing, I have swum into deep light-distances and
bird-wisdom came to my freedom:
but thus speaks bird-wisdom: 'Behold, there is no above,
no below! Fling yourself above, out, back, weightless
bird! Sing! speak no more!'

$(Z$, p. 247)[11]

The implicit analogy drawn in the letter between the Futurist
poet and Nietzsche's protagonist suggests that Zarathustra
may be numbered among the many and diverse *personae*
("doubles") of Khlebnikov.[12]

The final one of the passages comes in a late work – the poem
"The Tree" ("Derevo"), which Khlebnikov wrote in Piati-
gorsk in November 1921, and which turns out to be especially
important for our purpose. There are several variants of this
poem. One of these was first published by Nikolai Khardzhiev
in 1940.[13] As the title indicates, the text consists of a poetic
depiction of a tree. In a brilliant projection of his own reactions
and views, Khlebnikov likens both its individual parts
(branches, leaves) and the tree as a whole to various events and
personages from current and past history.[14] In effect, the tree
becomes a partial double of the poet. The second (numbered)
part of the poem contains these lines:

And every morning Nietzsche echoes in the forest.
And every morning, sunshine beggar,
You take your glasses off and go after pennies.
(Kh. *CW* III, forthcoming)

(I kazhdoe utro shumit v lesu Nitsshe.
I kazhdoe utro ty solnechnyi nishchii,
Snimaia s ochei ochki, idesh' za kopeechkoi!)
(*NP*, p. 278)

Khlebnikov's word-plays, however elaborate, usually contain
a semantic core, and thus the appearance of Nietzsche's name
in a marked place in the line (as part of the rhyme-pair
"Nitsshe-nishchii") and identified with the tree itself, prompts
a search for both intratextual and intertextual motivations for
it. Identifying the tree with Nietzsche seems to be prompted by

the broad theme of the tree as a fighter in different spheres: the iconoclastic philosopher is an apt analogue for such a figure. At the same time, given the centrality of the tree in the poem, it seems reasonable to trace the source of the image to a passage in Nietzsche where a tree plays a major role. This may be found in *Thus Spoke Zarathustra*, in the section "Of the Rabble": "We build our nest in the tree Future; eagles shall bring food to us solitaries in their beaks!" (*Z*, p. 122).[15]

In the same poem, the double repetition of the word "morning" (*utro*), natural in view of the recurrent forest scene depicted in Khlebnikov's poem, may be secondarily motivated by the frequency with which this motif comes up in Nietzsche's writings: be it in the 1881 collection of aphorisms, *The Dawn*, or in *Zarathustra*, where dawns appear at various moments in the text, for example, the beginning of "The Sign" (*Z*, p. 333).

Taken in a fuller context, the previously cited lines from "The Tree" reveal further connections between the poem and Nietzsche's thought, especially since Nietzsche is mentioned:

> You spin out night's oxygen into a sinewy drag-net
> And challenge the firmament!
> The resonant thwack! of a stick with a thousand leaves!
> And even the moon's at fault:
> In the meshes of the drag-net,
> Night's colors glitter
> With the thick silver of fish scales.
> And every morning Nietzsche echoes in the forest.
> And every morning, sunshine beggar,
> You take your glasses off and go after pennies.
> The stars – even the ones up there –
> Conversed all night of fair-haired herds.
> There are fights and fights,
> And the justice
> Of a forest outlaw's fist.
>
> (Kh. *CW* III, forthcoming)

The "night conversation of the stars" is a clear echo of Lermontov's best known lyric poem,[16] but the nature of this conversation, "of fair-haired herds" (or "blond herds" ["o belokurom skote"]), as well as the following lines ("There are fights and fights, / And the justice / Of a forest outlaw's fist"

["Est' draka i draka / I pravo kulaka / Lesnogo galakha," *NP*, 278]), is somewhat obscure. A look at another variant of the poem expands the context somewhat: "You spin out night's oxygen into a sinewy drag-net: / In the meshes of the net, night's colors glitter like fish, / Where the stars become legends of fair-haired herds. / I am sure a blond beast taught the tree its behavior" (Kh. *CW* III, forthcoming) ("Ty tianesh' kislorod nochei moguchim nevodom, / V iacheiakh nevoda sverkaet ryboi sineva nochei, / Gde zvezdy – predan'e o belokurom skote. / Veriu; dal nravy derevu zver' belokuryi").[17]

But it is a fragment from "The Tree," ultimately discarded by the poet, which fully clarifies Khlebnikov's meaning. The following passage originally followed line 34 in the version of the poem we have concentrated on: "Some blond beast taught the tree its behavior; / Kindness and mercy are witless as chickens" (Kh. *CW* III, forthcoming) ("Derevu nravy dal zver' belokuryi, / Milost' i nezhnost' glupy kak kury)" (*NP*, p. 452). These two lines bring the reader squarely into the realm of Nietzschean philosophy and psychology. Khlebnikov refers here to the celebrated "blond beast,"[18] the being at the core of the so-called noble races whose psychology and ethics are opposed to the slave morality of Judaism-Christianity (*GM*, pp. 40–41).[19] This image, and the concept of the noble man, are part of a critique of Christian (Jewish) morality, which Nietzsche claims was born out of the *ressentiment* of slaves. Khlebnikov's pithy formulation, "Kindness and mercy are witless as chickens," catches the essence of Nietzsche's attack on pity and other related Christian virtues. The Futurist poet uses it in the several variants to build a more or less explicit opposition between the tree, which behaves as if taught by a beast of prey, and the stars, a synecdochic replacement for the sky as a whole, which are linked with cattle – that is, the natural target of a predator.

With this source of the Khlebnikov text clarified, some other elements in "The Tree" fall into place. In particular, there are the lines from its beginning, "Your sharp thorns lash us, putting out eyes, scratching / The servile human face" (Kh. *CW* III, forthcoming) ("Ty mechesh' ostrye koliuchki, chtob

ochi vykolot' / Liudiam vytsarapat' litso raba," *NP*, 277),
which are usually interpreted in political terms. This is
natural, since Khlebnikov is writing at the end of the Civil
War. However, they can also be related to the attempt by the
Nietzsche-like tree – a *persona*, a double of Khlebnikov himself –
to change his audience's psychology, to bring home to them the
true nature of human society during this period.
There is a crucial parallel between the tree and Khlebnikov
himself. The "protagonist" of the poem assumes a *heroic stance*
and thus expresses once again a mythologem which was central
for Khlebnikov's model of the world, and which helped define
to a significant degree the group myth of early Futurism. Two
passages from the version of the poem published by Khardzhiev clarify this theme:

> Fighting over open spaces, bright with shaman's eyes,
> Impaling night on the black points of your branches,
> Tree, you have terrified the grove: space drowses on
>   your curves.
> The Cossack rider, his long hair streaming, flies across
>   the field,
> The lance in his hand trembles with war-fervor.
> You tap at the windows of the starry sky.
> But the darkness has no eye.
> . . .
> You fight for spatial volume, seem to seek
>   Lobachevskian space,
> And the young seek a sword to swear an oath on.
>   (Kh. *CW* III, forthcoming)

"The Tree" and its imagery is but one example, late in Khlebnikov's life, of a series of thematically-related works which
began years before, and which involve different expressions of
the mythologem of a heroic duel with a potentially superior
opponent. This mythologem was particularly important for
Khlebnikov's writings before World War I,[20] though variants
of it, with a different content, can be found in his late works as
well.
   The mythologem is articulated most extensively in Khlebnikov's first "supertale," "The Otter's Children" ("Deti
Vydry," 1914). The term "supertale" or "supersaga"

(Schmidt – *sverkhpovest'*, *zapovest'*), coined by Khlebnikov, was used by him to designate a new genre, in which an assortment of works, diverse in genre and contents, often written and published previously, is brought together and joined into a larger whole, a second-order montage. "The Otter's Children" is composed of numerous texts, created between 1911 and 1913, which are assembled into six sections, each of which is termed a *parus* ("lacunar," though usually translated as "sail"). The sections include prose tales, a theatrical sketch, a narrative poem, a philosophical disquisition in verse, and a poetic "dialogue of the dead." The title, "The Otter's Children," refers to its two eponymous protagonists (a brother and a sister). In the course of the work, they travel through time, and stop in different historical epochs, where they meet various characters. The text opens in the days of the world's creation, as imagined by a minor Siberian people, the Orochi; it ends within the soul of Khlebnikov, identified with the Son of the Otter. In the process, Khlebnikov has an opportunity to describe his early ideas on historical cycles and to polemicize with economic and biological determinism (Marx and Darwin).

In spite of the diversity of both genre and contents, "The Otter's Children" as a whole possesses a major cohesive element. This is provided by the Son of the Otter, who, starting with his role as a culture hero in the beginning of the work, serves as a model of heroic behavior emulated by the many other *dramatis personae*. Whether facing a cosmic body during the days of the world's beginning, an enemy army in war, or Time itself in trying to grasp its "laws," the positive message is the same. Thanks to the Son's explicit identification with Khlebnikov in the last section, "Deti Vydry" essentially becomes a glorification of courageous action, no matter what the cost to oneself. This message is consistent with the self-images propagated by the Hylaeans.

Significantly, the heroic figures in the "supertale" are differentiated from the great mass of people, although the poet's "spokesmen" call for everyone to behave in this way. This opposition and call for transformation is expressed very clearly in Section Five, in a discussion of the Futurists' (Futurians') mastery of time and the help they may lend struggling humanity as a whole:

> They beg in vain: give back the world
> we once had, free from cogwheels and bolts –
> the Futurian merely adjusts a screw,
> seeking to build a shield that fits.
>
> He knows he can build what he wants,
> and number offers him support.
> When lightning strikes, or avalanche,
> the masses shout: "It's not our fault!"
>
> Oh man! Forget humility!
> See there! Like an ancient axle creaking,
> barely able to grease its friction
> or manage its missing points,
>
> alone, alone! a feeble constellation
> comes to passionate grips with destiny –
> There! Go there, you statuesque young man,
> be older brother to that stricken hind!
>
> (Kh. *CW* II, p. 296)

The stance of opposition between the Hylaeans and the rest of society is expressed elsewhere in Khlebnikov. Thus, in the polemical essay "!Futurian" (1914, unpublished), it is central to the poet's slashing attack on his literary opponents and on journalistic and literary critics. Khlebnikov's jibes at the mob-like opposition are filled with echoes of Nietzsche's motifs as well as style:

> We rang for room service and the year 1913 answered: it gave Planet Earth a valiant new race of people, the heroic Futurians....
>
> But every line we write breathes victory and challenge, the bad temper of a conqueror, underground explosions, howls. We are a volcano. We vomit forth black smoke....
>
> We have made it very clear that 20th century man is dragging around a thousand-year-old corpse (the past), doubled over like an ant trying to move a log. We alone have given man his own true stature and tossed away the truss of the past (the Tolstois, the Homers, the Pushkins)....
>
> For us, all freedoms have combined to form one fundamental freedom: freedom from the dead, i.e. from all these gentlemen who have lived before us....

Above the dark precipice of our ancestors, beneath looming masses of rock, the entire country picks its way on goat feet down the steep cliff of the present; it steps surefootedly on ledges in the wall – allusions we have majestically let fall, our three-line Korans (for instance "Incantation by Laughter" and "We want to get close to the stars"), skipping from one foothold in the wall to the next, occasionally stopping to rest, elegant as a mountain goat. Eagles watch over its progress. (Kh. *CW* II, pp. 260–62)

This may be juxtaposed with, for example, the following passage in *Zarathustra*: "I do not call cold-spirited, mulish, blind, or intoxicated men stout-hearted. He possesses heart who knows fear but *masters* fear; who sees the abyss, but sees it with *pride*. He who sees the abyss, but with an eagle's eyes – he who *grasps* the abyss with an eagle's claws: *he* possesses courage" (*Z*, p. 298).

World War I muted considerably the shrillness and militancy of early Futurism, while the magnitude of losses of life prompted Khlebnikov to seek to determine the "laws of time" with ever greater urgency. The figure of the Futurist (Futurian) is transformed, while the Hylaeans are replaced in Khlebnikov's worldview by the Presidents of Planet Earth (*predsedateli zemnogo shara, predzemshary*) or by the ranks of the Martians (inspired by H. G. Wells). Still, the opposition between the small band of the select fighters and their opponents – now increasingly "the old men" (deemed responsible for the war), and the states which have engaged in the mass slaughter of human beings – is as sharp as ever, and is expressed in a range of texts.

One of these is "An Appeal by the Presidents of Planet Earth," which contains a particularly bitter attack on the "governments of space" (*gosudarstva prostranstva*), counterposed to the forthcoming "governments of time" (*gosudarstva vremeni*). The following passage is typical of its polemics:

Your space government of sinister plunder, you kings and kaisers and sultans, is as different from our society as the hand of an ape burned by its unknown fire god is different from the hand of a rider calmly holding the reins of bridled fate. (Kh. *CW* I, p. 334)

Such a posture is strikingly similar to Nietzsche's highly negative views on the state:

But the state lies in all languages of good and evil; and whatever it says, it lies – and whatever it has, it has stolen. Everything about it is false; it bites with stolen teeth. Even its belly is false. Confusion of the language of good and evil; I offer you this sign as the sign of the state. Truly, this sign indicates the will to death! Truly, it beckons to the preachers of death. (Z, p. 76)

Nietzschean overtones again appear in the proclamation "The Trumpet of the Martians" (1916), signed by Khlebnikov and several of his associates:

... We are uncompromising carpenters, and once again we throw ourselves and our names into the boiling kettles of unprecedented projects.

We believe in ourselves, we reject with indignation the vicious whispers of people from the past who still delude themselves that they can bite at our heels. Are we not gods? And are we not unprecedented in this: *our steadfast betrayal of our own past*, just as it barely reaches the age of victory, and our steadfast rage, raised above the planet like a hammer whose time has come? Planet Earth begins to shake already at the heavy tread of our feet ... (Kh. *CW* I, p. 321)

Before World War I, the heroic myth of Hylaea was closely related to Khlebnikov's ideas about the Russian people and Russian culture. These are clearly expressed in an early pro-grammatic essay, "The Burial Mound of Sviatogor" ("Kurgan Sviatogora," 1908), where Khlebnikov polemicizes with the Symbolists and with broader cultural and political forces which, he feels, have turned Russia toward the West, and away from its true cultural identity. He calls for a return by Russian culture to its original pristine condition, where it expressed a native, rather than an alien Western spirit. Images from two sources are fused together in the argument: the folk *bylina* about the death of the primal Russian hero Sviatogor and the transfer of some of his strength to Il'ia Muromets, and the geological conception of the descent of the Eurasian plain from a former sea-bed (formed by the retreat of glaciation). Equa-ting the sea to Sviatogor, and the Russian people, now living in its former boundaries, to the younger hero Il'ia, Khlebnikov offers an elaborate cultural hypothesis. According to his view, the Russians, the present inhabitants of Eurasia, have been shaped in the image of the original hero, but have been prevented from fulfilling their natural, heroic destiny by the influence of the West. An amelioration of their situation can be effected by linguistic experimentation (neologisms, etc.), which can bring about a mystical union between the Russian people and the land they inhabit.

A key element in the essay is the notion of *national archetypes*, which extends into the sphere of psychology. The word "will" (*volia*) and its derivatives recur frequently in the text:

We are executors of the great sea's will
. . . .
And the vast extent of our comutual countenance, is it not the lawful inheritor of the vast extent of the ancient sea?
. . . .
The defiant one desires to see himself enrolled among the tribe of the defiant.
. . . .
And must we not reproach even the great Pushkin because in his work the sounding numbers of the life of the nation – the sea's inheritor – have been replaced by numbers from the life of nations subservient to the will of the ancient islands.
. . . .
Let us consider the rays of earthly wills. If we rest content with a borrowed light, then we consign ourselves to outer darkness, and the good rays will remain forever at the service of neighboring nations. We must not stint in nearness to divinity – even to one whose existence we deny, even to one we ourselves may have willed into existence. (Kh. *CW* I, pp. 234–36)

As in the case of the myth of the Futurist hero, Khlebnikov's notion of the national archetype, of what the Russians have been in the past and what they should be in the future, revolves around self-definition, overcoming one's current state by an act of will. Evidence for this is found in various texts. To cite but one: a passage from a 1912–13 article, "Monuments," where Khlebnikov enumerates his ideas about the kind of monuments that should be put up throughout Russia:

Erect a monument to Ilya Murometz – to the might of the Russian people in his native village of Karacharov. Thus will the government express the hope that Russians will lead their lives on the model of their hero, and mothers will give birth to heroes, inspired by the stone erection. (Kh. *CW* I, p. 238)

It is noteworthy that the passage emphasizes a people's ability to define themselves, to consciously shape their psychology and life.

The concept of national psychological archetypes leads back to the first of the passages where Nietzsche is mentioned, the quote from "Garden of Animals," and to some information concerning the origins of this work, which Khlebnikov first discussed in a letter of June 10, 1909 to Viacheslav Ivanov:

> What have I been doing these last few days? I went to the zoo, where I had the strangest vision of some kind of connection between Buddhism and a camel, and between Islam and a tiger. After a brief reflection I arrived at a formula: natural species are the offspring of belief, and religions are infantile species. One and the same rock has split humanity into two currents, which has given us Buddhism and Islam, and also split the unbroken core of animal nature, giving birth to the tiger and the ship of the desert.
>
> In the camel's calm visage I read the open book of Buddhism. On the face of the tiger certain slashes proclaim the law of Mohammed. From such perceptions it is not difficult to affirm that species are species because the animals that comprise each of them have a specific vision of the Godhead. The religious beliefs that agitate us are merely pale impressions of forces at work eons ago, forces that at some point created the species. There you have my somewhat exalted view of the matter. I think it can be appreciated only by one who has ascended mountaintops himself. (Kh. *CW* I, p. 46)

Khlebnikov's wide-ranging interests and knowledge were noted above. He was not only a poet, but a professionally trained ornithologist and botanist; a talented student of mathematics; a reader in a variety of fields. Different sources (or no sources at all) may be posited for the passage just cited. However, in the context of a letter to Ivanov, a figure who served as an important conduit for Nietzsche's ideas into Russian culture, and in the context of the subsequent insertion of the Nietzsche reference into the text of "Garden of Animals," it is possible that Nietzsche's writings played some role in shaping Khlebnikov's thinking about and depiction of differences between various species and faiths, and between separate peoples – "men of the continent" (Russians) and "men of the islands" (Westerners). Again, the likely source are

Nietzsche's views concerning the differences in ethical systems of different peoples, and the varied ways in which their "will to power" manifests itself. A passage from *Zarathustra*, Part I, "Of the Thousand and One Goals," one of Nietzsche's first explicit discussions of the "will to power," is illuminating:

> No people could live without evaluating; but if it wishes to maintain itself it must not evaluate as its neighbour evaluates.
>
> Much that seemed good to one people seemed shame and disgrace to another: thus I found. I found much that was called evil in one place was in another decked with purple honors ...
>
> A table of values hangs over every people. Behold, it is the table of its overcomings; behold, it is the voice of its will to power ... (*Z*, pp. 84–85)[21]

The preceding discussion has established the likelihood of Nietzsche serving as an important source for Khlebnikov's key ideas concerning national psychologies and destinies, and for his conception of the Futurist, the *budetlianin*.[22] The very title of the Hylaeans' famous manifesto, *A Slap in the Face of Public Taste*, may be regarded as a Nietzschean expression of their heroic spirit, a reflection of a provocative stance of a self-defined group of higher men who will lead Russian society to its true destiny.

Additional evidence reinforces this connection. The image of the "blond beast," the lion, discussed in connection with "The Tree," occurs in early Khlebnikov also, most notably, at the very center of the poem "The Tangled Wood" ("Trushchoby," 1910):

> The tangled wood was full of sound,
> The forest screamed, the forest groaned
> With fear
> To see the spear-man beast his spear.
>
> Why does the hart's horn hang heavy with
> Hazard, the moving mark of love?
> Arrow's flying glitter hits a haunch,
> And reckons right. Now beast is broken
>
> To his knees, beaten to the ground.
> His eyes look deep at death.
> The horses clatter, snort and chatter:
> "We bring the Tall Ones. Useless to run."

Useless only your exquisite motion,
Your almost feminine face. No action
Can save you. You fly from rack and ruin,
And searching spear-man follows fast.

Panting horses always closer,
Branching antlers always lower,
Twangling bowstrings over and over,
Nor hart nor help, from hurt and hazard.

But he rears abruptly, bristles, roars –
And shows a lion's cruel claws.
With lazy ease he touches, teases –
Teaches the trick of terror.

Acquiescent and still,
They fall to fill their graves.
He rises rampant. Regal
Regard. Observing the bodies of slaughtered slaves.

(*KT*, pp. 22–23)

An early publication of "The Tangled Wood" contained an
annotation: "The hart, transformed into a lion, is the image of
Russia." The poet suggested that his text be read as an ideological allegory, most likely prompted by Khlebnikov's frust-
ration and anger about Russia's condition following its defeat
in Manchuria and the trauma of the 1905 Revolution. The text
also mirrored his hopes, increasingly inspired by an extreme
nationalist ideology, for a drastic change in the country's
political orientation. However, the central image of the poem
may also be associated with the Nietzschean conception of the
"blond beast," and thus with Khlebnikov's broader views on
the true nature of the Russian people – one of the "noble,"
"knightly," "warrior-like" races. This image may in fact
reflect a specific passage in Nietzsche's writings, the section
"Of the Three Metamorphoses" in *Zarathustra*, Part I:

... But in the loneliest desert the second metamorphosis occurs: the
spirit here becomes a lion; it wants to capture freedom and be lord in
its own desert.
    It seeks here its ultimate lord: it will be an enemy to him and to its
ultimate God, it will struggle for victory with the great dragon....
(*Z*, pp. 54–55)

One may trace another link between Nietzsche and Khlebnikov, particularly with regard to the self-definition of the Hylaeans. As recognized by many of their older competitors, the Symbolists, a salient characteristic of Zarathustra is his levity – so opposed to the bearing of priests and scholars. Thus, in the section "Of the Higher Man," Zarathustra addresses himself to this class of individuals, who must strive towards the ideal of the Superman and "learn to laugh" (Z, pp. 305–6). His statement, and similar ones elsewhere in Nietzsche's work, may have inspired one of Khlebnikov's best known poems, the neologistic "Incantation by Laughter" ("Zakliatie smekhom"), where almost all the words are derived from the Russian word for laughter, *smekh*:

> Hlahla! Uthlofan, lauflings!
> Hlahla! Uthlofan, lauflings!
> Who lawghen with lafe, who hlaehen lewchly,
> Hlahla! Ufhlofan hlouly!
> Hlahla! Hloufish lauflings lafe uf beloght lauchalorum!
> Hlahla! Loufenish lauflings lafe, hlohan utlaufly!...
>
> (KT, 20)

Viewed in isolation, the proposed link between the neologistic poem and Zarathustra's laughter may appear tenuous.[23] However, support for this hypothesis is found elsewhere in Khlebnikov: a passage in a letter by him to Aleksei Kruchenykh, in which he discusses the text of Kruchenykh's "opera" "Victory over the Sun." This work is itself a variation on the basic heroic myth of Khlebnikov and the Futurists as a group, and Khlebnikov had written the prologue for it. In the letter, he comments on one expression used by Kruchenykh, revolving around the coinage "laufling" (*smekhach*):[24]

The same youthful attack and youthful extravagance are audible in "Make a laugh / Light a fire," ["ogni zazhgli smekhachi" – H.B.] that is, the extravagance of youth carelessly flinging the required sense and meaning in concise words, and disinterestedly serving destiny by propagating its commands, combined with a cool indifference to the fate of that propagation. True, I'm afraid that Old Believers here refers not only to the class of people who follow the old ways, but also to upholders of oldfashioned taste in general, but I think that in this case too you were writing under the pressure of two minds: the conscious and the subconscious; and consequently with the single point of a double pen you were referring to the original Old Believers. These two places, as long as they are correctly understood, are valuable for an understanding of Russia in general; an understanding which the Russians themselves (it is their tribal characteristic) do not in fact possess. And so the meaning of Russia consists in this: "Old Believers beat / From within / With fire with brand," with a heat accumulated by their ancestors, while their children the Lauflings have lit the fires of laughter, the sources of joy and happiness. (Kh. *CW* I, pp. 71–72)

Laughter then, the joyful laughter of Zarathustra helped inspire the iconoclastic stance of Hylaea, manifested both in its publications and its public escapades,[25] a stance which differentiates it so fundamentally from all other groups competing in the literary marketplace of pre-World War I Russia. But there was another motif in Nietzsche which likely inspired Khlebnikov and his colleagues: the previously quoted passage from "Of the Rabble," with its image of the *tree Future.*

In his study of Mandelstam, Omry Ronen suggested that this passage served as an inspiration to the early period of Futurism,[26] and pointed in particular to a section in Khlebnikov's autobiographical and autocommentatory essay "Self-Statement," written in 1919, in connection with Khlebnikov's and Roman Jakobson's work on preparing an edition of Khlebnikov's writings:

Little things are significant when they mark the start of the future, the way a falling star leaves a strip of fire behind it; they have to be going fast enough to pierce through the present. So far we haven't figured out where they get that speed. But we know a thing is right when it sets the present on fire, like a flint of the future. There were nodes of the future in "The Grasshopper," in "BO BEH O BEE," in "Incantation by Laughter" – a brief appearance by the fire god and his joyful gleam. Whenever I saw old lines of writing suddenly grow dim, and their hidden content become the present day, then I understood. The future is creation's homeland, and from it blows the word god's wind. (Kh. *CW* I, p. 147)

Ronen's comments are directed at the final sentence of this passage, with its magnificent image of the future as the homeland of the poetic word (an image which also has another association – that of *kamikaze*, literally, 'divine wind', that destroyed the fleet of Kublai Khan during his attempted invasion of Japan).[27] One should also note Khlebnikov's mention of "Incantation by Laughter" and the epithet "joyful" or ("jolly") (*veselyi*) – both elements prominent in Nietzsche's writings, and likely to have been imported from there into Futurism.

The most challenging and most moving aspect of the Nietzsche–Khlebnikov problem involves "Zangezi." This is Khlebnikov's last and most ambitious "supertale," "assembled" in January 1922, which offers a panorama of both his theories on language and history and examples of diverse ways in which these can be implemented. As echoes of Russia's Civil War resound in the distance, the eponymous protagonist, a poet-prophet living in the mountains, unfolds his visions to a gathered crowd, which includes devoted pupils, the merely curious, and the mockers. Zangezi is the last of Khlebnikov's "doubles" – a moving figure, who voices the poet's own doubts, his fears for the fate of his manuscripts (a sore point with Khlebnikov at the end of his life), and his thoughts about suicide. His name, as Grigor'ev has proposed, is intended as a major "geographical symbol": it fuses the names of two great rivers from two different continents, the Zambezi and the Ganges.[28]

As a figure, Zangezi owes much to the East, in particular to the Indian tradition of the teachers of wisdom, such as the great exponent of Vedanta, Śaṅkara (788–820).[29] His connection with Nietzsche's Zarathustra may be seen in their common use of provocation with regard to their audience and themselves, and their readiness to doubt and challenge all doctrine, including their own. Like Zarathustra, Zangezi is sometimes mocked by his listeners: "He's an idiot! A fool! The sermons of a forest fool! What about cows? Does he at least keep a herd of cows?" (Kh. *CW* II, p. 335). Yet at other times, these same non-believers acknowledge: "Obscure. None too comprehensible, either. And yet – the lion's claw is visible in all of this! You can sense its presence somehow! A scrap of paper, and on it engraved the fates of nations for someone possessed of superior vision!" (Kh. *CW* II, p. 337).

At the end of Part II of *Zarathustra*, the hero has gone through his "dark night of the soul," and has abandoned his friends. Only later, after he has thought through his ideas to their logical conclusion, he regains his spirits and is ready to march into the world and spread his message: "Thus spoke Zarathustra and left his cave, glowing and strong, like a morning sun emerging from behind dark mountains" (*Z*, p. 336). Zangezi's path is different. His great moment comes in Section (Plane) Nineteen, when, mounted on a horse, he offers stunning visions of himself ("I have rivers for hair!" "I am the master carpenter of time" [Kh. *CW* II, p. 364]) and commands mankind at large ("Trumpet the charge, humanity / Round up the herd of wild horses! / Saddle and bridle the Cavalry of Sound!" [Kh. *CW* II, p. 368]). Yet this is followed by the "play" "Sorrow and Laughter" (Plane Twenty), and the death of one of the two players, Laughter. In the Epilogue (Plane Twenty-One), a newspaper article carries the news of Zangezi's suicide. The poet-prophet's final appearance turns tragedy into buffoonery ("Zangezi lives! It was all just a simpleminded joke!" [Kh. *CW* II, p. 374]), but the optimism is decidedly forced.

Of course, while reading the final pages of *Zangezi* we cannot help recalling the real conclusion life would soon provide to art: Khlebnikov's painful death in an isolated village near Novgorod followed a few months later (June 28, 1922). Nietzsche's tragedy – the years of madness – was of a different order, yet, like Khlebnikov's fate, it too endows his writings with existential authenticity.

NOTES

1 A major translation of his writings into English is currently being published. See Velimir Khlebnikov, *Collected Works*, I: *Letters and Theoretical Writings*, trans. Paul Schmidt, ed. Charlotte Douglas (Cambridge, MA, 1987); *Collected Works*, II: *Prose, Plays, and Supersagas*, trans. Paul Schmidt, ed. Ronald Vroon (Cambridge, MA, 1989) (henceforth Kh. *CW* I and Kh. *CW* II). Translations

from the final, unpublished volume of the *Collected Works* are cited parenthetically in the text as (Kh. *CW* III, forthcoming). I am grateful to Paul Schmidt for permission to use them in this article. Also see Velimir Khlebnikov, *The King of Time*, trans. Paul Schmidt, ed. Charlotte Douglas (Cambridge, MA, 1985) (henceforth *KT*). An overview of Khlebnikov's life and thought is provided by Raymond Cooke's excellent *Velimir Khlebnikov: A Critical Study* (Cambridge, UK, 1987); also see Henryk Baran, "Velimir Khlebnikov," *European Writers: The Twentieth Century*, ed. George Stade, vol. X (New York, 1990), pp. 1331–64.

2 See Edith W. Clowes, *The Revolution of Moral Consciousness: Nietzsche in Russian Literature, 1890–1914* (DeKalb, IL, 1988).

3 Khlebnikov's frequent use of puns, word-play in general, may owe something to Nietzsche's playful practice, but specific textual proof is not available at present.

4 See Viach. Vs. Ivanov, "The Category of Time in Twentieth-Century Art and Culture," *Semiotica* 8:1 (1973), pp. 1–45.

5 See the extensive discussion of the poet's relationship to 20th century scientific trends in: Viach. Vs. Ivanov, "Khlebnikov i nauka," *Puti v neznaemoe: Pisateli rasskazyvaiut o nauke. Sbornik dvadtsatyi* (Moscow, 1986), pp. 382–440.

6 A recently published text from 1904, "Enia Voeikov" (other titles "Principia," "In the Struggle with Species," "In the Struggle of the Individual with the Species," etc.), confirms Khlebnikov's early interest in philosophy. In this work, a primary source is Spinoza, though the young author also mentions Plato, Descartes, Newton, Leibniz, and Schopenhauer. See N. A. Zubkova, "Iz rannei prozy V. V. Khlebnikova (po materialam fonda Otdela rukopisei Publichnoi biblioteki)," *Issledovaniia pamiatnikov pis'mennoi kul'tury v sobraniiakh i arkhivakh Otdela Rukopisei i Redkikh Knig: Sbornik nauchnykh trudov* (Leningrad, 1988), pp. 151–78.

7 Recently, the subject of the relationship between Futurism – including Khlebnikov – and Nietzsche's heritage has been discussed by Bernice G. Rosenthal, "A New Word for a New Myth: Nietzsche and Russian Futurism," *The European Foundations of Russian Modernism*, ed. Peter I. Barta (Lewiston, NY, 1991), pp. 219–48.

8 See Svetlana Ia. Kazakova, "*Tainstvo dal'nikh* – 'dionisicheskaia' p'esa Velimira Khlebnikova," *Russian Literature* 27:4 (May 15, 1990), pp. 437–52. In her discussion, Kazakova, who presents the text of "The Mystery of the Distant Ones" (previously only referred to or briefly cited by scholars), points to a likely textual connection between this work and *The Birth of Tragedy*.

82 HENRYK BARAN

9 This work, and its relationship to Nietzsche's writings, are discussed in a recent article by A. E. Parnis, "Viacheslav Ivanov i Khlebnikov. K probleme dialoga i o nitsshevskom podtekste 'Zverintsa'," *De Visu* o (1992), pp. 39–45. The present study and the contribution by one of Russia's leading Khlebnikov specialists were prepared independently of each other.

10 See Susan Ray, "Afterword: Nietzsche's View of Russia and the Russians," *Nietzsche in Russia* (Princeton, NJ, 1986), ed. B. G. Rosenthal, pp. 399–400.

11 On the theme of flight, see also ζ, pp. 210–11.

12 On this aspect of Khlebnikov's poetics, see Ronald Vroon, "Metabiosis, Mirror Images and Negative Integers: Velimir Chlebnikov and his Doubles," *Velimir Chlebnikov (1885–1922): Myth and Reality*, ed. Willem G. Weststeijn (Amsterdam, 1986), pp. 243–90.

13 Velimir Khlebnikov, *Neizdannye proizvedeniia*, ed. N. Khardzhiev and T. Grits (Moscow, 1940), pp. 277–79. This edition is henceforth cited parenthetically in the text as *NP*.

14 The imagery in the poem is discussed in detail by Johannes Holthusen, "Die Sphäre der Metaphern in Velimir Chlebnikov's Gedicht 'Derevo,'" *Russian Literature* 9:1 (January 1981), pp. 23–46.

15 First suggested by Omry Ronen, *An Approach to Mandel'štam* (Jerusalem, 1983), p. 182. This analysis does not exclude others, which focus on internal relationships of elements of the text, or other motifs drawn from history and culture.

16 "Vykhozhu odin ia na dorogu ..." The relevant line is "And star talks with star" ("I zvezda s zvezdoiu govorit").

17 Velimir Khlebnikov, *Sobranie proizvedenii*, 5 vols., ed. N. Stepanov (Leningrad, 1928–33), III, p. 255. This edition is henceforth cited parenthetically in the text as *SP*.

18 The usual Russian rendition of the German *blonde Bestie* is "belokuraia bestiia." See E. Trubetskoi, "Filosofiia Nitsshe," *Voprosy filosofii i psikhologii* (May–June 1903), p. 270. As he frequently does elsewhere, Khlebnikov has slightly transformed the expression.

19 That this passage is the source for Khlebnikov's lines was first pointed out by Holthusen, "Die Sphäre der Metaphern," pp. 41, 45.

20 See Henryk Baran, "Temporal Myths in Xlebnikov: From 'Deti Vydry' to 'Zangezi,'" *Myth in Literature*, ed. A. Kodjak, K. Pomorska, S. Rudy (New York University Slavic Papers, vol. V) (Columbus, Ohio, 1985), pp. 63–88.

21 The commentary to "The Garden" in a major recent Russian edition of Khlebnikov notes the likelihood that *Zarathustra* influenced the text. See V. Khlebnikov, *Tvoreniia*, ed. V. Grigor'ev and A. Parnis (Moscow, 1986), p. 679.

22 Khlebnikov's anti-Western, Russocentric ideology is reflected in his coinage of the word *budetlianin*, as a replacement for *Futurist*, which for him was linked with concessions to the priority of Marinetti and Italian Futurism over the Russian group. As seen in some passages above, Paul Schmidt uses the term *Futurian* to convey this difference.

23 First suggested, in general terms, by the Italian Slavist Angelo Maria Ripellino, *Poesie di Chlébnikov: Saggio, antologia, commento* (Torino, 1968), p. 179.

24 For a discussion of this word, and related coinages involving the core meaning of "laughter," see V. P. Grigor'ev, *Slovotvorchestvo i smezhnye problemy iazyka poeta* (Moscow, 1986), pp. 181–89.

25 Such as the challenges by Hylaea members to their audience at public readings, or the publicity strolls through the main streets of Moscow staged by the Futurists. See Vladimir Markov, *Russian Futurism: A History* (Berkeley and Los Angeles, 1968), pp. 132–41.

26 *An Approach to Mandel'stam*, p. 182.

27 Khlebnikov, who had a keen interest in Asia in general, and in Japan in particular, was well-aware of both the historical situation and the meaning of the term.

28 Khlebnikov considered many variants of the name, with other associations. See Grigor'ev, *Slovotvorchestvo i smezhnye problemy*, pp. 222–34. Also see *Tvoreniia*, p. 697.

29 See Grigor'ev, *Slovotvorchestvo i smezhnye problemy*. Also see Baran, "Temporal Myths in Xlebnikov," pp. 78–85.

CHAPTER 3

Apollonianism and Christian art: Nietzsche's influence on Acmeism

Elaine Rusinko

In *The Joyful Brotherhood* (*Veselye brat'ia*), an unfinished novella written by Nikolai Gumilev around 1917, the central figure is an urban intellectual who submerges himself in the life and religion of provincial Russia. Motivated by curiosity and the desire for adventure, and confident that his higher education will help him make important ethnographic discoveries, he sets off on his adventure taking provisions for his journey – a toothbrush, cigarettes, and a volume of Nietzsche.[1]

For Gumilev and the other Acmeists, Nietzsche was as basic an intellectual commodity as he was for the emblematic hero of this curious story. They absorbed Nietzsche's ideas, along with the philosophy of Bergson and other fashionable ideologies, from the intellectual atmosphere of the Symbolist period. In distinction to Russian Symbolism, however, Acmeism contributed an original interpretation of Nietzsche that emphasized the Apollonian principle over the Dionysian in style and philosophy. By developing Nietzsche's concept of the Apollonian, Acmeism was able to reconcile Hellenism and Orthodox Christianity in a poetic valorization of reality.

Acmeism was a post-Symbolist poetic movement. Its adherents rejected theurgy and mysticism; their esthetics emphasized craftsmanship and earthly reality. The theoretician and leader of the Acmeists was Nikolai Gumilev (1886–1921), and the movement's outstanding poets were Osip Mandelstam (1891–1938) and Anna Akhmatova (1888–1966). There were also three minor poets who called themselves Acmeists: Sergei Gorodetsky (1884–1967), co-founder of the movement and author of a manifesto of Acmeism, Vladimir Narbut (1888–1944), and

Mikhail Zenkevich (1891–1969). Though the active, public life of the movement was short (its manifesto is from 1912 and the group remained intact only until the beginning of World War I), Mandelstam and Akhmatova continued to develop the basic elements of Acmeist esthetics throughout the Soviet period. Because their emphasis on esthetics, individualism, and the primacy of the word conflicted with the tendencies of Soviet politics and culture, the movement was proscribed under Stalin. Gumilev was executed by the Bolsheviks, Mandelstam died in a Stalinist camp, and Akhmatova was denounced in 1946 and prohibited from publishing for long periods. The work of the major Acmeists began to appear in the Soviet Union only with the relaxation of political-cultural repression in the 1960s, and the rehabilitation of Gumilev began only in 1986. Throughout the Soviet period, however, the Acmeist poets were known and admired by lovers of Russian literature for the uncompromising moral determination and "manly will" that Acmeism brought to poetry.

   The basic doctrine of the movement was set forth in Gumilev's and Gorodetsky's Acmeist manifestos, published in the first 1913 issue of the journal *Apollo* (*Apollon*, 1909–17). Mandelstam clarified and redefined Acmeism in his essays "The Morning of Acmeism" (written in 1913, but not published until 1919) and "On the Nature of the Word" (1922). Characterized by clarity of language and a visual orientation, Acmeist poetry depicts concrete objects from nature and art, in opposition to the Symbolists' emphasis on abstract and otherworldly subject matter. Acmeism was grounded in traditional world culture and defended basic Christian ethical values: love of God and one's neighbor and the moral courage to uphold God's commandments. Though the initial pronouncements stressed poetic ideals (form, equilibrium, and concrete imagery), Mandelstam defined Acmeism more broadly as "a moral force," "a social phenomenon," and "a yearning for world culture."[2] Of the Acmeists, perhaps Akhmatova was least affected by Nietzsche's philosophy. Still, her poetry has been praised for "showing man in a heroic light,"[3] and certainly her dedication to art and memory in the

Stalinist period reflects the values of "courage, steadfastness, and determination" (*muzhestvennost'*) that Acmeism appropriated from Nietzsche. As this capsule summary of the movement's theory indicates, Acmeism stressed the Apollonian principle, as elaborated by Nietzsche in *The Birth of Tragedy*, adapting it and combining it with other elements of Nietzsche's life-affirming philosophy, while rejecting the Dionysian essence.

This essay will examine the adaptation of Nietzsche in the development of Acmeist theory, and will therefore concentrate on the work of the theoreticians of the movement. Gumilev and Gorodetsky had undergone an intensive period of Nietzscheanism in the early years of their careers.[4] In his search for a world-view, Gorodetsky turned to mystical anarchism, which was heavily influenced by Nietzsche.[5] His first collection of poetry, *Iar'* (1906), named for a pagan deity created by the poet, had as its central theme a poeticization of the elemental strength of primeval man. Deriving his inspiration from ancient Slavic folklore, Gorodetsky created original mythical images which echoed pagan beliefs, traditions, and customs and, in the spirit of Nietzschean individualism, glorified self-affirmation and self-determination. His heroes demonstrate superhuman strength and innate morality as they cheerfully combat the forces of nature in a world free of the restraints of government, law and social convention. Written in a fresh and playful style similar to that of folk poetry, Gorodetsky's first book was a reflection of the Nietzschean impulse behind mystical anarchism, which purported to reconcile individual freedom and social harmony. Viacheslav Ivanov acclaimed it "a literary event."[6] Though Gorodetsky's association with Acmeism was short-lived and of questionable impact (he subsequently accommodated himself to the Soviet regime and renounced his attachment to Acmeism), his early attraction to Nietzsche was undoubtedly one of the sources for the primitivist element of Acmeism, which became known by the name of Adamism.

In contrast to Gorodetsky's interest in mystical anarchism, Nietzsche's impact on the early Gumilev manifested itself not as a coherent doctrine, but as an amalgam of ideas and attitudes. Nietzsche's appeal to the leader of the Acmeists seems to have been personal and esthetic, and Gumilev utilizes Nietzschean themes and images throughout his work. The sun, arrows, fire, eagles, lions, and superman-like heroes are most predominant in the early poems, but they persist through his mature poetry. Nietzsche's emphasis on creative individualism and personal freedom is reflected in Gumilev's conquistador persona and in his favorite themes of valor and adventure. Moreover, the Superman posture Gumilev liked to affect in his own life has been attributed to the influence of Nietzschean ideals. According to Irina Odoevtseva, who knew him in postrevolutionary Petrograd, Gumilev assimilated many of Nietzsche's precepts. She quotes him as saying, "It is possible that if I let myself, I would be kind, but I don't allow myself that ... Kindness is not a masculine quality. One must be ashamed of it as of a weakness."[7] Compare Zarathustra's comment in the section "On War and Warriors": "They call you heartless: but your heart is true, and I love the modesty of your kindheartedness. You feel ashamed of your flow, while others feel ashamed of their ebb" (*Z*, p. 74).

In addition to the profusion of Nietzschean imagery, there are direct echoes of Nietzsche in the poetry of Gumilev's first collection *The Path of the Conquistadors* (*Put' konkvistadorov*, 1905): "The Song of Zarathustra" ("Pesn' Zaratustry," *SS* I, p. 5), "To the People of the Present" ("Liudiam nastoiashchego"), and "To the People of the Future" ("Liudiam budushchego," *SS* I, p. 35). Note, for example, the following stanzas from an untitled poem, where the poet's persona, "a forgotten, abandoned god," is counselled by a vague voice from above:

> My tired and pale brother, to work!
> Sacrifice yourself to the earth,
> If you want the mountainous heights
> To burn in the midnight gloom.
>
> If you want the bright distances
> To unfold before the ailing people,
> Take the days of silent and burning sorrow
> Into your powerful soul.

> Be a light blue, pre-dawn sacrifice...
> In the dark abyss soundlessly burn...
> And you will be the Promised Star,
> Heralding the coming dawn.
>
> (*SS* I, p. 40)

Compare Zarathustra: "I love those who do not first seek beyond the stars for reasons to go down and to be sacrifices: but who sacrifice themselves to the earth, that the earth may one day belong to the Superman" (*Z*, p. 44).

Though Gumilev later dismissed his first collection as juvenile and chose not to republish it with the rest of his work, the warrior pose and conquistador persona for which he became famous persist into his last collection, published posthumously in 1921. Nietzsche's concept of *amor fati* is particularly apparent in the strain of virile Romanticism that informs such poems as "My Readers" ("Moi chitateli"). Here the poet characterizes his readers as "strong, vicious, merry," choosing examples from his actual experience – an exotic tribal chieftain, a naval lieutenant, an assassin, those who are "true to our planet."

> I don't insult them with neurasthenia,
> Or embarrass them with heartfelt warmth.
> I don't bore them with significant hints
> About what's left in an egg when it's eaten;
> But when bullets whistle all around,
> When waves crack into ships,
> I teach them not to be afraid,
> Not to fear, and to do what they must.
>
> And in their last hour,
> When a red mist clouds their view,
> I will teach them to recall straight away
> All of cruel, lovely life,
> Our beloved, alien earth,
> And, standing before God
> With wise and simple words,
> To await calmly His judgment.
>
> (*SS* II, p. 60)

Gumilev's dedication to the Apollonian principle is apparent here in his basic agreement with Nietzsche that it is this element in art that enables man to face the horrors of existence without becoming "rigid with fear" (*BT*, pp. 22, 104). Many additional examples of Gumilev's attraction to the idea of *amor fati* can be found in his poems and stories, as well as in his biography. The most famous are those in which he seems to prophecy his own violent death (*SS* II, pp. 10, 14, 48; IV, pp. 141–52), accepting it ("It is an incomparable right to choose own's own death," *SS* I, p. 55), as Nietzsche admonished:

One perishes by no one but oneself. Only "natural" death is, for the most contemptible reasons, an unfree death, a death at the wrong time, a coward's death. From love of *life* one ought to desire to die differently from this: freely, consciously, not accidentally, not suddenly overtaken. (*TI*, p. 88)

For the development of the artistic philosophy of Acmeism, though, it is Nietzsche's insistence on loyalty to the earth that is most important. The poem immediately following "My Readers," the closing poem of Gumilev's last collection, repeats those ideas expressed in the Nietzschean poems of *The Path of the Conquistadors*. "Starry Terror" ("Zvezdnyi uzhas," *SS* II, p. 62) depicts the demise of a primitive tribe's superstition against looking directly at the night sky for fear of the demons who, it is believed, inhabit it. Enlightenment comes through the experience of a child, who is brought as a sacrifice to the sky dweller, but who comes away unscathed, seeing nothing more threatening than stars. Finally, the entire tribe looks up to the sky, "And the whole tribe / Lay down and sang, sang, sang." However, the poet's sympathy seems to be with the old patriarch, for whom the end of the superstition is the loss of a meaningful illusion, and for whom the people's fascination with the sky signifies a betrayal of man's proper realm, the earth. He grieves for the time when people looked

> To the plain, where their herds grazed,
> To the water, where their sail skimmed by,
> To the grass, where their children played,
> But not to the dark sky, where there sparkle
> The inaccessible, alien stars.

This recalls Gumilev's justification of the Acmeist rejection of mysticism: "The whole beauty, the whole sacred meaning of the stars lies in the fact that they are infinitely far from earth and that no advance in aviation will bring them closer" (*SS* IV, p. 174). Even more closely it recalls Zarathustra's exhortation to "remain true to the earth" (*Z*, p. 42). This particular teaching of Nietzsche's is in accord with the basic postulates of the Acmeist program. Acmeism, said Gorodetsky, is "a struggle for this world."

This world made of time, volume, and form, this planet – the earth. By filling the world with "correspondences," Symbolism essentially transformed it into a phantom whose importance is determined only by the degree to which other worlds are visible through its translucencies. Symbolism depreciated its great intrinsic worth.[8]

Since the Acmeists developed this world view as a rebuff to Dionysian Symbolism, they instinctively identified it with the Apollonian. Their connection with the journal *Apollo*, which for a time was considered an organ of Acmeism, made the opposition explicit. Gumilev's sympathies are revealed as early as February 26, 1909, in a letter to his mentor Valery Briusov (1873–1924): "I have been to see Viacheslav Ivanov three times, but have not fallen into the Dionysian heresy."[9]

The relationship of Acmeism to Viacheslav Ivanov is a complex topic requiring further study, but a comment is relevant here in view of Ivanov's well-known attraction to Nietzsche. The relationship between Ivanov and most of the future Acmeists goes back to the founding of the journal *Apollo* in 1909. Of the composition of the editorial board, the founder of the journal, Sergei Makovsky, states simply, "It is curious that both of my senior associates in the creation of the journal, Viacheslav Ivanov and Innokenty Fedorovich [Annensky], were at heart zealous adherents not of Apollo but of his antipode Dionysus."[10] Their participation in the new journal may well have been more pragmatic than principled. Makovsky needed their reputation and professional expertise, while Annensky and Ivanov needed a forum to express their ideas and expand their influence, since the older Symbolist journals *The Scales* (*Vesy*) and *The Golden Fleece* (*Zolotoe runo*) ceased publication in 1909. Ivanov, for example, soon moved his customary poetic "evenings" from the "tower" with which they had long been identified to the editorial offices of *Apollo*, giving them a more professional character as meetings of the "Society of Zealots of the Artistic Word" (*Obshchestvo revnitelei khudozhestvennogo slova*), known by the "Apollonians" as the "Poetic Academy." With the addition of Blok and Kuzmin to the editorial board, *Apollo* effected a remarkable unification of Petersburg poets, which, however, proved to be short-lived. Before the year was over, *Apollo* was the scene for what has become known as the "crisis of Symbolism." Prompted by Ivanov's well-known essay "The Precepts of Symbolism" ("Zavety simvolizma"), presented at the Poetic Academy in March and published in the May–June, 1910 issue of *Apollo* together with Blok's accompanying article "On the Contemporary State of Russian Symbolism" ("O sovremennom sostoianii russkogo simvolizma"), the open debate that ensued over the goals of Symbolism marked the dissolution of the movement. When Briusov's polemical response, "About 'Servile Speech,' In Defense of Poetry" ("O 'rechi rabskoi,' v zashchitu poezii," 1910) was published in the next issue, it won the allegiance of Gumilev and the rest of the editorial staff. This was the end of Ivanov's active role in *Apollo*. According to Makovsky he had never wielded great influence, since the younger generation reacted reservedly to his poetry and responded more favorably to Annensky (*Portrety*, p. 276). A further quarrel with Ivanov in 1911 over Gumilev's poem "Prodigal Son" ("Bludnyi syn") and its relation to "myth-creation" prompted Gumilev and Gorodetsky to create the Poets' Guild in opposition to Ivanov's "Poetic Academy."[11] The declaration of Acmeism as a doctrine and a school was announced in December 1912 at the Stray Dog café and published in *Apollo* in 1913.

In spite of the differences in their poetic philosophy, however, Ivanov and the Acmeists shared a personal affection and mutual professional admiration. Ivanov came close to making a trip to Africa with Gumilev in 1909, and, in the words of Olga Deschartes, Ivanov "all his life ingenuously and unalterably loved the three representatives [of Acmeism]."[12] The dispute between them centered around Ivanov's acceptance (and the Acmeists' rejection) of Nietzsche's notion of

Dionysian self-transcendence. In this sense, the essence of the Acmeist revolt against Symbolism can be understood as an argument over Nietzsche. To be sure, Nietzsche has a prominent place in Gumilev's Acmeist manifesto, "Acmeism and the Legacy of Symbolism" ("Nasledie simvolizma i akmeizm," 1913, *SS* IV, pp. 171–76). Since this was the primary manifesto for the movement, I will analyze it in some detail, including comments from the other theoreticians of Acmeism as appropriate. The very terminology used by Gumilev alerts the reader to the Nietzschean subtext. In the introduction of the manifesto he presents the issue as a "revaluation of values and reputations that were not so long ago indisputable" (*SS* IV, p. 171). The phrase as used by Gumilev is deliberately ironic, since the values being revalued here are largely Nietzsche's, as popularized by the Russian Symbolists.[13] Acknowledging Acmeism's debt to Russian Symbolism, Gumilev recognizes their common ancestor in French Symbolism, but he discerns in the latter what he calls a "non-Romanic, non-national, alien base."

> The Romanic spirit is too beloved of the element of light, which separates objects, which draws lines clearly and precisely; but this Symbolist merging of all images and objects and the changeability of their appearance could have arisen only in the misty shadows of Germanic forests. (*SS* IV, p. 172)

Echoing Nietzsche, he goes on to suggest that Symbolism in France is a direct result of the Battle of Sedan. However, whereas Nietzsche nationalistically saw the German victory in the Franco-Prussian war as a liberation, "the elimination of everything Romanic" and the return of the German spirit to itself (*BT*, pp. 138, 121), Gumilev expresses the point of view of the vanquished Romanic spirit, deploring the imposition of Germanic ideals on French culture.

Aligning Acmeism firmly with the French or Romanic spirit, he announces, albeit in rather vague terms, some of the formal principles of Acmeism: a new, freer verse, a new vocabulary with a stable content based on living, popular speech (as opposed to "the imitation of music," *BT*, p. 54), and a "lucid irony, which does not undermine the roots of our faith" to replace "that hopeless German seriousness that our Symbolists so cherished" (*SS* IV, p. 173). (Here Gumilev also alludes to the anti-Christian nature of Nietzsche's ideas as incompatible with the philosophy of Acmeism, a notion he expands in the ideological core of the manifesto.) Finally, in a transparent jibe at Viacheslav Ivanov, he rejects the emphasis on the symbol in favor of Appollonian balance, "the full coordination" of poetic devices through careful craftsmanship. Thus, he declares, "It is more difficult to be an Acmeist than a Symbolist, just as it is more difficult to build a cathedral than a tower" (*SS* IV, p. 173). As Ivanov's "tower" characterized the Symbolist stage of Russian poetry, the equilibrium of forces in the unity of the architectonically complex Gothic cathedral was to become emblematic of the Acmeist poetic style.

Apart from its rather vague references to poetic form, Gumilev's manifesto was considered deficient (by contemporaries and in subsequent scholarship) as an expression of the new movement's philosophy. Though stated in an authoritative tone, his desultory maxims do not readily form a coherent argument. A recognition of the Nietzschean subtext, however, fills in some of the apparent gaps in the exposition of the manifesto's philosophical core. In fact, to a certain degree the manifesto can be read as one side of a debate, with Ivanov and the Nietzsche of *The Birth of Tragedy* as silent interlocutors.

Gumilev mentions Nietzsche as one of the "forefathers" of German Symbolism, which posited an "objective goal or dogma" for man in the universe. According to Gumilev,

This showed that German Symbolism did not sense the intrinsic value of each phenomenon, which needs no justification from without. For us, however, the hierarchy of phenomena in the world is merely the specific gravity of each of them, the weight of the most insignificant being still immeasurably greater than the absence of weight, non-existence, and for that reason, in the face of non-existence, all phenomena are brothers. (*SS* IV, p. 173)

Gumilev is obviously objecting here to the Dionysian emphasis on "fusion with primordial being" (*BT*, p. 65). The collapse of individuation that results is, according to Gumilev, a corollary to Nietzsche's famous dictum that "it is only as an esthetic

phenomenon that existence and the world are eternally justified" (*BT*, p. 52). To this Gumilev responds that there is no
need for justification. Existence is justification enough, and as
an Apollonian artist, he takes pleasure in the very existence of
the phenomenon, in the *principium individuationis*, of which
Apollo himself is "the glorious divine image" (*BT*, p. 36). As
Mandelstam put it, the Acmeist poet stands in awe of the law of
identity, A = A. "Love the existence of the thing more than the
thing itself and your own existence more than yourself: that is
Acmeism's highest commandment" ("The Morning of
Acmeism," *CCPL*, p. 64).

This insistent belief in the existence and dignity of individual
things is in direct contrast to the Symbolists' emphasis on
mysticism, their theurgical understanding of art, and their
(especially Ivanov's) refusal to "accept the world." Nietzsche's
theories on esthetics played an enormous role in the development of the central idea of Russian modernism, that is, the
importance of art in bringing closer to consciousness the mysteries that lie beyond the corporeal world.[14] Of course, the
Symbolists' position represents a certain transposition of
Nietzsche's thoughts, blended as they were with ideas of Soloviev, Merezhkovsky, and various occult philosophies. Rather
than disentangling the various strains of influence behind the
principle to which he objected, Gumilev found it convenient to
simplify his argument by identifying theurgical Symbolism
wholly with Nietzsche. The Symbolists' concentration on the
Dionysian element in Nietzsche to the virtual neglect of the
Apollonian made it easy for Gumilev to reject Symbolism and
Nietzsche together, even though Acmeism identified with
many of Nietzsche's life-affirming principles.

The Acmeists, then, insisted on the intrinsic value of each
phenomenon and, like Zarathustra, accepted experience in its
totality.[15] Accepting no externally imposed system of value, the
Acmeists, as Apollonians, still speak of a hierarchy of phenomena, but a hierarchy based on nothing more than the "specific
gravity" of each phenomenon. That is, Acmeism emphasizes
the weight and corporeality of phenomena and accepts the
Apollonian restraint represented by the force of gravity.

Gumilev seems to identify Zarathustra's aspirations toward escaping gravity by dancing and flying with Symbolism's allegorical flight into abstraction and another world. In Zarathustra's song on the Spirit of Gravity, he says, "He who will one day teach men to fly will have moved all boundary-stones; all boundary-stones will themselves fly into the air to him, he will baptize the earth anew – as 'the weightless'" (*Z*, p. 210).

As if in answer, Acmeism took the boundary-stone as the base of its edifice, and Mandelstam claims, "Acmeism is for those who, inspired by the spirit of building, do not, like cowards, renounce their own gravity, but joyously accept it in order to arouse and exploit the powers architecturally sleeping within ... We cannot fly, we can ascend only those towers which we build ourselves" ("The Morning of Acmeism," *CCPL*, p. 62). Man's role in the world, then, is to struggle against non-existence by creating structures of buildings and poems, and in this conscious, laborious effort mankind is united, not in a spontaneous, self-transcending mystic oneness, but in a universal brotherhood of phenomena. In Mandelstam's words, "There is no equality, there is no competition, there is only the complicity of all who conspire against emptiness and non-existence" ("The Morning of Acmeism," *CCPL*, p. 64).

The next, central, paragraph of Gumilev's manifesto is interesting for its argumentative content and the combative style of its assertions, which seem almost to be hurled at a silent interlocutor.

We would not dare to force an atom to bow to God, if this were not in its nature. But, feeling ourselves to be phenomena among phenomena, we become part of the world rhythm, we accept all the forces acting on us and, in our turn, we create forces ourselves. It is our duty, our will, our happiness, and our tragedy to guess each hour what the next hour may be for us, for our cause, for the whole world, and to hurry its coming. And as our highest reward, which never for an instant escapes our attention, we dream of the image of the last hour, which will never come to pass. However, to rebel in the name of other conditions of existence here, where there is death, is just as strange as for a prisoner to break down the wall, when in front of him there is an open door. Here ethics becomes esthetics, expanding into the latter's sphere. Here individualism at its highest tension creates community. Here God becomes a Living God, because man has felt himself worthy of such a God. Here death is a curtain, separating us, the actors from the audience, and in the inspiration of the play, we disdain the cowardly peeping into the future, the "what will happen next?" As Adamists we are partly forest beasts and in any case we will not give up what is animal in us in exchange for neurasthenia. But now it is time for Russian Symbolism to speak. (*SS* IV, pp. 173–74)

As though with a great sigh, Gumilev finishes his tirade directed at the Dionysian emphasis of Nietzsche and turns to a discussion of its heritage in Russian Symbolism, the use of the national adjective serving to stress the thematic transition. Before following his train of thought, however, the arguments presented here beg for elucidation. Again, a recognition of the subtext is helpful.

Gumilev begins with an acceptance of the natural world as a "given" and man's place in it as "part of the world rhythm." While the Dionysian spirit's perception of reality is accompanied by a "striving for the infinite" (*BT*, p. 141), the Apollonian response to the natural world is to accept its limits and to act, to become a force among others, and to live on to see what life has in store. There are echoes here of the concluding section of *The Birth of Tragedy*: "In [Apollo's] name we comprehend all those countless illusions of the beauty of mere appearance that at every moment make life worth living at all and prompt the desire to live on in order to experience the next moment" (*BT*, p. 143). However "the next moment" for Gumilev is but one in a progression leading to "the last hour, which will never come to pass." This understanding of time sounds similar to Nietzsche's notion of "eternal recurrence," in that it motivates an extraordinary heightening of the importance of each moment of existence. However, in rebuttal to Nietzsche's recourse to esthetics, Gumilev's "justification" of the world involves a Christian understanding of time in which each moment holds the potential for an eschatological fulfillment. Though on the surface Acmeism's increased sensitivity to the texture of existence is similar to Nietzsche's, it arises from an opposite source.[16]

Gumilev goes beyond the "esthetic" justification of the

world to the ethical, since in his world, "here where there is death," ethics has expanded into the realm of esthetics, that is, art must be justified ethically as well as esthetically. He had expounded this theme in an earlier essay "The Life of Verse" ("Zhizn' stikha," 1910), which was in part a response to Viacheslav Ivanov's "Precepts of Symbolism." In this, his first published essay, Gumilev upholds an extreme Apollonian view of art, accepting the proposition, perhaps from Nietzsche, that "purity is suppressed sensuality, and it is beautiful." But he insists that any attitude toward art must be "chaste." He defines the concept of chastity (*tselomudrennost'*) idiosyncratically as "the right of every phenomenon to be valuable in itself, not to require justification of its existence, and another, higher right – to serve others" (*SS* IV pp. 158–59). Thus, the phenomena of the world, among them art and literature, are justified intrinsically, but also by the ethical principle, here stated somewhat vaguely, of service to others. That these two "rights" are one and the same is explained by Mandelstam.

In the Middle Ages man considered himself just as indispensable and just as bound to the edifice of his world as a stone in a Gothic structure, bearing with dignity the pressures of his neighbors and entering the common play of forces as an inevitable stake. To serve meant not only to act for the common good. In the Middle Ages a man unconsciously recognized the plain fact of his own existence as service, as a kind of heroic act. ("Francois Villon," *CCPL*, p. 59)

This is consistent with the Apollonian world view, in the sense that Apollo is the "ethical deity" (*BT*, p. 46), and the Acmeists more than once reproached Symbolism for its "amoralism."[17] However, in the manifesto in which he announces the movement to replace Symbolism, Gumilev refers to the ethical justification of art and existence only in passing. Of greater interest here is the eschatological justification, and this is his ultimate refutation of the otherworldliness of Symbolism. He claims that there is no need "to rebel in the name of other conditions of existence here, where there is death." That is, the focus on and the justification of life in this world is possible not as an escape from death, but *because* "here there is death." Gumilev is being deliberately provocative with this seemingly paradoxical statement. He does not elucidate any particular Acmeist understanding of death in his manifesto, but there are relevant hints of such a philosophy elsewhere in Acmeist writings, particularly in Mandelstam's essay "Pushkin and Scriabin" (1915).

This essay, which Mandelstam at one time considered his most important article,[18] was characterized by Nadezhda Mandelstam as a "certain polemic with Viacheslav Ivanov-Nietzsche and his (sic) Dionysian understanding of art."[19] Jane Gary Harris describes it as "a more mystical-religious-philosophical statement of his basic esthetic tenets, indeed of his Acmeist views juxtaposed against the esthetic tenets of Symbolism ... Mandelstam focuses on the experience of 'illusion' or esthetic consciousness and poetic craft as opposed to the religious experience and 'pure music'" (Jane Gary Harris, commentary to Mandelstam, "Pushkin and Scriabin," CCPL, p. 598). Harris comments that Mandelstam seems to be invoking Annensky's tradition while opposing Ivanov's, but one might also say that he is invoking the Apollonian principle as opposed to the Dionysian.

Mandelstam specifically characterizes Scriabin's talent as Dionysian. He sees Scriabin as "the most extreme revelation of the Hellenistic nature of the Russian spirit possible....a *mad Hellene*" (Mandelstam's italics, "Pushkin and Scriabin," CCPL, p. 91), and goes on to discuss Scriabin's music, which allows an apparent, though unstated, correlation with Nietzsche. Noting the fear and distrust of music among the ancients, Mandelstam focuses on Nietzsche's recognition of the practical impossibility of purely Dionysian music. Such pure music would be shattering in its evocation of primordial universality and its unbearable representation of suffering and pain, which is the Dionysian truth about the world. Hence, the chief function of the Apollonian element of tragedy is to shield the spectator against the full impact of the music (BT, pp. 125–26). Mandelstam recognized that Scriabin's music approached the Dionysian, particularly in the "wordless, strangely mute" chorus of Prometheus (CCPL, p. 91). Scriabin's biographer E. A. Hull describes the musician's aspirations in his famous orchestral tone-poem "Prometheus: Poem of Fire" as follows: "[Scriabin] is apparently striving to obtain by means of his music that state of ecstasy which the true mystic realizes can only be obtained when a perfect union with the divine has been achieved."[20] By analogy, this striving for Dionysian transcendence in Scriabin is the basis for Mandelstam's Acmeist condemnation of Nietzsche's Dionysianism and Viacheslav Ivanov's theurgical Symbolism.

Though Mandelstam's sympathy is clearly with the Apollonian rather than the Dionysian principle, like Gumilev he agrees with Nietzsche that it does not provide a sufficient justification of the world and of art. What does provide justification for Mandelstam, as for Gumilev, is the existence of death, but Mandelstam goes beyond Gumilev to provide an explanation, however obscure, of how death alters the Apollonian–Dionysian duality.

The Christian world is an organism, a living body. The fabric of our world is renewed through death. We must struggle against the barbarism of our new life, for in the new life which is flourishing, death is unvanquished! As long as death exists in the world, Hellenism will exist, for Christianity *Hellenizes death* . . . Hellenism, impregnated with death, is Christianity. (Mandelstam's italics, "Pushkin and Scriabin," *CCPL*, p. 94).

To inject the concept of death into the Hellenic world is to infuse it with the understanding of grace, redemption, and salvation which is part of the Christian world view. As Gregory Freidin writes, "The Greeks, who had realized the ideal of beauty, were unaware of the beauty and special significance of death known to Christians." In his definition of Christianity as "Hellenism impregnated with death," Mandelstam "was trying to combine the best of both worlds."[21] The Christian world does not fear the Dionysian spirit, because it is confident in its salvation, as Mandelstam explained once again through the analogy of music.

Pure music was unknown to the Hellenes; it belongs completely to Christianity . . . Christianity did not fear music. The Christian world smiled as it spoke to Dionysus: "All right, try it, just order your

Maenads to tear me to pieces: I am wholeness, I am individuality, I am indivisible unity!" ("Pushkin and Scriabin," *CCPL*, p. 94).

Even in this polemic with him, the inescapable impact of Nietzsche is evident in the fact that the "Christian world" here opposes Dionysus with distinctly Apollonian traits of integrity and individuality.

In the final analysis, both Mandelstam and Gumilev perceived Nietzsche's unstated hostility to Christianity in *The Birth of Tragedy* and answered this and his subsequent anti-Christian arguments with a defense of Christianity in art. Gumilev does so tacitly, describing the Christian world as "here where there is death." Here we see the merging of ethics and esthetics and the creation of civic society (*obshchestvennost'*, not *sobornost'*, that is, an architectonic organic system rather than a mystical community), taking place in the realm of the Living God, not in the world of Zarathustra where God is dead. As a result of the existence of death, the "play of life" as seen by Gumilev is one in which there is a definite separation of actors and audience, not the "great sublime chorus of dancing and singing satyrs" that Nietzsche saw in Greek tragedy (*BT*, p. 62). Nietzsche's reaction to Greek drama – "we felt as if only a parable passed us by, whose most profound meaning we almost thought we could guess and that we wished to draw away like a curtain in order to behold the primordial image behind it" (*BT*, p. 139) – is answered by Gumilev's refusal to "peep into the future."

Acmeism adamantly refuses to look behind the curtain, because this is, in fact, not a world of dissonance and ugliness that requires a veil of Apollonian illusion to be made bearable, nor is the Apollonian transfiguration "mere appearance," as Nietzsche would have it. Acmeism revises the Apollonian perception of the world as offered by Nietzsche by "impregnating" it with death, or grace. To the Acmeists, the beauty of the phenomenal world *is* metaphysical truth because a living God is present in it, and not beyond or above it. As Nadezhda Mandelstam wrote, "For the Christian, the link between the empirical world and the higher one is ensured not by means of symbols, but through revelation, the sacraments, grace, and – most important of all – through the coming of Christ. Christ is not a 'Symbol'."[22] Thus, the Acmeists had a sacramental view of the earth as a "God-given palace" ("The Morning of Acmeism," *CCPL*, p. 63), since Christ had lived on it and sanctified it. That is, Acmeism counters Nietzsche and theurgical Symbolism with the basic Orthodox belief that God is the author of the created world, which is beautiful and significant because of his presence. And Gumilev finishes his polemic with Ivanov/Nietzsche by alluding to the alternate name by which the Acmeists were known, Adamists, its Biblical origin countervailing against the Greek *akme*.

In "Pushkin and Scriabin," Mandelstam explicitly describes the features of "Christian art," with implicit references to Nietzsche's view of tragedy as redemption (*BT*, p. 125).

Christian art is action, always based on the great idea of redemption. It is an "imitation of Christ" infinitely varied in all its manifestations, an eternal return to the single creative act that began our historical era. Christian art is free. It is "art for art's sake" in its fullest meaning. No necessity of any kind, not even the highest, darkens its bright inner freedom, for its prototype, that which it imitates, is the very redemption of the world by Christ. Thus, neither sacrifice, nor redemption in art, but rather the free and joyous imitation of Christ is the keystone of Christian esthetics. Art cannot be sacrifice, because a sacrifice has already been made; it cannot be redemption because the world, along with the artist, has already been redeemed. (*CCPL*, p. 91)

Mandelstam's use of the phrase "eternal return" here is provocative, since this passage from "Pushkin and Scriabin" radically reinterprets Nietzsche's concept. The "redemption" of the past, which Nietzsche finds in eternal recurrence, is superfluous in the world of Christian art, as is the justification of the present. Redemption and sacrifice were achieved by the Son of God during his sojourn on earth, and the role of man and the artist is to imitate him by accepting the limits of the world, and rejoicing in its beauty as a God-given gift. As Gregory Freidin notes, from this point of view, poetry is also a form of the imitation of Christ. "In the symbolic and anagogical sense, it is the poetry of resurrection. In this art form ... such an indisputable fact as death endows one's art with the ultimate meaning and sanction."[23]

That this "Christian" attitude to art and the world bears more than a slight similarity with the Apollonian principle is not coincidental. If Viacheslav Ivanov wanted to reconcile Christianity with Dionysianism, seeing Dionysus as a precursor of Christ, the Acmeists sought no such synthesis. They understood Christ as a true person who shared their own humanity and their own world. Nonetheless, his attitude toward and acceptance of that condition (as they understood it) was essentially Apollonian, and their role was to imitate Christ. In that sense, though they themselves would undoubtedly reject any hint of religious syncretism, one might say that the Acmeists saw Orthodox Christianity as the fulfillment of Apollonianism.

The balance of Gumilev's Acmeist manifesto is directed at the otherworldly aspirations of theurgical Symbolism, to which Gumilev responds with the famous assertion that "the unknowable, by its very definition, cannot be known" (*SS* IV, p. 174). In contrast to Western theology, which attempts to justify the existence of God, Gumilev appeals to Orthodox apophatic theology, which forbids positive or rationalistic explanations of the deity and which requires that He be defined only by negation. The insistence on the impossibility of describing the absolute transcendence of God thus preserves an element of ineffability in God's relation to man. This is entirely consistent with the Apollonian orientation, which is presented by Nietzsche as more orderly than its Dionysian antipode, but not, strictly speaking, any more rational.[24] In the context of Nietzsche's *Birth of Tragedy*, Gumilev's emphasis on accepting the unknown and relishing "the feeling of not knowing ourselves" may also represent a defense against the charge of Socratism.

There are many other aspects in which Acmeism opposes Nietzsche's Dionysian principle and its manifestation in theurgical Symbolism. It exalts masculinity. It accepts social, ethical and political responsibilities, like the virgins of Apollo who "remain what they are and retain their civic names," as opposed to the dithyrambic chorus, "timeless servants of their god who live outside the spheres of society" (*BT*, p. 64). (Mandelstam viewed Acmeism as a social phenomenon, as opposed to the cosmic aspirations of Symbolism.) Acmeism values "domesticity" over mystery, appreciating Euripides as a "domestic writer" ("On the Nature of the Word," *CCPL* p. 127), rather than reproaching him for the degeneration of tragedy (*BT*, pp. 79–86). Finally, the Acmeists insist on the adequacy of language, opposing the primacy of music with the power of the word. All of these topics deserve treatment in a more detailed discussion of the relationship between Acmeism and Nietzsche, with further elaboration of the separate effects that the ideas of Nietzsche had on the individual Acmeist poets. However, Nietzsche's greatest impact on Acmeism was in the impetus he provided for the formation of a world view and esthetic philosophy that opposed theurgical Symbolism. The other elements of influence, easily apparent in the imagery and thematics of their poetry, are the logical outcome of that position.

The well worn volume of Nietzsche packed in the traveling bag of the adventuresome hero of Gumilev's *Joyful Brotherhood* was soon lost, along with his toothbrush and his intellectual arrogance (*SS* IV, p. 124). The Acmeists made a great show of their ostensible rejection of Nietzsche because of his identification with the Dionysian world view and Viacheslav Ivanov's brand of Symbolism, and his hostility to Christianity. Still, by emphasizing the Apollonian, the Acmeists appropriated and reworked the elements of Nietzsche's philosophy that appealed to them, and, paradoxically, they come closer to the essence of Nietzsche's life-affirming philosophy than the Symbolists, whose one-sided adherence to the Dionysian fueled their rejection of the material world.

Gumilev comments on relationships of influence in a late poem entitled "The Master Artists' Prayer" ("Molitva masterov," *SS* II, p. 56), where he agrees with Nietzsche that the only followers worth having are those who resist their masters.

> We welcome those who insult and abuse,
> But to flatterers we say, "No!"

Fawning reviews and the crowd's acclaim
Are useless for the creation of sacred things.

The Acmeists were indeed resistant followers, but the critical
stance they took to Nietzsche's teachings proved to be highly
productive for their art and a significant step in the development of Russian literature.

NOTES

1 N. Gumilev, *Sobranie sochinenii*, ed. G. P. Struve and B. A. Filippov, 4 vols. (Washington, 1962–68), IV, p. 103. Henceforth cited
   parenthetically in the text as *SS*.
2 Osip Emilievich Mandelstam, "On the Nature of the Word" ("O
   prirode slova"), *The Complete Critical Prose and Letters*, ed. Jane
   Gary Harris, trans. Jane Gary Harris and Constance Link (Ann
   Arbor, 1979), p. 131. Henceforth cited parenthetically in the text
   as *CCPL*.
3 N. V. Nedobrovo, "Anna Akhmatova," *Russkaia mysl'* 7 (1915),
   repr. Anna Akhmatova, *Sochineniia*, ed. G. P. Struve and B. A.
   Filippov, 3 vols. (Paris, 1983), III, pp. 473–95.
4 A study of the influence of Nietzsche on the poetry of Gumilev is
   sorely wanting. For Nietzsche's influence on Gumilev's drama,
   see two articles by Elaine Rusinko: "An Acmeist in the Theater:
   Gumilev's Tragedy *The Poisoned Tunic*," *Russian Literature* 31
   (1992), pp. 393–414, and "Rewriting Ibsen in Russia: Gumi-
   lyov's Dramatic Poem 'Gondla,'" *The European Foundations of
   Russian Modernism*, ed. Peter Barta (Lewiston, NY, 1991), pp.
   189–218. The impact of Nietzsche on Mandelstam is complex; see
   Clare Cavanagh's chapter on Mandelstam's view of history in this
   volume.
5 See B. G. Rosenthal, "The Transmutation of the Symbolist
   Ethos: Mystical Anarchism and the Revolution of 1905," *Slavic
   Review* 36 (December 1977), pp. 608–27.
6 Cited in S. I. Mashinskii, "Sergei Gorodetskii," Sergei Gorodetskii, *Stikhotvoreniia i poemy* (Leningrad, 1974), p. 2.
7 *Na beregakh Nevy* (Washington, 1968), p. 114. Odoevtseva states
   that she was introduced to Nietzsche by Gumilev, who lent her his
   own volumes of the philosopher's works. She recalls, "Nietzsche
   had an enormous influence on Gumilev. His affected cruelty, his
   scorn for the weak, and the tragic heroism of his world view was
   appropriated from Nietzsche" (p. 72). There is also evidence of
   Gumilev's attraction to Nietzsche in the biographical notes com-

piled by Pavel Lukhnitskii, published in Vera Lukhnitskaia, *Nikolai Gumilev: Zhizn' poeta po materialam domashnego arkhiva sem'i Lukhnitskikh* (Leningrad, 1990), pp. 9, 37, 66, 80.

8 S. M. Gorodetskii, "Nekotorye techeniia v sovremennoi russkoi poezii," *Apollon* 1 (January 1913), p. 48.

9 N. S. Gumilev, *Neizdannye*, ed. Gleb Struve (Paris, 1980), p. 60.

10 Sergei Makovskii, *Portrety sovremennikov* (New York, 1955), p. 128.

11 Nadezhda Mandelstam, *Hope Abandoned*, trans. Max Hayward (New York, 1974), pp. 38–39.

12 O. A. Deschartes, commentary to Viacheslav Ivanov, *Sobranie sochinenii* (Brussels, 1971), I, p. 848. For the relationship between Ivanov and the Acmeists, see Sheelagh Graham and Michael Basker, commentary to Nikolai Gumilev, *Neizdannoe i nesobrannoe*, ed. M. Basker and S. Graham (Paris, 1986), pp. 253–56.

13 In the same spirit, to support the Acmeist dedication to the traditions of world culture, Mandelstam proposed that "Affirmation and justification of the real values of the past is just as revolutionary an act as the creation of new values," "Storm and Stress," in *CCPL*, p. 176.

14 Ann M. Lane, "Nietzsche Comes to Russia: Popularization and Protest in the 1890s," *Nietzsche in Russia*, ed. B. G. Rosenthal (Princeton, 1986), p. 63.

15 This aspect of Acmeism is best represented by the two lesser known poets, Vladimir Narbut and Mikhail Zenkevich. Zenkevich's 1912 collection *Wild Purple* (*Dikaia porfira*) was praised by Gumilev for the poet's "contentment with the earth" (*SS* IV, p. 290). Both poets demonstrate a "genuine fascination with ugliness" and are relentless in their glorification of the grotesque (*SS* IV, p. 300). Still Gumilev insists that they express in such poetry "vigorous life-affirmation," celebrating as Nietzsche did, in the words of John Burt Foster, "the fullness of being that can result from any open-eyed avowal of the negative aspects of life," *Heirs to Dionysus: A Nietzschean Current in Literary Modernism* (Princeton, 1981), p. 81. A discussion of this "primitivist" aspect of Acmeism can be found in Elaine Rusinko, "Adamism and Acmeist Primitivism," *Slavic and East European Journal* 1 (1988), pp. 84–97.

16 Nietzsche's eternal recurrence was salient for Akhmatova's and Mandelstam's artistic use of poetic memory and synchronic understanding of history (cf. Mandelstam's "joy of recurrence," *CCPL*, p. 114). But the Acmeist concept is a Christian transposition of Nietzsche's idea. See Gregory Freidin's discussion of Mandelstam's Mnemosyne as "a Christian cousin of Nietzsche's

eternal recurrence" in *A Coat of Many Colors: Osip Mandelstam and his Mythologies of Self-presentation* (Berkeley, 1987), p. 80.

17 Nadezhda Mandelstam, *Hope against Hope*, trans. Max Hayward (New York, 1970), p. 278; O. E. Mandelstam, "On the Nature of the World," *CCPL*, p. 131; Gumilev, *SS* IV, p. 321.

18 N. Mandelstam, *Hope against Hope*, p. 175.

19 N. Mandelstam, *Hope Abandoned*, p. 126.

20 E. A. Hull, *A Great Russian Tone-Poet: Scriabin* (London, 1921), cited in *CCPL*, p. 601. See also Ann M. Lane, "Bal'mont and Skriabin: The Artist as Superman," *Nietzsche in Russia*, ed. Rosenthal, pp. 195–218.

21 Freidin, *Coat of Many Colors*, p. 72.

22 N. Mandelstam, *Hope Abandoned*, p. 44.

23 Freidin, *Coat of Many Colors*, p. 80.

24 M. S. Silk and J. P. Stern, *Nietzsche on Tragedy* (London, 1981), p. 162.

CHAPTER 4

Armchair anarchists and salon Supermen: Russian occultists read Nietzsche

Maria Carlson

At the turn of the century, a certain element within the Russian intelligentsia desired to escape the materiality of existence and find some alternative to what it considered the spiritual sterility of Marxism, positivism, and dogmatic religion. Friedrich Nietzsche was one of the few European philosophers it found appealing. Russian Theosophists, Anthroposophists, and other occultists derived a unique, distinctly mystical reading of Nietzsche, and through the caprice of history their ideas survived to influence the philosophy of culture that emerged from the chaos of the Bolshevik Revolution. Their reading was essentially apolitical, but it strengthened the apocalyptic and religious interpretation of Nietzsche first promulgated by the Russian Symbolists and the God-seeking philosophers. The occultists' reading of Nietzsche was not particularly profound, but it reinforced certain aspects of the Nietzschean idea that would eventually become, under other names, a part of Soviet mythology.

Perhaps the most philosophically sophisticated of the occultists were the Theosophists and Anthroposophists. Theosophy as an organized movement was begun in 1875 by Helena Petrovna Blavatsky (1831–91), an eccentric Russian expatriate then living in New York City. Assisted by her friend, Colonel Henry Olcott (1832–1907), this unusual woman founded a Society that soon claimed thousands of faithful believers worldwide. Theosophy,[1] as Mme. Blavatsky outlined it in her major work, The Secret Doctrine (1888), provided its adherents with a highly-structured, neo-Buddhistic world-view that claimed to reconcile religion, philosophy, and science and thereby restore the sense of cosmological unity which modern man had lost. A syncretic, mystico-philosophical system with a strong moral ethic and a well-defined sense of spiritual "progress," Theosophy claimed to accommodate all faiths because it was ostensibly founded on a single, ancient esoteric tradition, long hidden from ordinary mortals, from which all subsequent religions derived. It was the most philosophically influential occult trend of the late nineteenth century.

By the 1890s Theosophy had spread to Russia, where it attracted numerous adherents from among the petty gentry, aristocrats, civil servants, professionals, and intelligentsia. The Russian chapter of the Theosophical Society, headquartered in St. Petersburg, received its charter only at the end of 1907 (after Russian censorship banning such societies was lifted), but by then many Russians had become members of the Society's numerous European branches. In 1913 the prominent Theosophist Dr. Rudolf Steiner (1861–1925) broke away from the Theosophical Society to establish a separate Anthroposophical Society, which looked more to the Western occult tradition and Wagnerian mythopoesis for its content without entirely rejecting neo-Buddhist cosmology. By that time, there were probably several thousand Russian Theosophists and Anthroposophists. Considering how small the Russian educated class was on the eve of the First World War, the philosophical occultists represent a significant portion of it.

Russian adherents of Theosophy and Anthroposophy in the two decades preceding the Revolution included several prominent members of the God-seeking intelligentsia, among them the poets Konstantin Bal'mont and Max Voloshin; the composer Aleksandr Scriabin; the painter Vassily Kandinsky; the writer Andrei Bely; the occultist Anna Mintslova, who inveigled poet and scholar Viacheslav Ivanov into Theosophy; the philosopher P. D. Uspensky. The brothers Vladimir and Vsevolod Soloviev (the philosopher and the novelist, respectively) had a passing interest in Theosophy, as did the philosopher Nikolai Berdiaev. Whether supportive or disdainful of Theosophy, most members of the Russian intelligentsia were familiar with its basic tenets.

The reception of Nietzsche by the occultists was based primarily on a single work. Most had thrilled to *Thus Spoke Zarathustra*, recognized its hero as the Zoroastrian prophet described in Mme. Blavatsky's *The Secret Doctrine*, and knew it immediately for a "spiritual parable." They felt they shared with Nietzsche the imperative need to find new values to replace dead, decaying values; the attempt to create meaning for a life that seemed meaningless; the notion of the elite "Superman," standing out from the "common herd;" the rejection of dogmatic Christianity; and escape from the trap of eternal recurrence. Feeling themselves to be spiritually superior, middle-class Theosophists and Anthroposophists were dismayed by the thought that they might be considered "tame and bourgeois," part of the "common herd;" Nietzsche gave them the opportunity to become armchair anarchists and salon Supermen.

The occultists' understanding of Nietzsche was enthusiastic, but all too often superficial and naive, as they reduced his philosophy to fit the tenets of their own. Nietzsche's views of eternal recurrence, for example, were diametrically opposed to the Theosophical concept of Karmic law, but this did not deter those Theosophists who interpreted it as an expression of reincarnation or even messianism. Theosophists turned Nietzsche's amorality into mystical freedom and ignored his pessimism. They transformed his Superman into a Mahatma and his *amor fati* into pantheistic submissiveness. Many felt that they alone could truly understand Nietzsche: "Nietzsche as an individual and as a writer, however, must remain insolvable to those who have not studied the phenomena of psychism and of mediumism. For he was mediumistic without knowing it, and he allowed himself to think that his psychic experiences were unique and conclusive."[2] Nietzsche would probably have been appalled to see himself identified as "our brother in the ranks" in the obituary written for him by the editor of *Theosophical Review*.[3]

The major Theosophical interpreter of Nietzsche in Russia was Petr Demianovich Uspensky (1878–1947). A mathematician by training and a writer by profession, Uspensky was the

Russian Theosophical Society's most prominent philosopher, speaker, and author until he became fascinated by the neo-Sufism of Georges Gurdjieff (1866–1949) shortly after the outbreak of World War I. Uspensky's interest in Nietzsche preceded his interest in Theosophy. Like many of his contemporaries, Uspensky came under the influence of fashionable Nietzscheism and its terminology during his adolescence, when he first read *Zarathustra*. He was soon afterward swept up by mysticism, "higher dimensions," psychology, the history of religions, and occultism, but did not lose his interest in Nietzsche. By 1907 he was seriously involved with Theosophy, a logical step, given that both Nietzsche and the Theosophists were influenced by Schopenhauer and Buddhism. He soon developed a reputation as "the most independent and talented Theosophical writer" in Russia.[4]

Uspensky's major philosophical contribution was his theory of multiple dimensions, first described in his book, *The Fourth Dimension* (St. Petersburg, 1910; 2nd rev. edn. 1914) and later expanded in *Tertium Organum* (St. Petersburg 1911; 2nd rev. edn. 1916). According to Uspensky, *Maya* (the World Illusion of the Hindus) causes man to perceive only three spatial dimensions and one linear dimension of time. In reality there are other time dimensions invisible to man's physical senses, but visible to the "supersensible sight" of the "new man" who has developed his "higher self." Eternity is such another time dimension; the Superman (a sort of Theosophical Zarathustra) is such a "new man." Uspensky's philosophy of higher dimensions attempts to join Western philosophy to Eastern mysticism; in this he adheres to the Theosophical Idea. "The major content of the Theosophical system," he concludes, "must be considered *synthetic philosophy, revolutionary morality, and the doctrine of the superman* [*sverkhchelovek*].[5] His mystical mathematics would later prove important for Russian abstract art.

Refracting Nietzsche through the prism of Theosophy, Uspensky focused on two fundamental Nietzschean ideas – the Superman and eternal recurrence – as relevant to Theosophical thought. At first Uspensky equated Nietzsche's concept of eternal recurrence with the Theosophical notion of reincarnation. Reincarnation is an evolutionary process which, "according to the understanding of this doctrine [Theosophy], is the evolution, the perfection, the *ascent along the path to the Superman.*"[6] That Uspensky interpreted the Nietzschean eternal recurrence in terms of the wheel of reincarnation is also clear in his book *The Symbols of the Tarot* (*Simvoly Taro*, 1912), in which he interprets the tenth Arcanum, "The Wheel of Fortune," with the aid of *Thus Spoke Zarathustra*:

And I heard the voice of the animals of Zarathustra:
Everything goes, everything returns; eternally rolls the wheel of being. Everything dies, everything blossoms forth again; eternally runs the year of being. Everything breaks, everything is united anew; eternally builds itself the same house of being. Everything parts, everything meets again; the ring of being remains eternally true to itself.[7]

This simplistic reading of eternal recurrence as reincarnation did not please Uspensky for long. He soon expanded the idea of eternal recurrence to include the notion of cyclical time as taken by the eclectic Theosophists from the Indic Vedas and the Pythagoreans. Uspensky refers to Pythagoras's *two* categories of recurrence: (1) a recurrence of seasons, movements of heavenly bodies, growing cycles, etc. (repetition in perceived time), and (2) the recurrence of time itself, where all that has been will be again, exactly as it was before (repetition in eternity). "The Pythagoreans," points out Uspensky, "distinguished between these two ideas, which are confused by modern Buddhists [Theosophists] and were confused by Nietzsche."[8]

To refine his (and Nietzsche's) notion of eternal recurrence, Uspensky returned to his original work on multiple dimensions. He concluded that eternal recurrence can be mathematically proven only in the fifth dimension: *three-dimensional space + time + eternity.* Even if Uspensky did not always find himself in total agreement with Nietzsche, he was able to reach his conclusions only with the German philosopher's poetic aid (*Thus Spoke Zarathustra*):

Nietzsche contributed a great deal to the popularization of the idea of eternal recurrence, but he has added nothing new to it. On the contrary, he introduced several wrong concepts into it, as for instance his calculation, which mathematically is altogether wrong, of the mathematical necessity for the repetition of identical worlds in the universe. But although he made mistakes in the attempts to prove his theories, Nietzsche emotionally felt the idea of eternal recurrence very strongly. He felt the idea as a poet. And several passages in his *Zarathustra*, and in other books where he touches upon the idea, are perhaps the best he ever wrote.[9]

Under the spell of *Zarathustra*, Uspensky tried to express his interpretation of eternal recurrence in a literary medium. In 1917 he published a novel, *Kinemodrama (ne dlia kinematografa)*, which he subtitled "an occult tale from the cycle 'Eternal Recurrence'" (translated into English in 1947 as *The Strange Life of Ivan Osokin*). On the title page of the Russian edition is a picture of the Tenth Card of the Tarot, "The Wheel of Fortune," which a brief introduction defines as the symbol of eternal recurrence. The novel's epigraphs are taken from Uspensky's own *Tertium Organum* and Nietzsche's *Zarathustra*.

In 1913 Uspensky published an expanded version of two lectures he had read in St. Petersburg in January and February 1912; the more important of these was "On the Superman" ("O sverkhcheloveke").[10] In his lecture, Uspensky explicitly connected the idea of the Nietzschean Superman, which he considered to have been contained in "all parallel symbolic systems, 'hermetic philosophy,' in all [traditions of] 'western occultism,' and in Masonic teachings," with the "New Man" of Theosophy. Without precisely defining terms, Uspensky claims that Theosophy is nothing less than the morality of the Superman. Nietzsche's Superman, claims Uspensky, is in fact "very close to the idea of the 'Initiate' of Western occultism."[11] Uspensky equates the Superman with the "Initiate" in the sense that the Initiate is one who is in a state of constant spiritual evolution toward a "higher self;" that is his fundamental understanding of the Superman as well. In his subsequent discussion, Uspensky selects various passages from *Zarathustra* to support this view of the Superman.

The Superman that Uspensky constructs in his essay is by no

means identical to Nietzsche's; on some points, Uspensky's Superman even represents a serious misreading of Nietzsche. Following Nietzsche, Uspensky posits a Superman with a high level of intellectual development and understanding of idealist philosophy; his Superman also boasts a supra-individual [*sverkh-lichnoe*] development of the "higher" emotions (which Uspensky defines not only as esthetic, moral, and social, but also religious, in a traditional Christian sense). Uspensky points out that:

The negation of morality in the idea of the Superman is frequently connected with Nietzsche's name. But Nietzsche is completely innocent in this. On the contrary, it is possible that no one inserts as much true morality into the philosophy of human existence and into the notion of the Superman as Nietzsche does. He destroyed only the old morality, he fought against ready-made forms of morality. He taught that morality should be *created* and should live in the heart of man, and not be taken, ready-made, in one and the same form, and made obligatory for all and for always. [Uspensky decides that] Nietzsche protests against morality as *external law*, and demands morality as an inner feeling.[12]

Uspensky's Superman has a strong and conscious will and a sense of the "higher self," great love of mankind and people, faith in the future, and an inability to betray his own conscience. Unlike Nietzsche, who places his Superman beyond the constraints of traditional Christian morality, Uspensky never questions the Christian ethic's influence on the formation of the conscience or morality of the Theosophical Superman. Finally, the Superman needs to engage in the right kind of labor (Uspensky's Superman engages only in creative and artistic work).

Uspensky's Superman is the result of spiritual evolution. "You must seek the Superman within yourself, in your soul," he writes, for the image of the Superman represents "man's 'higher self,' his *higher consciousness*."[13] All of these characteristics of the Superman were now evolving, in Uspensky's view, within the enlightened inner circles of the Theosophical Society. It is entirely possible that Uspensky never read Nietzsche's *The Antichrist* and so did not see his comment in

Section 4: "Mankind does *not* represent a development toward something better or stronger or higher in the sense accepted today." Nietzsche grants that occasionally "we really do find a higher type," but terms this a "fortunate accident," not a line of evolutionary development. In his essay Uspensky totally misses Nietzsche's sense of quest and question, his attempt to move beyond traditionally accepted constructs. Uspensky also lacks Nietzsche's sense of humor: laughter is not a feature of Uspensky's humorless and stuffy spiritual Superman. He implicitly rejects the Nietzschean element of tragedy and pessimism and does not understand Nietzsche's concept of freedom (to exercise the will to power). Uspensky reads Nietzsche strictly as a mystic philosopher. Uspensky's tendentious, "corrected" model of the Nietzschean Superman assumes an evolutionary progress of the spirit, based on a neo-Buddhistic model of reincarnation, toward a traditional Christian concept of the good and the beautiful. While he explains that the Superman's path into the future "is not at all a *path to happiness*, but, on the contrary, an approach to a new, great suffering, because the Superman *is* superhuman suffering," Uspensky makes it clear that this suffering is redemptive. Thus Uspensky's "Theosophized" concept of the Superman develops a decisively Christian dimension: "The Superman *without Golgotha*, without crucifixion – external or internal – is impossible."[14] Theosophy, in Uspensky's reading, has become more than the morality of Nietzsche's Superman; it is now his religion.

Uspensky's essay, "On the Superman," is essentially a tendentiously-presented formula for generating an improved Christian Superman with distinctly Victorian preconceptions. There is even an element of "mystical Darwinism," in Uspensky's position: his Superman emerges as a "class" and even as a "race." Furthermore, his Russian, "Christianized" reading of the Superman dove-tailed neatly with the "New Man" emerging in the enthusiastic writings of the Russian socialists and "God-builders." Certain dimensions of the "New Soviet Man" of subsequent Bolshevik mythology (faith in the radiant future, the redemptive power of labor, the perfectibility of mankind) clearly stem from the various efforts of the Russian "God-builders" and "God-seekers" (including occultists) to romanticize and/or "spiritualize" Nietzsche's Superman.

Uspensky himself must have regretted his original, juvenile reading of Nietzsche, because when he revised this essay in 1929 for inclusion in his major work, *A New Model of the Universe*, he made radical changes in it. He abandoned the notion of evolution as progress (as opposed to change), and edited out much of the unsophisticated enthusiasm for occultism and the sentimental Theosophical maunderings about new races and creative labor. The "formula" for a self-righteous Superman is gone; a less literal understanding of Zarathustra's "mercilessness" (his ruthlessness toward the weak, the vulgar, and the mediocre) has taken its place. Uspensky did not, however, abandon entirely the religious dimension of his redefined Superman and continued, in his future works, to polemicize with Nietzsche specifically on this point:

All this lack of understanding of Nietzsche is curious and characteristic because it can only be compared with Nietzsche's own lack of understanding of the ideas of Christianity and of the Gospels. Nietzsche understood Christ according to Renan. Christianity was for him the religion of the weak and the miserable. He rebelled against Christianity, opposed Superman to Christ, and did not wish to see that he was fighting the very thing that had created him and his ideas.[15]

In embracing this point of view, Uspensky reveals that he is both a Theosophical and a profoundly Russian interpreter of the Nietzschean idea in the context of the Russian religious renaissance on the eve of Revolution. Like Dmitri Merezhkovsky, Andrei Bely, and Viacheslav Ivanov, he sought to integrate the ideas of Nietzsche into the philosophy of speculative mysticism. Uspensky's Theosophical reading of Nietzsche did one more thing: it presented a Nietzsche cleansed of the hubris, amorality, decadence, and pessimism that offended many middle-class Russians. This modified reading of Nietzsche would later help make certain aspects of his world view more acceptable to the essentially middle-class, even Victorian, personal morality of the rulers of the new Soviet state.

Theosophy's interest in Nietzsche was shared by its Germanic offshoot, Anthroposophy. Anthroposophy's "Christian Theosophy," relieved of oriental passivity and imagery, appealed to Russian Theosophists. Its leader, Dr. Steiner, claimed that Russia had a special mission: it was destined to play a major role in the renewal of world culture. This point suited the Russian intelligentsia's own sense of messianism very well. Thus Steiner attracted those Russian "God-seekers" who rejected the Buddhist hegemony of Theosophy, but who were also dissatisfied by the "Westernizing" elements in Russian culture, preferring to build on the Slavophile idea without returning to tradition or reactionary xenophobia. By emphasizing the Russian "creative will" as the means by which a stagnant Russian (and world) culture would be transformed in the future, Steiner, himself influenced by the Nietzschean idea of cultural creativity, attracted those who wanted to see in Russian culture an outwardly-directed synthesis of the finest features of both East and West.[16]

Like Uspensky, Steiner was greatly interested in Nietzsche, and Nietzsche continued to influence the Russian Anthroposophists through Steiner's writings. The author of several books on Nietzsche, including *Friedrich Nietzsche: Ein Kämpfer gegen sein Zeit* (1895), translated into English as *Friedrich Nietzsche: Fighter for Freedom* [1960, 1985]), Steiner frequently referred to Nietzsche in his lectures and had actually met him in 1894.[17] Impressed by Nietzsche's "immense spirituality," Steiner saw great consistency in what he termed Nietzsche's "spiritual development," the "aloofness" of his soul from his body. But unlike the Theosophists, who focused almost exclusively on Nietzsche's "spirituality," Steiner viewed Nietzsche primarily as a cultural landmark, a man "whose tragic destiny it was to participate in the scientific age of the latter half of the nineteenth century and to be shattered by its impact. He *sought* the spirit in that age but found *nothing*."[18]

While he admired Nietzsche, Steiner did not agree unconditionally with Nietzsche's philosophical position; in fact, he found it "the opposite of my own conviction." For Steiner, Nietzsche was a cultural extreme; he represented the pole opposite to Goethe, who more closely approached Steiner's own views: "Goethe *found* the spirit in the reality of nature; in his dream of nature, Nietzsche *lost* the spirit-mythos."[19] Steiner interpreted Nietzsche's formulation of the eternal recurrence and the Superman as "the suffering of a person who is prevented from reaching understanding of the evolution of humanity and of the true being of man by the convincing arguments of natural science at the end of the nineteenth century."[20] In viewing Nietzsche as a victim of the very positivism against which he fought, Steiner showed himself to be more discerning than those Theosophists who were so ready to accept Nietzsche as "our brother in the ranks." Nietzsche's own brand of positivism apparently spoke to an element of "superstitious positivism" within Theosophy. Steiner, although he admired Nietzsche, realized that their ways did not lie together. He could explain the phenomenon that was Nietzsche from the point of view of Anthroposophical "spiritual science," but had to conclude that Nietzsche, although a martyr to his time, "produced no new ideas for a world conception."[21]

The Russian Anthroposophists followed Steiner's interpretation of Nietzsche as a cultural icon, not a spiritual leader. The most interesting and best-known Russian Anthroposophical reading of Nietzsche is that of the writer Andrei Bely (1880–1934). Bely had lived in the Anthroposophical community in Dornach, Switzerland, and worked there on the building of the first Anthroposophical temple, the Goetheanum. During this period of great upheaval in Russian culture (1912–23), Bely continued to write about Nietzsche and the crisis of culture and consciousness in numerous works: in his articles for *Works and Days* (*Trudy i dni*),[22] in his series *At the Pass: Crisis of Thought, Crisis of Life*, and *Crisis of Culture* (*Na perevale: Krizis zhizni, Krizis mysli*, both Petrograd, 1918, and *Krizis kultury*, Petrograd, 1920), and in as-yet-unpublished manuscripts. Nietzsche continued to interest Bely until his death in 1934.

Like the Theosophist Uspensky, Andrei Bely had admired

Nietzsche since adolescence, when he worshipped Nietzsche as a sacred figure, a symbol of the dying and resurrected Dionysus and, ultimately, of the martyred Christ Himself. In the early days of Symbolism, Bely felt that "for a whole group of Russian Symbolists Nietzsche was, in his time, a transition to Christianity. Without Nietzsche, the prophecy of neo-Christianity would not have arisen among us."[23] In this position, Bely reflected the tendency of the God-seeking intelligentsia to replace Nietzsche's philosophical dimension with a religious one, in which eternal recurrence becomes an expression of messianism, the Superman a version of the God-man, and amorality, mystical freedom.

With time, the influence of Steiner, and a more sophisticated acquaintance with the German philosopher's work, Bely re-evaluated his own conception of Nietzsche and came to see mystical Christianity and Nietzscheanism as opposites. Nietzsche continued to be an important figure for Bely, but he was no longer a Christ figure; now Nietzsche was the greatest representative and martyr of the crisis of European culture. He was the poet who wrote the great poem of the spirit, *Thus Spoke Zarathustra*. But although Nietzsche was able to identify the symbols of the spirit, he was unable to interpret them; he was unable, wrote Bely, to "unite the two paths: the path of the line and the path of the immovable circle, into the spiral."[24] Nietzsche erred in assuming that the realm of the spirit was imaginary, and thus he became trapped in matter, the martyred victim of prevailing scientific materialism; unable to transcend them, he was crucified by his own thoughts, Bely wrote in 1918.[25] And so Bely denied Nietzsche his earlier status as prophet; instead, Nietzsche became one of several major milestones on the borderline between the old culture and the new. In this role he was assimilated into Bely's emerging philosophy of culture.

Saturated with Anthroposophical doctrine, Bely returned to Russia in 1916 and remained there during the years of Revolution and Civil War. From 1916 to 1921 he was an active and influential member of numerous artistic and philosophical enterprises, speaking to gatherings of the Proletkult and giving specialized lectures at meetings of the Moscow Anthroposophical Society. He was also a founding member of Vol'fila (The Free Philosophical Association, 'Volnaia Filosofskaia Assotsiatsiia'), which existed in Petrograd from 1919 to 1923. Vol'fila was an organization of writers, philosophers, academics, and artists, some with Theosophical and Anthroposophical backgrounds, others with more general interests in religion, philosophy, and philosophy of culture. Members and participants of Vol'fila, to name just a few in addition to Bely, included Aleksandr Blok, Kuz'ma Petrov-Vodkin, N. O. Lossky, Mikhail Matiushin, Olga Forsh, Margarita Sabashnikova, and others. The Petrograd Vol'fila had a counterpart in Moscow, the Free Academy of Spiritual Culture ('Vol'naia Akademiia Dukhovnoi Kultury'), whose membership included Gustav Shpett, Nikolai Berdiaev, Mikhail Gershenzon, Boris Vysheslavtsev, and Fedor Stepun. Some were Theosophists and Anthroposophists; many were sympathizers; all represented idealist philosophical tendencies.

By 1920, the meetings of Vol'fila attracted as many as 1,000 listeners to each lecture. The range of topics included proletarian culture, the philosophy of Symbolism, Campanella's *City of the Sun*, neo-Platonism, the philosophy of creativity, and Anthroposophy as a means of self-cognition. Apparently none of the numerous public lectures of Vol'fila was devoted specifically to Nietzsche, but the name of the German philosopher was frequently mentioned in discussions of the philosophy of culture in general and the direction of contemporary Russian culture in particular. For four crucial years, from 1919 to 1923, Russian Anthroposophy and the Nietzschean idea had a platform from which they could contribute to the emerging intellectual profile of the new Soviet culture.

The Moscow Free Academy of Spiritual Culture had been organized in 1918 by Nikolai Berdiaev (1874–1948). An idealist philosopher with strong occult and religious interests, Berdiaev was well-acquainted with Nietzscheanism. But like the Anthroposophists, to whom he was bound by ties of friendship and a mutual interest in speculative mysticism, he could not agree with Nietzsche's fundamental position: "Nietzsche and I always diverged on one major point, and that was that Nietzsche's primary orientation was '*diesseits* [on this side],' he wanted to be 'true to the earth,' ... My primary orientation was '*jenseits*' [on that side]."[26] Like the Anthroposophists, he concluded that Nietzsche was actually an intellectual positivist, not a mystic, as the Theosophists saw him.

The dialogue with Nietzschean ideas in the Free Academy was continued indirectly. Berdiaev's friend and colleague, the philosopher and critic Fedor Stepun (1884–1965), was among the first Russians to read Oswald Spengler's important *Decline of the West* (*Untergang des Abendlandes*, 1918), a work strongly influenced by Nietzsche's philosophy. Stepun lectured on Spengler in the Free Academy. He criticized Spengler's cultural pessimism (inherited from Nietzsche) and optimistically assumed that the war and the Russian Revolution would bring Europe to its senses and result in a new spiritual renascence.[27] In 1922 Berdiaev, Stepun, Semen Frank (1877–1950), and Ia. M. Bukshpan published four essays on Spengler's work under the title *Oswald Spengler and the Decline of Europe* (*Osval'd Shpengler i zakat Evropy*), in which they reaffirmed the idealist, "spiritual" position that was the hallmark of the Free Academy.

This period of open dialogue among idealism, Nietzscheanism, and occultism did not last beyond 1923. The disbanding of the Russian Theosophical Society became a priority for the new regime almost immediately after the Revolution. Anna Kamenskaia (1867–1952), the Society's President, had continued the intellectual and philanthropic activities of the Society and publication of its major journal, *The Theosophical Herald* (*Vestnik Teosofii*, 1908–18), in spite of persecution, paper shortages, and the closing of the Society's offices. But Kamenskaia refused to collaborate with the Bolsheviks or to spread their "materialist message" in her *Theosophical Herald*, and in June 1921 she fled across the Finnish border; many of her colleagues (including P. D. Uspensky) had already emigrated. In Switzerland she continued her long career in Theosophy as President of the Russian Theosophical Society Outside Russia. The Anthroposophists, although less visible than the Theosophists, experienced a similar pattern of arrests, exile, and self-imposed silence. By 1923 the platform for open dialogue was all but gone.

Moscow's Free Academy of Spiritual Culture was disbanded in late 1922; Petrograd's Vol'fila was closed early in 1923; the Theosophical and Anthroposophical Societies, the Tolstoians, and other mystical and occult groups were permanently disbanded by official decree in 1923; the presses that published mystical and occult literature were closed; occult books and the works of "subversive" philosophers (like Nietzsche) had been removed from library shelves as part of a new move by the Bolshevik regime to eradicate the idealist, mystic, formalist, and "bourgeois intellectual" element from its midst.

In spring 1922 a new "anti-religious front" was formed. The young Soviet regime attacked occult and religious groups with a series of publications calculated to "historicize" religion and "demystify" it. Large numbers of "undesirable elements" – writers, philosophers, critics, academics – were exiled to Western Europe (among them Russia's leading religious and idealist philosophers: Nikolai Berdiaev, Fedor Stepun, Sergei Bulgakov [1871–1944], Boris Vysheslavtsev [1877–1954], and Semen Frank). This coincided with attacks on mysticism by major figures of the new regime, such as Trotsky's virulent criticism of Anthroposophy in *Literature and Revolution* (*Literatura i revoliutsiia*, 1923). There were also assaults on the occult societies in the newspapers. The official campaign against the "decadent bourgeois intelligentsia" signaled the end of the period of relatively open philosophical inquiry and the beginning of Soviet ideological hegemony.

After the closing of Vol'fila and the occult societies, the center of Anthroposophical activity shifted briefly to the experimental Second Studio of the Moscow Art Theatre (MKhAT). Several of its members were Anthroposophists, including actor-director Mikhail Chekhov (1891–1955), who headed MKhAT's Studios I and II from 1918 to 1928, when he emigrated in the wake of accusations that he was using the Studio to disseminate Anthroposophical doctrines inconsistent with MKhAT's world view. Chekhov staged Andrei Bely's

Anthroposophical drama *Petersburg* in 1925, as well as two Anthroposophical plays by actress and dramatist Nadezhda Bromley (1889–1966): *Archangel Michael* (*Arkhangel Mikhail*, 1922) and *King of the Square Republic* (*Korol' kvadratnoi respubliki*, 1925). Chekhov based his acting method on Steiner's concept of the "Higher Self." The MKhAT Studio II was an unlikely pulpit for the Movement, but Anthroposophical ideas stayed alive there.

The post-revolutionary legacy of Theosophy and Anthroposophy, still bearing a residue of the Nietzschean idea, also continued to live in Russian art of the avant-garde. Uspensky's eclectic mysticism exerted an influence not only on the work of Vassily Kandinsky, but also on Russian Cubo-Futurism, especially on the painting of Mikhail Matiushin (1861–1934) and Kazimir Malevich (1878–1935), and the poetry of Aleksei Kruchenykh (1886–1968).[28] In their abstract art they realized Uspensky's suggestion that "from the fourth dimension it should be possible to see the cube simultaneously from all sides and from the inside, as if from the center, even though in three dimensions it might seem totally untransparent."[29] In developing his theories of the fourth and fifth dimensions (in which linear time and three-dimensional space are shown to be an illusion), Uspensky had been influenced not only by Charles Hinton, R. M. Bucke, and Mme. Blavatsky, but also by Nietzsche.[30] Eternity becomes another dimension, visible to the "new man" with "supersensible sight," the man who realized his "higher self," the Superman. In the work of these abstract artists, the remnants of the Nietzschean idea that persisted in Theosophical thought had been estheticized by the reality of political ideology, but had not disappeared altogether.

By 1928, both the God-seeking and the God-building elements of the Russian intelligentsia, those who introduced and disseminated the Nietzschean idea in all its Russian hypostases, were effectively rendered impotent. This line of development appeared to have no future in the further evolution of Soviet Russian culture. The occultists were in exile or had been silenced; still others silenced themselves. The Russian variant of the Nietzschean idea that they had helped to shape, however, seeped by osmosis into the emerging mythology of the new Soviet state.

NOTES

1 A distinction exists between "theosophy" as "divine wisdom," a philosophical tradition of speculative mysticism, and "Theosophy" as an organized, religious-philosophical movement dating from 1875.
2 E. T. H[argrove], "Nietzsche and Mme. Blavatsky," *Theosophical Quarterly* [New York] 6:4 (April 1909), p. 340.
3 *Theosophical Review* [London] 27:128 (October 15, 1900), p. 102.
4 Nikolai Berdiaev, "Tipy religioznoi mysli v Rossii," *Russkaia mysl'* 11 (1916), p. 1 (2nd pagination).
5 P. D. Uspenskii, *Chetvertoe izmerenie: opyt issledovaniia oblast' neizmerimogo* (St. Petersburg, 1910), p. 95. This and all subsequent emphases are Uspensky's.
6 P. D. Uspenskii, *Chetvertoe izmerenie*, p. 89.
7 P. D. Ouspensky, *The Symbolism of the Tarot*, in his *A New Model of the Universe* (New York, 1971; orig. 1931), p. 213.
8 P. D. Uspensky, "Eternal Recurrence and the Laws of Manu," in his *Model*, p. 411. Nietzsche refutes the Pythagoreans in "Vom Nutzen und Nachteil der Historie," pt. 2, in his *Unzeitgemässe Betrachtungen (UT)*.
9 Ouspensky, *Model*, pp. 409–10.
10 P. D. Uspenskii, *Vnutrenii krug ("O poslednei cherte" i "O sverkhcheloveke")*; *dve lektsii* (St. Petersburg, 1913). The first essay, "O posledenei cherte," subtitled "Teosoficheskaia ideia v russkoi literature," is a review of Mikhail Artsybashev's novel, *U poslednei cherty* (1910–11). Artsybashev vulgarized the Nietzschean idea in his sensationalistic, frequently erotic novels.
11 Uspenskii "O sverkhcheloveke," pp. 83, 84.
12 Uspenskii "O sverkhcheloveke," pp. 103, 104.
13 Uspenskii "O sverkhcheloveke," p. 139.
14 Uspenskii "O sverkhcheloveke," p. 125.
15 P. D. Ouspensky, "Superman," in his *Model*, p. 113. Ernst Renan, author of *La Vie de Jésus* (1863), depicted Jesus as an exclusively historical personage, denying His divine essence.
16 For further discussion of this point from an Anthroposophical point of view, see Nikolai Belotsvetov, *Religiia tvorcheskoi voli* (Petrograd, 1915).
17 Nietzsche's sister, Elizabeth Förster-Nietzsche, asked Steiner to

catalog Nietzsche's library and to work in the archives (Rudolf Steiner, *An Autobiography*, trans. Rita Stebbing [Blauvelt, 1977], p. 223).

18 Steiner, *Autobiography*, p. 227.

19 Steiner, *Autobiography*, pp. 226, 228.

20 Steiner, *Autobiography*, pp. 228.

21 Rudolf Steiner, *Friedrich Nietzsche: Fighter for Freedom* (Blauvelt, 1985), p. 212.

22 Especially in Bely's two articles, "Liniia, krug, spiral' – simvolizma" and "Krugovoe dvizhenie," *Trudy i dni* 4/5 (1912), pp. 13–22, 51–73.

23 Andrei Belyi "Nastoiashchee i budushchee russkoi literatury," in his *Lug zelenyi* (Moscow, 1910), p. 81.

24 Andrei Belyi, *Na perevale III: Krizis kul'tury* (Petersburg, 1918), p. 40.

25 Ibid., p. 55.

26 Nikolai Berdiaev, *Samopoznanie* (Paris, 1983), pp. 142–43.

27 Fedor Stepun, *Byvshee i nesbyvsheesia*, II (New York, 1956), pp. 275–77.

28 For the Cubo-Futurists' union of the neo-Buddhistic notion that higher consciousness and "supersensible sight" can be achieved by organic evolution, with Uspensky's theory of multiple dimensions, see Charlotte Douglas, "Beyond Reason: Malevich, Matiushin, and Their Circles," *The Spiritual in Art: Abstract Painting 1890–1985* [Exhibition Catalog] (New York, 1986), pp. 186–87.

29 P. D. Uspenskii, *Chetvertoe izmerenie*, p. 29.

30 To secure his case Uspensky quotes from *Thus Spoke Zarathustra*: "Being begins in every Now, around every 'Here' rolls the sphere of 'There.' The middle is everywhere. Crooked is the path of eternity" (P. D. Ouspensky, *Model*, p. 213).

PART II

Nietzsche and Soviet Initiatives in the Arts

CHAPTER 5

Nietzschean leaders and followers in Soviet mass theater, 1917–27

James von Geldern

During the years of Civil War, Soviet Russia was gripped by what Viktor Shklovsky called "theatromania";[1] amateur theaters appeared in every corner of society. Soldiers fresh from battle declaimed Danton's fiery rhetoric in plays about the French Revolution; bureaucrats donned tattered clothes for dramas of peasant life; Marxists played aristocrats in Molière's satires. The theater of the masses reached its ultimate form in mass spectacles, where thousands of untrained actors recreated the October Revolution on the city squares. Everyone, it seemed, had caught the bug.

The cherished dream of socialists was coming true: the people, who had languished in ignorance so long, were creating a culture of their own. Like the socialist order that inspired it, the new culture would be democratic and egalitarian; perhaps it would surpass even the Greeks! Nadezhda Krupskaia, Lenin's wife and an administrator of popular culture from 1920, seemed to think so; the blooming of amateur theater proved to her that Russia had become a "new Athens."[2] And she was not alone in that belief.

The Bolsheviks had set culture on a new course. It would not mushroom just because its spores fell on fertile ground; it would be created and cultivated. The only question was how. Should the working class be allowed to control its own cultural expression, or should it be guided by a vanguard? Who should do the creating: the working class or its representatives? The debate was often furious, even though it was conducted on both sides by Bolsheviks. It echoed old contentions: would socialist culture be a harmonious celebration of proletarian power or a struggle for the future; would it belong to workers alone, or include others? Amongst these "others" was the intelligentsia, whose uncertain future was a matter of great concern. In the debate on the new culture they heard reflections of an old "eternal" question: the relationship of the intelligentsia and people. Intellectuals wondered if the revolutionary people needed them, and what their own contribution might be.

In the decades before the Revolution, Nietzsche had offered answers to these questions, and his influence, often covert, was felt in post-revolutionary debates. His *The Birth of Tragedy* had come to pre-revolutionary Russia as a revelation. It described a Hellenic culture divided between two spirits, the measured Apollonian and the chaotic Dionysian, that came together in tragic drama. Culture flourishes only when the two spirits are joined in a single expression. Russians projected Nietzsche's duality onto their own society: the intelligentsia was Apollonian, the people were Dionysian. Read this way, *The Birth of Tragedy* (*BT*) offered a divided nation the hope of unity; and it offered relevance to an intelligentsia that felt left behind by history. In Nietzsche's cultural equation, the people provided the impulse and emotion, the intelligentsia guidance and expression. The cultural debates following the October Revolution only made Nietzsche more relevant; the older intelligentsia could counter radical belligerence with the vision of *BT*. Let the workers act; let them project their visions on stage: if amateur theatricals were to be the foundation of a new culture, they would have to be guided by the intelligentsia. The intelligentsia (the part that chose to join the new order) was not asking the workers to leave the stage; they only wanted to help. If Nietzsche was right, the collaboration would yield a truly great culture.

Nietzsche's often contradictory influence could be found on all sides of the debate after the Revolution. When Bolsheviks and intellectuals who had come to maturity before the 1905 Revolution spoke of a cultural balance, *BT*'s optimism could be heard. When younger radicals from Prolekult, who had come of age after 1905, spoke of creating an exclusively proletarian culture, glimmers of *The Will to Power* could be seen (reflected by Georges Sorel). When those same radicals produced plays in which revolutions were propelled by a single strong individual, the influence of *Thus Spoke Zarathustra* was evident. Underlying all this was the question of who should lead and who should follow. Nietzsche was present in the debate; but his Russian readers used him in many ways. What will be discussed here is not what Nietzsche was, but how he was read and how he was used.

THE OLDER GENERATION

The generation of Russians that came to maturity before the Revolution of 1905 was profoundly influenced by *BT*, and it shared an enthusiasm for mass drama. The enthusiasm cut across ideological boundaries. The older Bolsheviks who administered Soviet culture immediately after the Revolution, such as Anatoly Lunacharsky (1875–1933), Pavel Kogan (1872–1932) and Vladimir Friche (1870–1929), saw mass drama as the summit of socialist culture. Their contemporaries the Symbolists had even greater aspirations. Symbolists had been among the first to suggest mass drama as a modern equivalent to the Greek drama. Vsevolod Meyerhold (1874–1940), Andrei Bely (1880–1934) and Georgy Chulkov (the "mystical anarchist," 1879–1939) had appeared – along with Lunacharsky – in the anthology *Theater: Book on the new theater* (1908); and Viacheslav Ivanov (1866–1949) had forcefully advocated the mass national drama in his early anthology *By the Stars* (1909) and the later *Furrows and Boundaries* (1916).[3] The connection was odd and always fragile, yet as members of a single generation they shared many acquaintances and ideals. Some of them could be found drinking tea together at Ivanov's Wednesday night salon; their articles often appeared in the same anthologies and journals. The Symbolists and older Bolsheviks discussed the same questions; and when they disagreed, as they often did, it was in a common language.

Neither group would have objected to the statement that great changes must come to Russia; opinions diverged as to how, when, and by whom. Speculation on the culture of the future – after the changes – brought them even closer. Theater, all would have agreed, would be the preeminent art of the future; and it would be a tragic theater that rivaled the Greeks, expressing a harmony of purpose and will. Ivanov envisioned a theater in which the entire nation would merge in a single all-embracing mythic experience; Lunacharsky saw theater expressing the united will of a socialist nation;[4] Friche thought theater would disappear entirely, to be replaced by festivals and choral dances.[5] The only difficulty socialism would introduce to culture was, as Aleksandr Bogdanov (1873–1928) noted, that it would make tragedy altogether unthinkable: tragedy thrives on a divided spirit, socialism heals divisions.[6]

Each imagined a culture of marble monuments and cathartic tragedies, very much like the culture of ancient Athens, at least, like the ideal Athens first described by Winckelmann, and much later by Wagner. The older Russian generation sought an undivided society in which free citizens devoted their spare time to the cultivation of the arts and humanities. It could be socialist, or it could be Christian: the differences seemed to fade as the vision moved farther into the future.[7] Athens was always a model.

Which Athens was it? Winckelmann and Wagner, Hegel and Marx had all shaped the Russian understanding to some degree. Yet there was also a strong native tradition led by the classicists Tadeusz Zielinski and Innokenty Annensky, who had appreciated Nietzsche; and most important was Nietzsche himself and his *BT*. The second half of this book, which predicted the renaissance of German culture from the spirit of music, was received more avidly in Russia than in Western Europe. According to the Russian reading of *BT*, the culture of the future would be born in ecstatic communal "Dionysian" rites, and be given crystalline artistic form by an individual, the "Apollonian" artist.

Nietzsche's formulation had two advantages over other versions of the Hellenic ideal. First, he recognized the unfettered, chaotic emotions that catalyze social upheaval: precisely those impulses that fascinated and worried the intelligentsia. Wagner, who in his youth had greeted the Revolution of 1848, was uncomfortable with disorder. The upheaval of 1848 was for him an aberration, which would lead to a higher stability;

society would be "conservative anew."[8] *BT*, on the other hand, saw revolutionary intoxication not as a temporary aberration but as an eternal impulse, the Dionysian. Its other advantage was a satisfactory resolution of the split between the people and the intelligentsia. The Russian intelligentsia had always been conscious of its special historical role as a counterforce to the ruling autocracy. It felt responsible for the fate of the nation, particularly of the common people. Yet the essential bridge to the people that would justify the intelligentsia's self-vision had never truly materialized; and it sometimes seemed it never would. The Hellenic myth of an organic, harmonious society offered a solution; in Nietzsche's version, it demanded the collaboration of Dionysus and Apollo, simple folk and intelligentsia, commune and individual. *BT* was even more attractive than Wagner had been. It allotted the intelligentsia an active role in culture, equal to that of the people. Wagner, after all, had said that the "*Volk* holds the Life-force, which arrogant intellect must return to," and that "intellect has only exploited the inventions of the *Volk*."[9]

Nietzsche afforded the intelligentsia a more desirable understanding of their role in the chaos of revolution. His opposition of Apollo and Dionysus was reread by the Russians as the opposition of the intelligentsia and the people; artists and intellectuals would take the people's chaotic revolutionary spirit and shape it into constructive expressions. Ivanov believed that an artist's need to be unique could be realized only by immersing himself in the people's culture, and that this unity would create a true national drama.[10] Lunacharsky too saw in popular drama a "moment of orgiastic exultation," the return to a primeval oneness.[11] Of the many intellectuals who understood their epoch through Nietzsche and Wagner, the most notable was the Symbolist Aleksandr Blok (1880–1921), whose essay, "The Intelligentsia and the Revolution" (January 1918) described the Revolution as a Dionysian movement of nature, the call of which must be heeded and answered by the intelligentsia.[12] Revolution was Nietzsche's "music," and art would be an instrument tuned by the new song. The intelligentsia, roused by the life-force of the people, would "wake from its deep sleep and be greeted with thoughts cleansed by the [Apollonian] dream."[13]

When the October Revolution arrived, many older-generation intellectuals, both socialist and Symbolist, saw a realization of their visions. One of the crowning glories of Russian revolutionary culture was its mass spectacles, theatrical displays that filled the city square with thousands of actors and viewers. The people relived great moments of struggle and victory as they watched, and if reports are to be believed, they swarmed onto the stage to join in the celebrations. Avid readers of *BT* saw mass spectacles as a socialist analogy to Nietzsche's Athenian tragedies. Mass dramas were spontaneous manifestations of popular joy; the entire nation, people and intelligentsia, merged in a single, like-minded impulse.

Lunacharsky, Kogan, Friche, and Ivanov all held positions in the administration of mass festivals, and Nietzsche's guidance was evident in their rhetoric. Ivanov, delivering the keynote address at the December 1919 Congress on Worker-Peasant Theater, spoke of socialist theater in language he had been using for a decade and a half: it would be classless, created by the intelligentsia and people alike. Oddly enough for a speech applauded by most Bolsheviks in the audience, Ivanov advocated a return to the religious sources of drama: choral chants and ecstatic rituals of unification.[14] Lunacharsky saw mass spectacles as an opportunity to awake Dionysian creativity in the people, as can be seen from a plan he submitted to the Moscow Soviet for the 1918 anniversary festival. He proposed "repeating the emotional experience of the October Revolution." The festival would be "split into three parts: struggle, victory, the intoxication of victory ... Initially the mood culminates, then attains its high point [!] and ends in general gaiety ... Festivals should not only be official, as May Day was, but should have deep internal sense. The masses should re-experience the revolutionary impulse."[15]

The clearest imprint of Nietzsche was to be found in the plan for a May Day celebration made by Kogan, who was director of the National Bureau for Mass Spectacles and Festivals:

For the festival, we must attract the participation of both proletarian collectives (Red Army units, worker unions, etc.) and individual artists, poets, musicians – but only those ideologically inclined toward workers – who can merge with them in a single creative impulse. These people of art are the leaders of the masses, they awaken the creative urge and find appropriate forms to express the masses' enthusiasm.

In turn, the proletarian collectives contribute internal content – i.e. revolutionary passion – to the festival: that intoxication, orgiasm, without which mass theatrical action (*deistvo*) cannot exist.[16]

To the older generation, mass spectacles encouraged a healthy collaboration of people and intelligentsia, which promised to engender a national dramatic theater rivaling the Greeks.

THE YOUNG RADICALS

Older Bolsheviks occupied the upper rungs of the Soviet cultural hierarchy after the Revolution, but there was a younger generation that had matured after the disappointing Revolution of 1905, impatient with their leadership. They disagreed with a policy of moderation: now, they thought, was the time to create a new culture, and they asserted their right to a monopoly. The most vociferous radicals were the day-to-day leaders of Proletkult such as Platon Kerzhentsev (1881–1940), Pavel Lebedev-Poliansky (1881–1948), and Valerian Pletnev (1886–1942) (not its older-generation founders Bogdanov and Lunacharsky), and the avant-garde Futurists, led by Vladimir Mayakovsky (1893–1930). Radicalism was in fact all that united them: Proletkultists and Futurists disagreed on the nature of socialist culture and the ways to get there;[17] yet they were together in rejecting moderation. Nowhere was their dissent stronger than in their treatment of the creative balance cherished by the older generation, and described in *BT*. Proletkultists thought the new culture should be exclusively proletarian; Futurists felt that only they, the artists, could create it.

Though Bogdanov valued the contributions of sympathetic

intellectuals,[18] younger Proletkult leaders thought that the old-line intelligentsia was forever alien to working-class culture. Whatever the motive, any effort at accommodation was doomed. As Kerzhentsev said, "in the theater, as in other fields, the psychology of the new class can be reflected only when the creator is a representative of that class. However talented and sensitive a bourgeois actor is, there will always be psychological boundaries separating him from the proletariat."[19] Kerzhentsev was one of the foremost advocates of mass spectacles in revolutionary Russia. His popular book on the topic, *Creative Theater*, went through five editions in the years 1918–23. Still, even in the shared ideal of mass drama, the differences of the two generations were glaring: for Kerzhentsev, it was not a vehicle for national reunification, as Ivanov believed, but self-activity (*samodeiatel'nost'*) and class struggle. He saw the proletariat flooding the streets spontaneously to celebrate its own history. There could be no thought of accepting intelligentsia guidance. "In these years of sharp social conflict and revolutionary struggle, it is silly to speak of some sort of classless 'actions' [*deistva*: Ivanov's favorite word] and particularly of triumphal celebrations which unite all levels of the population ... We must for the time being speak specifically of proletarian or peasant celebrations."[20]

Most of the younger Proletkultists betrayed a deep familiarity with Wagner and Nietzsche. In many cases, such as Kerzhentsev, it was a first-hand acquaintance; but even where the knowledge was second-hand, the German thinkers were fundamental to determining the agenda of cultural debate.[21] Such was the case with the dialectic of spontaneity and consciousness that was a well-spring of Soviet cultural formation.[22] It was yet another transcription of the Dionysian–Apollonian, people–intelligentsia opposition. The notion expressed itself politically in the debate over Party-control and worker-control; and culturally, in the tug-of-war between intelligentsia and proletariat. That the younger Proletkult leaders demonstrated an inclination for spontaneity should be no surprise. Kerzhentsev saw bursts of spontaneous creativity

in mass festivals, as in the Petrograd celebration of May Day
1920: "The most gripping moment was when . . . a tremendous
chorus of workers of all nationalities sang the *Internationale*. The
electrified mass of the people broke through the cordon . . .
dashed to [the stage] and joined the singing. A huge choir was
created, spectators mixed with the actors."[23]

Ivanov might have called it a merging (*sliianie*); Kerzhentsev called it self-activity. What Kerzhentsev, who actually
spent the day in Moscow, could not have known was that the
crowd did not merge with the actors, but stopped itself (spontaneously) before the stage, recognizing the limits of theatrical
convention. The production had not been created by the
masses, but by professionals of the theater and opera, for whom
the division of stage and audience was essential.

Obviously, there were some contradictions between theory
and practice. Members of both generations had nothing but
praise for the notion of mass drama: for some, it was a ritual
unification of the nation; for others, it expressed the class will of
the proletariat. Mass spectacles proved to be neither. The
Soviet state handed production over to professional directors
who exerted dictatorial control over the masses that performed
the plays. The line between leaders and followers was distinct.

The contradiction between theory and practice was most
glaring in two dramas written by radicals in the years 1918–19:
Mayakovsky's *Mystery-Bouffe*, a celebration of revolution
directed by Meyerhold; and Petr Kozlov's *Legend of the Communard*, the banner piece of the Petrograd Arena of Proletarian
Creativity. Both addressed the role of leaders and followers in
revolution; both glorified individual leaders and minimized the
role of followers. Here again Nietzsche's imprint could be
found; this time not that of *BT*, but of *Thus Spoke Zarathustra*.

Perhaps the only consistent thing in Mayakovsky was his
radicalism. He ardently heralded the subordination of artists to
the proletarian state in his "Second Decree on the Army of the
Arts;" but he could just as ardently deride his proletarian
critics. The influence of Nietzsche's *Zarathustra* on his work
before and after the Revolution has already been noted;[24] his
heroes stood proudly above the masses, ready – like Christ – to

suffer their misunderstanding. *Mystery-Bouffe* offered the proletariat a similar leader.[25] The play was a depiction of revolution on the model of the Biblical Deluge. The old world is destroyed by a flood; representatives of the bourgeoisie and proletariat are brought together on board an ark. At first the old classes are in power, but the workers soon effect a coup. Yet they are confused; what happens after the Revolution? An answer is provided only by the miraculous appearance of "A Simple Man" (played in the 1918 production by Mayakovsky), who leads them through Hell and Heaven to the Promised Land of socialism, where workers and their worktools dance in an ecstatic festival of unity.

Mayakovsky's influence was felt in *Legend of the Communard*, where a similar Nietzschean hero made an appearance.[26] The Arena was directed by Aleksandr Mgebrov (1884–1966) and Victoria Chekan (1893–1974), actors who had first gained fame at a time when Nietzsche was finding a Russian audience. The play was written by Petr Kozlov (1885–1935), a common soldier in the Red Army and *samouchka* (self-taught) playwright, who nevertheless had written a decadent-Symbolist play, *Above Life*, in prewar years.[27] The Nietzscheanism that influenced Mgebrov and Kozlov in their prewar youth saw the meaning of life in individual moments of creative ecstasy (Dionysianism without collectivity) and it elevated beauty, *esthetic* beauty, to the summit of values. It resembled, in fact, the Nietzscheanism of Fedor Sologub.[28] *Legend* was, like *Mystery-Bouffe*, a dramatic representation of revolution. In it, oppressed workers are saved from factory life by the appearance of the Communard, a pure and handsome young Superman clad in Greek garb. Led by the Communard, the workers embark into the desert in search of their Promised Land (the play is not localized, but the Biblical Exodus is an obvious model). They languish and suffer in heat and starvation, and eventually want to turn back. Only the overpowering will of the Communard keeps them going; at his urging they go forward and reach their destination, the land of socialist plentitude.

Critics had nothing but scorn for the play – one called it, after Sologub, a "created legend"[29] – but it was the most successful Proletkult play of the Civil War, which suggests that the popular audience found it a reflection of their revolution. What neither *Mystery-Bouffe* nor *Legend* offered was the balanced model of culture that *BT* had given the older generation, one in which leaders and followers contributed equally to the creation of a new society.

A NIETZSCHEAN SOLUTION

As the Civil War drew to a close in 1920, there was still much confusion in Soviet cultural administration. The means of artistic production had been nationalized, yet policy itself varied. Proletkult remained powerful; conservatives like Friche exerted a great deal of control; and even the Futurists were still influential. Mass dramas, which bore their finest fruit in the summer and fall of 1920, reflected much of the confusion. They were, judging by newspaper accounts, joyous manifestations of the popular will, spontaneous outpourings of the people's dramatic instinct. Yet these people's dramas were created by professional directors; the directors made sure to stifle spontaneity (imagine ten thousand people improvising at once!), and they used army conscripts, not volunteers, as actors.[30]

The position of Proletkult and Futurism was weakened in November 1920 when Lenin sponsored a "Letter on the Proletkults," which condemned the pretensions of all radicals to a monopoly on cultural creation. Their funding was cut significantly and direction of popular culture passed on to new organizations, foremost of which, Glavpolitprosvet (Central Political Education), was created in the reorganization of Narkompros (Commissariat of Education).[31] The centralization of culture put control firmly in the hands of the older generation: Lunacharsky, Krupskaia, and others, people who had often been horrified by the artistic radicalism of the younger generation. The new apparatus rewrote the equation of cultural development; once again, popular effort would be directed from above by the politically enlightened intelligentsia. Cultural funding was more evenly spread over a variety of programs: education, professional theater, propaganda, and working-class culture. Large-scale efforts like the mass spectacles, which had been sponsored in the Civil War years by the Army, municipal soviets, the International, and other well-funded organizations, lost their patrons. In the years of NEP, mass spectacles did not disappear; rather their function was redefined. They became strictly amateur, organized by workers' clubs from their own considerable resources without the assistance of professionals. The most active producers in Soviet Russsia were the workers' clubs of the Petrograd Politprosvet, whose artistic director was Adrian Piotrovsky (1898–1938). Piotrovsky had been a theater instructor for the Red Army and co-director of some of the greatest mass spectacles of the Civil War years. He shared the general enthusiasm for mass theater, but he had seen first-hand how little popular participation there was.

Piotrovsky was an anomaly possible only in the first years of the Revolution, a classical scholar deeply imbued with Hellenic values, and a fervent believer in the Bolshevik Revolution.[32] He had been imbued with the Nietzschean ideals of Ivanov's generation, yet he saw the many ways these ideals did not fit the new society. In effect, he was the final participant in the long debate that first brought *BT* to prerevolutionary Russia, interpreted it to answer the needs of that society, and then reworked it again for the Revolution. By the time the debate reached its final stages during NEP, the Nietzschean trace was slight; yet the original inspiration of *BT* should be clear. The seeds planted by Nietzsche once again offered a resolution to the question of leaders and followers.

Piotrovsky's Nietzscheanism was almost a birthright; he was the (illegitimate) son and student of Zielinski, the great classicist of Petersburg University and colleague of Ivanov, who was teacher of Acmeists, Futurists, the great scholar Mikhail Bakhtin, and a conduit of Nietzsche's ideas to much of the Symbolist generation. It was to Zielinski and Ivanov that Meyerhold (the great director and future leader of "October in the Theater") turned for instruction during his Symbolist period. Another student of Zielinski, Sergei Radlov (1892–1958), had been Piotrovsky's colleague in the direction of mass spectacles in 1920.

The mass dramas of Civil War Russia owed much to the Nietzscheanism of Zielinski and Ivanov; it was in fact believed that the dramas were a socialist equivalent of the rites of Dionysus.[33] Piotrovsky would himself admit the influence.[34] He attributed considerable importance to public festivals; in fact, he claimed Soviet Russia would be, like Athens, a "theatocracy."[35] Yet many ideas had to be reworked if they were to engender socialist theater. Often, Piotrovsky returned directly to Nietzsche, avoiding the agency of Ivanov and Lunacharsky's generation. Ivanov's ideal, like Wagner's, had been essentially non-urban, with its reliance on the "people" (*narod* or *Volk*); Nietzsche had spoken of the city, which was more appropriate for a proletarian culture. Furthermore, Nietzsche's description of the tension between the Apollonian and Dionysian could be readily conflated with the Marxist language of class struggle, while Ivanov rejected class struggle.

The problem of leaders and followers, unresolved by the older Nietzscheans and younger radicals, could be broken down into two questions of psychology: the psychology of creativity and of sponsorship. Bolshevism had always been stronger on history than psychology. It had a clear idea of Marxist historical principles; less clear was how the principles would be translated into a mass impulse. One answer had been Lenin's notion of *samodeiatel'nost'*, which assumed the people would spontaneously react to an objective historical reality, but also assumed the response would comply with the Party's conscious direction. Nietzsche, on the other hand, offered a powerful psychology of creative activity. In *BT*, he had described the creative act as a balance of Dionysian frenzy and disciplined artistic consciousness. It was both spontaneous and conscious. Socialists like Georges Sorel in France and the God-builders (Lunacharsky, Gorky, and their ally Bogdanov) in Russia combined Marxist history with Nietzschean psychology. They believed that in each historical period the strength of the dominant class could be traced to a guiding ideal or myth. The Greeks had been inspired by their religion; the working class was motivated by socialism.

Piotrovsky's reading of *BT* and the God-builders suggested that the kinship of ancient Hellenes and modern proletariat (the ascendant classes of their times) begged for the development of a Soviet equivalent to Hellenic drama. The Dionysian (religious) principle of Athens would be reborn in the collective (social) principle of socialism. Just as the Greek religion had its ecstatic rites which, according to *BT*, gave birth to the drama, Soviet socialism had its own ecstatic rites – the so-called *mitingi* (mass political rallies) – from which mass drama would evolve. Here was the logic of Piotrovsky's frequent (and unfounded) claim that "festivals were born in mass rallies;"[36] they were the Apollonian expression of a Dionysian impulse.

Crucial to Soviet cultural policy was the question of how artists would be inspired to convert popular impulses into art. There had to be a mechanism – historical, cultural, or psychological – by which the artist could remain an individual yet embody the will of the people. Proletkult and the Futurists had been unable to strike a balance; even Nietzsche had not discussed the mechanism in *BT*. At the advent of NEP, Piotrovsky revived a concept first developed by Ivanov that would become central to Soviet thinking in the late twenties (particularly among the avant-garde): the doctrine of "command" (*zakaz*).[37] Ivanov had filled the gap in Nietzsche's reasoning with the claim that any artist, if he is to be a true artist, will instinctively understand and respond to the needs of his time. "Command" represented an internal compulsion, and it could express itself in any number of ways: the specific request of a patron or a more general desire to serve the people.

Ivanov's "command" offered considerable possibilities to Soviet culture: it maintained the Nietzschean balance between artist and people. Yet post-October cultural politics saw a shortcoming in the insistence on artistic autonomy. Ivanov was adamant that artists often resist the prevailing political and social climate. Even a critic like Kogan, who, although a Bolshevik, was very much of Ivanov's generation, could not accept the subordination of art to the state; he called for a "command theater" (*teatr na zakaz*) that would "*create* the new forms of [socialist] life."[38] But Piotrovsky was not so hesitant. He updated the term to incorporate the voice of the working class: the abstract notion of "command" was modified to "social command," which in practice – on the assumption that the Party was the voice of society – became Party command. Citing Athens and Renaissance Italy (Nietzsche's ideal urban cultures), Piotrovsky agreed that the great artist must respond to the command of his society; yet, unlike his predecessors, he gave "command" a specific identity. The Revolution had created a new "client class," the proletariat; and Piotrovsky called for the appropriation (*ogosudarstvlenie*) of artistic command by the workers' state.[39]

This last addition to the debate begun twenty years before by *BT* suggested ways in which Soviet culture could, as Athenian culture once had, develop from the seeds of popular ferment. Piotrovsky claimed that in times of social upheaval "self-activity" takes over the development of national culture and renews it.[40] Piotrovsky used the term differently from both Lenin and Proletkult; to him it meant non-professional cultural activity. He interpreted the dialectic of amateur and professional on the model of Nietzsche's Apollo and Dionysus,[41] and saw amateur (self-active or *samodeiatel'nyi*) theater as the embryo of Soviet drama. With the advent of NEP, he organized the Petrograd Politprosvet network of workers' clubs into a city-wide system called the United Artistic Circles ('Edinyi khudozhestvennyi kruzhok': acronym EXK). To Piotrovsky it was theater "born of the crowd," as the Greek tragedy had been born of popular religion.[42] It was not an imitation of the professional; it had its own esthetics, and its own expressive system.[43]

THE DEBATE BEARS FRUIT

A theory does not guarantee successful practice; Piotrovsky had to translate the Nietzschean dialectic into the reality of theatrical administration. Somehow, the creative impulse of the masses had to be released, and it had to be given expression under the tutelage of educated leaders.

EXK regained the Nietzschean balance lost in the radical controversy. Its administrative structure was such that the

masses' unorganized impulse was guided by club instructors –
the conscious vanguard. Upon joining the club, members were
asked to choose one of several circles: dramatic, artistic,
musical, or political. Initial instruction was carried out exclusively in this circle, and dealt only with the given craft. Once
initial instruction was completed, projects were begun; it was
through work on a project – usually a celebration of one of the
new Soviet holidays (Paris Commune Day, International
Youth Day, etc.) – that Piotrovsky's cultural myth was
enacted. Synthesis came when the various circles were united
in the festival production. Thus, festival dramas served a cultural function similar to that of the Greek tragic drama: unifying, shaping, and expressing a popular impulse. The basis of
EXK theater was described, as in Ivanov's Hellenic model, as
choral art; it would be a "synthesis of choral music, the [poetic]
word and creative play."[44] The chorus, in an important ideological equation, was identified with the "people;" this was
another favorite notion of Ivanov, but one that Nietzsche had
sniffed at as "an arty cliché." (*BT*, p. 56).

Amateur political theater in Soviet Russia was, of course,
not a simple application of Nietzschean principles. EXK envisioned the collaboration of people and intelligentsia along
the lines of *BT*; but divergence was most marked when the
notion of "command" was introduced. Piotrovsky had first
introduced it to Soviet thinking to establish direction in the
free creative process described by Nietzsche; it created a hierarchy of values in an egalitarian system, and allowed the best of
Proletkult and Futurism to be combined. Command came into
the EXK process at the production stage. A synthetic choral
art was created by merging all club circles into one, yet there
was a hierarchy within the synthesis. The process was begun by
a patron-commander (*zakazchik*): the political circle – defined
as the primary circle in the club – met to choose a theme for the
holiday, e.g. "From Paris to the Petrograd Commune."[45] The
political circle was the embodiment of the "social command;"
with the theme chosen, it would order a scenario from the
dramatic circle.[46]

After the scenario had been developed, each circle elected a representative; the representatives distributed the tasks demanded by the scenario among themselves: painting posters, performing background music, and so on. These tasks were then assigned to individual members of each circle.[47] Club work originated with basic instruction; it developed into a synthetic dramatic performance (poetry, music, dance, gymnastics, and sport) under the guidance of club directors (the intelligentsia); and the evolution was controlled by the "command" of its political circle. There was a structure to maintain the balance of spontaneity and consciousness, club members and director, people and intelligentsia.

As a footnote to demonstrate how deeply the Greek model inspired EXK, we might note that Piotrovsky instituted a series of contests in Petrograd like the Athenian drama contests that first uncovered the talent of Aeschylus. In Petrograd, each club competed for a position in one of several festival presentations. The victors advanced to the national drama contest conducted during the newly instituted Spartakiad. Greek tragic contests were part of the Olympic Games, dedicated to the gods of Olympus; the games of Soviet socialism honored a slave, Spartacus.[48] There were, as in Olympus, athletic contests; political rallies replaced the religious rites of the Greeks; and mass spectacles were the Soviet equivalent of the Hellenic tragic drama.

EXK shared many of Proletkult's most radical dogmas: it insisted that its members maintain factory jobs, and that the circles perform their own plays without the help of professional playwrights and directors. Yet it also avoided pitfalls that had crippled Proletkult. Proletkult claimed it would create an entirely new culture, and that the artists of the future would emerge from its amateur charges. When its actors gained experience, they wished to become professionals; yet Proletkult doctrine excluded professionals from the creation of the proletarian theater.[49] Its cultural policies did not allow for creative evolution. Proletkult members were often resentful of the restriction; and when they sought the opportunity to develop into skilled artists, they had to leave the organization (as the film directors Sergei Eisenstein, Gregory Aleksandrov, and others did). According to EXK doctrine, Soviet dramatic culture would grow from the efforts of amateurs, whose skills were to be perfected and passed on to the professional theater.[50] Piotrovsky's program, inspired by the Nietzschean dialectic, provided for the evolution of amateurs into full-fledged artists.

The fertility of the debate that began with Nietzsche, passed through the generation of Ivanov and Lunacharsky, and ended in NEP with the creation of EXK is evident in its contributions to theatrical culture of the late 1920s. There was a strong and mutual influence between professional and non-professional theaters during NEP; and sometimes it was unclear who influenced whom. Both EXK and Meyerhold were developing a theater accessible to popular audiences that addressed contemporary issues; and both cultivated devices such as the "social mask" (one-dimensional social characters), choral reading, gymnastics on stage.[51] EXK's most important contribution to the professional theater was an acting-style called "role alienation" (*otnoshenie k obrazu*), another development of the creative psychology described in *BT*. Nietzsche's tragic poet had a double identity; he was immersed in Dionysian frenzy while maintaining an Apollonian distance from the images he created. Double identity was a foundation of EXK acting. Stanislavsky's methods were still very influential in the 1920s; they demanded a complete identification of the actor and role he played. Yet, as Piotrovsky asked, what was a proletarian actor to do when given the role of a bourgeois character? Identifying with the character would be socially and politically harmful (if not impossible). "Role alienation" allowed the worker-actor to play "outside" a character, periodically emerging from the role to comment on the situation as a worker. Piotrovsky's theory was known to Meyerhold and the leftist playwright Sergei Tretiakov, and it was probably through the latter that Bertolt Brecht became aware of it. He adopted it as the principle of "alienation," which lay at the foundation of his esthetics.

EXK also allowed its members to make their own contributions to the professional theater. Freed from the limitations of Proletkult, EXK actors graduated to the professional ranks in both the central cities and the provinces. In an encouraging development foreseen and guided by Piotrovsky, select EXK circles grew into professional theaters; and the Gleron Circle of Petrograd, of which Piotrovsky was patron,[52] became the nucleus of the famous TRAM (Theater of Worker Youth) movement that spread around the entire country.[53] The Leningrad TRAM, directed by Mikhail Sokolovsky and sponsored by Piotrovsky, was a theater staffed by actors who still worked in factories. TRAM's plays, all written by club members, concerned only worker life and its social issues. No professional actors and directors were allowed; the worker-actors would play only themselves before an audience of workers like themselves. TRAM was tremendously popular in the late 1920s; many thought that it would make a contribution to the Soviet theater equal to that of the Civil War mass spectacles.[54] While this might have been overambitious, TRAM was one of the most innovative theaters of the late 1920s; it revived the dormant tradition of popular political theater, reclaimed the role of the people in the creation of socialist culture, and brought new blood into the professional ranks. The Nietzschean cultural paradigm had come a long way since its initial appearance in Russia; many changes were introduced as *BT* was reread by each generation. Yet the core of its Russian reading, the balance of spontaneous inspiration and consciously-guided expression, remained vital until the end of NEP.

NOTES

1 Viktor Shklovskii, "Drama and Mass Spectacles" ("Drama i massovye predstavleniia") *Khod konia* (Berlin, 1923), p. 61.

2 Nadezhda Krupskaia, "Glavpolitprosvet and Art" ("Glavpolitprosvet i iskusstvo"), *Pravda*, February 13, 1921, p. 1.

3 See Ivanov's "The Spear of Athens" ("Kop'e Afeny"), "Presentiments and Portents" ("Predchuvstviia i predvestiia"), and "The Theater of the Future" ("Teatr budushchego"), *Po zvezdam* (St. Petersburg, 1909). In his later anthology see "On the Essence of Tragedy" ("O sushchestve tragedii") and "The Esthetic Norm of Theater" ("Esteticheskaia norma teatra"), *Borozdy i mezhi* (Moscow, 1916). See also *Teatr. Kniga o novom teatre* (St. Petersburg, 1908).

4 Anatolii Lunacharskii, "Socialism and Art" ("Sotsializm i iskusstvo"), *Teatr: kniga o novom teatre* (St. Petersburg, 1908), pp. 7–40.

5 Vladimir Friche, "Theater Now and in the Future" ("Teatr v sovremennom i budushchem obshchestve"), *Krizis teatra* (Moscow, 1908), pp. 157–85.

6 Aleksandr Bogdanov, *Red Star* (Bloomington, 1984), p. 87.

7 See in particular Anatolii Lunacharskii, *Religiia i sotsializm*, 2 vols. (St. Petersburg, 1908–11).

8 "The Art-Work of the Future," in Richard Wagner, *Works* (London, 1909), I, p. 59.

9 Wagner, *Works*, I, pp. 74, 80. For Wagner's great influence on revolutionaries, see Bernice Glatzer Rosenthal, "Wagner and Wagnerian Ideas in Russia," *Wagnerism in European Culture and Politics*, ed. David Large and William Weber (Ithaca, 1984), pp. 227–36.

10 Ivanov, "The Poet and the Crowd" ("Poet i chern'"), *Po zvezdam*, p. 41.

11 Lunacharskii, "Socialism and Art," p. 28.

12 Aleksandr Blok, "Intelligentsia i revoliutsiia," *Sobranie sochinenii* (Moscow, 1961), VI, pp. 11–20.

13 Blok, *SS*, VI, p. 14. On Blok's relation to Nietzsche, see E. L. Bel'kind, "Blok and Viacheslav Ivanov," *Blokovskii sbornik* (Tartu, 1972), II, pp. 367–70; and Evelyn Bristol, "Blok between Nietzsche and Soloviev," *Nietzsche in Russia*, ed. Bernice G. Rosenthal (Princeton, NJ, 1986), particularly pp. 158–59.

14 Nikolai L[vov], "Congress on Worker-Peasant Theater," ("S"ezd po raboche-krest'ianskomu teatru"), *Vestnik teatra*, 44 (1919), p. 3.

15 "The Festival of the Revolution" ("K prazdniku revoliutsii"), *Vechernie izvestiia Moskovskogo soveta*, September 26, 1918, p. 3.

16 "Plan for the first popular drama-festival" ("Plan pervogo narodnogo deistva-prazdnestva"), *Vestnik teatra* 46 (1919), p. 5.

17 Bengt Jangfeldt, *Majakovskii and Futurism, 1917–1921* (Stockholm, 1977), pp. 72ff.

18 See Aleksandr Bogdanov, "What is Proletarian Poetry" ("Chto takoe proletarskaia poeziia") and "On the Artistic Heritage" ("O khudozhestvennom nasledstve"), *Iskusstvo i rabochii klass* (Moscow, 1918).

19 *Bolshevik Visions: First Phase of the Cultural Revolution in Soviet Russia*, ed. William G. Rosenberg (Ann Arbor, 1984), p. 428.

20 Pavel Kerzhentsev, *Tvorcheskii teatr* (Moscow, 1920), p. 162.

21 For Kerzhentsev's intellectual relationship to Wagner and

Nietzsche, see my *Bolshevik Festivals, 1917–1920* (Berkeley CA, 1993), pp. 28–30. Zenovia A. Sochor, "A. A. Bogdanov: In Search of Cultural Liberation," *Nietzsche in Russia*, ed. Rosenthal, pp. 293–314, deals with the question of Nietzsche and his influence on Bogdanov and Proletkult.

22 Katerina Clark, *The Soviet Novel: History as Ritual* (Chicago, IL, 1985), pp. 15–24, and passim.

23 Pavel Kerzhentsev, "Mass Theater" ("Massovyi teatr"), *Vestnik teatra* 65 (1920), p. 4.

24 See Bengt Jangfeldt's chapter in this volume, as well as Bernice Glatzer Rosenthal, "A New Word for a New Myth: Nietzsche and Russian Futurism," *The European Foundations of Russian Modernism*, ed. Peter Barta (Lewiston, NY, 1991), pp. 219–50.

25 Vladimir Maiakovskii, *Misteriia-Buff* (Petrograd, 1918).

26 Petr Kozlov, *Legenda o kommunare* (Arkhangelsk, 1923); for an account of the production, see Aleksandr Mgebrov, *Zhizn' v teatre* (Leningrad, 1932), II, pp. 48–94, and David Zolotnitskii, *Zori teatral'nogo oktiabria* (Leningrad, 1976), pp. 314–23.

27 Nikolai Petrov, *50 i 500* (Moscow, 1960), p. 15.

28 See particularly his "Theater of Single Will," *Russian Dramatic Theory from Pushkin to the Symbolists*, ed. Laurence Senelick (Austin, 1981).

29 Mikhail Zagorskii, "Legenda o kommunare," *Vestnik teatra* 56 (1920), p. 9.

30 Sergei Radlov, *Stat'i o teatre* (Petrograd, 1922), p. 39.

31 See Sheila Fitzpatrick, *The Commissariat of Enlightenment* (Cambridge, 1970), chapters 7–9.

32 For a brief biography, see the introduction to Adrian Piotrovskii, *Teatr. Kino. Zhizn'*, ed. Anatolii Trabskii (Leningrad, 1969).

33 See, e.g., Evgenii Riumin, *Massovye prazdnestva* (Moscow, 1927), p. 5.

34 *Istoriia sovetskogo teatra*, ed. Aleksei Gvozdev (Leningrad, 1933), p. xxvi.

35 Adrian Piotrovskii, "Theater of the Entire People" ("Teatr vsego naroda. Teatral'nyi kruzhok"), *Zhizn' iskusstva*, May 20–21, 1920, p. 1.

36 See, for example, *Massovye prazdnestva* (Leningrad, 1926), p. 55; also Vsevolod Vsevolodskii-Gerngross, *Istoriia russkogo teatra* (Leningrad, 1929), II, p. 389. Radlov emphatically denied the claim: Radlov, *Stat'i o teatre*, p. 39.

37 See Ivanov's "On Merry Craftsmanship and Intelligent Merriment" ("O veselom remesle i umnom veselii"), *Po zvezdam*.

38 Pavel Kogan, "Teatr na zakaz," *Vestnik teatra* 66 (1920), pp. 4–5.

39 Adrian Piotrovskii, "The Artist and the Client" ("Khudozhnik i zakazchik"), *Za sovetskii teatr* (Leningrad, 1925), 22–24.
40 Adrian Piotrovskii, "Anniversaries" ("Godovshchiny"), *Petrogradskaia pravda*, November 9, 1923, p. 5. For the same hypothesis in reference to the Greeks, see his contribution to *Istoriia evropeiskogo teatra* (Leningrad, 1931).
41 *Istoriia sovetskogo teatra*, p. xxv.
42 *Massovye prazdnestva*, p. 73.
43 See Adrian Piotrovskii, "Toward a Theory of Amateur Theater" ("K teorii samodeiatel'nogo teatra"), *Problemy sotsiologii teatra* (Leningrad, 1926), pp. 121–24.
44 Adrian Piotrovskii, "Edinye khudozhestvennye kruzhki," *Za sovetskii teatr*, pp. 7–8.
45 Piotrovskii, "Edinye," p. 7.
46 Grigorii Avlov, *Klubnyi samodeiatel'nyi teatr: evoliutsiia metodov i form* (Leningrad, 1930), p. 146.
47 See the articles in *Edinyi khudozhestvennyi kruzhok* (Leningrad, 1925).
48 Adrian Piotrovskii, "The Games of May" ("Maiskie igry"), *Zhizn' iskusstva*, July 15 1924, p. 5.
49 See V. Kerzhentsev, "O professionalizme," *Gorn* 4 (1919). The dilemma would last into NEP: S. Lukovskii, "Theater Studios, Circles, and Action-Cells" ("Teatral'naia studiia, kruzhok ili deistvennaia iacheika," *Rabochii klub* 1 (1924), p. 12.
50 Stefan Mokul'skii, "On Amateur Theater" ("O samodeiatel'nom teatre"), *Zhizn' iskusstva*, July 15, 1924, pp. 6–7.
51 *Problemy sotsiologii iskusstva*, pp. 126–27.
52 Pavel Marinchik, *Rozhdenie komsomol'skogo teatra* (Moscow, 1963), pp. 80–82, etc.
53 See V. M. Mironova, *TRAM: Agitatsionnyi-molodezhnyi teatr 1920–30-kh gg.* (Leningrad, 1977), or Konstantin Rudnitsky, *Russian and Soviet Theater, 1905–1932* (New York, 1988), pp. 203–5.
54 Rudnitsky, *Russian and Soviet Theater*, p. 204.

CHAPTER 6

Revolution as an esthetic phenomenon: Nietzschean motifs in the reception of Isaac Babel (1923–32)

Gregory Freidin

My natural readers and listeners
are even now Russians,
Scandinavians and Frenchmen –
will it always be that way?

F. Nietzsche, *Ecce Homo* (p. 321)

Nietzsche, the Russian Nietzsche imprinted in the consciousness of Russian intelligentsia, holds the key to Babel's success in
the 1920s. A few juxtapositions will suffice to amplify the
presence of Nietzschean overtones in the reception of Babel's
fiction:[1]

Dare to devote some thought to the problem of restoring the health of
a people which has been impaired by history, to how it may recover
its instincts and therewith its integrity. (*H*, p. 25)

Babel:

Before saying goodbye, the Chief of Staff wrote a resolution over his
grievance: "Restore the above-described stud to its primordial
status." ("The Story of a Horse"[2])

Nietzsche:

You say it is the good cause that hallows even war? I tell you: it is the
good war that hallows any cause.
   War and courage have done more great things than charity. Not
your pity but your courage has saved the unfortunate up to now.
(*Z*, p. 74)

Babel:

Afonka stuck the papers into his boot and fired a shot into Dolgushev's mouth. "Afonya," I said with a pathetic smile, and rode up
to the Cossack, "I just couldn't do it." "Get away," he said, turning

pale, "I'm gonna kill you! You jerks with specs, you take pity on us folks like a cat pities its mouse ..." ("The Death of Dolgushev," p. 67)

Nietzsche:

Only where the state ceases, does the man who is not superfluous begin: does the song of necessary man, the unique and irreplaceable melody begin.
  There the state ceases – look there my brothers. Do you not see it: the rainbow and the bridges to the overman? (Z, pp. 77–78)

Babel:

"Where does police begin," he screamed, "and Benya end?" "Police ends where Benya begins," replied reasonable people. ("How It Was Done In Odessa," p. 169)

Alexander Blok:

Man is a beast; man is a plant, a flower; he shows the qualities of extreme cruelty, seemingly inhuman, animal cruelty, and the qualities of primordial tenderness – equally inhuman, almost vegetative ... ("The Collapse of Humanism"[3])

Babel:

You are tiger, lion, cat. You can spend the night with a Russian woman and the Russian woman will be satisfied. ("How It Was Done in Odessa," p. 165)

THE IRONY AND THE PATHOS OF THE REVOLUTION

It is a truth universally acknowledged that postrevolutionary Russian prose, with its palpable verbal texture and penchant for paradox – two key features of Babel's art – was a direct heir to the literary patrimony of the preceding decade. Continuity extended to other areas as well, not least because most of the stars who graced the post-1917 horizon had either been launched on their course before the Revolution (Babel, for one), or had been shaped by and matured in the twilight years of the Russian Empire (Zoshchenko, Olesha, Lunts). But even though they were rooted in the literary institutions of the old regime and largely unfettered by the new ones,[4] these authors could not write, could not afford to write, in Zoshchenko's understated phrase, "as though nothing had happened."[5] The work-horse solution for this dilemma, common in a period of rapid change, was the deployment of the ironic mode.[6] By and large, the ironic effect was produced by the use of local dialects and a densely metaphoric style (the "ornamental prose") or by using the technique of *skaz*.[7] Both approaches were a foil for the stylistically "unmarked" prose and the "standard" literary Russian associated inevitably with the centralized order of the departed state.

Likewise, in searching for forms of emplotment, writers could no longer draw sustenance from the certainties of affirming or denying the truths of religion, science, progressive secular ideologies of the Enlightenment, not to mention everybody's tried-and-true favorite, the oppression of the old regime. Instead, they tended to structure their narratives along the lines of irreconcilable conflict and paradox, pitched a few ironic registers below Dostoevsky's high tragedy or the Symbolists' fascination with an apocalyptic mêlée (Blok's *The Twelve*, Pilniak's *The Naked Year* or Vsevolod Ivanov's *Dityo* can serve as prime examples). This ironic trend in the culture, which had bade farewell to the world of the old regime, provided a nurturing environment for Nietzschean paradigms, which had been deeply, at times seamlessly, assimilated (as well as contaminated) by the Russian intelligentsia.[8] The resurgence of "the new barbarism," provoked by the Great War[9] and culminating in the Civil War, made Nietzschean formulae particularly useful for making sense out of what was perceived as both an epochal cataclysm and an epochal opportunity for fundamental renewal. In the shadow cast by the iconic hammer-wielding proletarian of the socialist revolution a trained eye could discern the outlines of the *philosopher with a hammer*. For the contemporary Russian intellectuals, even those sitting in "opposite corners" (e.g., Ivanov and Gershenzon,[10] Schloezer and Voronsky, Lunacharsky[11] and Blok) this blurring of the outlines was not a matter of confusion. On the contrary, for a member of the Russian intelligentsia, nurtured on the ideology of populism, it made perfect sense.

Little effort, then, was required of Babel's contemporaries to recognize in his stories that took Russia by storm in 1924–25 an articulation of this radically antinomian, Nietzschean vision of the Russian Revolution – a culmination of the world-historical drama, its irony based on "pushing down that which was falling,'" its pathos inspired by the mind-boggling magnitude of the destruction and the desperate anticipation of the dawning of a new age. That antinomy *was* the Revolution, and to a Nietzscheanized mind, it could be "justified," made supremely acceptable, to use the formulation in *The Birth of Tragedy*, "as an esthetic phenomenon." A close look at contemporary reviews of Babel shows that for many critics, his stories did just that.

One of the first Soviet admirers of Babel's new fiction, Iakov Benni, saw this clearly and boldly declared that Babel managed to resolve the gaping antinomies of the revolution, indeed, to justify them through art, nothing but art:

The abiding contradiction, especially powerful at the time of revolution, the contradiction between art and life is resolved by Babel simply through the sense of the inevitability and the ultimate completeness [*tselesoobraznost'*] of art [. . .] The tormenting contradictions, greeting Babel the dreamer at the threshold of life, cannot repel him even when life appears before him as the passionate, cruel, crude, seething struggle. Babel looks back, sees something and forgets himself . . . At that point Babel the artist remains alone, standing face to face with the radiant, seething, reality, magnificent in its self-generated, legitimary, [*samozakonnost'*] . . . reality, not a tiny shade of which, be it sound, color, pain, joy, tragedy as much as laughter, can escape the artist, who has become all eyes. [. . .] His stories overwhelm one with their authenticity: a strange echo of the familiar laughter of a "tiny little Gogol" combined with the great intensity of the justification of sacrifice . . .[12]

Of all the Soviet critics, Benni was one of the least equivocal in praising Babel for establishing the Revolution's Nietzschean credentials as an esthetic phenomenon ("the self-generated legitimacy of reality," "completeness of art," etc.). Others, who came after him, were more or less oblique or, as happened often enough, were not even aware of their Nietzschean vocabulary. The question that I will address is how contemporary criticism managed to assimilate Babel's fiction – an acknowledged postrevolutionary masterpiece yet patently Nietzschean in its language, sentiment, and emplotment – to the ostensibly Marxist Bolshevik scheme for Soviet art. The story of this assimilation is, in a sense, a case study in the formation of the intelligentsia consciousness, its growing acceptance, however grudging, of the Bolshevik regime during the period of the "breather" (*peredyshka*), as Lenin so aptly christened the NEP.

THE BABEL EXPLOSION

Proportion, symmetry, sense of scale and measure – they are easily discarded under the spell of Babel's art. So it was with the critical response to the paradoxically hyperbolic and spare stories, which would later form the *Red Cavalry* and *Odessa* cycles following their first appearance in 1923. In Shklovsky's unfailingly astute phrase, 1923–24 were the years of the first blush of the reader's "romance" with Babel.[13] And a romance it was; for what, short of an infatuation, can explain why G. Lelevich, one of the most blustering and unromantic critics of the *On Guard* (which is blustering and unromantic indeed), would so sweetly serenade Babel after debunking unceremoniously such giants of postrevolutionary Russian prose as Ilia Ehrenburg, Vsevolod Ivanov, Nikolai Nikitin, and Boris Pilniak.[14] "Of all the fellow-traveler fiction," Lelevich wrote in his "1923: A Literary Summing-Up,"

the fragments by Babel, which have appeared in the periodical literature during the past year, represent the most interesting phenomenon, one most deserving of our attention. [...] No one has yet conveyed in fiction that image of Budennyi's troopers, with their heroism, their instinctive revolutionary consciousness, with their devil-may-care, guerrilla, Cossack spirit. There is not an iota of idealization. On the contrary – an ever-so-slight smile is present everywhere, but at the same time the reader receives the impression of *enormous revolutionary power*.[15]

Coming from the pen of Lelevich, these were the words of love indeed (Babel was the only writer in Lelevich's survey to merit a whole separate section). What is more, Lelevich's panegyric was one of the earliest critical appraisals in which Babel was praised for presenting the Revolution as an eruption of the primordial will to power, a motif that would receive its supporters and detractors later on.

Not to be outdone in patronizing a promising new talent, Aleksandr Voronsky, Lelevich's nemesis among the Bolshevik literati, argued, eschewing, as he put it, "all exaggeration," that Babel was "a new milestone on the circuitous and complicated road along which contemporary literature was moving toward Communism."[16] The magnitude of Babel's achievement was recognized by the émigré press as well,[17] most notably by Prince Sviatopolk-Mirsky. Mirsky, who was situated at the opposite end of the cultural-political spectrum from his two Bolshevik colleagues and treated Babel as a consummate artist indifferent to ideology, unwittingly echoed Lelevich in a review of the first edition of *Red Cavalry*:

Among all the "Soviet writers" who have become famous since 1922, Babel, it seems, is the most famous, perhaps – without any exaggeration – the only truly popular author; for one, he is just about the only writer read outside Russia "for pleasure," not merely to keep abreast of what is happening "on the other shore." And this perception, one must admit, is fully justified: indeed, Babel is the only fully mature craftsman among the "fellow-travelers," the only one writing "for the reader" as well as "for himself." Other craftsmen, such as Pasternak, think the least about the reader, concentrating on their new artistic goals, whereas popular writers, like Seifullina, think least of all about their duty as artists and write in order to satisfy the communist demand.[18]

And so it went. By 1926, when *Red Cavalry* appeared in its first edition, the volume of ink and newsprint devoted to the critical appraisal of this short fiction, as one contemporary acknowledged in amazement, had easily exceeded the volume of Babel's own published work.[19] For a while, it seemed as though Babel's star would never stop rising. In 1927, Viacheslav Polonsky, perhaps the most authoritative and least dogmatic Marxist critical voice of the late 1920s, pronounced with a somber finality: 'In Soviet literature, Babel has rightly come to

occupy an exalted position. The very existence of *Red Cavalry* is
a factor that defines the development of literary art."[20]

BOLSHEVIZED NIETZSCHE: A CULTURAL MOTIF

All the vicissitudes of Babel's literary career notwithstanding,
Red Cavalry and *Odessa Tales* have remained to this day the
jewels in the crown of postrevolutionary Russian literature. In
this regard, the praise lavished on them at the time of publication has limited heuristic value for one studying Nietzschean
elements in Soviet culture. It is another matter when this
remarkably expeditious response is located in the context of the
cultural debates of the 1920s. Highly politicized, these debates
involved not only a sorting out of a variety of blueprints for
building a new culture but, more importantly for the purposes
of the present discussion, revolved around determining the
status of the Revolution in the eyes of the intelligentsia. Those
who had accepted the Revolution as a preordained (the Hege-
lian *gesetzmässig*) or, at least, complete and mature (*gesetzt*)
event, i.e., the Bolsheviks and people close to them, were trying
to convert to their faith those, the majority, who were possessed
by varying degrees of doubt. As in the case of major philosophical systems which, since Kant, could not be considered complete unless they accounted for the beautiful, the Bolshevik
vision of Russia's "socialist revolution" required some form of
legitimation in the esthetic sphere as well. The Revolution
could not quite be considered *real*, so went the argument, if it
failed to give birth to "new art" – a "red Lev Tolstoi," as
contemporary wits would put it.

Whether they belonged to those who, in matters of esthetics,
put their trust in History and were more or less satisfied with
"organic" cultivation of Soviet art (among them, Trotsky,
Voronsky, Lunacharsky, Polonsky, the champions of the
"fellow-travelers"), or whether, like the members of LEF or
the *On-Guardists*, they wished to employ more intrusive tech-
niques, the agronomists of the Soviet culture garden became
captives of their own cerebral expectations and schemes.
Theirs was a barely concealed anxiety that the revolution, or

more precisely, the authenticity of the Bolshevik version of it, could be called into question if Soviet writers failed to produce new works rivaling in quality and profundity the best of the Imperial achievement (cinema, a new art form, could escape the severity of this test).

To put it differently and compactly, the Bolshevik position regarding art, especially literature, an authoritative and consecrated art form in Russia, combined two contradictory messages. On the one hand, art was able to express the very essence of social forces, "serving the purpose of analyzing," as Lunacharsky put it, "the reality of our milieu." "For us, Marxists," continued the People's Commissar of Enlightenment, known to harbor a weakness for the *philosopher with a hammer*, "the freedom of a [major] artist implies his highest engagement with the social forces. After all, we do not believe in an abstract free will. When man expresses himself freely, he gives the optimal expression to those social forces which exert their influence on him."[21] On the other hand, "art *was* a social force" in its own right, because "sometimes consciously, sometimes unconsciously, a writer becomes a preacher [...] he selects his facts in such a way that they would move the reader toward a particular conclusion."[22]

The latter point is a clear evocation of Bogdanov's theories which assigned art pretty much the same function as the "sacred" possesses in Durkheim – a force constitutive of a society.[23] The Russian intelligentsia's traditional privileging of *belles-lettres* no doubt played a crucial role in this theoretical elevation of literature to the lofty status of a civil religion.[24]

The task that the Bolshevik culture-mongers thus set themselves was not merely to win writers over to their ideological position in order that they might preach, or prophesy, the Bolshevik gospel, but also so that they might do so "freely" – under the compulsion of the invisible hand of the hegemonic working class. The former task represented an attempt at a political and ideological conquest of the intelligentsia. The latter involved the Bolsheviks' monistic compulsion to subject the historical authenticity of the *socialist* revolution to an ordeal by art. Indeed, it would have been far more convenient for the

Bolsheviks to accept the Formalists' view of art as an "autonomous series." Yet they would not let go, insisting, as Lunacharsky put it, that "all art was ideological as long as it is prompted by a powerful feeling, which, as it were, compels the artist to invade, to seize souls, to expand the power of his *dominant* [*dominanta*] over them."[25] This task, if we are to use a Nietzschean scheme, amounted to an esthetic justification of the Bolshevik Revolution – a justification deemed all the more precious if its source could be identified as coming from someone other than a brother-in-Marx. Babel – the author and his fiction – fit the bill, if ever so ambiguously and imperfectly.

THE PARADOX OF BABEL CRITICISM

As late as 1932, Sviatopolk-Mirsky, the same critic who five years earlier had singled out Babel as an unrivaled star of Russian letters writing under, not to say despite, the Bolsheviks,[26] was now declaring from the high rostrum of *Literaturnaia gazeta* that Babel's achievement was proof positive of the historical legitimacy of the Bolshevik Revolution and one of the factors persuading him to return from his self-imposed exile in the West.[27] For those who followed Babel's reception in the 1920s, Mirsky's earlier insistence on Babel's supreme estheticism – "his stories create a purely literary, esthetic impression; ideology for him is a constructive device" – was not necessarily incompatible with his later view that Babel's fiction legitimated Soviet achievement.

Apart from providing a basis for an esthetic legitimation, Babel's writings functioned as an artistically perfect paradox, a device capable of generating an endless critical discourse on the contradictions of the Revolution – a whetstone on which various critics sharpened their theoretical and ideological knives. Indeed, critics experienced a virtual compulsion to explain, classify, dissect, and reassemble his stories, ostensibly to guide the "infatuated" reader and, implicitly, to assimilate the paradox of the Revolution which seemed to have erupted with a mesmerizing force and undeniable authenticity in Babel's short fiction.

Much of what was written about Babel in Soviet Russia in the 1920s was informed, if not shaped, by key ideas associated with Nietzsche's teaching: that human existence may be justified only as an esthetic phenomenon (*The Birth of Tragedy*), a motif popularized by the Russian Symbolists; that the Christian ethic, with its ascetic ideal and *ressentiment*, represents an insidious ploy of the weak and unhealthy to suppress "life" and thus dominate the healthy and the strong (*The Genealogy of Morals*, assimilated through the turn-of-the-century debates); and that "life and action" must be served by history "to the advantage of a coming age," and not the other way around ("love of the distant one" in *Zarathustra*, elaborated in *On the Advantage and Disadvantage of History For Life*, and echoed by, among others, M. O. Gershenzon in his repartees to Viach. Ivanov).[28] In 1926, the year *Red Cavalry* was published, Lunacharsky had no compunction in acknowledging Nietzsche's appeal, specifically, his "militancy, his spirit of exaltation," and his own solidarity with Nietzsche's "contempt for petty-bourgeois morality and Christian romanticism"[29] – terms easily identified with the Populist humanism of Russia's cultural elite.

Babel's representation of the Revolution, deriving its authority from the intelligentsia's privileging of verbal art, retained the revolutionary paradox of cruelty for the sake of happiness on the intellectual level, but Babel the artist was able to reconcile this contradiction mimetically at the plane of art, appealing to the heavily "Nietzscheanized" esthetic sensibility of the intelligentsia. In Babel's fiction, to paraphrase the famous formula of Lévi-Strauss, the intelligentsia's "inability to connect two kinds of relationships" – that is the human abyss of the present and the all-too-distant radiant peaks, was "overcome (or rather replaced) by the assertion that contradictory relationships are identical inasmuch as they are both self-contradictory in a similar way."[30] Applied to the reception of Isaac Babel, this formula might run as follows: the cruelty of the Revolution and Civil War was to the beauty, or sublimity, of art what backward ravaged Russia was to the super-modernity of socialism. To puzzle out this mythic grasp of experience, which *Red Cavalry* exemplified, was the thankless task of the contemporary critic.

FERSTEN-LIEBE AND THE POETRY OF BANDITRY

"Love For the Distant" (*"Liubov' k dal'nemu"* 1924) was the title of an early essay on Babel, penned by a Bolshevik historian and sociologist, Iakov Shafir.[31] This miniature critical meditation on the few *Red Cavalry* stories that had appeared by 1924 has the distinction of being the only one in Soviet Russia to establish a direct link between *Red Cavalry* and one of Zarathustra's famous commandments, which Shafir uses as his title, albeit ironically and in a Marxist key. The sacrifices in the name of the Revolution, however harsh and inhuman they may have been, were made for the sake of future generations, not at their expense, as in the Great War with its lip service to humanist ethics. To this extent, at least, one could use Nietzsche with profit. So went the drift of Shafir's position from which he proposed to examine Babel. The value of Shafir's observations cannot be overestimated for yet another reason: he was one of the more prominent students of contemporary Soviet readership and, rather than offer an esthetic evaluation or elaboration of *Red Cavalry*, he treated the work pretty much as a slice of life served up *au naturel*, without any sauce of artistic mediation.[32]

In an observation that would become a commonplace of Babel criticism, Shafir pointed to a key aspect of Babel's Nietzschean strategy: to justify the perpetrators of cruelty by surrounding them with the "enormously heroic, in the best sense of the word, pathos." As far as I know Shafir was the only one to see this strategy as originating in a nexus of specifically Nietzschean motifs, namely, justifying existence as an esthetic phenomenon. While lauding Babel's achievement, Safir was enough of an orthodox Marxist to draw a line between a Nietzschean and a Marxist justification of violence.

With the delicacy befitting a critic taking on a popular idol, he gently chided Babel for leaning too much toward the former, perhaps even confusing the two. According to Shafir,

Babel not only failed to denounce vengeance, but he tended to see in it an appropriate means for righting the wrong. For Babel, he wrote, wreaking vengeance was tantamount to "restoring social justice."

Thereby vengeance becomes humanized. This attitude toward vengeance is profoundly "of the people" [*narodno*], but is has nothing in common with the attitudes of conscious proletarians, who are guided in their behavior and actions exclusively by the considerations of rational expediency [*tselesoobraznost'*]. Alas, not only does our artist depict vengeance as an act of the greatest justice in the minds of the Balmashevs [the story "Salt," G. F.], but it would seem that he himself perceives vengeance as justice. If we are not mistaken on this point, this is where we must take issue with Babel's fiction. But this is just an aside.[33]

In the atmosphere of the ever-intensifying literary squabbles, even this gentle critical aside drew blood – not much, but enough to attract Vladislav Veshnev (Przeslavski), a Bolshevik rigorist from the journal *Young Guard* (*Molodaia gvardiia*). A rather astute and not entirely unsympathetic reader of Babel's stories, Veshnev adopted a position of one who had the interests of Soviet youth at heart, a position that compelled him to sound a note of caution amid the chorus of acclaim greeting the appearance of yet another piece of Babel's short fiction. Himself a writer of short fiction,[34] Veshnev did not mince words. Babel's popularity among the young, who could recite by heart pages from *The Tales of Odessa*, could lead to dire consequences, propagation of the ideals of "bestial banditry," for example, a transparent allusion to Nietzsche's Superman. Hence, "The Poetry of Banditry" (1924), as Veshnev unceremoniously entitled his critique.[35]

Unlike other critics, who praised Babel's ability to balance the intelligentsia's humanistic morality with the Cossack justice "beyond good and evil," Veshnev insisted on Babel's privileging the former over the latter. In a surprisingly Nietzschean move, he accused Babel of insolence in his attempts to justify the revolutionary violence of the Cossacks with such petty bourgeois concepts as right and wrong: "Herein lies the key to the understanding of Babel's art. First of all, we must note that Babel approached the revolution with a moral criterion. This alone is bad enough. Morality has no jurisdiction over revolution. On the contrary, revolution has jurisdiction over ethics."

Veshnev was equally hard to please when it came to esthetics: "Look how hard Babel is trying! In what luxuriant, colorful, subtle poetry does he cloak the bloody cruelty of the red heroes of the civil war." Indeed, Babel's greatest offense was in trying to justify the Revolution at all. How dare he, one can almost hear Veshnev exclaiming, imagine that the Revolution needs any justification at all: "Revolution is justified 'immanently,' by the meaning it itself generates (*sobstvennym svoim smyslom*)." This was a tall *Nietzschean* order, one that even the author of *Red Cavalry* would find difficult to fill.

ALEKSANDR VORONSKY

The founder and editor of *Red Virgin Soil* and the guardian angel of the fellow-travelers, Aleksandr Voronsky was one of the first and most astute readers of Babel and one of the cleverest mystifiers of Babel's Nietzschean motifs. Whether these mystifications were intentional or merely unwitting is beside the point. What matters is that they provide us with one of the best early examples of what we might call the Soviet crypto-Nietzscheanism. From the outset of his 1924 essay devoted to Babel,[36] Voronsky presented him as an author who is decidedly "Soviet" – a metonymous qualifier that becomes a legitimating synecdoche once it is paired with such a potent term of the Sovietese as "achievement." "Babel," Voronsky was unequivocal, "is a new achievement of the post-October Soviet literature" ("Babel," p. 148). The same claim is repeated a few pages later: "Babel is a very big hope of the Russian, contemporary, Soviet literature and already a big achievement." The Bolshevik Revolution could take credit for Babel and to that extent, at least, it was esthetically justified. To drive his point home, Voronsky informs his readers that Babel became a serious author only recently – an exaggeration, to say the least, since Babel's prerevolutionary publications in

Gorky's *Letopis'* were singled out by contemporary critics as were Babel's regular contributions to Gorky's anti-Leninist *Novaia zhizn'*.[37] Let us now take a close look at the character of this "hope and achievement" of *Soviet* Russian literature, as Voronsky defined it.

Voronsky's yardstick for measuring and the ultimate antecedent of Babel was Lev Tolstoi. Like Tolstoi, Babel is capable of isolating an insignificant detail, making it "more expressive of the *essence*," than any amount of digression can achieve "Babel," (p. 150). Generically, too, Babel and Tolstoi share a penchant for the "epic," although Babel, Voronsky admitted, did not intend to produce a "comprehensive, esthetically precise [*sic*] epic representation of the actual Red Cavalry Army by means of emphasizing its essential spirit and qualities, as, for example, Tolstoi had done in *War and Peace*" ("Babel," p. 155). Like Tolstoi, Babel works in the "classical, if modernized, tradition" ("Babel," pp. 147, 149). To be compared to Tolstoi would be high praise for any author, and Voronsky's virtual insistence on the legitimacy of this comparison bestowed on Babel's controversial art a certificate of what Pasternak later referred to as "safe conduct." Indeed, for many contemporary Marxist critics, Tolstoi possessed such exemplary authority that his art was virtually allowed to transcend its class origins.[38] Hence Voronsky's flattering juxtaposition functioned as an implicit acknowledgement that with regard to Babel criticism based on the "class approach" just would not do.

No less important (whether Voronsky intended it or not), Tolstoi, whose name served as a work horse hitched to most contemporary literary theories,[39] provided a cover for dealing with Babel's apparent Nietzscheanism, not as a liability, but as a most powerful asset. Like Tolstoi, Babel was a "physiological writer."

What is sacred for Babel is the immediacy [*dannost'*],[40] actuality, life, and primitive character of human interests, urges, passions, desires, psychology – everything that is commonly referred to as crude animal instincts. The sacred immediacy [of life for Babel] has nothing to do with the acceptance of life according to the formula: "everything real is rational and everything existing is real." [This pointedly anti-Hegelian characterization of Babel, too, may suggest a Nietzschean subtext, *G.F.*] Babel is a pagan, a materialist, and an atheist in his art. He is alien to the Christian, idealistic world-view which treats flesh, matter as something base, sinful, while treating "spirit," "spirituality" as solely valuable essence of human life ("Babel," p. 151)

These qualifiers could have as easily been applied to Tolstoi (Tolstoi's "physiologism" was a topos of literary criticism in the 1920s), and since Shestov's brilliant analysis, they could have as easily defined the philosophical ground that Tolstoi shared with Nietzsche. "As in *War and Peace*, so in *Anna Karenina*," wrote Shestov,

not only does Count Tolstoi refuse to accept exchanging life for the Good, but he considers such an exchange unnatural, false, hypocritical, ultimately eliciting the opposite of the desired reaction even in the best human being.[41]

Reveling in the retelling of and quoting from Babel's famous anti-Dostoevskian parodies, "The Sin of Jesus" and "A Tale About a Wench," Voronsky rehearsed Nietzsche's categorical indictment of the "value of the value pity" (*GM*, I, p. 6; *Z*, I, p. 16, II, p. 3) and the life-denying "fantasies" and "spirituality." True, Babel is an estheticist, Voronsky readily conceded, but his estheticism, unlike that of the decadents, possesses a full-blooded Dionysian energy:

Babel's [...] estheticism has already earned him the attribute of a semi-decadent. Babel is no decadent. The truth lies elsewhere: in his fiction, the dreamer clashes with the realist, who has intuited the deep truth of the immediate, actual life, perhaps crude, but full-blooded and blossoming.

His characters are not mere brutes, murderers and marauders, but powerful men seeking their own version of justice – "concrete, entirely earthly, unreflective and instinctive." These words, which deny the validity of the distinction of "good and evil" while affirming that of the "good and bad'" for life, could have been lifted from *On the Genealogy of Morals*. But instead of crediting Nietzsche, Voronsky links these Babelian *Bestiaen* to the folk and literary tradition of Russia's "truth-seekers" (*pravdo-iskateli*), very likely having in mind the itinerant "philosophers" from the lower depths such as Gorky's Nietzscheanized *bosiaki*, Chelkash, Sharko and Malva.[42] Whatever his cultural loyalties, Babel's narrator, according to Voronsky, also renounced *ressentiment*. With great pathos, Voronsky quotes from the opening of "Pan Apolek," singling out for emphasis the attributes of *ressentiment*: "the sensuality of the *dreamy anger*, bitter disdain for the dogs and the swine of humanity, the fire of the *silent and intoxicating* revenge – I have sacrificed them to the new god" ("Babel," p. 153). That god is "life," in the Nietzschean, post-Darwinian understanding of the term, the immediate present that does not live "*at the expense of the future*" but itself is a payment for "*the highest power and splendor* actually possible for the type man" (*GM*, Preface, p. 20). Like his character "Apolek," wrote Voronsky,

Babel treats the natural in man as the summit of creation, he writes about the truth of the "wenches" like Arina and Kseniia, about the truth of Afonka Bida, about the triumph of life in the moment of mortal battles. For he knows that Kseniias and Arinas are the fertile producers of life, but in the Alfreds, there is "plenty of play but ain't nothing serious," for one must be proud of the natural in human being, whereas disdain for the crude wench-life, attempts to follow Jehovah's example and create out of oneself some little worlds, amount only to "blasphemy and lordly arrogance" of the little Alfreds and spectators without the binoculars. (p. 153)

Voronsky stepped on the most dangerous ground when he turned to "Gedali," a story that echoes closely Nietzsche's demystification of the ethic of charity, equality, and, by implication, the socialist ideals as the slave morality of *ressentiment*. Even in their outward appearances as dark and out-of-the-way places, Gedali's Dickensian "old curiosity shop" and the residence of his Braclav Rabbi ("Rabbi") come perilously close to Nietzsche's subterranean "workshop," a version no doubt of the satanic mills, "where ideals are manufactured" (*GM*, I, p. 14). "They tell me," goes the passage in *GM*, "their misery is a sign of their being chosen by God; one beats the dogs one likes best." "Blessed is the Lord," announces Rabbi Motaleh of Braclav, as he "breaks the bread with his monkish fingers."

"Blessed is the God of Israel for he has chosen us among all the peoples of the world" ("The Rabbi"). This is an intensely ironic moment – to have the traditional blessing pronounced by a leader of a religious culture, just a hair's breadth away from its total demise. Highlighting the "monkish fingers'" and the "breaking of bread," Babel followed in Nietzsche's footsteps. He conflated the Hebraic ritual of the Hasidim with the Christian Eucharist and had both echo in Gedali's vegetarian War-Communist wish for "the International of kind people where each soul would be registered to receive a ration according to the top category." Voronsky quoted this passage, an expression of "slave morality" par excellence, and left it hanging in the air, with but a brief comment saying simply that Gedali and his milieu belonged wholly to times past.

"Babel's main theme," Voronsky summed up his appreciative critique, "is Man, with a Capital 'M,' Man, who under the influence of the Revolution, has emerged from the lowest depths" ("Babel," p. 160). In the long shadow cast by this new "Man" – the pinnacle of Bolshevik Futuristic anthropology, reminiscent of Trotsky's vision in *Art and Revolution* – one can readily discern the features of Nietzsche's Superman.

CONFUSION OF TONGUES

Voronsky pretty much set the tone for the Bolshevik reception of Babel. And while Babel's "Nietzscheanism" remained the focal point in criticism, some found it more unsettling than did Voronsky. Georgy Gorbachev, a critic who shared many of Voronsky's views, commended Babel for his invaluable contribution to the creation of the "new linguistic culture" and his "service to the cognition of life, development of technique, new expressiveness." This was no mean achievement, "for language," as Gorbachev went on to explain in the spirit of Nietzsche's *On the Genealogy of Morals*, "represents the most important tool of enlightenment and communication among the masses, which have entered a period of great cultural and social ferment."[43] Still, Gorbachev was apparently too much of a dialectician to accept comfortably Babel's penchant for sharp contrasts and paradox, the essential components (according to Georg Simmel's popular view[44]) of Nietzsche's individualism and his yearning for *distance*, lacked any suggestion of the possibility of a resolution at a higher plane:

The most interesting thing for Babel is combining in one person, group, or action that most contradictory quality – the paradoxical nature of existence. Almost all the stories by Babel are paradoxical, especially, in *Red Cavalry*. [...][45]

And while one could find a certain consolation in the fact that "Babel's paradoxes were recouped by the dialectic of the Revolution," Gorbachev chided the author for leaving no textual clues to that effect, indeed, even tempting the reader with a purely esthetic treatment of the Revolution.

Marxist strictures notwithstanding, Gorbachev the reader must have been deeply affected by Babel's fiction, and we see him slip eventually into a more appropriate analytical mode reminiscent of Nietzsche's Dionysian understanding of tragedy and its subsequent "reprise" in Bakhtin:[46] "Both style and structure of Babel's stories are pitched to a humorous key; his stories, as a rule, prompt laughter. But in the majority of Babel's stories, there gleams through the laughter a serious thought or a description of the tragic, terrifying and at the same time beautiful, powerful, burgeoning, and victorious life."[47]

As Gorbachev moved toward his conclusions, however, the Bolshevik Marxist in him once again took the upper hand, even if the Nietzschean temptation was not altogether banished:

But, of course, most of all *Red Cavalry* tells the story of Babel the writer, the raconteur and the virtually irreplaceable protagonist of the stories: an *intelligent*, who has long ago become disillusioned about the old values; a skeptic, who has rejected old ideologies; a connoisseur of unusual situations, life's most exuberant manifestations, beautiful, strange and funny but always exuberant; an adventurer and the lover of the "spicy;" a cynic and estheticist [...] a spiritual brother of the author of *Sentimental Journey* and *Letters Not About Love*, that adventurer, witty thinker, cynic, mischief-maker and estheticist. ("O tvorchestve," p. 282).

What could have attracted this estheticist to the Bolsheviks? Interestingly enough Gorbachev produces a catalogue of Nietzschean virtues possessed, he proudly insists, by the Bolsheviks themselves: "Life is on our side, and so is freshness, power [*silia*], and youth, [lack of] prejudice" (p. 283).

If Babel's public pronouncements in support of "us," Gorbachev went on, indicated the author's desire to make his art truly revolutionary, Gorbachev had a recipe for him. Instead of indulging in the sight of existence "laid bare," with its conjuncture of "primitive desires" and the revolutionary "ideology," Babel must convert his muse to a "revolutionary romanticism,"

the romanticism of a conscious struggle under the banner of communism, the world-view that bravely looks straight in the eye of reality, unblinking in the face of difficulties of mistakes, muck and blood partially covering its way, but also the world-view that dictates to its envoys a buoyant readiness for sacrifices of all kinds for the sake of that inevitable result of the struggle – that "kingdom of the future" before whose might and joy pale all the miracles of the fairy tales and all romantic dreams ever created by mankind. ("O tvorchestve," pp. 284ff.)

Abram Lezhnev,[48] a prominent critic of the Voronsky camp (he belonged to "Pereval"), begged to differ with Gorbachev's assertion of Babel's amoral estheticism. Like Voronsky, and, if to a lesser extent, Gorbachev himself, Lezhnev used as his point of departure Babel's stupendous achievement, not its compatibility with a specific Marxist scheme. Where Gorbachev demanded that Babel transform at once the apparent antinomy of the Revolution into a Bolshevik dialectic, Lezhnev showed a far greater, Nietzschean appreciation for the irreconcilable paradox of the times. "Babel knows about the necessity of cruelty," wrote Lezhnev in 1926,

no less than those who criticize him. In his work, it is justified ("Salt," "The Death of Dolgushev"), justified with the revolutionary pathos. His cavalrymen are no brutes; otherwise *Red Cavalry* would have amounted to a libel of the Cavalry Army. But the justification of cruelty – in a strange and conflicting way – exists side by side with his rejection of it. This contradiction cannot be resolved.[49]

Except, he might have added, in the Bolshevik will to power. Lezhnev introduces another Nietzschean motif when he turns to Babel's penchant for achieving the effect of epiphany by presenting his characters at the moment of an unbearable nervous tension or breakdown (*proryv*) – the moments when the cavalrymen "lose control over themselves." In those moments, "what is dormant, what cannot be uttered, what we can only guess about" comes to the surface. That here Lezhnev reaches out beyond Freud to Nietzsche can be gauged by what he includes in the list of the "repressed" that returns in the moments of the Cossack's Dionysian frenzy: "The elemental force of popular song that has been passed from generation to generation (the epileptics in Babel begin to speak in the figures and rhythm of a folk song), and the love the Cossack feels for his quiet native farmstead, and the enthusiasm of a participant in a revolutionary struggle ..." ("I. Babel," p. 84)

Curiously and characteristically, Lezhnev's acceptance of or, rather, tolerance for Nietzschean antinomies and his yearning for the primordial are intertwined with a naive biographical moralism with a Dostoevskian twist. Assuming, quite erroneously, as we now know, that Babel's narrator and the author were identical, Lezhnev found an explanation and a psychological excuse for Babel's focus on cruelty in the author's alleged childhood experience in a pogrom.[50] Lezhnev was referring to the stories "First Love" and "The Story of My Dovecot" (dedicated to Gorky), published in 1925 and ultimately intended as part of a long autobiographical fiction in the Gorky mold.[51]

BABEL'S RECEPTION OF BABEL, OR LIUTOV ROUTINIZED

Babel's turn to the theme of childhood, presented, as in *Red Cavalry*, in the first-person narrative voice, stemmed, I am inclined to think, from Babel's own attempts at assimilating his earlier triumphs to the new expectations of the literary establishment and the reader under NEP. Life, it seemed, was returning to normal. The extraordinary, not to say Dionysian, intensity of existence under the conditions of revolution and civil war, with its manifest self-legitimation (*samozakonnost'* as in Benni, Veshnev, above), were gradually yielding to quotidian predictability. As a sociologist would put it, charismatic authority generated in the depths of the revolutionary experience was undergoing routinization, partly, by being transformed into a new "revolutionary tradition," partly, because of the emerging institutions of bureaucracy and law which were letting in through the back door, so to speak, some of the condemned "petty-bourgeois" luxuries, among them, individual psychological motivation. One of the sure signs of this process, related directly to Babel, was an article by I. Ilinsky, "Legal Motifs in Babel's Writings" (1927),[52] a study of popular conceptions of law and justice underlying the actions and sensibilities of Babel's protagonists.

The fictional continuity between the narrator of *Red Cavalry* and the narrator of the childhood stories, suggesting an identity between the boy victim and Liutov, makes this hypothesis highly plausible. If this was indeed the case, as I believe it was, Babel was merely taking the cue from his patrons and supporters among the critics: he was covering the Nietzschean tracks of *Red Cavalry* and *The Tales of Odessa* by having them blend with the more conventional mentality of the peaceful, still "vegetarian," period of NEP. What the "childhood" stories seemed to be saying was that Liutov the man, Liutov the boy, and, by implication, their creator were not merely Nietzschean "adventurers and estheticists" (Gorbachev, Veshnev), inscrutably alien to the conventional view of life, but adults scarred deeply by the cruelties of the old regime at the most impressionable time of life, their childhood. Psychological and sociological motivations were now called upon the supplement the pure poetry of Babel's prose that struck the first readers of *Red Cavalry* as "completeness of art" (Benni).

Nietzschean motifs, individualistic, anti-statist, esthetic to the core, were growing ever fainter, barely discernible above the beat of the kettle-drums of the Stalinist superstate.

NOTES

1 For Babel's Nietzscheanism see James E. Falen, *Isaac Babel, Russian Master of Short Story* (Knoxville, 1974). See also my "Fat Tuesday in Odessa: Isaac Babel's 'Di Grasso' as Testament and Manifesto," *The Russian Review* 40: 2 (1981), pp. 101–21, and "Isaak Babel," *European Writers: The Twentieth Century* (New York, 1991).

2 All citations of Babel's texts, unless otherwise noted, are from *Izbrannoe*, intro. by L. Poliak, comment by E. Krasnoshchekova (Moscow, 1966). All translations are mine.

3 A. Blok, *Sobranie sochinenii v shesti tomakh*, ed. M. A. Dudina et al., IV (1982), p. 346.

4 B. Eikhenbaum, "V ozhidanii literatury," *Russkii sovremennik* 1 (1924), pp. 280–96. See also his "V poiskakh zhanra," *ibid.* 3 (1924), pp. 228–31.

5 M. Zoshchenko, "Literatura dolzhna byt' narodnoi," in his *1935–1937* (Leningrad, 1937), p. 394. Cited in M. Chudakova, *Poetika Mikhaila Zoshchenko* (Moscow, 1979), p. 70.

6 See M. Chudakova, "Puti slova v proze 1920-kh-1930-kh godov," *Poetika Mikhaila Zoshchenko*, pp. 98–130. See also my "Dying As Metaphor and the Ironic Mode," in *The Coat of Many Colors: Osip Mandelstam and His Mythologies of Self-Presentation* (Berkeley, Los Angeles, London, 1987).

7 I define *skaz* as a first-person narrative which contains elements of vocabulary and grammar which (1) are not normally associated with published literature and (2) define the narrator as a social inferior of the implied reader.

8 See discussion in *Nietzsche in Russia*, especially, the Preface by George Kline and the Introduction by Bernice Glatzer Rosenthal. For the Nietzscheanism of Viacheslav Ivanov, a key figure in the Russian Symbolist movement, see Patricia Ann Mueller-Vollmer's Ph.D. Thesis, "Dionysos Reborn: Vjaceslav Ivanov's Theory of Symbolism" (Stanford University, 1985) and my "In Place of a Biography," *Coat of Many Colors*, pp. 155ff.

9 See, e.g., A. Voronskii, "Iz sovremennykh nastroenii (po povodu odnogo spora)" *Krasnaia nov'* 3 (1921), p. 247.

10 Viach. I. Ivanov and Mikhail O. Gershenzon, *Perepiska iz dvukh uglov* (Petersburg, 1921). Voronskii, "Iz sovremennykh literaturnykh nastroenii," *Krasnaia nov'* 3 (1921), pp. 244–55. P. S. Kogan, "Viach. Ivanov i M.O. Gershenzon, 'Perepiska iz dvukh uglov'" (review), *Pechat' i revoliutsiia* 3 (1921); Mikhail Kuzmin, "Mechtateli," in his *Uslovnosti: Stat'i ob iskusstve* (Petrograd,

1923). Sloezer, "Russkii spor o kul'ture," *Sovremennys zapiski* 11 (1922), pp. 197, 207.

11 A. Lunacharskii, "Simvolisty," in his *Ocherki po istorii russkoi literatury* (Moscow, 1976), pp. 433ff.

12 Ia. Benni, "I. Babel'," *Pechat' i revoliutsiia* 3 (1924), pp. 136 and 139.

13 Victor Shklovsky's view of Babel was similar to that of Benni and Mirsky and lies squarely in the esthetic sphere, i.e., in the category of the "justification of existence as an esthetic phenomenon." Consider: "Russian literature is as gray as a siskin, it needs raspberry-colored riding breeches and leather shoes the color of heavenly azure. [. . .] What literature needs is concreteness and to be cross-fertilized with the new style of life," V. Shklovskii, "Kriticheskii romans," *Lef, zhurnal levogo fronta iskusstva* 6 (1924), p. 152.

14 G. Lelevich, "1923 god: Literaturnye itogi," *Na postu* 5 (1924), pp. 82–87.

15 G. Lelevich, "1923 god: Literaturnye itogi," p. 87.

16 A. Voronskii, "I. Babel' i L. Seifullina," *Krasnaia nov'* 5 (1924), p. 281.

17 M. Tseitlin, "Obzor zhurnalov," *Sovremennyia zapiski* 20 (1924), pp. 434–35, and his "Krasnaia nov'," *Sovremennyia zapiski* 25 (1925), pp. 477–79.

18 D. Mirskii (Sviatopolk-Mirskii), "I. Babel'. *Rasskazy*. Gosudarstvennoe izdatel'stvo. Moskva-Leningrad. 1925" (review), *Sovremennyia zapiski* 26 (1925), p. 485.

19 A. Leznev, "I. I. [sic] Babel': Zametki k vykhodu 'Konarmii,'" *Pechat' i revoliutsiia* 6 (1926), p. 82.

20 Viach. Polonskii, "Babel'," in *O literature (Izbrannye raboty)* (Moscow, 1988), p. 78. Originally published as "Kristicheskie zametki o Babele," *Novyi mir* 1 (1927).

21 A. V. Lunacharskii, "Znachenie iskusstva s kommunisticheskoi tochki zreniia," *Nachalo puti: Iz sovetskoi literaturnoi kritiki 20-kh godov*, ed. O. V. Filimonov, (Moscow, 1987), p. 10. First published in *Rabochii put'* (Omsk) 229 (December, 21 1924).

22 Lunacharskii, ibid., p. 4.

23 Cf. Venus de Milo in Bogdanov's *Iskusstvo i rabochii klass* (Moscow, 1918): "The temple was the center of the community, and the goddess was the center of the temple. Therefore she was the center of organization of the collective."

24 G. Freidin, "Authorship and Citizenship: A Problem for Modern Russian Literature" *Stanford Slavic Studies* 1 (1987) and in an essay, "Justification of Literature: Christianity and Authorship

in the Modern Russian Tradition," *The Russian Review* 2 (1993).
25 A. V. Lunacharskii, "Formalizm v nauke ob iskusstve," *Pechat' i revoliutsiia* 5 (1924), p. 23.
26 Sviatopolk-Mirsky, "I. Babel'. *Rasskazy*," p. 486.
27 D. S. Mirsky, *Literaturnaia gazeta*, September 12, 1932.
28 Gershenzon and Ivanov, *Perepiska iz dvulh uglov*. For a "Nietzschean" reading of this celebrated volume see B. Schloezer (Shletser), "Russkii spor o kul'ture," *Sovremennye zapiski* 11 (1922), pp. 195–211.
29 A. Lunacharsky, "Simvolisty" (1926), p. 443.
30 Claude Lévi-Strauss, "The Structural Study of Myth," in his *Structural Anthropology*, trans. Claire Jacobson and Brooke Grundfest Schoepf (New York, 1963), p. 216.
31 Shafir, "Liubov' k dal'nemu."
32 See his *Ocherki psikhologii chitatelia* (Moscow and Leningrad, 1927). The book deals with the popular attitudes to the work of selected "classics," i.e., Pushkin, Gogol, Lermontov, Turgenev, Goncharov, and Gorky.
33 Shafir, "Liubov' k dal'nemu."
34 V. Veshnev, *Rasskazy* (Moscow, 1927).
35 V. Veshnev (Vl. Przhetslavskii), "Poeziia banditizma," *Molodaia gvardiia* 7–8 (1924), pp. 274–80.
36 A. Voronskii, "Babel'," in his *Iskusstvo videt' mir: Portrety, stat'i* (Moscow, 1987), pp. 146–62. Pages, given in parentheses, refer to this edition. The essay was first published as "Babel', Seifullina," *Krasnaia nov'* 5 (1924).
37 Babel's contributions to *Novaia zhizn'* were reprinted in *Zabytyi Babel': sbornik maloizvestnykh proizvedenii I. Babelia*, ed. and comp. Nikolas Stroud (Ann Arbor, MI, 1979).
38 See, for example, A. V. Lunacharsky's use of Tolstoi as ally in his polemic with the Formalists. Lunacharskii, "Formalizm v nauke ob iskusstve," *Pechat' i revoliutsiia* 5 (1924), pp. 25ff.
39 E. J. Brown, *The Proletarian Episode in Russian Literature: 1928–32* (New York, 1971), pp. 66ff. Samuel David Eisen, "Fox to Fox: Viktor Shklovsky's appeal to Tolstoi in the Twilight of NEP" (MA Thesis, Stanford University, 1989).
40 Cf. H. Bergson, *Essai sur les données immédiates de la conscience* (Paris, 1889), in English translated as *Time and Free Will*. Bergson was an acknowledged influence on Voronsky. See "Estetika Bergson i shkola Voronskogo," *Literature i iskusstvo* 1 (1930). The Russian word, *dannost'*, however, may as easily refer to Nietzsche's sense of life eliciting *amor fati*.

41 L. Shestov (Shvartsman), *Dobro v uchenii gr. Tolstogo i Fr. Nitsshe: Filosofiia i propoved'* (Petersburg, 1900), p. 7.
42 Cf. Platonov's *pravdoiskateli*, Voshchev in *Kotlovan*, Mekar from the *Bedniatskaia khronika*, etc.
43 Georgii Gorbachev, "O tvorchestve Babelia i po pobodu nego," *Zvezda* 4 (1925), pp. 270–86; quote is from p. 275.
44 Georg Simmel, "Fridrikh Nitsshe: Etiko-filosofskii siluet," trans. N. Iuzhin, in A. Rihl and G. Simmel, *Nitsshe* (Odessa, 1898), p. 148.
46 On Babel, Nietzsche, and Bakhtin, see G. Freidin, "Fat Tuesday in Odessa, pp. 1906–7.
47 G. Gorbachev, "O tvorchestve Babelia," p. 276.
48 See G. Belaia, *Iz istorii sovetskoi literaturno-kriticheskoi mysli 20-kh godov: esteticheskaia kontseptsiia "Petervala"* (Moscow, 1985). See also E. J. Brown, *The Proletarian Episode in Russian Literature: 1928–32* (New York, 1971), p. 97 and passim.
49 Lezhnev, "I. Babel," p. 85.
50 Cf. Natalie Babel, " Introduction,"in I. Babel, *The Lonely Years: 1925–1939 (Unpublished Stories and Private Correspondence)* (New York, 1964).
51 See my discussion of Babel's "autobiographical fiction" in "Isaac Babel," pp. 1886–87 and 1892–93.
52 I. Il'inskii, "Pravovye motivy v tvorchestve Babelia," *Krasnaia nov'* 7 (1927), pp. 231–40.

CHAPTER 7

Nietzschean implications and superhuman aspirations in the architectural avant-garde

Milka Bliznakov

I love him who works and invents that he may build a
house for the superman ...

$(\mathcal{Z}, \text{p. } 44)$

Architecture, a fusion of art, technology, and necessity, was in
the forefront of the new Soviet culture from the beginning of its
development in the 1920s. Actual construction, however, was
limited because of lack of funds until the Five-Year Plan
(1928–32). During the Cultural Revolution (1928–31), which
accompanied the heroic efforts to fulfill this plan, the theoretical debate about the physical form of Soviet cities and buildings reached its peak. Ideas derived from Nietzsche's philosophy were a prime factor in this debate. Indeed they had
influenced the theoretical search for a new architecture since
1919.

The problem of defining Nietzsche's influence on the architectural avant-garde of the 1920s is inherent in the process of
design, whereby ideas are translated into visual forms, rather
than expressed in verbal statements. The architect must satisfy
the pragmatic requirements of the building program, deal with
economic and legal limitations, consider structural and
environmental restrictions, and despite these constraints,
design an esthetically pleasing building. Ideological, philosophical, and esthetic influences are subconscious. During the
process of design, the architect envisions physical elements such
as forms, shapes, colors, materials, and structures, and thinks of
methods to unite them into a coherent totality. Verbal explanations of the design, added after the design is completed,
usually aim to clarify the project for the clients (public or

private) in terms they could understand, or in words they would like to hear. In Russia of the 1920s (as in Bulgaria of the late 1940s, where this author lived), clients were representative of state organizations which had no criteria for judging the esthetic merits of an architectural design; instead, they expected the design to be justified by popular slogans or quotations from Marxist literature. Most state officials, however, were not familiar with the voluminous pronouncements of Marx and Lenin, hence unequipped to challenge the architects' claim that their work was the visual manifestation of Marxist dogma. Neither were the architects experts on Marxist philosophy nor on philosophy in general; therefore, verbal explanations and architectural projects need to be critically analyzed for hidden meaning and buried influence, especially since Nietzsche was never mentioned by name.

Marxist literature was not a useful guide for artists and architects aiming to create the visual forms of the new Soviet culture. Neither Marx, Engels, nor even Lenin specified the architectural forms of a socialist society. During the New Economic Policy (NEP) period, the Soviet government encouraged a relative tolerance towards various artistic schools and expressions, taking the position that no literary movement, school, or group, could be singled out to speak in the name of the Party. In 1921, Anatoly V. Lunacharsky (1875–1933), the Commissar of Enlightenment (1917–29), clarified the official Policies in the Fields of the Arts and concluded that "every help should be given to original endeavors in the field of the arts."[1] Artists, therefore, felt free to seek inspiration and guidance among the wide range of authors easily available at the time, from Charles Fourier (1772–1837) and Mikhail Bakunin (1814–76) to Petr Kropotkin (1842–1921), Richard Wagner (1813–83), and Friedrich Nietzsche (1844–1900).[2]

Petr Kropotkin had already envisioned an alternative to capitalist urbanization. In his *Fields, Factories and Workshops* (published in Russian in 1918), the state as a political institution is replaced with a decentralized federation of agro-industrial towns. Since Marxists and anarchists agreed that the State would disappear under Communism, Soviet planners and designers were tempted to borrow some anarchist ideas for this distant future. This is evidenced by proposals of the so-called urbanist faction in Gosplan, whereby the population was to be resettled in agro-industrial towns of some forty to sixty thousand people living together in large communal houses. These schemes were the first to be dismissed in 1931 by the Party.

Projections into the future, such as utopias and science fiction, were very popular during the Cultural Revolution. Utopias were a likely source for inspiration for two reasons. First, they usually included a physical environment which reflected and supported the social system envisioned by the author. Thus, a relationship between ideology and architectural environment was established and sustained. Widely-read descriptions of utopias reached all segments of the population, spreading attractive images of an exciting and desirable future. Second, the grandiose goals of the Five-Year Plan called for "the actualization into practice of all that until recently was [considered] fantasy and utopia."[3] One anarcho-Nietzschean utopia serving as a channel for Nietzsche's influence and also suggestive of Fedorov's ideas on the conquest of nature is Aleksandr Kuprin's "A Toast."

Aleksandr Kuprin (1879–1938), a protégé of Maksim Gorky and member of his Wednesdays (Sreda) group, wrote his three-page story, "A Toast," in 1906. The toast was given at a New Year celebration on the eve of the year 3106 commemorating the 200th anniversary of the "world-wide anarchist union of free people". The festivities were located at the North Pole inside a magnificent structure of glass, marble, and steel, adorned with exotic flowers and luxuriant trees more like a beautiful botanical garden than a public hall. An engineer from the North Pole raised his glass in homage to Man and "his immortal mind ... There are no restraints on our minds and nothing bars the fulfillment of our desires ... Our work is our delight. And our love, liberated from the shackles of servitude and triviality, is like the love of flowers, free and beautiful. Our only master is human genius!"[4]

This toast was communicated to the South Pole through

two-way giant television. Technological advancements and unlimited energy (from the earth's magnetic fields among other sources) had freed man from undesired labor. State, national, and religious institutions had been replaced by free professional associations supporting the development of individual talents and creativity. The model was clearly a Nietzschean "Superman" engineer who could change the world to a paradise. For architects, who were able through their creativity to add an artistic dimension to engineering, the leaders of civilization were the architects. Nietzsche had correctly admired the architect as representing:

neither a Dionysian nor an Apollonian condition: here is the mighty act of will, the will which moves mountains, the intoxication of the strong will, which demands artistic expression. The most powerful men have always inspired the architects; the architect has always been influenced by power. Pride, victory over weight and gravity, the will to power, seek to render themselves visible in a building ... (*TI*, p. 74).

The supremacy of architecture was also advanced by Oswald Spengler. Stating that "architecture of the grand style ... is naturally the early art in all Cultures"[5] and that "great architecture of the early period is ever the mother of all following arts; it determines the choice of them and the spirit of them,"[6] Spengler destined architecture to play the leading role in the development of a new culture. The problem of creativity in a mass society had concerned Nietzschean Marxists such as Maksim Gorky, Lunacharsky, and Bogdanov. It became of paramount significance when, with the initiation of the First Five-Year Plan, architects were charged to envision a socialist lifestyle and to design the physical environment which would support and enhance this lifestyle. This challenge was too important for the architects not to seek information from non-Marxist alternative projections into the future. Directly or indirectly, consciously or subconsciously, Nietzsche was a likely source of influence. The "Nietzschean Marxists'" belief that socialism would elevate everyone to his full, god-like potential was paralleled by the architects' claim that a well-designed environment could achieve similar goals.

Although Nietzsche's books were removed from the libraries' shelves after 1923, they were still available in private collections and probably were read with great interest, especially since they were banned. When Nietzsche was banned in my native Bulgaria some thirty years later for example, even those who had never heard his name before began looking for his books. Many of us memorized entire chapters before passing over one of his books to the next reader. For those who could not read Nietzsche directly, secondary sources of his thought were readily available. Foreign publications in art and architecture were also accessible.[7] Russians who traveled abroad brought back information to share with friends and colleagues, and Western firms and technical specialists were involved in major architectural projects in the Soviet Union. By 1930, about one thousand foreign architects, mostly Germans, were known to be working there and their number increased during the Second Five Year Plan (1933–37).

This study surveys only a few leading avant-garde architects willing to "smash the old tablets of values" in order to "inscribe new values on new tablets" (Z, pp. 51–52). They attempted to define these new values in architectural terms – first by restructuring all inclusive total works of art for the new man, and then by transforming men into creative individuals who would actively participate in restructuring their own environment and in building their new civilization. The rise of a kind of individualism during the Cultural Revolution and the Constructivists' assertion in 1931 that "each dwelling is a manifestation of an individual's personality" is the last homage paid to Nietzsche before the architectural avant-garde was suppressed.

Constructivism in art and architecture is broadly used to cover the Modernist movement in Russia and often misused to imply unity. Actually the strength of the Russian avant-garde was in the variety of creative outbursts in all artistic fields. The common ground for the avant-garde was its rejection of previous cultures, its negation of existing values, and its search for a new civilization. Two groups played leading roles in the propagation of a new architecture, the Constructivists who formed in 1925 the Society of Contemporary Architects (Obedinenie sovremennykh arkhitektorov, abbreviated as OSA), and the Rationalists who organized in 1923 the Association of New Architects (Assotsiatsiia novykh arkhitektorov, abbreviated as ASNOVA). These groups were preceded, however, by the Commission for Sculpture Architecture Synthesis (Sinskulptarkh), formed in May, 1919. Soon this group expanded to include painters and was renamed Zhivskulptarkh, an abbreviation of Painting–Sculpture–Architecture Synthesis.[8] The group experimented with the idea of synthesizing the arts into a total work, a *Gesamtkunstwerk*, in numerous sketches, some of which were displayed in 1920 at the Nineteenth State Exhibition in Moscow. Nikolai Aleksandrovich Ladovsky (1881–1941), the spokesman of the group, presented his visualization of the theme "Architectural Manifestation of a Communal House" (Illustration 7.1) with his Credo attached to the drawing. "Technology creates wonders. Architecture also must create wonders. The wonders of antiquity were built with slave labor and the main factor was the quantity of labor. The space where contemporary wonders of architecture would dwell would be built by art and the main factor will be the quantity of intelligence. Space, not stone, is the material of architecture ..."[9]

Substituting labor with art and intelligence, i.e. with creativity, and stone with the experience of space, brings to mind Nietzsche in his definition of architecture as "victory over weight and gravity" (*TI*, p. 74).

The members of Zhivskulptarkh were included in the Institute of Artistic Culture (Inkhuk), formed in May 1920 to advise the government on policies concerning the visual arts. Although Zhivskulptarch was dissolved, Ladovsky formed a "working group" of Inkhuk architects and prepared a research program to examine the influence of space, form, and color on the human psyche.[10] He spent the rest of his life developing what he termed "the psychoanalytical method of design." Through this rational method, Ladovsky maintained, architects would be able to organize spaces which would evoke

7.1 Nikolai Ladovsky, Architectural Manifestation of a Communal House, 1920.

feelings and emotions and promote human action and participation in cultural activities. Ladovsky applied his method to architectural education in the Basic Division of the Higher State Art-Technical Studios (Vkhutemas),[11] to architectural design within the Association of New Architects (ASNOVA), and to planning and urban design after 1927. In 1928 Ladovsky founded the Union of Architects-Urbanists (ARU), and restated the importance of the psychological influence of architecture in ARU's declaration.

The activities of contemporary man are constantly linked with architectural surroundings. The architectural edifices of the city, even when casually observed, directly influence the feelings of the "consumer." Architecture, through form and appearance, thus shapes [man's] specific world outlook. The Soviet State must make use of architecture as a powerful means for the organization of the psychology of the masses.[12]

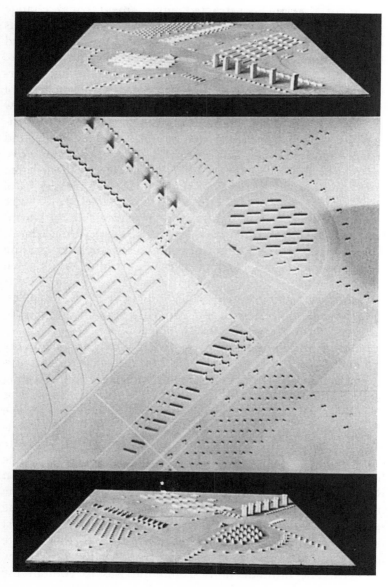

7.2 Nikolai Ladovsky, Project for the new industrial town Kostino near Moscow, 1927.

Confident that the constructed environment could change man's behavior and eventually transform society, architects affirmed their leading position among the arts and justified their continuous search for new architectural forms.

An early proposal (1927) to organize work, housing, cultural, and recreation facilities into a perceptually clear scheme of distinctive zones was Ladovsky's project for Kostino, a new industrial town for 25,000 inhabitants near Moscow (Illustration 7.2). The town and each of its zones could expand independently, yet all facilities would remain at walking distance. The inhabitants were offered a variety of housing to satisfy the individual needs of single factory employees or of large farmers' or workers' families. Man-made elements were sensitively integrated into the natural environment, and farmland wrapped around cottages without a perceivable edge.[13] The economy of psychophysical energy used in understanding the purpose and spatial arrangement of a building or of a town Ladovsky named "Architectural Rationalism." The architects pursuing this design goal called themselves Rationalists, though critics of their work also called them Formalists, already a term of opprobrium.

Building individual houses for each family, as Ladovsky proposed, was not consistent with Marxist doctrine as interpreted by many politicians and architects. The prevailing model for housing the industrial workers, during the 1920s, was broadly based on Fourier's phalanstery. The house-commune (dom-kommuna), as this housing structure for numerous inhabitants was called, consisted of minimal apartments for private activities, while collective facilities satisfied public needs. The house-commune was to alleviate the grave housing shortage in Russian cities by reducing the individual dwelling to the minimum, in some cases to a fifty-square-foot bedroom. At the same time, this new housing type was a response to the Marxist postulate about the eventual disappearance of the private family unit and its replacement with the social unit of fellow workers. The ultimate house-commune was to contain the services of an entire neighborhood within one structure, as Fourier had proposed over half a century earlier.

Most of the research on the socialist transformation of every-day life and on the house-commune as a tool for the acceleration of this transformation was accomplished by the members of the Society of Contemporary Architects (OSA).[14] The Standardization Section of the Construction Committee (Stroikom RSFSR), organized in 1928, was headed by OSA's theoretician, Moisei Iakovlevich Ginzburg (1892–1948). Within three months, Ginzburg's group of four OSA members produced five types of housing units in several variations to be prefabricated and speedily assembled on sites all over Russia. In addition to economic and technical considerations, the housing units were to ease "the transition to a new, socially superior way of life."[15] The new house-commune, with its cultural and recreational facilities, was a major factor of social transformation. The housing units, developed by Ginzburg's Stroikom group,[16] were actually individual apartments of the so-called "transitional type," intended to help the inhabitants transcend their old habits, "overcome" their previous selves by voluntary measures, as Nietzsche had urged (*Z*, p. 75). According to Ginzburg: "It is impossible at present to compel the occupants of a building to live collectively, as some of us have intended to do in the past, usually with negative results ... We consider it absolutely necessary to incorporate certain features that would stimulate the transition to a socially superior life, stimulate, not dictate."[17]

Two of the Stroikom housing units were combined in Ginzburg and Milinis' Narkomfin (Narodnyi Komissariat Finansyi) house-commune (1928–30). Originally constructed for the Commissariat for Finances (Illustration 7.3), this communal house was taken over by the Soviet of People's Commissars (Sovnarkom). Apparently, even the members of the highest Soviet resented communal living. As Ginzburg confirmed, most of the families did not eat in the common dining room, but took their food from the communal kitchen and ate in the privacy of their small apartments.[18]

In 1926, the Society of Contemporary Architects (OSA) began the publication of its monthly magazine, *Contemporary Architecture* (*Sovremennaia arkhitektura*, abbreviated as *SA*) under

7.3 Moisei Ginzburg, Narkomfin (Sovnarkom) housing complex, Moscow, 1928–1930.

the editorship of Moisei Ginzburg. In its fourth issue, this magazine launched a public opinion poll about communal living. The six questions addressed to anyone who cared to respond were:

(1) How do you envision the physical environment of the workers' new way of life, and what do you consider unnecessary objects of petty-bourgeois origin?

(2) In your opinion which are the new aspects of the mode of living? Which new needs are already forming, and which do you consider [to be] dying out?

(3) Which aspects of everyday life should remain private, separated as personal for the individual, and which should be reorganized as collective for society?

(4) What is your opinion about communal food preparation which will free women from domestic labor ...?

(5) What is your opinion on public education and on the upbringing of children ...?

(6) Do you have any specific proposal for the organization of individual leisure?[19]

The published responses, by workers and civil servants, all hailed the freedom of women from domestic chores and the public education of children. Significantly, all insisted on preserving as much privacy for the individual as possible.

The new mode of life requires clear separation between the collective and the individual and [differentiation] between the physical environment of each. The physical environment for the personal aspects of everyday life must include everything that promotes an active will [aktivnosti voli]. The creative development of an individual demands a spacious room filled with light and sun and equipped with all the necessary furniture (well manufactured and comfortable) ... The standards for physical and intellectual labor must be somehow differentiated ...[20]

This demand for individual privacy and carefully designed environment, activating the human will, probably indicated the urban dwellers' longing for solitude, yet it sounded as an echo of Nietzsche:

Association with people imposes no mean test on my patience: my humanity does not consist in feeling with men how they are, but in enduring that I feel with them.

My humanity is constant self-overcoming.
But I need *solitude* – which is to say, recovery, return to myself, the breath of a free, light, playful air (*EH*, p. 233).

Collectivization of public life and behavior-modification of large groups was to be accomplished not in the privacy of the home but in a new building type, the worker's club. As El Lissitzky (1890–1941), a member of ASNOVA, explained:

The growing needs in this area [compelled us] to provide all the age groups of the working masses with facilities for recreation and relaxation after a day's work, i.e., a place to store up new sources of energy [soziale Kraftwerk] . . . The aim of the club is to liberate man and not oppress him as was formerly done by the Church and the State . . . These were the power sources of the old order. Their power can only be transcended by establishing new power sources belonging to our new order . . .[21]

Such a "club of a new social type" was designed in 1928 by Ivan Leonidov (1902–59), a student of Ladovsky and an OSA member. The enormous complex of educational, research, cultural, recreational, and information facilities was located in a park. "Outside the club . . . all political and economic news of the day, all the activities of the club and its scientific institutes are flashed on screens or reported over loudspeakers, for the purpose of ensuring high quality instruction and the broadest possible diffusion."[22]

The club was a participatory educational and cultural complex, where workers were not to be entertained or amused, but "should instead arrive at a realization of their potentialities by their own effort,"[23] insisted Lissitzky, echoing Nietzsche's call for self-overcoming and the God-builders' trust in man's ability to elevate himself. Although many leading architects designed workers' clubs, few integrated all "cultural activities of the workers for the constant broadening of their initiatives,"[24] as did Leonidov's 1930 project for the Palace of Culture (Illustration 7.4). Designed on the site of the former Simonov Monastery in Moscow, this club was "an organizer of the entire system of political enlightenment and cultural education in the neighborhood . . ."[25] The complex was not an architectural monument for passive contemplation, but follow-

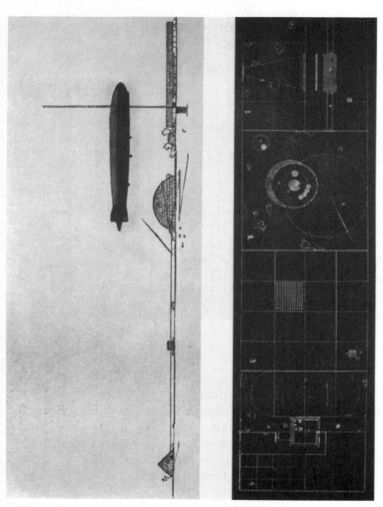

7.4 Ivan Leonidov, Project for Palace of Culture, 1930.

7.5 Ilia Golosov, Zuev Club, Moscow, 1927–1928.

ing Ladovsky's teaching, was conceived as a living architectural organism functioning integrally with the people using it, arousing their vitality, enriching their sensitivities, and developing their creative potentials.

Unfortunately, none of Leonidov's clubs was actually built, although, between 1927 and 1931, several trade unions constructed smaller clubs for their members, such as the Zuev Club (1927–28) in Moscow by Ilia Golosov (1883–1945) (Illustration 7.5). Konstantin Melnikov (1890–1974) was best known for his workers' clubs, many in Moscow – Kauchuk Factory Club (1927), Rusakov Factory Club (1927), etc. – or near Moscow – the Pravda Club (1928) for the porcelain

7.6 Konstantin Melnikov. Pravda Club for the porcelain factory in Dulevo, 1928.

7.7 The Vesnin brothers, Likhachev Factory Club, Moscow, 1930–31.

factory in Dulevo (Illustration 7.6). The Vesnin brothers, Leonid (1880–1933), Viktor (1882–1950), and Aleksandr (1883–1959) designed two of the largest clubs, the Likhachev Factory Club (1930–31; Illustration 7.7) and the Political Prisoners Club (1931–34), yet they house only a small portion of the activities envisioned in Leonidov's projects.

Thus, avant-garde architects became the "revaluators of values." Their destiny was not only to transform themselves and become creators but also to transform humankind to creative individuals. Yet, those potentially creative individuals were images "sleeping in the stone ... in the hardest, ugliest stone!" (*Z*, p. 111). Clubs, like the educational institutions, were to drill into the hardest of individuals to free their creative will. Thus, workers were to spend their free time in the club. Reading and seminar rooms, workshops and art studios, gave every worker the option to design his own educational and recreational activities. The clubs were to be managed by the workers themselves, thus releasing their abilities for self-organization and their leadership potentials.

Many proponents of the Cultural Revolution viewed it as liberation from traditional authorities, social structures, and cultural values, an ideal which meshed, not only with "Nietzschean" individuality, but also with the socialist vision of freeing humanity from the tyranny of hunger and thereby removing obstacles to creativity and personal development.

The forced collectivization of agriculture during the First Five-Year Plan (1928–32) and the resulting migration of the peasantry to towns and cities in search of industrial employment resulted in an unprecedented social change. Sheila Fitzpatrick emphasizes the "enormous upward social mobility, as peasants moved into the industrial labor force, unskilled workers became skilled, and skilled workers were promoted into white-collar managerial positions and higher education."[26] The aggressive recruitment of workers' and peasants' children into technical and higher education created a new proletarian intelligentsia. Although this mobility has been noted by Soviet and Western historians, its liberating psychological and behavioral aspects have not been adequately examined.

For centuries the family, the clan, the tribe had control over the development and the behavior of its members. Deviations from established norms, individual preferences and desires, were neither tolerated nor allowed to develop. Paradoxically, in their desire to destroy traditional social structures, including the family, which suffocated individual development, the Soviet authorities were unintentionally elevating the individual as the most important social unit. Lonely workers or peasants far away from home had neither the familiar support of relatives and friends, nor their restrictive control. In an unfamiliar urban school, or in a distant factory, or on an isolated new construction site, they were on their own. They could count only on their own resourcefulness; they could define their own preferences and behavioral norms; they were free to become individuals. Nietzsche claimed that the cultivation of obedience is due to the fact that "ever since there have been human beings there have also been human herds (family groups, communities, tribes, nations, states, churches), and always very many who obey compared with the very small number of those who command" (*BGE*, p. 102).

Those who command were not only few, but also far away in Moscow and usually behind the Kremlin walls. New factories and new industrial towns spreading all over the country were competing to attract a labor force from the dislocated rural population. Housing to accommodate these peasants-turned-workers was urgently needed. This housing, the architects believed, should transform the unconstrained peasants into the creators of the new civilization. Their faith did not find support in Marx's contempt for the peasant, but in Nietzsche's tribute to him:

I think the finest and dearest man today is a healthy peasant, uncouth, cunning, obstinate, enduring: that is the noblest type today. The peasant is the finest man today; and the peasantry should be master! (*Z*, p. 258).

The so-called "socialist transformation of everyday life" ("sotsialisticheskaia rekonstruktsiia byta") became especially important during the Cultural Revolution. Russian horizons of expectation helped channel the reception of Nietzsche and provided guidance for transforming human herds into self-confident workers building new settlements and a new civilization. During the course of 1929, Ginzburg and many OSA members abandoned the communal house as a "superior way of living" in favor of a separate house for each individual as the most appropriate environment to "**liberate the personality and create optimum conditions for its full development**."[27] The impetus for this new search came within the Section for Socialist Resettlement, organized in 1929 as part of the State Planning Commission (Gosplan), the most powerful organization for economic development. The same year Ginzburg's research group was moved from the auspices of the Russian Republic to the Section for Socialist Resettlement in order to participate in the physical planning of the entire Soviet Union.[28] The theoretician of the Section, economist Mikhail (or Moisei) A. Okhitovich (1896–1937), joined the Society of Contemporary Architects and published his "Notes on the Theory of Resettlement" in the Society's periodical *SA*.

Reviewing the historic development of human societies, Okhitovich concluded that:

working together led in primitive societies to residing together. In contemporary society, however, working together with others promotes the development of the individual person [lichnost']. Man is born individually, not collectively. He eats, drinks, sleeps, dresses, etc. – in other words he *consumes* always individually. The higher the society develops, the greater the right of the individual to consume; let us not forget that socialism means *abundance* of goods ... With the disappearance of private property disappears only the bourgeois, capitalist form of personality; but personal property, personal consumption, personal initiative, personal legs, personal head and brain, these will not disappear ... Individualism is the product of technical, not social division of labor. Proclaiming individualism, without recognizing its debt to society, as does Max Stirner, means being enthusiastic about the effect while holding the cause in contempt. Praising the [social] collective, and ignoring the individual, is like eulogizing the Russian language while forbidding the pronunciation of [separate] Russian words. This is how our contemporary Stirnerists [Stirneriantsy] have turned upside down this specific brand of Proudhonian communalism ...

The individual is not a mathematical unit [to be counted, reported in statistics, etc.] but an [independent] social unit ...[29]

Thus Okhitovich offered a Marxist justification of the individualism associated with Nietzsche. Okhitovich defined the development of personal aptitudes and talents as an outcome of and a necessity for technological development and progress. He distinguished between the selfish egotism of capitalist society and the self-realization, individual growth, and free choice made possible by socialism. Okhitovich probably shared Nietzsche's belief that "people were the creators at first; only later were there individual creators. Indeed, the individual himself is still the latest creation" (Z, p. 85).

The Section for Socialist Resettlement was to find solutions to the pressing problem of urbanization and to develop a conceptual scheme for the future transformation of the Soviet Union to an industrialized communist state. The Section's proposal called "socialist population resettlement" was a theoretical solution eliminating the conflict between town and village which Karl Marx attributed to the antagonistic classes of the capitalist system and which Friedrich Engels foresaw disappearing under socialism. The proposed resettlement system assumed the withering of the capitalist city and village. Instead, it offered a uniform dispersion of the urban and rural population over the entire Soviet territory, thereby creating a townless, fully decentralized, and evenly populated country. This process of deurbanism was already evident in advanced industrial countries (especially in Australia and north America), Okhitovich pointed out, and was due to man's natural desire to "return to nature," an inclination which now could be fulfilled by new means of transportation.[30] The Constructivist architects supporting Okhitovich's theory of deurbanism found several occasions to transform the theoretical premises into actual design proposals. The best examples are two 1929 competition projects, one for a model Green City (designed by Moisei Ginzburg and Mikhail Barshch) and the other for the new town of Magnitogorsk (by Moisei Okhitovich, Mikhail Barshch and others). With Promethean zeal both projects scattered the population over the land and replaced the individual room of the communal house with a separate dwelling for each individual. The slogan of both was: not communal houses but "community of houses." In Ginzburg's words:

The house-commune canonized a pre-determined way of life for its inhabitants; in contrast, these two projects upheld the principle of providing options for a variety of free associations among the people who are housed together. The actual mode of living would generate a variety of solutions in various forms depending on the individual peculiarities, interests, needs and possibilities of the inhabitant in each dwelling.

The Magnitogorsk project resolved the above problem in the following manner: a free-standing dwelling for each human being if he lives alone; free-standing dwellings for groups of various sizes, from one couple to any desired fraternity – professional or voluntary union of co-workers; yet in all cases a separate dwelling, surrounded by space and greenery, permeated by light and sun, freed from being squeezed into the narrow limits of the city block.[31]

This vision of freedom to create and to live alone in light and sun is an echo of Nietzsche's thoughts on the need for solitude (*EH*, p. 233). The designers of Magnitogorsk, squeezed in Moscow's crowded quarters, were probably thinking like Nietzsche:

But where is your inner worth when you no longer know what it means to breathe freely? When you no longer have the slightest control over yourselves? ... Against all this, everyone should think in his heart: Sooner emigrate and in savage fresh regions seek to become master of the world, and above all *master* of myself; keep changing location as long as a single sign of slavery still beckons to me ...[32]

The housing units for Magnitogorsk were easy to move and to assemble. Only the structural parts were standardized. Thus, the authors of the project offered choices according to personal taste, as well as the possibility of changing the dwelling over time (Illustrations 7.8 and 7.9). "Taste changes, culture changes, prosperity changes; the dwelling should also grow and change ..."[33] The explanatory notes to this project contain many assertions about the importance and the rights of the individual, and above all, his right to associate with others by his free will. For example:

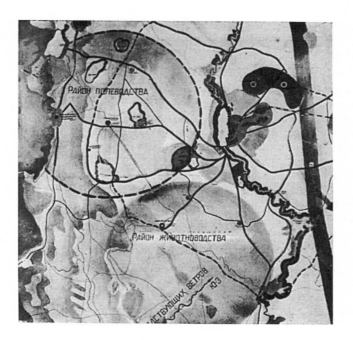

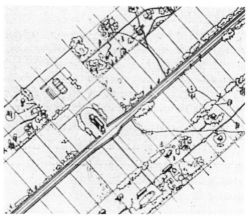

7.8 Moisei Okhitovich, Mikhail Barshch, Nikolai Sokolov, Viacheslav Vladimirov, Nina Vorotyntseva, Competition project for the new town of Magnitogorsk, 1930.

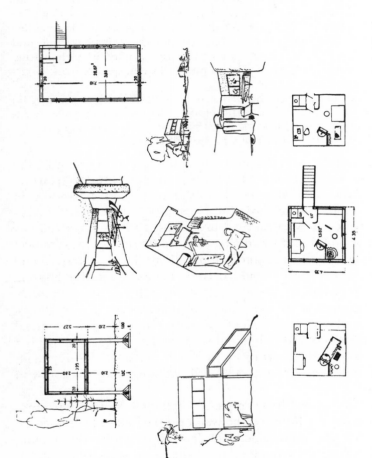

7.9 Moisei Okhitovich, Mikhail Barshch, Nikolai Sokolov, Viacheslav Vladimirov, Nina Vorotyntseva, Competition project for the new town of Magnitogorsk, 1930. Housing units.

One's personality could develop fully and completely in no other place except one's own home.[34]

and:

Personal preferences are expressed not only in food and clothing but also in the dwelling: in its size, form, arrangement, remodeling. The dwelling is not only a place for sleeping, but also a place for creative work ... The bonds with society are not in sleeping, sitting, and staying together, not in consuming together, but are in participating in the common process of production, even when [people work] apart from each other ...

We abolished only the personal household but not the person; actually not even individual property ... we design a separate dwelling for the individual worker, yet we realize that nothing prevents him from joining his dwelling to those of others.[35]

To accomplish this voluntary organization of communities the architects designed ribbons of individual cottages, starting from Magnitogorsk's industrial complex, and expanding in many directions towards future employment centers (industrial parks, mining, agriculture). The authors relied on the necessity of building roads and infrastructure to connect employment centers and supply them with materials and goods. These roads would become logical spines for housing development. The system would eventually distribute industry and people evenly over the entire territory. The cottages, supported on stilts and floating above ground, could be joined together or erected individually, thus identifying each member of society and allowing for privacy, personal development, intellectual growth, and, above all, voluntary association with others.

In the "Green City Project," explained Moisei Ginzburg, "where up to a hundred thousand people had to be housed on a limited site, the problem [of density] was solved by joining the dwelling units into long rows and at the same time providing daylight and contact with the open space and greenery on two opposite sides [of each dwelling]."[36]

These continuous ribbons of housing units raised on stilts could be erected quickly with minimal disturbance of the land (Illustrations 7.10, 7.11, 7.12). At the same time the space

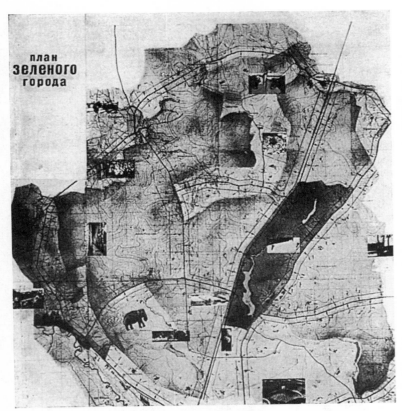

план
зеленого
города

7.10 Moisei Ginzburg, Mikhail Barshch, Competition project for Green City, 1930. Master plan.

under the units provided covered pedestrian walkways on the ground and secured unobstructed view and privacy for the individual inhabitants above. Each unit, glassed entirely front and back, "looks spacious and closely related to nature. Sunrise and sunset, nature all around – these are not luxuries but the satisfaction of undeniable human needs ... The window walls could fold and the housing unit transformed to a covered terrace surrounded by greenery. The room almost loses its specific geometric form and dissolves into nature ... The dwelling becomes linked with limitless space ..."[37]

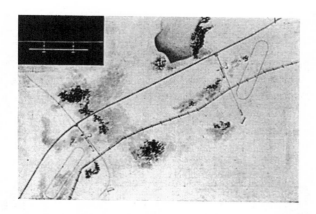

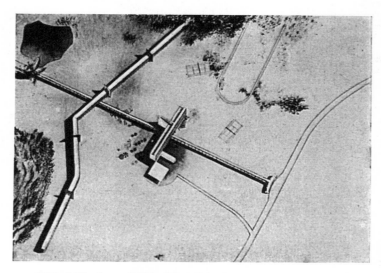

7.11 Moisei Ginzburg, Mikhail Barshch, Competition project for Green City, 1930. Linear arrangement of housing units parallel to roads.

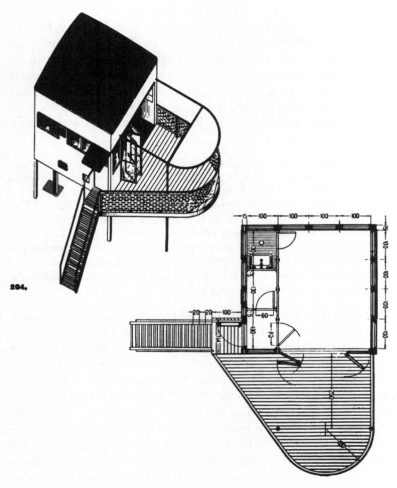

7.12 Moisei Ginzburg, Mikhail Barshch, Competition project for Green
City, 1930. Housing units.

The Green City competition, sponsored by the Moscow Communal Economic Administration, was actually for the design of a summer resort in the outskirts of Moscow. Ginzburg and Barshch, however, took this opportunity to demonstrate how Moscow itself could be transformed into a socialist city by decentralizing industry and by dispersing its population. They argued that well designed dwellings in constant contact with nature would transform the Russian cities into year-round resorts.

When a man is sick, he is given medicine, but prevention is better than cure ... When a city is in a bad shape ... noise, dust, lack of light, air, and sun, etc., it is necessary to administer medicine: a summer cottage, a health resort, a vacation in A GREEN CITY. This is the medicine ... This dual system of poison and antidote is precisely the capitalist system of contradiction. It should be compared with the socialist system – prophylactics, a system requiring the destruction of the city ... and the resettlement of mankind in a way that solves the problem of labor, rest, and culture as a single continuous process of socialist living ...[38]

This grandiose project replaced all existing concepts of human settlements with "a new universe in which every single conquest of the human genius will be fully utilized," an idea Ginzburg had already expressed in his 1924 treatise *Style and Epoch*.[39] Was Nietzsche among these conquests? Ginzburg's argument sounds like Nietzsche's: "What at home began to degenerate into dangerous discontent and criminal tendencies will, once outside, gain a wild and beautiful naturalness and be called heroism."[40] Ginzburg was assured by Oswald Spengler that Russia would be the cradle of the new civilization following the decline of Western (or "Faustian") culture. The Russian translation of *The Decline of the West* appeared in 1923, just as Ginzburg was working on his treatise and naming Spengler as one of his sources. Other Constructivist theoreticians, such as Nilolai Tarabukin, also drew on Spengler to support their arguments.[41]

The visionary schemes for a new way of life were not the lonely attempt of a small group of architects to project their imagination into a foreseeable future. During the Cultural

Revolution specialists in many fields, as well as complete amateurs, made proposals for new communities and for new ways of living. And, more surprisingly, the antiurbanists' research was supported by important state agencies, patronized by high officials, and accepted even by the Communist Party because it broadly corresponded with the utopian vision implicit in the Party's First Five-Year Plan.[42] Sabsovich had an official post in the State Planning Commission (Gosplan), Ginzburg headed the State research laboratory, and Nikolai Miliutin, another supporter of individual dwelling units, chaired the Section on Socialist Resettlement, Housing, and Way of Life of the Communist Academy's Institute of Economics. Miliutin, who also edited the periodical *Soviet Architecture* (*Sovetskaia arkhitektura*), aired his own view on housing in the first issue of this journal:

The dwelling unit ... should serve not only for sleeping, as some authors believe. It must serve for: (1) sleep; (2) learning; (3) individual rest and eating; (4) keeping personal belongings; (5) personal hygiene, etc ...
   Each dwelling unit, with no exception, must always house one single individual regardless of who is going to use it and how; therefore, each unit should have a separate entrance.[43]

Miliutin's schemes for socialist towns (Sotsgorod), however, consisted of large communal houses with individual rooms. Still, he published in the same issue the views of other architectural factions more interested in the welfare of the individual than the collective. Nikolai Ladovsky insisted that the "organization of the dwelling of everyday life is much more complex than it seems at a superficial glance. Differences among people depend on work, age, physiology, psychology; there are also the elderly, the handicapped, etc.; and all require different, not the same, type of housing ..."[44]
   In their declaration of 1931 the Constructivists restated their concerns for individual freedom more emphatically:

We consider the highest social form of living not the old-fashioned family structure and not the forced communal life with its mechanically grouped people but a new mode of voluntary bond on the basis of common work and cultural interest, on personal companionship and intimacy between individuals, because only such associations could facilitate the maximum blossoming of each person and consequently the blossoming of the collective society ... Each dwelling is a manifestation of an individual's personality or, if inhabited by a group, of a social personality ...[45]

The Central Committee of the Bolshevik Party demonstrated its support for individual homes in the 1930 Decree by attacking the supporters of super-collectivization and the construction of large communal houses.

The Central Committee notes that along with the movement for a socialist way of life there are highly ill-founded, semi-fantastic, and, hence, extremely harmful attempts of certain comrades (Sabsovich, Larin, etc.) to surmount "in one leap" all the obstacles on the road to the socialist reconstruction of everyday life, obstacles rooted ... in the economic and cultural backwardness of the country ... These attempts ... are linked with recently-published projects for ... complete collectivization of every aspect of the workers' life: feeding, housing, education ... etc. ...[46]

The decree required new rules "for the construction of workers' settlements and individual homes," demanded "green belts to be provided between the industrial and residential zones," and encouraged "the construction of housing through building cooperatives using the resources of the population itself."[47] This decision of the Central Committee encouraged the organization of a shareholding company "Green City" which approved thirteen of the original sixty-one standardized units proposed in the Green City Competition for experimental construction at one sector of the Green City site.[48] This shareholding company founded a Brigade for Socialist Resettlement (including OSA members headed by Ginzburg and Okhitovich) to supervise construction, although only a few units were actually constructed during 1931.[49] Paradoxically, the promotion of individualism and personal creative development by this group was not attacked in any of the Party decrees guiding the architectural changes during the early 1930s. Only the rival architectural organization, the Union of Proletarian Architects (Vsesoiuznoe Obedinenie Proletarskykh Arkhitektorov, abbreviated as VOPRA), launched a campaign against the Constructivists. Founded in 1929 by young militant architects, VOPRA was involved mainly in political rhetoric and criticism. Sabsovich was criticized as a "petit-bourgeois revisionist" for his assertion that "the collective is something external to the individual."[50] The theory of deurbanism and population resettlement was denounced as "Chaianovism" (that is, promoting Aleksandr Chaianov's peasant anarchism),[51] Okhitovich was accused of "wild Trotskyism,"[52] and Ginzburg's defense of individual dwelling was castigated as a "typical Kautsky Menshevik argument."[53]

Nietzsche was never mentioned either by promoters or by critics of individualism. Yet the Rationalists' and Constructivists' persistent experiments with the psychological transformation of man through creative design were strikingly Nietzschean. Architects, knowingly or not, echoed Nietzsche's view that "the conditions [exist] for the production of a stronger type, we are now able to comprehend and consciously *will*; we are able to create the conditions under which such an elevation is possible" (*WP*, p. 477).

The resurgence of individualism and the architects' attentiveness to individual needs and personal freedom occurred within the particular atmosphere of Russia's Cultural Revolution. Many Soviet and Western scholars have simply dismissed this non-Marxist trend either as petit-bourgeois or as utopian. Some explain the failure of the entire Modernist movement in Russia by economic and technical deficiencies,[54] others blame Stalinism and the conservatism of his bureaucracy.[55] S. Frederick Starr relates these visionary proposals to "the romantic anarchism that flowered so luxuriantly during the years 1929 and 1930"[56] and to a psychological crisis among the architects, a "wishful attempt to liberate themselves from the impending threat of being swallowed by an impersonal and centralized union dominated by their opponents,"[57] the members of VOPRA, many of whom became leaders in Stalin's Socialist Realism.

As previously stated, these arguments are tinted by knowledge of subsequent developments, for during the Cultural Revolution no one could have predicted the events of Stalin's era. Indeed, the first Five-Year Plan prompted many to believe that the Dictatorship of the Proletariat would soon be over and with rapid industrialization the country would be transformed to a social paradise.[58] Rapid industrialization and collectivization of agriculture had set the rural population in motion, dislocating family members, and resettling peasants on new construction sites away from family, kin, and tribe. Children of deserving workers and peasants sent during the 1920s to colleges and universities in distant cities were graduating and filling ranks of the Cadres.[59] The mobility of the population found expression in the design of almost movable homes.

A disguised individualism actually continued during the 1930s. For the selected few this individualism was expressed in private dachas surrounded by nature. For the masses such individualism took the form of an individual facade with "its unique architectural appearance" for each apartment building. Furthermore, all new housing had to consist of separate apartments for individual families.[60] Although this decree made it imperative for new housing to have separate apartments, housing shortages, especially in large cities, forced families to share apartments. Architecture continued to be regarded as the leading art, though not for the creation of a new civilization but for the ornamentation (*oformlenie*) of engineering structures. The Moscow subway testifies to what Spengler calls "meaningless, empty, artificial, pretentious architecture and ornament,"[61] marking the final stages in the decline of a civilization.

NOTES

1 A. Lunacharskii, "Tezisi khudozhestvennogo sectora NKP i Ts. K. Rabis ob osnovakh politiki v oblasti iskusstva," *Iskusstvo* 1 (1921), p. 20.

2 Five volumes of Bakunin's *Selected Works* (*Izbrannye sochineniia*) were published between 1919 and 1922, followed in 1923–28 by three volumes of *Materials for the Biography of M. Bakunin* (*Materialy dlia biografii M. Bakunina*), and several collections of his works. In addition, numerous biographies of Bakunin appeared during the 1920s and 1930s. Petr Kropotkin, who returned to Russia in

June 1917 and died there in February 1921, saw many of his works published in Russian for the first time, starting in 1918 with his *Fields, Factories, and Workshops*. Richard Wagner's *Art and Revolution* (1849) was translated into Russian in 1906. For Wagner's influence in Russia, see Bernice G. Rosenthal, "Wagner and Wagnerian Ideas in Russia," *Wagnerism in European Culture and Politics*, ed. David Large and William Weber (Ithaca, 1984).

3 *Goroda sotsialisma i sotsialisticheskaia rekonstruktsiia byta* (*Socialist Cities and the Reconstruction of Everyday Life*, ed. B. Lunin (Moscow, 1930), p. 3.

4 A. Kuprin, "A Toast," *Pre-Revolutionary Russian Science Fictions: An Anthology* (*Seven Utopias and a Dream*), ed. Leland Fetzer (Ann Arbor, MI, 1982), p. 183.

5 Oswald Spengler, *The Decline of the West*, trans. Charles Francis Atkinson (New York, 1932), p. 129. I am indebted to Bernice Glatzer Rosenthal for drawing attention to Spengler's influence in Russia.

6 Ibid., p. 224.

7 In 1926 Berlin's *Wasmuth's Monats Hefte* had 600 subscribers in the Soviet Union, followed in popularity by *Städtebau* and *Der Industriebau*. From England came the *Architectural Review*, *The Architect*, and *The Studio*; from France, *La Construction moderne*, *Le génie civil*, *L'Architecture*, and *Art et decoration*; from the United States, *American Architect*, *Architectural Forum*, *Engineering News Records*, *Pencil Points*. See A. I. Dimitriev, "Inostrannye arkhitekturnye zhurnaly," *Stroitelnaia promyshlennost'* 10 (1926), pp. 738–39.

8 Originally the Commission consisted of one sculptor, Boris D. Korolev (1884–1963) and seven architects, among them Nikolai Ladovsky and his lifelong friend Vladimir F. Krinsky (1890–1971). Before the end of 1919 the group included Alexander Rodchenko, Aleksandr Shevchenko, and, according to some sources, also Liubov Popova and Nadezhda Udaltsova.

9 N. Ladovskii, "Credo," *Mastera sovetskoi arkhitektury ob arkhitekture*, I, ed. M. G. Barkhin (Moscow, 1975), p. 344.

10 N. Ladovskii, "O programme rabochei gruppy arkhitektorov," ibid., pp. 346–47.

11 The Higher State Art-Technical Studios (Vkhutemas) were founded in 1920 through the reorganization of the Free State Art Studios (SVOMAS). The latter were the outcome of the integration in 1918 of the Moscow Institute of Painting, Sculpture and Architecture, and the Stroganov School of Art and Applied Art.

12 "Deklaratsiia ARU," *Ezhegodnik literatury i iskusstva na 1929 god* (Moscow, 1929), pp. 552–55. Ladovsky's theory of the psycho-

logical influence of architecture was influenced by the research of Wilhelm Max Wundt, the founder of physiological psychology.

For Ladovsky's work see Milka Bliznakov, "Nikolai Ladovsky: The Search for a Rational Science of Architecture," *Soviet Union/Union Sovietique* 7, part 1–2 (1980), pp. 170–96.

13 This 1927 design is illustrated in N. Ladovskii, "Proekt planirovki trudkommuny Kostino," *Stroitelstvo Moskvy* 7 (1929), pp. 14–17.

14 OSA was annexed at the time of its foundation in 1925 to the State Academy of Artistic Sciences (GAKhN). Among its founding members were the Vesnin brothers, the Golosov brothers: Panteleimon (1882–1945) and Ilia (1883–1945), and the economist Leonid M. Sabsovich.

15 Moisei Ginzburg, "Slushali: problemy tipizatsii zhilia RSFSR," *SA* 1 (1929), p. 4. An in-depth study of the Stroikom units is in Anatole Kopp, *Town and Revolution: Soviet Architecture and City Plan* (London, 1970), pp. 130–44.

16 The group consisted of M. Barshch, V. Vladimirov, A. Pasternak, and G. Sum-Shchik.

17 Ginzburg, "Slushali: Problemy tipizatsii zhilia RSFSR," p. 5.

18 M. Ginzburg, *Zhilishche* (Moscow, 1934), p. 82.

19 *SA* 4 (1926), p. 109. The same questionnaire was republished in *SA* 5–6 (1926), p. 111 and in *SA* 3 (1927), p. 102. An additional seven questions were addressed to construction specialists and dealt with materials and methods of construction. A translation of the entire questionnaire is in Kopp, *Town and Revolution*, p. 246.

20 From O. D. Kameneva's response, *SA* 1 (1927), p. 24.

21 El Lissitzky, *Russland, Die Rekonstruktion der Architektur in der Sowjetunion* (Vienna, 1930), quoted from *Russia: An Architecture for World Revolution*, trans. Eric Dluhosch (Cambridge, MA, 1970), pp. 43–44.

22 Ivan Leonidov, "Organizatsia raboty kluba novovo sotsialnovo typa," *SA* 3 (1929), pp. 106–13. The facilities included laboratories, lectures, museums, exhibitions, sports, games, military exercises, meetings, sociopolitical campaigns, action campaigns for a new way of life, competitions, cinematic exhibitions of new films, a planetarium, etc.

23 El Lissitzky, *Russia*, p. 44.

24 Ivan Leonidov, "Dvorets Kultury," *SA* 5 (1930), p. 4.

25 Ibid., p. 4.

26 Sheila Fitzpatrick, "Editor's Introduction," *Cultural Revolution in Russia, 1928–1931* (Bloomington, 1978), p. 3.

27 Ginzburg, *Zhilishche*, p. 148. Bold face in original.

28 Among the Constructivist members of the section were: K. N. Afanasev, M. O. Barshch, V. N. Vladimirov, I. F. Milinis, S. V. Orlov, G. G. Savinov, N. B. Sokolov, G. A. Zunblat.
29 M. Okhitovich, "Zametki po teorii rasseleniia," *SA* 1–2 (1930), pp. 12–13. Okhitovich's editorial in the same issue, "Kuda idti," is translated in Kopp, *Town and Revolution*, Appendix 4.
30 M. Okhitovich, "Ne gorod a novyi tip rasseleniia," *Goroda sotsializma i sotsialisticheskaia rekonstruktsiia byta*, pp. 153–55. The deurbanist movement is discussed in M. Bliznakov, "Urban Planning in the USSR: Integrative Theories," *The City in Russian History*, ed. M. Hamm (Lexington, KY, 1976), pp. 243–56.
31 Ginzburg, *Zhilishche*, p. 148.
32 Nietzsche, *The Dawn* in *The Portable Nietzsche*, trans. Walter Kaufman (New York, 1968), pp. 90–91.
33 M. Barshch, V. Vladimirov, M. Okhitovich, N. Sokolov; with G. G. Vegman, N. P. Vorotyntseva, Kalinin, Pavlov, A. L. Pasternak, G. G. Savinov, "Magnitogorsk," *SA* 1–2 (1930), p. 48.
34 Ibid., p. 54.
35 Ibid., pp. 55–56.
36 Ginzburg, *Zhilishche*, p. 148.
37 M. Barshch and M. Ginzburg, "Zelenyi gorod. Sotsialisticheskaia rekonstruktsiia Moskvy," *SA* 1–2 (1930), p. 31.
38 Ibid., p. 17. The argument in favor of deurbanism is discussed at length in Kopp, *Town and Revolution*, pp. 178–84.
39 Moisei Ia. Ginzburg, *Stil i Epokha* (Moscow, 1924), p. 148. The influence of Spengler is discussed by Anatole Senkevich, Jr., in his introduction to the English publication of this book. Moisei Ginzburg, *Style and Epoch* (Cambridge, MA, 1982), pp. 23–25.
40 Nietzsche, *Dawn*, p. 91.
41 N. Tarabukin, *Ot molberta k mashine* (Moscow, 1923).
42 The official support lent to radical antiurbanist proposals is convincingly demonstrated in S. Frederick Starr, "Visionary Town Planning during the Cultural Revolution," *Cultural Revolution in Russia 1928–1931*, ed. Sheila Fitzpatrick (Bloomington, IN, 1978), pp. 207–40.
43 N. Miliutin, "Zhilishchno-bytovoe stroitelstva SSSR," *Sovetskaia arkhitektura* 1–2 (1931), pp. 3–4.
44 N. Ladovsky, "Planirovka Avtostroia i Magnitogorska v Uze," *Sovetskaia arkhitektura* 1–2 (1931), p. 22.
45 SASS (Sektor Arkhitektorov Sotsialisticheskogo Stroitelstvo), "Na novom etape," *Sovetskaia arkhitektura* 1–2 (1931), p. 101.
46 Decree of TsK VKP (b). "O Rabote po perestroike byta," published in *Pravda*, May 29, 1930, immediately reprinted in *SA*

1–2 (1930), p. 3. It is translated in full in Kopp, *Town and Revolution*, Appendix 10.

47 Kopp, *Town and Revolution*, p. 260.

48 "Protokol No. 38 Rasporiaditelnogo zasedaniia prezidiuma Gosplana RSFSR. 4 Oktiabria 1930," *SA* 6 (1930), p. 17.

49 Two of the erected housing units are illustrated in S. O. Khan-Magomedow, *Pioniere der sowjetischen Architektur* (Dresden, 1983), p. 387.

50 A. Mikhailov, "VOPRA," *Sovetskaia arkhitektura* 3 (1930), p. 53.

51 E. Iaroslavskii, "The Dreams of the Chaianovs and Soviet Reality," *Pravda*, October 18, 1930, as quoted in Starr, "Visionary Town Planning," p. 238. Aleksandr Chaianov, an agricultural economist, wrote in 1920 an anarchist utopia *Journey of my Brother Alexei to the Land of Peasant Utopia*, where the Moscow of 1984 had been transformed into a large park with small communities set in it. Though better known for his economic theories, Chaianov wrote several fictional works and novels during the 1920s. He died in a concentration camp in 1939.

52 "Deklaratsia VOPRA" (VOPRA's Declaration), as translated in Kopp, *Town and Revolution*, p. 213.

53 Mikhailov, "VOPRA," pp. 53–54. Okhitovich responded to this accusation in "Marksistkaia zashchita kommunalnogo sotsializma," *SA* 5 (1930), p. 6. Okhitovich probably died in a concentration camp in 1937.

54 See, for example, Bruno Zevi, *Storia dell' architettura moderna* (Turin, 1950). The author accuses the Modern architects of designing in complete disregard of the actual technical and economic conditions in Russia at the time.

55 Kopp, *Town and Revolution*, pp. 227–28.

56 Starr, "Visionary Town Planning," p. 222.

57 Ibid., p. 224.

58 Leonard Moiseevich Sabsovich, a member of Gosplan and the leading spokesman for the urbanist faction of the town planning movement, insisted that within only fifteen years, the Soviet Union would become a federation of small agro-industrial towns. See his *SSSR Cherez 15 let. Gipoteza generalnogo plana, kak plan postroeniia sotsialisma v SSSR* (Moscow, 1929).

59 Sheila Fitzpatrick, *Education and Social Mobility in the Soviet Union, 1921–1934* (Cambridge, MA, 1979).

60 "O tipe zhilogo doma" (Decree of July 14, 1932), *Stroitelstvo Moskvy* 8–9 (1932), page opposite 1.

61 Spengler, *Decline of the West*, Table II.

CHAPTER 8

Nietzscheanism and the return of Pushkin in twentieth-century Russian culture (1899–1937)*

Irina Paperno

This study reveals the presence of Nietzschean ideas in one of the central paradigms of Russian culture – the twentieth-century cult of Pushkin. My method can be best described by a metaphor suggested by John Foster: digging up the buried Nietzsche. Believing that symbolic thinking and rhetorical organization are among the driving forces of intellectual history, I proceed by uncovering Nietzschean associations contained in the conceptual structure, phraseology and imagery of the debates on Pushkin in the first third of the twentieth century.

The image of Pushkin as the progenitor of Russian culture and as the absolute expression of the Russian spirit, present in Russian culture since the 1830s, acquired special meaning and significance at the beginning of the twentieth century. For contemporaries, the new era, with its dramatic historical developments and artistic and spiritual revival, appeared as a clear parallel to the beginning of the nineteenth century – the glorious Age of Pushkin. The desire to relate the two periods, viewed as the Golden and Silver Ages of Russian culture respectively, and to revive (or relive) the Age of Pushkin left a powerful imprint on the culture of the time.[1] Students of twentieth-century culture speak of the myth of "centennial return" as an integral part of the cultural self-consciousness.[2] In this atmosphere, Pushkin emerged as one of the dominant cultural symbols and assumed a mythic role. The established term for this phenomenon is Pushkinism, or Pushkinianism, a concept which connotes a cult of Pushkin with overtones of religious worship. In the words of Lidia Ginzburg, Pushkinism was "a system of values of a liturgical type."[3] It involved an attitude toward Pushkin, the poet and the man, as a universal model for the resolution of an infinite variety of literary and real-life problems.

The chronological boundaries of this phenomenon are roughly marked by two anniversaries and the cultural events surrounding them: the Centennial of Pushkin's birth in 1899 and the Centennial of Pushkin's death in 1937. Having arisen around the turn of the century, the cult of Pushkin extended into the 1920s and '30s; it demonstrates the essential continuity of Silver Age and Soviet culture.

A Nietzschean undercurrent can be discerned in the very idea of the return of the Pushkin Age that emerged at the turn of the century, as this return can be viewed as a manifestation of Nietzsche's doctrine of "eternal recurrence." The vagueness of Nietzsche's concept of "eternal recurrence" invited various, and at times idiosyncratic, interpretations. One of them, the notion of the circular movement of time ("the ring of recurrence"), implied that each moment in the present recreated a moment in the past and thus viewed "eternal recurrence" as a repetition of both history and individual life.[4] This interpretation also involved the belief in the resurgence of past cultures in contemporary life. Nietzsche in *The Birth of Tragedy* proclaimed his belief in the imminent rebirth, or return, of Greek antiquity. A Russian equivalent was the expectation of the return of the Golden Age of Russian culture, a sentiment supported by the atmosphere of the Centennial of Pushkin's birth that coincided with the turn of the century. The analogy between the Age of Pushkin and ancient Greece and a view of Pushkin as "an ancient Hellene" became commonplace. Thus, in Russian culture, Nietzschean "eternal recurrence" appeared as "centennial return" – the return of the Age of Pushkin.

While the cult of Pushkin was reinforced by Nietzschean influence, Nietzsche's ideas received additional corroboration in the Pushkinian connection. The men of the Silver Age "recognized" in Nietzsche a Russian prototype – Pushkin. It was Dmitri Merezhkovsky who established the image of

Pushkin as a Russian equivalent of Nietzsche. Merezhkovsky's 1896 essay "Pushkin" (reprinted in *Eternal Companions* [*Vechnye sputniki*], 1899), written at the height of his Nietzschean period, can be regarded as the first text of Pushkinism. Merezhkovsky doubtless had in mind Dostoevsky's speech at the dedication of the Pushkin monument in 1880, in which Dostoevsky defined the essence of Pushkin – the "prophetic revelation" in Russian life – as his ability to resolve the world's contradictions and reconcile opposites, and saw in this the universal character of Pushkin's genius; Pushkin is a universal man (in Dostoevsky's words, "vsechelovek"). Merezhkovsky offered a Nietzschean interpretation of Dostoevsky's thesis: Pushkin is a Russian solution to the tragedy of dualism dramatized by Nietzsche and symbolized by the Apollonian–Dionysian polarity, a creative genius capable of synthesizing an antithesis into a unity, of reconciling such opposites as paganism and Christianity, spirit and flesh, art and life, the East and the West (or Russia and the West), and the ultimate opposing forces – Dostoevsky's God-man and Man-God "Bogochelovek i Chelovekobog", or Nietzsche's Apollo and Dionysus, or Christ and Antichrist. In this sense, Merezhkovsky saw in Pushkin a genius who transcended Nietzsche (before Nietzsche), or who was, in a manner of speaking, super-Nietzsche.

Moreover, for Merezhkovsky, Pushkin represented an embodiment of a major Nietzschean value: cultural creativity. Treating Pushkin as the creator of Russian culture, Merezhkovsky perceived an affinity between Pushkin and Peter the Great, whom he regarded as the ultimate manifestation of the Nietzschean superhuman creative will in European history.[5]

Discussing Nietzschean ideas in the introduction to his book *L. Tolstoi and Dostoevsky* (*L. Tolstoi i Dostoevskii. Zhizn' i tvorchestvo*, 1900), Merezhkovsky wrote: "For us, Russians, the appearance of the new Apollo and Dionysus had a special significance for it reminded us of the vision of the young Pushkin [...]" He then quoted Pushkin's poem "In the Beginning of My Life I Remember a School ..." ("V nachale zhizni shkolu pomniu ia ..., 1830) with its images of two Greek gods, Apollo and, most probably, Dionysus (the statues in the garden). As if defending Nietzsche against his Russian critics, Merezhkovsky affirmed that "what could be taken for something alien, foreign, sickly-decadent, Nietzschean is our very own, native, eternal, Russian, Pushkinian, what we had, have and will have."[6] Consequently, the appearance of Nietzsche in Russian culture can be viewed as a return of the Russian prophet of Apollo and Dionysus – Pushkin. Thus, the two symbols – Pushkin and Nietzsche – appear to be interchangeable. In the cultural mythology of the Silver Age the image of Pushkin acquired stable Nietzschean connotations and "Pushkin" was frequently used as a codeword for Nietzsche.[7]

For many Symbolists, a Nietzschean interpretation of Pushkin's image involved a view of the artist in general and of Pushkin in particular as Nietzsche's Superman (*sverkhchelovek*). Andrey Bely, in his collection of essays, *Arabesques* (1911), developed an esthetic doctrine based partly on Nietzsche. He viewed art (Symbolist art) as the creation of life, of the new world, and of the new man. He asserted that the artist must create in himself, through his art, an image of the man of the future, make himself into a Nietzschean Superman, or a "new man." Even though Bely did not directly refer to Pushkin, Pushkin's image was implicitly present in his theory. The title of Bely's collection refers to Gogol's collection of essays, *Arabesques* (1835). Bely replayed Gogol's ideas, which were presented in terms of German Romanticism, in a Symbolist and Nietzschean key. The focal point of Gogol's *Arabesques* is his essay "A Few Words about Pushkin" ("Neskol'ko slov o Pushkine," 1832), in the opening lines of which he introduced the concept of Pushkin as the new Russian man essential for the fulfillment of Russia's historical mission: "Pushkin is an extraordinary phenomenon. He is perhaps a unique revelation of the Russian spirit: he is a Russian man in the ultimate stage of development, such a person as may appear two hundred years from now." Subsequent generations of Russian writers viewed these words as prophetic. Dostoevsky opened his speech on Pushkin with these words; Merezhkovsky used the same words for the opening of his essay "Pushkin." Viewed against this background, Pushkin assumed for Bely the role of the Nietzschean new man.

To summarize, in Silver Age culture an array of Nietzschean themes became an inextricable part of Pushkinism: the eternal recurrence, deliberate cultural creation, the view of Pushkin as a reconciler of opposites, and a view of Pushkin as Superman, or a Nietzschean new man. These themes received further development in the culture of the 1920s and '30s; their treatment varied with the circumstances and context in which they appeared. In postrevolutionary culture Pushkin became a symbol in relation to which contemporaries interpreted the Revolution and established their ideological allegiances.

The February 1921 commemoration in Petrograd of the eighty-fourth anniversary of Pushkin's death called forth some of the most important reactions to the birth of Soviet culture on the part of the prerevolutionary cultural elite. For many of them it marked the death of an era of Russian culture.[8] Aleksandr Blok gave a speech "On the Calling of the Poet" ("O naznachenii poeta"), in which he presented Pushkin's death as a symbolic event: caused by the lack of "freedom" (Pushkin's "secret freedom" of art), which for the poet was the lack of air, it signified the death of his culture. In conclusion, Blok referred to cultural bureaucrats ("chinovniki") who, by infringing upon this freedom, stood in the way of the poet's calling – a hint at the contemporary situation and at the intrusion of the new Soviet state into art. Nietzschean connotations of Pushkin's image manifested themselves in this speech. Echoing Bely, Blok maintained that the ultimate goal of art and the ultimate task of the poet – the task of Pushkin – is to create new, superior breeds of men. This Nietzschean idea found the clearest expression in the drafts for the speech contained in Blok's diary for 1921, where he defined the calling of the poet as "obtaining the human [...] from a rapidly declining breed called 'the human race,' which is obviously imperfect and should be replaced by a more perfect breed of beings. Everything obtained and selected in this way by art is obviously deposited somewhere and should serve for the formation of the new beings."[9]

A younger contemporary of the Symbolists, Vladislav Khodasevich (1886–1939), in his anniversary speech, "The

Swaying Tripod" ("Koleblemyi trenozhnik"), given shortly
before he left Soviet Russia, also discussed the death of the
culture. Khodasevich considered the commemoration of February 1921 as a historical divide, the "brink of time": "We are
present at the change of the two epochs. The old Russia, that is,
the Pushkin Russia, has suddenly and abruptly moved away
from us ... The Petrine and Petersburg period of Russian
history has come to an end; whatever lies ahead, the past will
not return. A return is unthinkable both historically and
psychologically." Khodasevich predicted that this moment of
Russian history would be marked by an "eclipse of Pushkin's
sun" and reminded his audience of the first eclipse with Pis-
arev's nihilist attack on the Pushkinian tradition in the 1860s.
The new eclipse, claimed Khodasevich, was caused by the
appearance of people formed in the cataclysmic events of the
war and revolution, people for whom genuine understanding
of Pushkin was inaccessible. "They are not apostates or
degenerates," wrote Khodasevich, "they are simply new
men."[10] For Khodasevich, unlike Blok, the Nietzschean notion
of the new man had a pejorative connotation; the realization of
Superman in the new Soviet man meant the end of the Russian
cultural tradition associated with the name of Pushkin. The
commemoration of Pushkin's death in 1921 marked the
approach of the ultimate and final death of Pushkin, the
creator or the demigod (Khodasevich's words) of Russian
culture.

The Nietzschean undercurrent is present not only in such
ideologically charged texts as the Pushkin speeches of February
1921 but also in works of literary criticism devoted to Pushkin.
Beginning with the 1920s, the rapidly proliferating critical and
scholarly studies devoted to Pushkin's life and works evolved
into a separate discipline, Pushkinistics (*pushkinistika*). Its
Nietzschean background can best be illustrated by reviewing
the background of the central achievement of the branch of
Pushkinistics concerned with the investigation of Pushkin's
biography, V. V. Veresaev's *Pushkin in Life* (*Pushkin v zhizni*,
1926), subtitled "Character – Attitudes – Habits – Appearance
– Clothing – Circumstances." This monumental compendium

of documentary evidence on Pushkin's life enjoyed enormous popularity.

An ideological opponent of the Russian Symbolists, Vikenty Veresaev [Smidovich] (1867–1945), a writer, literary critic, and translator, was actively involved in the intellectual quests of the time. At the beginning of the twentieth century, when Nietzscheanism made ancient Greece into one of the central cultural symbols, Veresaev developed an interest in classical philology and the culture of ancient Greece, especially the Hellenic philosophy of life in relation to beauty and art.[11] According to Veresaev, Hellenic (Homeric) culture possessed the secret of the "harmonious transformation of life into beauty and art," creating "living life" ("zhivaia zhizn'," Dostoevsky's phrase). He opposed the Hellenic "living life" to the Hellenistic (Alexandrian) "decadent" estheticization of life and to its contemporary equivalent, Nietzschean decadence (including its Russian, Symbolist variant), which, he claimed, turned human life into a lifeless artifact. Veresaev expounded his views in a series of studies under the general title *The Living Life* (*Zhivaia zhizn'*), which included *The Living Life. On Dostoevsky and L. Tolstoi* (*Zhivaia zhizn'. O Dostoevskom i L. Tolstom*, 1910), the latter a reaction to Merezhkovsky's 1900 study of Tolstoi and Dostoevsky; *Apollo, the God of Living Life* (*Apollon, bog zhivoi zhizni*, 1913); and *Apollo and Dionysus* (*On Nietzsche*) (*Apollon i Dionis* [*O Nitsshe*], 1914). His study of Pushkin's life, or, in his words, the book on the "living Pushkin," was originally intended to conclude this sequence. Veresaev saw in Pushkin a perfect incarnation of the Hellenic ideal of the harmonious transformation of life into art, which he opposed to the artificial, stultifying estheticism of contemporary decadence. (This intention, however, was not realized – a matter for later comment.) Thus, in the 1910s, working with such Nietzschean themes as the estheticization of life, Apollo and Dionysus, the tragedy of antithesis, Veresaev developed his theory to counter Nietzsche and viewed Pushkin as an anti-Nietzschean symbol.

By the time Veresaev's *Pushkin in Life* appeared (1926), Pushkinistics, like many other areas of literature, was an arena of literary wars. In Pushkinistics, the wars centered around the

issue "Pushkin the man versus Pushkin the poet." The issue
had been discussed since the 1890s, when the problem of the
relation between life and art (or between artist and man)
acquired a special importance. Pushkin, who was mythicized
as a reconciler of the antithetical elements and as the ideal of
the man-artist, became the model for the reconciliation of art
and life, artist and man. Most of the major cultural figures of
the 1900s–1920s were actively involved in vigorous discussions
of these issues, which contributed to the elaboration of the
Nietzschean theme in the Pushkin myth. Veresaev's *Pushkin in
Life* provoked a polemic which became an important component in these debates. Veresaev's major opponent was the
already emigrated Vladislav Khodasevich. The controversy
was a part of the intellectual interchange between Soviet and
émigré writers that dominated the 1920s.

   In order to fully understand the meaning of the debates of
the mid-1920s on Pushkin, man and poet, it is necessary to
review their prerevolutionary background. Vladimir Soloviev
began the polemic. He developed his view of Pushkin to
counter the Nietzsche-inspired cult of the poet, which he
viewed as idolatry. In his essay "The Fate of Pushkin"
("Sud'ba Pushkina," 1897), directed specifically against Merezhkovsky's "Pushkin," Soloviev opposed the conception of
Pushkin as a man of superhuman wisdom. He insisted on the
separation of Pushkin's life and works, and stressed the contrast
between Pushkin the poet of genius and Pushkin the man
endowed with many human imperfections that ultimately
resulted in his death in a duel. Andrei Bely viewed the problem
of artist and man in terms of the Nietzschean problem of the
split in man and maintained that the persona of the poet
embodied the idea of inner unity, a unity achieved by erasing
the line between art and life. Bely found an example of such
an artist in a contemporary Symbolist poet – Valery Briusov.
But Briusov was for him a contemporary correlative, or a
double, of Pushkin. Viewed through Briusov as through a
prism, Pushkin appeared to Bely as a Nietzschean image of
the poet who had achieved inner harmony by acting as the
creator of his own self and life.[12]

The Symbolist tenet of making one's own life a work of art (*zhiznetvorchestvo*), a by-product of Nietzschean estheticism, found practical realization in such concrete attempts at deliberate organization of private life as the renowned love triangle (starting in 1904) involving Bely, Briusov, and the writer Nina Petrovskaia, known largely due to a critical account given by Khodasevich in the essay "The End of Renata" ("Konets Renaty," 1928, in *Nekropol'*). In this essay Khodasevich claimed that Symbolism failed to create a harmonious unity of art and life, artist and man. In each individual the "artist" and the "man" were in conflict with each other and struggled for dominance. Characteristically, Khodasevich used Pushkin as material to further develop his conception of the relation between man and artist. In Pushkin Khodasevich found a perfect realization of the ideal of harmonious, organic synthesis of life and art that remained unattainable for the Symbolists.[13] In the 1920s Khodasevich devoted considerable attention to the investigation of Pushkin, becoming a professional Pushkinist. In his Pushkin studies Khodasevich tried to integrate the facts of Pushkin's life and his works.

In the 1920s, in the context of Pushkinistics, the issue of man and artist was translated into a methodological problem facing the new discipline: the interrelation between biographical material and poetic texts in the study of Pushkin. As a general principle, Pushkinistics accepted the separation of life and works in literary analysis. Khodasevich vehemently attacked the principle of separating the man from the poet which gave rise to two extremist approaches to Pushkin: Formalism and "biographism" (his term). Formalism separated works from life and studied exclusively the formal properties of Pushkin's texts; "biographism" studied exclusively the facts of Pushkin's life. Beginning with "The Swaying Tripod," Khodasevich launched a series of attacks on the Formalist School, which he viewed as a characteristic phenomenon of Soviet culture.[14] According to Khodasevich, the Formalists (like the Futurists) are secret enemies and slanderers of Pushkin. Giving primacy to form in the study of Pushkin is as unsound as giving primacy to social content (the sin of the realist critics of the 1860s); therefore Formalists are "Pisarevists turned inside out" ("*pisarevtsy naiznanku*"). Khodasevich attacked Veresaev's postrevolutionary works as an example of pure "biographism." During the 1920s, Veresaev changed and repudiated his initial conception of Pushkin as the epitome of a harmonious synthesis of man and artist, which had been inspired by prerevolutionary Nietzschean disputes. The *Pushkin in Life* that appeared in 1926 was not the book that he originally planned to write. In the introduction Veresaev emphasized that he separated Pushkin the man from Pushkin the poet. Consequently, in his reconstruction of Pushkin's image he relied solely on biographical evidence of a documentary nature, and did not include "poetic data," or the testimony of Pushkin's poetic works.

Khodasevich attacked *Pushkin in Life* in a review published in 1927 in the Paris emigre newspaper *The Latest News* (*Poslednie novosti*). Veresaev's Pushkin, he charged, was torn from his creations, consisted solely of his "character, attitudes, appearance and clothing," and thus was not the "living Pushkin," but the "dead Pushkin," or a "living corpse." Khodasevich concluded with an ideological argument condemning Veresaev as a Soviet author. Apparently he attributed Veresaev's change of position toward Pushkin to the "revaluation of values" brought about by the October Revolution. Khodasevich wrote: "the unnatural desire to present Pushkin without poetic creations (*bez tvorchestva*) is characteristic of the intellectual trends that are now enforced in Russia by the governing party."[15] These trends are Formalism and "biographical formalism" (or "biographism"), two methodologies characterized by "love of materials for the sake of materials." This argument was not only a reference to the methodological principles of these schools (the Formalist notion that art is "the deformation of verbal material," and Veresaev's positivist reliance on documentary materials), but also an intimation that materialistic (Marxist) philosophy propagated by the Bolsheviks was an undercurrent of the principle of separation of art and life in both of its extremes.

Veresaev, in turn, attacked Khodasevich's position in a series of articles on Pushkin collected under the title *In Two Planes* (*V dvukh planakh*, 1929). Here Veresaev maintained that, contrary to his earlier belief, there was no unity between "the two hypostases of Pushkin: the quotidian and the artistic." This idea served as a justification for the strategy he had adopted in *Pushkin in Life*. From this point of view, Veresaev opposed the practice of using Pushkin's poetry as biographical evidence and condemned Khodasevich's Pushkin studies as extreme examples of this. Resorting to ideologically charged language, Veresaev accused Khodasevich of "belief in the dogma of the absolutely autobiographical nature of Pushkin's creations."[16]

One of the central issues in the literary debates of the 1920s, the union and division of man and poet in Pushkin, incorporated many perennial problems in Russian culture which acquired special poignancy in the early Soviet period. Among the themes underlying this issue was the relation between Nietzscheanism and Christianity. Indeed, the debates over the two beings in Pushkin were projected onto the early medieval Christological debates concerning the two natures, the divine and the human, in Christ. Briefly, the essence of the Christological debates lies in the controversy between two main trends in Christian thought: the trend emphasizing Christ as a human being and that emphasizing Christ's divine nature. The first saw in Christ a man assumed by the divine Logos and implied a rationalization of Christianity. The second represented a mystical interpretation of Christianity involving the negation or limitation of the humanity of Christ. The formulation of the decree of Chalcedon in 451 reconciled these extremes in proclaiming the unity of Christ's person, "truly God and truly man," "the same perfect in godhead, the same perfect in manhood," two natures united in one, yet retaining in full their respective characteristics. The Chalcedonian formula read: "Christ [...] acknowledged in two natures without confusion, without change, without division, without separation."

The mid-nineteenth-century positivist and socialist revisions of Christianity, and in Russia specifically the influential anthropotheistic doctrine of Ludwig Feuerbach (1804–72), reopened the issue of the relationship between God and man. In Russia, the problem of God-man versus Man-God was a central concern of the ideological debates between Dostoevsky and the nihilists of the 1860s. Towards the end of the nineteenth century these debates reached their peak. Vladimir Soloviev issued his critique of the doctrines of "mangodhood," that is, the positivist revisions of Christianity, in his *Lectures on Godmanhood* (*Chteniia o bogochelovechestve*, 1877–81). At the same time, the influence of Nietzsche's philosophy reinforced the "nihilist" idea of the Man-God. Thus, Merezhkovsky, in his 1900 study of Tolstoi and Dostoevsky, wrote: "We could not fail to recognize the one who pursued and tormented Dostoevsky his whole life – to recognize the Man-God in the Superman." As noted earlier, Merezhkovsky saw Pushkin, whom Dostoevsky proclaimed to be a "prophetic phenomenon," as a reconciler of (in his words) "the two edges of the abyss" – the God-man and the Man-God. With these ideas in mind, Vladimir Gippius in his *Pushkin and Christianity* (1915) defined Pushkin as an organic part of Russian Christian life: "If Pushkin was, in fact, an extraordinary and a prophetic phenomenon in Russian life, then how can we fail to understand him from a religious perspective – as a phenomenon of religious life?"[17] Pushkin turned into a "laboratory" for the resolution of the quest for the new forms of synthesis between God and man.

From a Christological perspective, the debates over Pushkin the poet and Pushkin the man from the 1890s through the 1920s comprise two general trends: the rationalistic and the mystical. Veresaev's postrevolutionary documentary biographism represents the rationalistic trend in striving to reveal a full human being in Pushkin, to reveal, in Veresaev's terms, "Pushkin the living man, and not an iconized image of the 'poet.'" Within the trend of thinking Pushkin appears (paraphrasing Dostoevsky) as a Man-poet (*Chelovekopoet*). By contrast, the second trend, most clearly represented by the Symbolists, maintained the unity of the poet and the man and viewed poetic creation as a mystical, divine process. The artist was thus absolved from the concerns of everyday life and ethical judgement. In the Symbolist mystical art, the poet was as if disembodied, ceasing to be a human being. The Symbolist ideal is not Man-poet, but Poet-man (*Poetochelovek*). Khodasevich in his works on Pushkin written in the 1920s vehemently opposed all views and theories that departed from the notion of harmonious unity and perfect equilibrium between the two beings in Pushkin. In two little known articles, "On Reading Pushkin" ("O chtenii Pushkina," 1924) and "Debating Pushkin" ("V sporakh o Pushkine," 1928), published in the émigré journal *Contemporary Notes* (*Sovremennye zapiski*), in Paris, Khodasevich offered a precise, strictly defined formula of Pushkin's unity, a sort of Chalcedonian dogma of Pushkinistics. In "Debating Pushkin" Khodasevich wrote: "Pushkin's creations ("tvorchestvo") did not exist in isolation from his life, nor his life from his creations. There was a miraculous unity: life-and-creations (*zhizn'-i-tvorchestvo*)."[18] This formula implies the concept of elements that exist in a union without confusion and without division or separation. In the same article Khodasevich affirmed that Pushkin was perfect as both the poet and the man. In "On Reading Pushkin" Khodasevich defined the unity of Pushkin's being with a formula resembling the Christological formula of the "hypostatic union": "The 'Poet' and the 'man' are [*sut'* – a Church Slavonic word] two hypostases of one being." In conclusion, he explicitly alluded to the Christological projection, saying: "Certain high analogies are in order here."[19]

Thus, debates on the man and the poet in Pushkin in the 1920s brought about the resolution of one of the most important problems of Russian Nietzscheanism, the relations between Nietzsche's doctrine and Christianity. In Nietzsche's own view, expressed in his famous 1886 preface to *The Birth of Tragedy*, he founded "a radical counterdoctrine, slanted esthetically," to oppose what he called "the Christian libel on life." For Nietzsche, it was precisely the principle of "the purely esthetic interpretation of the world" that placed his doctrine "at the opposite pole from Christian doctrine, a doctrine entirely moral in purport." In the course of the Russian assimilation of Nietzsche, however, this point was radically reinterpreted, and the interpretation varied from writer to writer.

Soloviev, Nietzsche's major critic in turn-of-the-century Russia, welcomed the idea of Superman (understood as man's striving for infinite self-perfection through creative activity) in such works as "The Idea of the Superman" ("Ideia sverkhcheloveka," 1899) and "Lermontov" (1899), but he argued that the realization of Nietzsche's ideal was possible only within the traditional framework of this idea – Christianity. He specifically faulted Nietzsche's esthetic slant, his tendency to approach the world as a text and treat life as literature, and ascribed the limitations of Nietzsche's doctrine to the fact that Nietzsche was a philologist (or "super-philologist").[20] In the context of these ideas Soloviev opposed a Nietzschean cult of Pushkin.

In the 1900s, Merezhkovsky, who (like Soloviev) viewed Nietzsche as a religious philosopher, saw in Nietzsche's critique of Christianity a basis for the revitalization of religion. The development of an estheticized version of Christian doctrine preoccupied him at the time of his work on *L. Tolstoi and Dostoevsky*, with its Nietzscheanized image of Pushkin as a reconciler of Christ and Antichrist. (Merezhkovsky later repudiated his Nietzscheanism as a substitute for Christianity.[21])

Bely apparently saw the two systems (Nietzscheanism and Christianity) as compatible, freely combining Nietzschean and Christian concepts in his critical essays of 1907–10. Seeing no contradiction between the Nietzschean ideal of the artist as God and the Christian ideal of the deification of man, Bely used Nietzsche, Christ, and Pushkin as mutually interchangeable symbols.

Veresaev, a future Pushkinist, treated Pushkin in the 1910s as Nietzsche's antipode, and the philosophy of life associated with Pushkin as triumphant over the Nietzschean anti-Christian principle of emphasizing the esthetic and downgrading or ignoring the ethical. In the 1920s, with the birth of Soviet culture, Veresaev desanctified his Pushkin, viewing him as merely a man.

Looking back at these developments in the mid- and late 1920s, Khodasevich, an émigré, repudiated all of these views, striving to bring about "the triumph of Orthodoxy." In his polemical articles Khodasevich advanced an implicit view of Pushkin not as Nietzsche, but as the Christ of Chalcedonian dogma. His victory in the struggle over Pushkin meant for Khodasevich the triumph of Orthodox Christianity in its confrontation with Nietzscheanism and with the new, secularized ("materialistic") Soviet culture.

In the meantime, the new Soviet culture appropriated Pushkin as a symbol of the embodiment of the Russian spirit and an ideal model for man. In the early 1920s, the radical "Left Wing of the Arts" (Levyi front iskusstv, or LEF), an heir of Futurism, and the left wing of Proletkult echoed the Futurists' desire to "throw Pushkin overboard the ship of modernity." But most of the Soviet ideologues at that time looked for ways of incorporating Pushkin, like most of the other Russian classics, into Soviet culture.[22]

In the 1930s the appropriation of the Pushkin cult by official Soviet culture was completed, reaching its highest point in the grandiose, carefully orchestrated celebrations of the centennial of Pushkin's death in 1937. Many of the themes and images of the Pushkin cult of the preceding years found their way into the official manifestos of the Centennial, which were issued in January and February of 1937 by every Soviet journal and newspaper. A characteristic document illustrating the tendency to appropriate is an editorial that opened the first issue of *Literaturnyi sovremennik* for 1937, an essay entitled "The Glory of the People" ("Slava naroda"). The manifesto read:

Only our time [the age of Stalin] entirely and completely accepts Pushkin and Pushkin's heritage. V. Khodasevich, now an émigré and a traitor to the motherland, wrote in 1921 of the "approaching eclipse of Pushkin." [...] How miserable and false are his words! Only now Pushkin has become truly close to millions of hearts. For the new masses conquering the heights of culture Pushkin is an "eternal companion" ["vechnyi sputnik"] [...] The times when the theoreticians of Futurism, in a frenzy of leftism, demanded to "throw Pushkin overboard from the ship of modernity," have long gone and will never return. The remnants of decadent nihilism are deeply alien to the direction in which Soviet art is developing [...] alien to the Soviet country are the people who are still trying to follow the path of

Formalism and decadence ... The living Pushkin, the Pushkin living in his books, joined the ranks of those struggling for the high realist art.

While Khodasevich was rejected as a traitor, Futurism accused of excessive leftism, and both Futurism and Formalism associated with decadence and dismissed, such images of the Symbolist cult of Pushkin as "eternal companions" (Merezhkovsky's phrase) and "the living Pushkin" (the latter had a New-Testament connotation in the context of Symbolism) were naively incorporated into the Soviet discourse on Pushkin. The essay ends with a glorification of the superhuman qualities of Pushkin: Pushkin had a perfect command ("v sovershenstve vladel") of all the genres and all forms ... Every image and every event that he depicted bears an imprint of his individuality, the individuality that is boundless and can encompass the whole world.[23]

With the Pushkin cult of the 1930s, certain Nietzschean themes and images were legitimized and hence appropriated by official Soviet culture. Thus, the view of Pushkin as the creator of the new Russian man, which had been propagated in a Nietzschean context by the Symbolists, was adopted by one of the main Marxist ideologues, Anatoly Lunacharsky (1879–1933), who redefined it in connection with Soviet culture's Nietzschean aspirations to create the "new man." Explaining the significance of Pushkin in the introduction to the Soviet edition of Pushkin's collected works issued in 1931, Lunacharsky wrote that "Pushkin entered into life as a new Adam of sorts." He claimed:

[A hundred years after Pushkin's death] we quite realistically "dream" of the time when an average man would turn out to be richer in terms of his capacity to experience the world and to create than the people of the past [...] It is Pushkin who, among others, must become a teacher of the proletarians and peasants in the construction of their inner world [...] Every grain that is contained in Pushkin's treasury will yield a socialist rose or a socialist bunch of grapes in the life of every citizen.[24]

This essay was republished in a collection commemorating the Pushkin Centennial of 1937.

The themes of Pushkin as a creator of the new Soviet man was continued in an essay by N. Glagolev, "Pushkin and the Present" ("Pushkin i sovremennost'"), published in the jubilee issue of *The New World* (*Novyi mir* 1, 1937). Glagolev linked Pushkin as the new man with Chernyshevsky's conception of the "new man," which was rooted (as he claimed) in Feuerbach's idea of man's infinite striving towards self-perfection, thereby giving it a lineage acceptable to official Soviet culture. In his words, this new man is a "universal man" (*obshchechelovek*, Dostoevsky's concept). "These ideals," continued Glagolev, "turn into reality in front of our eyes [...] The new man, the man of the future is being born in the fire of the struggle of the working masses [...]" It is a man who is able to "conquer nature by the creative energy of the human thought."[25] In this Glagolev saw the significance of Pushkin's heritage in the Soviet present.

Another essay in the jubilee issue of *The New World* (*Novyi mir*) connected Pushkin with the image of the aviation hero which was advanced in high Stalinist culture (the mid-thirties) as "the most paradigmatic new man," an obvious echo of Nietzsche's Superman.[26] I. Rakhilo, in an essay entitled "Associations," relates a conversation about Pushkin that he has had with the cadets of a school of military pilots in 1933. "All of them were firmly convinced that were Pushkin to live in contemporary times, he would certainly be an aviator. [He has] all the typical traits of a fighter-pilot." The author comments: "Such are the associations that are evoked by Pushkin."[27] Thus, in the culture of the 1930s, the image of Pushkin evoked associations with the concept of the new Soviet man as Superman.

While Soviet ideologues saw Stalin's Russia as the glorious continuation of the Pushkinian tradition, their opponents in the West saw it as a betrayal of this tradition. In 1937 the Centennial of Pushkin's death was also solemnly commemorated by émigré writers. In Paris, Merezhkovsky, the progenitor of the Nietzscheanized cult of Pushkin, delivered a speech in which he returned to the ideas of his 1896 essay emphasizing the role of Pushkin who, along with Peter the Great, laid the foundations of Russia's historical mission as the reconciler of the East and the West. As if echoing Khodasevich's 1921 Pushkin speech, Merezhkovsky presented the death of the poet as a Nietzschean symbol of the death of God. Having given a promise of reconciliation, Pushkin "died like a God amidst the universe he had founded." Merezhkovsky then gave his assessment of the contemporary situation: "Never before has the Russian people [...] betrayed to such an extent as now the cause of Peter and Pushkin; opposed to such a degree the Russian East and the universal West [...]" But according to Merezhkovsky Pushkin represented not only Russia's past; Pushkin was also a pledge for the fulfillment of Russia's future greatness: Pushkin would fulfill what had been promised. At present Pushkin's most important role and mission was to reconcile the two Russias, the one in exile, and the one in captivity. Having added another antithesis to the scheme of Nietzschean polarities, Merezhkovsky reestablished Pushkin as a universal solution to all of Russia's ills: "Pushkin is the immutable proof of Russia's unity. He is the reconciler, the connector, the one who makes one out of two and destroys the barrier that stands between."[28] Thus, throughout the 1920s and 1930s, both Pushkin and Nietzsche were symbols used by both sides of the ideological confrontation between Soviet culture and its opponents. And with these developments of 1937, a period of Russian culture spanning the first three decades of the twentieth century, the period that was distinguished by the Pushkin cult, came to its conclusion.

In place of a final assessment of the interrelation between Pushkinism and Nietzscheanism, I would like to say that the dominant feature of both of these systems is a remarkable flexibility and versatility, a capacity to adapt to many functions, and to absorb a variety of concrete themes and problems. In his study of the Nietzschean current in West European modernism, John Foster emphasized this quality of Nietzsche's thought and described Nietzsche as "a remarkably Protean thinker." He claimed that one of the most impressive features of Nietzsche's influence is its role as "a meaningful context that draws together what might seem a host of random echoes."[29]

This quality of Nietzsche corresponds to a characteristic attributed as intrinsic to Pushkin in Russian cultural consciousness. This popular idea of Pushkin as Proteus implies a conception of Pushkin's "flexibility," understood in the broad sense as his unique ability to embody and encompass an infinite range of cultural values and problems that offer themselves to Russian society. In this sense, one can speak of the functional equivalence between Nietzscheanism and Pushkinism; a factor that contributed to the superimposition of these two paradigms within Russian culture.

NOTES

* I would like to thank David Shegold for his numerous suggestions for stylistic improvements.

1 Various aspects of this issue have been discussed in the essays collected in: *Cultural Mythology of Russian Modernism, From the Golden Age to the Silver Age*, ed. Boris Gasparov, Robert P. Hughes, and Irina Paperno (Berkeley, 1992). This collection contains my article, "Pushkin v zhizni cheloveka Serebrianogo veka," in which some of the problems discussed in this article have been treated in a different context.

2 See Iu. I. Levin, D. M. Segal, R. S. Timenchik, V. N. Toporov, T. V. Tsiv'ian, "Russkaia semanticheskaia poetika kak potentsial'naia kul'turnaia paradigma," *Russian Literature* 7/8 (1974), p. 48.

3 L. Ginzburg, "Variant staroi temy," *Neva* 1 (1987), p. 150.

4 On "eternal recurrence" in Russia see D. E. Maksimov, *Poeziia i proza Aleksandra Bloka* (Leningrad, 1975), pp. 74–83.

5 See Bernice Glatzer Rosenthal, *Dmitri Sergeevich Merezhkovsky and the Silver Age* (The Hague, 1975), pp. 70–72.

6 D. S. Merezhkovskii, *Polnoe sobranie sochinenii v 24 tomakh* (St. Petersburg, 1914), 9: viii, xii.

7 A characteristic example of infusing Nietzschean schemes with the Russian material pertaining to the Age of Pushkin appears in Andrei Bely's memoirs, *At the Beginning of the Century* (1933). Bely relates an episode that took place in 1904: Valery Briusov is reading him a verse from an old edition of Baratynsky ("Na chto vy, dni?", 1840): "What are you for, days? The vale of life will not change its phenomena. They all are known ... And the future promises only repetitions." The quote comes after a passage in which, naming the key words of the period, Bely puts the names of

Baratynsky and Tiutchev side by side with the names of Nietzsche and Erwin Rohde, and an image of an ancient Hellene who has been transferred into modern times. See A. Bely, *Nachalo veka* (Moscow–Leningrad, 1933), p. 28. Another example of substitution of Pushkin's name for Nietzsche's, as Joan Grossman has demonstrated, appears in a letter of Briusov to M. V. Samygin of July 1900, in which Briusov describes himself as a poet who has achieved the highest point (a Nietzschean self-image of poet as a creator and thinker): "'So. My noon has come' ['Tak, polden' moi nastal,' *Evgenii Onegin*]. Pushkin's words. I feel and recognize my strengths ...'" Grossman writes: "... to avoid a vulgar paraphrase of Nietzsche's prophet ... he instead had recourse to Pushkin: 'My noon has come.'" See Joan Delaney Grossman, *Valery Briusov and the Riddle of Russian Decadence* (Berkeley, 1985), p. 199.

8 On this anniversary see Robert P. Hughes, "Pushkin in Petrograd, February 1921," *Cultural Mythologies of Russian Modernism*, pp. 204–13.

9 A. Blok, *Sobranie sochinenii v 8 tomakh* (Moscow-Leningrad, 1960–63), VII, pp. 405–6.

10 V. Khodasevich, "Koleblemyi trenozhnik," in his *Stat'i o russkoi poezii* (Petersburg, 1922), pp. 113 and 115.

11 Veresaev translated Greek poetry, including Hesiod's *Works and Days* (a major literary source for the myth of the Five Ages of Man: Golden, Silver, Bronze, and so forth), and, following the example set by Merezhkovsky, undertook a symbolic trip – a "return" – to Greece. In 1918 Veresaev's translation of Hesiod (begun in the 1890s) received the Pushkin prize of the Academy of Sciences. A separate edition of the Russian *Works and Days* (entitled *Raboty i dni*) appeared in 1926, the same year as Veresaev's *Pushkin in Life*. As his model Veresaev took an earlier (and less complete) compendium of documents on Pushkin's life compiled by N. Lerner bearing a title borrowed from Hesiod – *The Works and Days of Pushkin* (*Trudy i dni Pushkina*, 1903).

12 A. Bely, "Venets lavrovyi," *Zolotoe runo* 5 (1906), pp. 43–50.

13 In his article, "In Memory of Gogol" ("Pamiati Gogolia," 1934), Khodasevich claimed that Pushkin was the first Russian writer who inextricably intertwined his private personality with his poetry. The first professional in Russian literature, the first true individualist, and the first romantic, Pushkin lived and died as a poet (in *Izbrannaia proza* [New York, 1982], p. 73).

14 On Khodasevich and the Formalists see John E. Malmstad,

"Khodasevich and Formalism: A Poet's Dissent," *Russian Forma-lism: A Retrospective Glance. A Festschrift in Honor of Victor Erlich*, ed. Robert L. Jackson and Stephen Rudy (New Haven, 1985), pp. 68–81.

15 V. Khodasevich, "Pushkin v zhizni" (Po povodu knigi V. V. Veresaeva)," *Poslednie novosti* 2122 (January 13, 1927).
16 V. V. Veresaev, "K psikhologii Pushkinskogo tvorchestva," *V dvukh planakh* (Moscow, 1929), p. 36.
17 V. Gippius, *Pushkin i khristianstvo* (Petrograd, 1915), p. 5.
18 V. Khodasevich, "V sporakh o Pushkine," *Sovremennye zapiski* 37 (1928), p. 275.
19 V. Khodasevich, "O chtenii Pushkina," *Sovremennye zapiski* 20 (1924), p. 232.
20 See V. Soloviev's "The Sunday Letters: Literature or Truth" ("Voskresnye pis'ma: slovesnost' ili istina," 1897) *Sobranie sochine-nii V. S. Solov'eva*, ed. S. M. Solov'ev and E. L. Radlov, vol. X (rpt. Brussels, 1966), pp. 3–80. A. Bely commented that Soloviev "disdainfully called Nietzsche 'super-philologist'" (see Bely, "Friedrich Nietzsche," *Arabeski* [Moscow, 1911], p. 89). The fact that Nietzsche was a philologist fascinated both Bely and his fellow Symbolist Viacheslav Ivanov (see his "Nietzsche and Dio-nysus," *Po zvezdam* (Petersburg, 1909, p. 5). On Soloviev's posi-tion see Anne M. Lane, "Nietzsche Comes to Russia: Populari-zation and Protest in the 1890s," *Nietzsche in Russia*, ed. Bernice Glatzer Rosenthal (Princeton, 1986), pp. 65–67. On Nietzsche's notion of life as literature see Alexander Nehamas, *Nietzsche: Life as Literature* (Cambridge, MA, 1985).
21 On Merezhkovsky see Bernice Glatzer Rosenthal, "Stages of Nietzscheanism: Merezhkovsky's Intellectual Evolution," *Nietzsche in Russia*, pp. 70–93.
22 On the early Soviet attitude toward the Russian classics see Robert Maguire, *The Red Virgin Soil* (Princeton, 1968), pp. 237–45, 293–301.
23 "Slava naroda," *Literaturnyi sovremennik* 1 (1937), pp. 7–8 and 9.
24 A. V. Lunacharskii, "A. S. Pushkin," *Pushkin. Sbornik kriticheskikh statei*, ed. A. G. Tseitlin (Moscow, 1937), pp. 269 and 290–91. First published in A. S. Pushkin, *Sobranie sochinenii v 5 tomakh* (Moscow-Leningrad, 1931–33). Compare Lunacharsky's famous description of the new Soviet man with Trotsky's prediction of Soviet superman in *Literature and Revolution* (*Literatura i revoluitsiia*, 1923) (see L. Trotsky, *Literature and Revolution* [Ann Arbor, 1960], pp. 255–56). On a Soviet Superman see Bernice Glatzer Rosenthal, "Introduction," *Nietzsche in Russia*, pp. 34–35. On

Lunacharsky's prerevolutionary attitudes toward Nietzsche see A. L. Tait, "Lunacharsky: A 'Nietzschean Marxist'?", *Nietzsche in Russia*, pp. 274–92.

25 N. Glagolev, "Pushkin i sovremennost'," *Novyi mir* 1 (1937), p. 229.

26 Katerina Clark described the aviation hero as "the most paradigmatic new man of the mid-thirties" in "Utopian Anthropology as a Context for Stalinist Literature," *Stalinism: Essays in Historical Interpretation*, ed. Robert C. Tucker (New York, 1977), p. 189, and in Katerina Clark, *The Soviet Novel: History as Ritual* (Chicago, 1985), pp. 124–29. Vladimir Papernyi, in *Kul'tura "dva"* (Ann Arbor, 1985), connected the aviation hero with Superman (see p. 74).

27 I. Rakhillo, "Assotsiatsii," *Novyi mir* 1 (1937), p. 45.

28 "Rech D. S. Merezhkovskogo," *Torzhestvennoe sobranie v den' 100 godovshchiny smerti Pushkina*, ed. V. A. Maklakov (Paris, 1937), pp. 14–15.

29 John Burt Foster, *Heirs to Dionysos* (Princeton, 1981), pp. 8 and 41.

PART III

Adaptations of Nietzsche in Soviet Ideology

CHAPTER 9

Nietzschean motifs in the Komsomol's vanguardism*

Isabel A. Tirado

In 1921 the members of the Komsomol (Communist Youth League) committee in Tot'ma district of Vologda province declared themselves adherents of Nietzsche's philosophy and even flaunted their affinity with the "Superman." Presumably, such an outright identification with Nietzsche was unusual for a Komsomol group: one can hardly expect a more incongruous mix than the Marxism-Leninism of the Communist Youth League and Nietzsche's philosophy. By then the philosopher had been anathematized as the exponent of a petty-bourgeois, nihilistic, individualistic world view, the herald of a "philosophy of a dying class" that could only harm the young generation. The fact that this incident took place in a district of Vologda province, one of the most backward areas of northern Russia, removed from the cultural centers of Moscow and Petrograd, suggests that Nietzsche enjoyed enough popularity among Communist youth to cause consternation in some Party and Komsomol circles. In early 1922, referring to the Vologda incident, Oskar Tarkhanov, a Komsomol leader, wrote:

Petty-bourgeois influences sometimes appear even inside our League. They express themselves both in the way of life of our activists and in the behavior of the masses of League members. Now and then these influences take the shape and character of all sorts of confused theories ... The last number of *Izvestiia Vologodskogo Gubpartkoma* reports that the Tot'ma Komsomol uezd committee declared itself "Nietzschean" and sports the toga of the "Superman." In this fashion, the philosophy of the dying class has found refuge within our League's walls.[1]

Given the politically sensitive nature of the subject, it would be almost impossible to establish the extent of the philosopher's popularity among the Komsomol. Yet Nietzschean concepts appeared in early Komsomol literature, particularly in the Komsomol poetry of the Civil War and the early 1920s. The pages of such journals as *Smena* (*The Young Generation*) and *Iunyi proletarii* (*Young Proletarian*) were filled with paeans to the Komsomol's role that evoked Nietzschean images.

The Komsomol's vanguardism – the League's claim to leadership in the revolutionary movement and in society in general – was a central tenet of the political culture of that mass organization. As the political leaders, industrial managers, and *intelligenty* to come of age after the Revolution, the Komsomol exerted influence far beyond its relatively limited, albeit rapidly expanding, membership. Through its network of cells and clubs, its press, and its public activities, the Komsomol became one of the most important revolutionary institutions to mold the identity, world view, and aspirations of Soviet youth.

YOUTH AS VANGUARD OF THE REVOLUTION

The Komsomol's first program (1918) defined youth as "the vanguard of the proletarian revolution," the most active and revolutionary part of the working class.[2] The first issue of the Komsomol journal, *Iunyi kommunist* (*Young Communist*) portrayed youth as the Revolution's advanced columns:

In Russia, as in the West, [youth] stands in the front ranks of the movement. Youth is more perceptive, and has not been poisoned by the prejudices and ideas of bourgeois society ... Youth is strong and brave. It understands that revolution is its own business and, knowing this, it gives thousands of brave warriors for a better future.[3]

Even in the provinces Komsomol collectives assumed such names as "Club of the Advanced Vanguard of the Revolution."[4] Komsomol literature portrayed the organization as being in the forefront of the Communist movement, often its most radical exponent and champion, a political vanguard. But the literature also used the word "vanguard" with its military connotation – as the advance guard leading troops.

The participation of youth activists in the barricades of 1917 and in the Civil War gave the youth league a militant and military identity from the start. For the purposes of this paper I am defining "vanguard" both as the forefront of a movement and as the head of troops. (I will not approach the League as an artistic or literary avant-garde of the Civil War and the NEP.)[5]

A vanguardist tone characterized the poems and other literature published by the Komsomol. Elsewhere I have delved into the political and economic forces that led to the emergence of the Bolshevik youth movement and how those forces interacted to shape the organization.[6] This article focuses on the vanguard motifs culled from poems, manifestos, and charters written by young poets and by members of the organized youth movement, which appeared in the youth press in the first years after the Revolution of 1917. Through this literature I seek to establish Nietzsche's work, in particular *Thus Spoke Zarathustra*, as one of the intellectual currents that helped form the Komsomol's vision of itself.

I do not argue that Nietzsche's was the main influence on the Komsomol's vanguardism. The components of that vanguardism – its anti-intellectualism, iconoclasm, vision of history – were shaped by many intellectual currents, the most important and obvious being Marxism-Leninism. Anti-intellectualism had popular pre-1917 roots. In his autobiography, the Bolshevik worker Semen Kanatchikov described the general distrust and animosity, mixed with admiration, that he and fellow working class radicals felt for the *intelligenty*. For many Komsomolites, anti-intellectualism merged with the rejection of the old order, the old "oppressive" classes, and their culture. Revolutionary iconoclasm, or the destruction of the symbols of the past, had diverse origins, ranging from the nihilism of the nineteenth-century revolutionary movement to the destructive peasant rampages aimed at all cultural and material symbols of the land-owning classes. During the first years of the Revolution iconoclasm took different if interrelated forms that were fed by the revolutionary events and idiom of the time.

While I have chosen only motifs that suggest Nietzsche's

influence, these motifs are typical of the Komsomol. Indeed, these themes were present in Komsomol literature during that early period and reflected the poets' selective adoption of Nietzschean concepts. Images of warriors and war, of the future, of determination and courage abound. Tracing Nietzsche's influence on the Komsomol presents special problems for the social historian who leaves aside high culture and its craftsmen's accounts of their artistic and intellectual indebtedness, preferring, instead, popular culture, whose origins are not as readily discernible. There are few direct references to Nietzsche in the poetry and in other Komsomol literature. One can assume, therefore, that those motifs and concepts found their way into Komsomol culture through intermediaries more often than through first-hand exposure to Nietzsche's work.

The works of Vladimir Mayakovsky, the beloved Futurist "poet of the Revolution," appeared frequently in the Komsomol press. Nietzsche's influence on Mayakovsky, recognized by his contemporaries and discussed in Bengt Jangfeldt's chapter in this volume, manifested itself in the poet's contempt for the past, his enmity toward philistinism, and his exaltation of the "new man" of the future, the prophet who was willing to sacrifice himself for new truths. Just before the Revolution, other Russian Futurists hailed the separation of the generations and called on "those who are closer to their death than to their birth surrender" to the "swords made of the pure iron of youth." To them, the older generation impeded "the locomotive of youth from taking the mountain that stands in its way."[7] These ideas became important components of the Komsomol's vanguardism.

Among the most important intermediaries were the "Nietzschean Marxists," Maksim Gorky, Aleksandr Bogdanov, and Anatoly Lunacharsky. The works of the immensely popular Gorky were a staple of almost every Komsomol reading list. Gorky's rebels appealed to youth, who found in his heroes' anti-intellectualism and rejection of bourgeois values their own cause. From its inception, the Bolshevik youth movement expressed contempt for the "philistine old order," and especially for bourgeois morality and values, for the intellectual and cultural canon, and for religion.

During the Civil War the Komsomol established close links with the Proletarian Culture movement (Proletkult), which was heavily influenced by Bogdanov. Founding members of the Komsomol, including Evgeniia Gerr and Ivan Tiutikov, were concurrently active in Proletkult. Bogdanov himself wrote articles for the youth press – among them, an essay on the emancipation of the individual under socialism for the journal *Molodaia gvardiia* ("Young Guard").[8] *Iunyi proletarii* ("Young Proletarian") published enthusiastic reviews of Bogdanov's novels *Red Star* and *Engineer Menni*, praising the preeminent role the works conferred to the liberated, creative individual in the construction of socialism.[9] At the height of its popularity during the Civil War, Proletkult had close to 500,000 members and over 1,000 clubs and studios. Even Vologda province, whose population was overwhelmingly illiterate on the eve of the Revolution, boasted a Proletkult branch as its first writers' organization.[10] Proletkult studios, clubs, and youth sections trained many young poets and writers, who embraced the movement's goal of smashing "bourgeois" culture and values and replacing them with a new proletarian culture and art. Some of these new artists published simultaneously in Komsomol and Proletkult organs, thus spreading the movement's influence over the Communist Youth League. Komsomol members felt Proletkult's influence even more directly after 1921, when the Proletarian Culture movement began to disintegrate and its clubs merged with school, trade union, and Komsomol ones.[11]

From its earliest days the Komsomol was intimately involved with Lunacharsky and the Commissariat of Enlightenment (Narkompros). The League received funds, teachers, and meeting places for its youth clubs and schools from the Commissariat. The Komsomol developed a complex relationship with Narkompros: it played the role of radical gadfly, often prodding the "bourgeois intellectual" adults working for the Commissariat to adopt a more radical reform of the educational system. In its cultural and educational activities the

Komsomol saw itself as a vanguard championing the new order – a young vanguard that considered itself intrinsically more radical than the older generation, even than many adults in the Party vanguard.

VANGUARD MOTIFS

Nietzsche hailed the historical role of youth, of "that first generation of fighters and serpent slayers which precedes a happier and more beautiful culture and humanity without having more than an inkling full of promise of this future happiness and beauty to come" (*H*, p. 63). What were the "Nietzschean" attributes of the young vanguard expressed in Komsomol literature? For Nietzsche youth played the decisive historical role by breaking with stultifying trends that spelt the death of a people. Youth was particularly suited for his mission due to its instinctive "fire, obstinacy, self-forgetting and love, [and] ... the heat of its sense of justice" (*H*, p. 57). With striking similarity, for the Komsomol the most important traits – those most often mentioned in the official literature and fiction of the youth movement – were energy, strength, courage, and determination; the most common image: youth as a warrior and a rebel. It was a male image, for there were almost no female representations of the vanguard in these early works. (This changed in the mid- and late 1920s when the Komsomol began to recruit young women more aggressively.) The image of a young warrior, which one would associate with the Civil War, in fact appeared in the youth literature of 1917. For example, the Manifesto of the Petrograd youth organization Trud i svet (Labor and Light), written that spring, called on its members "to man the barricades ... to deal a final blow to the remnants of infamous tsarism and the schemes of callous capitalism."[12]

For the Komsomol the war was hallowed by the cause of socialism, an inversion of Nietzsche's "good war that hallows every cause" (*Z*, p. 74). Yet, recalling Nietzsche, the Komsomol poems glorified war. In their depiction of war there was none of the inhuman, destructive carnage of the First World

War or the Civil War, but a liberating, heroic contest. The Komsomol poems celebrated war in terms that made more sense in Nietzsche's lifetime, when militarism was colored by what Peter Bergmann has called the "storybook wars" that spread throughout Europe from the 1850s to 1870.[13] Coming from a generation that witnessed the devastation wrought by the conflicts of their own century, such a portrayal of war may seem paradoxical. But the fact that the Komsomol gave a disproportionate number of volunteers to the Civil War, and that many members perished in the course of the combat that came to dominate revolutionary Russia, may explain the need to exalt that sacrifice.

The Komsomol warrior was fearless, callous, unbending, untiring, sometimes even invincible.[14] Like the superman, the young fighter shunned sleep. "Blessed are these drowsy men: for they shall soon drop off," exclaimed Zarathustra (Z, p. 58). The Komsomol warrior was not the somnolent, complacent man abhorred by Zarathustra. While the rest of society slept, the revolutionary warrior, seemingly alone in his watch, readied himself for the endless battles of an infinite number of tomorrows:

> Quietly I place my sword in its sheath
> In the silence before nightfall . . .
> Tomorrow, tomorrow, I guess
> A new battle will come my way.
> There is little rest,
> The long-awaited hours fly like instants.[15]

With their stress on a sleepless warrior's burden and their portrayal of others as complacent in face of imminent danger, these verses came closer to Nietzsche than to the mainstream revolutionary idiom which stressed collective watchfulness before the threat posed by capitalist militarism. Even more incompatible with mainstream Marxism-Leninism was the suggestion of an endless struggle without a resolution. In the poem "From the Haze of Contradictions" ("Iz mgly protivore-chii"), the same author, Dmitri Maznin, returned to the concept of recurrent events and gave a version of an endless dialectic, closer to Nietzsche's "eternal recurrence" than to the Marxist dialectic.

> The secret idea of contradictions
> I grasped gladly.
> I shouldered the inevitability
> Of centuries of eternal movement . . .
> And I understood, casting a rebellious glance
> At the distant chaos of the years:
> There is not quiet. Far away there are boundless
> Falls and victories.[16]

The Komsomol warriors were

> Waves on a stormy sea,
> Heaving, preparing for battle.[17]

The imagery and concepts in these verses echoed Nietzsche's future orientation. "So now I love only my children's land, the undiscovered land in the furthest sea: I bid my sails seek it and seek it" (*Z*, p. 144). Though this coupling of the future and new values with the young generation was hardly unique to Nietzsche, the motifs chosen by some of the Komsomol poets, particularly that of the raging sea, suggest a familiarity with Nietzschean themes, especially with his singling out the young, who were free of the prejudices and limitations of their fathers, to create the new values, and ultimately, a new type of man, "a new beginning" (*Z*, p. 55). In the words of a young Komsomol woman:

> We perish by the hundreds
> As sacrifices of the mighty blaze,
> but we are born by the thousands,
> just as passionate and inspired.
> Born in the whirlwind, in the storm,
> we live for the great struggle,
> [and] we die for the radiant beauty of the future.[18]

The elevation of youth to a determining historical role in Nietzsche's work was one of the currents that nurtured the Komsomol's proclivity for generational conflict and rebelliousness. "We are wrathful thunder," proclaimed another poem.[19] Youth's defiance and fury were coupled with a capacity for self-sacrifice for the future. In *Zarathustra* the young warriors represented the "first-born" who were "always sacrificed" for the future without seeking to "preserve themselves" (*Z*, p. 217). This image found expression in the following Komsomol verses:

> This song of a better destiny
> Kindled the rebellious warriors
> And we marched to the bloody battlefield . . .[20]

The warrior's recompense would be recognition from generations to come.

> And in future days a rapturous bard will sing
> Wonderful songs about us.[21]

Komsomol warriors were likened to

> A spring striving and searching
> For the new life of natural beauty.[22]

The young warrior prepared for the "final struggle" against capitalism specifically, but more generally, against the old order.[23] The struggle was waged against

> All that is old, powerless, and putrid,
> Replacing the old with its own
> Great beautiful, young creation.[24]

Komsomol poets depicted the past as oppressive in juxtaposition to the liberating future; the past was darkness, the future light. To them the past was like the fog, which the warrior vanquished "with sparkling bayonets," permitting the "sun's rays" to penetrate the mist of fog.[25] This may be compared to Nietzsche's "bright lightning flash of light [which] occurs within that encircling cloud of mist" as man transformed history (*H*, p. 11). The young warrior destroyed darkness and all those restraints that enslaved the nation:

> We dispel darkness, we destroy the laws
> that choke us and oppress us . . .
> Arise, slaves! Nations, arise!
> Bright days are beckoning![26]

The future was likened to the dawn:

> In the bright, fiery, beams
> Of the long-awaited dawn
> The liberated nation's heart
> Stirs with happiness.[27]

The fetters inherited from the past would be torn asunder and in their place a society would arise to provide "happiness without obstacles, life without fetters,"[28] a paradise on earth free from even memories of the past:

> In the sun-filled, flowering
> Earthly paradise of the future
> We won't recall
> The past ...[29]

This was not a repudiation of all of history, but only the "enslaving" past. The Komsomol literature exalted that past which provided liberating models for the future. A poem described a warrior being transported to "a bright paradise" where he met a Montagnard. The young warrior declared his solidarity with the French revolutionary and invited him to the corner tavern, where they discussed the imminent demise of all tyrants.[30] In keeping with Nietzsche's view of the necessity for a "monumental" type of history that would serve as a model for future generations, these verses drew a continuum between a radical of the French Revolution and the Komsomol warrior, who in Nietzsche's terms "live in timeless simultaneity, thanks to history, which permits ... cooperation ...; one giant calls to the other across the bleak intervals of ages ..." (H, p. 53).

Komsomol literature expressed an iconoclastic view of history. What linked the oppressive past with the liberating future was the bloody struggle of the present in which the young warrior played the determining role. For it was through his vital energy and his unconditional enmity towards the old order that the struggle could be taken to its victorious conclusion. Having triumphed, the young warrior would sweep the old world with a broom, cleansing it of all constraints, including God.

> Be brave, brothers, with brooms in your hands.
> Our descendants will remember us well.
> Storm the heavens! Storm the heavens!
> Fling your iron anger like a bomb.
> Storm the heavens! Storm the heavens!
> With a broom chase god into the sty.[31]

The cover of a 1923 issue of *Iunyi kommunist* ("Young Communist") showed a young Communist constructing the new society while toppling onion-domed churches. The editors interpreted the picture for their readers: "We the creators of the new society, who have a new ideology, find ourselves in the cruelest struggle against the remnants of the past," including the church and religion. This iconoclasm found expression even in official Komsomol documents: "The capitalist system is on the eve of destruction ... A new world is replacing economic, political, and spiritual slavery – a world of free labor and thought."[32] In this view of history, youth became "the bearer of a new epoch,"[33] the "regiments of the future," endowed with a vitality missing in the older generation.[34] At times youth's role was conceived in almost mystical terms. The young were called "forefathers of future revelations;"[35]

> Only we, the untiring will be entrusted
> With the key to the new epoch.[36]

In the spring of 1922 young readers were treated to the ruminations of a Zarathustra-like character in the pages of the Komsomol literary and artistic journal *Molodaia gvardiia*. In the story "Heathens," the young hero, isolated from other humans, lived in harmony with nature in exotic Alma Ata. Suggesting the philosophy of God-building developed years earlier by the Nietzschean Marxists, the colorful character called for the creation of a new religion for modern man. "This religion [will consider] the great essence [of people] God-like, and the human body saintly; its hymns ... will glorify the moment of love and conception, and its canon will affirm [human] passion."[37] This story appeared at the start of the anti-religious offensive which began that year and which featured noisy irreverent carnivals in which young people dressed up as Allah, Moses, priests, and other representatives of established religions. Religion, a pillar of the old world, and especially Christianity, were singled out for destruction. Komsomolites were only too eager to participate in militant atheistic activities.

The act of destruction was creative. And the destroyer-creator, for the Komsomol as for Nietzsche, was not an ivory-tower savant but an activist who transformed the world in which he lived. Yet what the young Komsomol warrior created was ultimately alien to Nietzsche's philosophy:

> Destroying all that prevented it
> From living and creating,
> [The creator] will build its own bright temple,
> The temple of brotherhood, based on equality.[38]

In these verses the creator-warrior declared his unity with "the people." Unlike Nietzsche's warrior, the Komsomol hero strove to erect "the temple of brotherhood," for Nietzsche the equivalent of the "herd" society, which represented the triumph of that detestable "last man" (Z, p. 130), who sacrificed creativity and freedom for the sake of material well-being. The Komsomol's vision had its roots in major currents of the Enlightenment as much as it did in socialism. Both the Enlightenment and socialism were anathema to Nietzsche, who saw in them a "plebeian antagonism to everything privileged and aristocratic" (*BGE*, p. 30). For Nietzsche, as for the Komsomol, the new order would permit the individual to develop his creativity in full. But for Nietzsche relatively few individuals ever could and should have the possibility to achieve their creative potential. For Nietzsche all such attempts at egalitarianism could only result in a leveling-down of society and cultural life, making it impossible for the exceptionally creative person to blossom.[39] And indeed powerful currents within the Russian Revolution stood for the razing down so feared by Nietzsche. Such movements as Makhaevism, with its strident anti-intellectualism and anti-elitism, or the peasants' destructive rampages against all signs of economic and cultural symbols of power played a notable role in the course of dismantling the prerevolutionary order in Russia.[40] Yet for the Komsomol, as for the mainstream Russian Communist movement, the Revolution's iconoclasm was only a means, a transition, to the empowerment of the previously disenfranchised. Like the "Nietzschean Marxists" before them, the Komsomol "asserted that social and political leveling does not have to be a leveling down, that in the socialist society of the future it will be a leveling up – bringing all men to the highest pitch of cultural creativity."[41] The new order would raise cultural and material levels for all toilers. In doing so, the old privileges and barriers to political and economic power and to culture would crumble and make way for "the bright kingdom of labor."[42]

Nietzsche's antagonism towards socialism made him an unacceptable influence over Soviet youth in general, and especially over the Komsomol. Party and Komsomol leaders found the exalted role that Nietzsche accorded youth especially problematic because of its potential for fomenting the Komsomol's vanguardism. At times the Komsomol writers' contempt for the old order was transformed into disdain for the older generation as well. In his poem "The Weak-Willed" ("Bezvol'nyi") Nikolai Fomin characterizes those whom the Revolution has passed by as old men:

> And you walk with a crooked back
> With a heavy, dark look,
> You're tired, like a soldier
> Who, day after day,
> Prepared for a needless parade.[43]

These verses may be compared to Nietzsche's characterization of that individual who could not transcend history or shake the burden of the past. The past, according to Nietzsche, "oppresses him ... it encumbers his gait like an invisible and sinister burden ..." (*H*, p. 9). Fomin chided the weak-willed:

> Only the austere,
> The hard and the young
> Who have broken the fetters
> Will toss up the surf
> And triumph.[44]

In a similar vein, Gerassim Feigin's "Krasnaia molodezh'" ("Red Youth"), which was written after the Civil War, called on the young to battle, concluding that

> Death in a bitter battle is brighter and younger
> Than the dull impotence of pitiful old men.[45]

The Komsomol came under sharp criticism for its members' categorical rejection of the old order. According to Bukharin, the Komsomol's iconoclasm, and by implication, its Nietzscheanism, were anachronistic legacies of the prerevolutionary intelligentsia, which negated its society's mores and values. Scornful of the past, the Komsomolites claimed to be ushering in new art forms and a new lifestyle. Viktor Klin believed that the Komsomol's iconoclasm had more recent roots in the Civil War. Regardless of its origins, Bukharin cautioned that the creation of the new *byt* required discipline and not the "petty-bourgeois" intellectual disorder and laxity displayed by the Komsomol. He chided them for thinking that a new culture could be constructed mechanically overnight; socialist culture and society would have to build organically on the cumulative past of human accomplishments.[46]

VANGUARDISM VERSUS COLLECTIVISM

The Komsomol's vanguardist claims were in tension with their quest to be an integral part of the collective creating the new socialist society. Paradoxically, the youth literature also depicted the young vanguard as part of the toiling nation, the sons of "great mother-labor, the rebelling nation," children of the "proletarian father," or as members of the Commune.[47] The most popular collectivist image was that of youth as the changing guard, the continuers of their fathers' and mothers' pursuits. This image was already present in works from 1917. "The adult generation of the working class lived through the horrors of the imperialist war; the war exhausted its strength, [and] sometimes it yields to feelings of fatigue."[48] This image became more prevalent in the literature of the Civil War.

> He who is young and strong
> Will relieve those who are weary![49]

Though the youth literature often focused on the individual warrior waging battle, it was understood that he was only a member in the columns of determined soldiers. This echoed the tension present earlier in the works of the Nietzschean Marxists. While Bogdanov and Lunacharsky embraced Nietzsche's idea of "man's historical transcendence," of the individual's role as creator and "shaper of culture," they felt that the transformation of society could be accomplished by individuals as part of the collective and not through Nietzsche's "radical individualism."[50] The Komsomol stressed unity in attaining the common goal of liberation, which was expressed as the quest for "the beauty of Life."[51] This unifying imagery was repeated in the third Komsomol program in 1920:

> The working class can fulfill the heroic task of saving humanity only in the event that ... it destroy the bourgeois state and organize its own power ... with the help of which it will deprive the bourgeoisie of its wealth, destroy bourgeois opposition, and lay the foundations for a new society, where humanity will be united and in harmony, a great working artel, without masters or rulers ... where each individual will be given the space to develop his talents and strength ... Not just one generation of workers will fight this struggle ... From the entrails of proletarian youth derive the cadres of young and fresh warriors who will overthrow capitalism.[52]

The tension underlying both of those motifs – vanguardist versus collectivist – had very concrete manifestations in the development of the youth movement. The socialist youth movement[53] emerged in 1917 as the organized expression of a particular sector of the working class that felt that its needs were ignored or actively resisted by the adult-male-dominated workers' movement. It championed such youth-specific issues as the six-hour day with paid time-off for studies, wage parity with adults, separate youth representation in factory committees and other workers' institutions, professional training, universal education, and the right to vote for eighteen-year-olds. That separatism soon gave way to vanguardist sentiments that were expressed from the inception of the youth movement and that were nourished by the organization's political radicalism. Komsomol historians boasted that in 1917 the socialist youth movement demonstrated its radicalism and revolutionary consciousness by adopting a Bolshevik line earlier than most "adult" organizations.

Yet from the beginning the movement's organizers faced the

dilemma of expressing those particularistic and vanguardist impulses while maintaining their ties and commitment to the larger workers' movement. Consistently, youth organizers felt that the movement's destiny was inextricably tied to the fate of the Revolution. Only the triumph of socialism, they felt, would allow youth to preserve the specific interests their movement had championed.

For that reason, the Komsomol met the needs of the new state for politically reliable personnel with boundless enthusiasm. By the end of the Civil War the League emerged as a critical institution of consensus building for the new society. Its main function, that of transforming consciousness, a central tenet of Marxist-Leninist political activism, placed the Komsomol in a privileged position in the Soviet state and gave it a special relationship to the Communist Party. The new order, Communism, could come about only if people's consciousness changed. To bring about that transformation in the new generation was the task of the Communist Youth League. The organization popularized the ideals and tasks of the state and the Communist Party through its network of youth clubs, factory schools, and secondary school branches. According to dominant sectors in the Party and the Komsomol leadership, the League could not carry out that task if it were to serve as an advocate for the particularistic interests of a special group or act as a vanguard in relation to the Party.

During the 1920s and, later, during the Stalin Revolution much of the Komsomol's rhetoric continued to posit youth as more revolutionary than the rest of the working class. In the political arena such vanguardist sentiments were in part responsible for the Komsomol's continued attraction to the various oppositions within the Party throughout the 1920s. In 1922 Trotsky, in his efforts to pit the young against the Old Guard which rejected his bid for power after Lenin's incapacitation, appealed to Communist youth by stating that they were "always ... the trumpet call of the proletarian Revolution."[54]

Emelian Yaroslavsky was not alone among Party leaders to bemoan the Komsomol's propensity to adopt all kinds of "harmful deviations" – presumably including Nietzscheanism

– under the influence of "anarchistic individuals," petty-
bourgeois and "lumpen" elements.[55] These "deviations"
found cultural and political expression in Komsomol circles.
This criticism was especially aimed at the urban Komsomol,
which developed a radical subculture distinct from that of its
more traditional rural counterparts. Urban Komsomolites
were especially leery of the compromise embodied in the New
Economic Policy (NEP) and resented the influx of peasant
recruits and their growing influence within the League. In
their "proletarian radicalism" many disaffected League
members juxtaposed themselves to the Party and the Komsomol leadership, which they felt had digressed from the true
path towards Communism by catering to "petty-bourgeois"
sectors of Soviet society. Many Party leaders were concerned
that this vanguardism on the Komsomol's part threatened the
Party's special relationship with the youth organization.[56]

In the mid-1920s and subsequently the Komsomol success-
fully channeled its vanguardism into the service of the collective and the state. League members assumed the role of
harbingers of a new materialist, modernizing, and secular
popular culture to the masses, young and old. They felt a sense
of mission: only their generation could construct the new
culture and new patterns of everyday life. And indeed the
Komsomol became identified as bearers of a new order and
new ways, its members' intransigence by no means universally
popular. Komsomolites were the first to introduce radios in
some villages and to use new farming methods and technology
in others. The Komsomol initiated new rituals and holidays,
such as Komsomol Christmas and Easter; their members
married in civil ceremonies (ZAGS) and refused to baptize
their children, preferring to dedicate their offspring in
"Octobering" ("oktiabrina") ceremonies. League members
served as advance guard in the campaigns against illiteracy
and against religion.

The literature of the mid- and late 1920s shed the Nietzscheanism that had been present in Komsomol works of the Civil
War and early NEP. Komsomol literature no longer focused on
the warrior, but on the massive social, cultural, and economic

changes wrought by the masses of workers and peasants. The peasant who adopted modern farming methods, the young woman who embraced the new customs and married the chairman of the local executive committee in a civil ceremony, these were the new subjects of Komsomol literature. In the late 1920s the Komsomol embraced the Cultural Revolution. The general malaise felt by many Komsomolites during the NEP, the perception of aimlessness and retreat from revolution, gave way to a renewed sense of purpose as the Komsomol sought to destroy the remnants of the hated past.[57] The period beginning in 1927–28 saw the revival of anti-religious and anti-intellectual campaigns. Komsomol literature of the Cultural Revolution (1928–32) used military imagery reminiscent of Nietzsche's warrior.[58] Yet this was not the Nietzschean hero fighting overwhelming odds but columns of "builders of socialism" and Komsomol soldiers fighting such concrete enemies as the bureaucrats in the department of education, the kulaks, industrial wreckers, and saboteurs.

The tone was just as monumental as that of the earlier works, but it was more practically-oriented than the heady vanguardism of the poetry and literature of the Civil War and early NEP. Though Komsomolites saw themselves as a vanguard and therefore an elite, as Communists their goal was to create a mass socialist culture and society, a goal inimical to Nietzsche's philosophy as it is usually understood.[59] Yet the philosopher, popular among Russian intellectuals before the Revolution, left his imprint on the first Komsomol generation. During the League's formative years, aspects of its vanguardism, so essential to the organization's self-identity, owed their origins to Nietzsche or to interpretations of his philosophy.

NOTES

* I am grateful to grants from William Paterson College and to a Ford Foundation Postdoctoral Fellowship for giving me time to write this article.

1 O. Tarkhanov, *Bol'shevistskii Komsomol; sbornik statei i rechei, 1921–1924 gg.* (Moscow, 1925), p. 61. On Vologda see "Tsentral'noe statisticheskoe upravleniie RSFSR," *Narodnoe knoziastvo Volo-*

godskoi oblasty za gody sovetskoi vlasti. Statisticheskii sbornik (Vologda, 1967), p. 3.

2 "First Program, and charter of the Komsomol (1918)," in Isabel A. Tirado, *Young Guard! The Petrograd Komsomol Organization, 1917–1920* (Westport, CT, 1988), p. 231.

3 *Iunyi kommunist*, 1 (1918), p. 2.

4 Records of the All-Union (Russian) Communist Party, Smolensk District, WKP 121 (1921).

5 I have used the definitions of "vanguard" and "avant-garde" provided in *Webster's New Collegiate Dictionary* (Springfield, MA, 1975), pp. 78 and 1293.

6 See Tirado, *Young Guard!*

7 V. Khlebnikov et al., "The Trumpet of the Martians" (1916) *Russian Futurism through its Manifestoes, 1912–1928*, ed. Anna Lawton (Ithaca, 1988), pp. 104–6.

8 George L. Kline, "'Nietzschean Marxism' in Russia," *The Boston College Studies in Philosophy* 2 (1968), pp. 166–83; in *Nietzsche in Russia*, ed. Bernice Glatzer Rosenthal, see the articles by Mary Louise Loe, "Gorky and Nietzsche: the Quest for a Russian Superman;" A. L. Tait, "Lunacharsky: A Nietzschean Marxist?;" and Zenovia Sochor, "A. A. Bogdanov: In Search of Cultural Liberation," pp. 251–311.

9 A. Bogdanov, "Trud i potrebnosti rabotnika," *Molodaia gvardiia* 5 (1923), pp. 109–10; I. Oksenov, "Chto chitat'," *Iunyi proletarii* (hereafter abbrev. *IUP*) 1–2 (January 1921), pp. 29–30.

10 E. A. Kondrat'eva, *Pisateli-Vologzhane (1917–1957)* (Vologda, 1958), pp. 4–5; *Narodnoe khoziastvo Vologodskoi oblasti*, p. 4.

11 Zenovia A. Sochor, *Revolution and Culture: The Bogdanov-Lenin Controversy* (Ithaca, 1988), p. 149.

12 "Manifesto of the All-District Council of Trud i svet," Tirado, *Young Guard!*, p. 220.

13 Peter Bergmann, *Nietzsche, the Last Antipolitical German* (Bloomington, IN, 1987), pp. 61–62.

14 N. Fomin, "Bortsam za pervenstvo truda," *Petrogradskaia pravda* (hereafter abbreviated *PP*), May 18, 1920.

15 D. Maznin, "Pesn' otdykha," *IUP* 1–2 (January 1921), p. 7.

16 Maznin, "Iz mgly protivorechii," *IUP*, January–February 1922, no. 1, p. 28.

17 Untitled verses by Evgeniia Gerr, *IUP*, December 16, 1917.

18 R. Bruker, "Za griadushchee," *IUP* 1–2 (January 1921), p. 23.

19 F. Isakov, "Dorogu," *PP*, December 14, 1920.

20 Evgenii Panfilov, "Edinenie," *PP*, August, 19, 1920.

21 D. Maznin, "Avangard," *PP*, January 27, 1920.

22 N. Fomin, "Iunost'," *PP*, September 5, 1920.

23 Vladimir Sobol', "Vpered," *Muza v krasnoi kosynke: Komsomol'skaia poeziia, 1918–1950* (Moscow, 1968), p. 19.

24 E. Gerr, Untitled verses, *IUP*, 16 (29) December 1917.

25 N. Fomin, "Iz pesen pobedy," *PP* December 21, 1920.

26 Sobol', "Vpered," *Muza*, p. 19.

27 Maznin and Fomin, "Molodoi rabotnitse," *PP*, April 20, 1920.

28 Gerassim Feigin, "Krasnaia molodezh'," *Muza*, p. 29.

29 Maznin, "Iunye kommunisty," *PP*, February 10, 1920; Bernice Glatzer Rosenthal "A New Word for a New Myth; Nietzsche and Russian Futurism," *The European Foundations of Russian Modernism*, ed. Peter Barta (Lewiston, NY, 1991), pp. 225 and 232.

30 Inn. Oksenov, Untitled verses, *IUP* 1–2 (1921).

31 V. Vorobei, "Komsomol'skii marsh," *IUP* 8–9 (1923), p. 12.

32 "First Program and Charter of the Komsomol (1918," Tirado, *Young Guard!*, p. 233.

33 N. Fomin, "K nam skoree," *PP*, February 17, 1920, p. 3; "Trud i svet's Manifesto," Tirado, *Young Guard!*, pp. 220–22.

34 Maznin, 'Iunye kommunisty," *PP*, February 10, 1920, p. 4.

35 Fomin, "Iunost'," *PP*, September 5, 1920, p. 3.

36 Maznin, "Avangard," *PP*, January 27, 1920, p. 4.

37 Pavel Nizovoi, "Iazychniki," *Molodaia gvardiia*, April–May 1922.

38 Gerr, Untitled verses, *IUP*, 16 (29) December 1917; Bergmann, *Nietzsche*, p. 63.

39 Kline, "'Nietzschean Marxism' in Russia," *The Boston College Studies in Philosophy* 2 (1968), p. 167.

40 Richard Stites, *Revolutionary Dreams: Utopian Visions and Experimental Life in the Russian Revolution* (New York, 1989), pp. 62–63, 74–75.

41 George L. Kline, "Foreword," *Nietzsche in Russia*, ed. Bernice G. Rosenthal (Princeton, 1986), p. xiv.

42 Maznin, "Avangard."

43 Nikolai Fomin, "Bezvol'nyi," *IUP* 1–2 (1922), p. 59.

44 Fomin, "Bezvol'nyi," p. 59.

45 Gerassim Feigin, "Krasnaia molodezh'," *Muza*, p. 29.

46 N. Bukharin, "Za uporiadochenie byta molodezhi" and Viktor Klin, "O tipe komsomol'tsa," *Byt i molodezh'*, ed. A. Slepkov (Moscow, 1926), pp. 6–9, 40–41.

47 For example see Evgeniia Gerr's verses in *IUP*, December 16, 1917.

48 "Trud i svet's Manifesto," Tirado, *Young Guard!*, pp. 220–22.

49 Maznin, "Iunye kommunisty," *PP*, February 10, 1920.

50 George Kline, *Religious and AntiReligious Thought in Russia* (Chicago and London, 1963), pp. 107–8; Zenovia A. Sochor, "A. A. Bogdanov: In Search of Cultural Liberation," *Nietzsche in Russia*, p. 299.

51 "Trud i svet's Manifesto," *Young Guard!*, p. 220.

52 "Third Program and Charter of the Komsomol (1920)," *Young Guard!*, p. 237.

53 The socialist youth movement initially brought together young workers, most of whom were not affiliated with political parties. Those who were affiliated politically belonged to the far left: Bolsheviks, Left-SRs, Menshevik-Internationalists, and Anarchists.

54 *Iunyi kommunist* 17–18 (1922), p. 1.

55 E. Yaroslavsky, "Za uporiadochenie zhizni i byta molodezhi," *Komsomol'skii byt*, ed. I. Razin (Moscow-Leningrad, 1927), pp. 105–8.

56 Slepkov's introduction to *Byt i molodezh'*, pp. 3–4.

57 *Cultural Revolution in Russia, 1928–1931*, ed. Sheila Fitzpatrick, (Bloomington, 1984), p. 3.

58 Ibid., p. 23. For example, see "Kak oni gotoviatsia k voine" and "Liogkaia kavaleriia v deistvii," *Komsomol'skaia pravda*, June 9, 1928.

59 Geoffrey Waite, "Zarathustra or the Modern Prince: The Problem of Nietzschean Political Philosophy," *Nietzsche heute: Die Rezeption seines Werkes nach 1968*, ed. S. Bauschinger et al., (Berne and Stuttgart, 1988), pp. 227–50.

CHAPTER 10

Nietzschean roots of Stalinist culture

Mikhail Agursky*

Although the USSR declared the total rejection of Nietzscheanism in 1933, when Hitler came to power, it was never truly abandoned there; internalized, it became an important undercurrent of Soviet culture. This chapter will treat the major tributaries of that undercurrent – the Nietzscheanism of certain Bolsheviks, Russian fellow-traveling writers, and Western writers, especially Jack London, showing how they converged in Stalinist Nietzscheanism.

BOLSHEVIK NIETZSCHEANISM

The formation of Russian Bolshevism coincided with the Nietzschean fever that infected Russians at the beginning of the century. Indeed, it can be claimed that the majority of Bolshevik intellectuals came under the influence of Nietzsche, an influence which varied only in intensity from one individual to another. Bogdanov and Lunacharsky, for instance, remained Nietzscheans after the Revolution and did their best to transmit their old Nietzschean values into the new society, implicitly or explicitly.

Lunacharsky, in a better administrative position to achieve the goal, lost no opportunity to express his ambivalent regard for Nietzsche. According to a Soviet historian, even in his last period he viewed some pages or chapters of Nietzsche as acceptable for any class which aspired to life, struggle and progress.[1] In 1928, in the introduction to M. G. Leiteisen's book *Nietzsche and Finance Capital*, Lunacharsky continued to claim that:

there is an affinity between some of Nietzsche's judgments and conclusions and our own. This certainly explains why we, Marxist-Communists, paid some enthusiastic tribute to Nietzsche in the dawn of our revolutionary movement ... While I personally have some reservations about the essence of Nietzsche's social trends I pay him tribute for his struggle against Christianity, against petty Philistine morality with its rumination, its pacifist toothlessness ...[2]

Lunacharsky also supplied an introduction to Stefan Zweig's novel on Nietzsche, Hölderlin, and Kleist, *The Master Builders*, published in Russian in 1932. This introduction, too, is ambivalent: it mentions some "excellent pages" of Nietzsche which specifically rebuked Germany for its attitude to its men of genius – among whom Lunacharsky lists Nietzsche.[3]

There were other committed Nietzscheans among the Bolshevik intelligentsia. The Soviet Commissar for Foreign Affairs until 1930, Georgy Chicherin (1872–1936), was one of them.[4] According to his recent official biography, he was a lifelong adherent of Nietzsche, and the biography relates how towards the end of his life he defended Nietzsche from charges of Fascism.[5]

As demonstrated in her autobiographical novel, written in 1919–21 but only recently published, the brilliant young writer and Bolshevik superwoman Larisa Reisner (1895–1926) was also a passionate Nietzschean. Married to the Soviet Commissar of the Navy, Fedor Raskolnikov, and mistress of Karl Radek, she was a prominent Soviet intellectual until her death from cancer. She wrote in 1921:

Nietzsche, the wise and mad Zarathustra who hated the powerful and the sated, was ingested by his own enemies ... Oh, enough of the useless perfection, enough of the incest between Heaven and Earth. The gods want resurrection and embodiment. The earth is full to overflowing with them, more so than in the time of the humanists ... It is impossible to grant giants a life-span of millennia and then sell them into eternal slavery. We will be strangled by the dreams with which we fill the air, not even providing them with living flesh. The Stone Guest of our spirit is approaching our doors to judge and to rule. He will not return to his cemetery, to his grave. We will have to take his granite hand and make a choice between a new life or complete irreversible destruction.[6]

Any discussion of Nietzsche's influence on Soviet society must consider Gorky, and not only in his early prerevolutionary period.[7] In fact, Gorky was an important transmitter of Nietzsche to Soviet society throughout his career, though his outlook was much too complicated to be reduced only to Nietzsche. It is true that towards the end of his life Gorky reconsidered some of his early naive Nietzscheanism, rejecting the vulgar form with its cult of power for its own sake. But he integrated other important aspects of Nietzsche in his literary and political activity and remained a Nietzschean until his death. One extremely important idea which he derived from Nietzsche was that of modern humanity as a bridge to future superhumanity, which incidentally did not differ greatly from the Noösphere of Teilhard de Chardin.[8]

Gorky accepted the Nietzschean definition of truth, repeatedly claiming that so-called natural laws exist only in the human imagination. He also accepted the Nietzschean condemnation of Christianity as slave morality: indeed, to be a "slave of God" was an utter humiliation for Gorky.[9] But, influenced by Merezhkovsky and Rozanov, he distinguished between historical and original Christianity. He claimed that Christ was the highest model of humanity, but was only future-oriented, and that in the meantime humanity needed Prometheus and even Antichrist. Later, Gorky tried to interpret Christ as a metamorphosis of Prometheus, since he regarded Christ also as a rebel against the Father.[10]

Now the possible impact of Nietzsche on Lenin himself can be legitimately examined. Although his published collected works contain only two explicit references to Nietzsche, both bibliographical,[11] Lenin's idea of overcoming Oblomov, or the remaking of Russian man, is entirely within the Nietzschean outlook.[12]

Nietzschean criticism of man and appeals to overcome him were extremely congenial to Lenin's contempt for the Russian national character. Inheriting his views from Russian radicalism via Chernyshevsky and Tkachev, Lenin saw the typical Russian as a passive, inert creature with an inherent slave morality, the most sinister manifestation of which was

Oblomov; he was especially critical of the Russian peasantry. Lenin dreamed of creating a Russian *homo novus*: his idea of social revolution was inseparable from his idea of a cultural revolution which would purge the new, perfect society of old human types that were unfit for the future. Not man as such should be overcome, according to Lenin, but specifically Russian man. The contemporary Russian people was merely raw material for the future, a Nietzschean bridge for the process of national reconstruction for which no moral criteria were needed. To Lenin, the remaking of Russia was more a problem of cultural anthropology than a problem of class struggle in the Marxist sense.

It was not Marxism but Nietzscheanism that supplied Lenin with the theory of human selection, since Marxism, as a part of German culture, regarded German proletarian efficiency as a model for other nations. The Bolsheviks operated within an entirely different society and their cultural considerations were fertile soil for the penetration of Nietzschean ideas into Bolshevik declarations of Marxism.

Gorky was very close to Lenin in his criticism of the majority of contemporary Russians, especially Russian peasants. He likely regarded them as subhuman, in part at least with Nietzsche's contempt for the herd. In 1921, after the famine relief appeal, Gorky hesitatingly suggested something close to a peasant purge in Russia. In 1922 he wrote:

The revolution, carried out by a numerically insignificant group of the intelligentsia at the head of several thousand workers it had educated – this revolution has furrowed the whole mass of the people with a steel plough so deeply that the peasantry can scarcely return to the old forms of life which have been reduced to dust forever; like the Jews that Moses led out of Egyptian slavery, the half-savage, stupid, ponderous people of the Russian villages and hamlets – all those almost terrible people of whom we spoke – will die out, and a new tribe will take their place – literate, sensible, hearty people.[13]

The idea of remaking the Russians into a superhuman community can be found everywhere in the Bolshevik culture of the 1920s. The novel *The Nineteen* (*The Rout*) (1927), by the young writer Aleksandr Fadeev (1901–56) – a Bolshevik since 1918, a favorite of Stalin, and a future Secretary-General of the Soviet Union of Writers – expressed this idea. The novel's main character, Osip Levinson, dreams of such reconstruction. Observing a flabby, indecisive Russian, Levinson muses:

> How unfortunate a country must be which produced so many men of his type, futile and worthless. Only with us, only in our country, Levinson thought ... could such lazy and spineless creatures ... be found; only in our country, where millions of people have lived for centuries under an indolent sun, in dirt and poverty, ploughing with primitive tools, believing in a vindictive and foolish God – only in such a country, where there is so little store of wisdom, could they exist ... And Levinson was moved, because these were his deepest and most intimate thoughts ... because he was urged by an over-powering desire, stronger than any other of his desires, to help to create a new, fine, vigorous man.[14]

Peter Scheibert notes in his article on Superman in the Russian Revolution that the elimination of subhumans was a general revolutionary objective.[15]

One aspect of early Bolshevik Nietzscheanism was a Dionysian interpretation of the Revolution. Gorky was very ambivalent towards such Nietzschean Dionysianism, admitting its existence, fascinated by it, but regarding it as a threat, a manifestation of an elemental force which should be kept under strict control.[16] In Nietzschean terms, Gorky identified with the Apollonian face of the human psyche. Nevertheless, any profound analysis of early Bolshevik collectivism, especially as manifested by Proletkult, shows that at bottom one can indeed distinguish the same Dionysian dissolution of personality in the collectivist superego.

An important expression of such Dionysian Bolshevik collectivism was the novel *Cement* (1925) by Fedor Gladkov (1883–1955), who had been a Bolshevik since 1906. One of the characters is a former Menshevik who joined the Bolsheviks during the Civil War and who almost unhesitatingly participated in the arrest of his father and brother. He is unexpectedly and seemingly undeservedly expelled from the Party during a routine purge. He does not rebel, but surrenders to the Party superego:

No personal life. What was his love, hidden in unseen depths? What were his problems and thoughts, which tortured his mind? All were survivals of an accursed past. All came from his father, from his youth, the romanticism of intellectuals. All this must be extirpated to the very root. These sick figments of the mind must be destroyed.[17]

Gladkov's ecstatic collectivism should not be removed from the general Nietzschean context. In 1928 he published a short novel, *With Bleeding Heart* (*Kroviu serdtsa*), which sounds like an attempt to imitate *Zarathustra*. Gladkov's protagonist, the worker Chizhov, instructs another character, a writer:

Art should go ahead of life, it should be a little bit above it. And you dig in the mire like beetles. Our life is vegetating in boredom. You do nothing to overwhelm us, to strike us, although you could cause the miraculous transformation of man by the power of your word. And man is a slave. He expects serenity and welfare. Slavery taught him obedience, calm, benevolent twilight – it accustomed him to flies, priests, the pigsty ... Don't let man be tired. Save him from comfort and sleep. Make him a permanent rebel against himself ... Why do you let man be silent? Don't let him forget even for a minute his great destiny as creator, builder, hero on the earth ... Man is an inextinguishable dream. He is the battle, the exploit, the eventual fall and victory.[18]

Several critics accused Gladkov of Nietzscheanism. The prominent leftist literary critic and former anarchist Iuda Grossman-Roshchin (1883–1934) commented: "On the one hand, man is a heap of vices and stagnation, and on the other, man has a surplus of energy and is always on the verge of exploding. Is not this an illiterate version of Nietzscheanism?"[19] Another critic accused Gladkov of "snub-nosed" Nietzscheanism.[20]

Another important aspect of early Bolshevik Nietzscheanism was anti-Darwinism. Indeed, Nietzsche himself preferred Lamarckism because it presumed biological activism, a creative element in evolution. From this viewpoint the evolutionary process is determined not by a selection of incremental changes but by a will for life, an effort, a creative impulse. In the Nietzschean context this signified that man, that is, Superman, could contribute to his own evolution by his own will. The laws of nature were relativized.

The Bolshevik Nietzscheans also expressed strong reservations about Darwinism. But one should take into consideration that it was very difficult, even dangerous, to come out publicly against Darwinism at that time, when it was part and parcel of the credo of every educated person in Russia. Moreover, Darwinism had been approved by Marx, who had called himself the Darwin of the social sciences. Reservations had to be expressed very cautiously. Gorky, for example, was never sympathetic towards Darwinism, but feared to criticize it publicly.[21] In a story he wrote in 1923, one of the characters, a student, says, "Darwin is a truth I don't like, just as I would not like hell if it were true."[22] In an article published in 1928, Gorky said that the Bolsheviks did not want to live according to Darwin,[23] because he had not left a place for human will. It is not surprising that Gorky supported the evolutionary theory of Nomogenesis suggested in 1921 by Lev Berg, who tried to explain evolution as a result of an immanent development inherent in nature.[24]

Ivan Skvortsov-Stepanov (1870–1928), a leading Bolshevik, actually contested Darwinism in his extensive writing on philosophy. Skvortsov-Stepanov had belonged to the left wing of the Bolshevik Party before the October Revolution and was close to Bogdanov; he was editor-in-chief of *Izvestia* until his death. According to him, nature cannot develop by incremental changes: only great leaps are productive. In his book on dialectical materialism he never mentioned Darwin.[25] This was certainly a way of tacitly expressing his support of Lamarckism.

BOLSHEVISM'S NIETZSCHEAN FELLOW-TRAVELERS

(1) The fascination of Bolshevik power

The aftermath of the October Revolution brought the majority of Russian non-Bolshevik Nietzscheans to Bolshevism. Always nationalist, the Russian Nietzscheans saw in the Bolsheviks not only a strong power that would eliminate the Russian flabbiness they hated, and not only power for its own sake, but also power for the sake of Russian power.

A few days after the October Revolution the second-rate Russian conservative writer Ieronim Iasinsky (1850–1931) visited Lunacharsky, the new Bolshevik Commisar for Education, to express his support for the Bolsheviks. Iasinsky was violently attacked for this by the non-Bolshevik press. In his article, "On Bolsheviks, Superman, and Frogs" ("O bolshevikakh, o sverkhcheloveke i o zhalakh"), Iasinsky informed his critics that he did not regard Bolshevism as a social-democratic movement, since it was a purely Russian phenomenon, the very opposite of Menshevism. He was attracted to the Bolsheviks, he said, because they represented a physically and morally bright and powerful type of Russian hero, and he stressed the Nietzschean influence that had led him to this conclusion. Later he formally joined the Bolshevik Party.

In turn, Iasinsky claimed, Lunacharsky was very enthusiastic about his visit. He said that Nietzsche was a fighter against pity and an apostle of courage, of comprehensive revaluation, of an impetuous drive towards the superior. Lunacharsky said that Iasinsky had taken "from a German wizard" all that was most militant, eagle-like, destructive, and creative.[26]

Nikolai Gredeskul (1864–?), a professor of social science and former Rector of Kharkov University, was a founder and prominent member of the Cadet Party. He, too, quickly accepted the October Revolution as a Russian national revolution. In his zeal he joined the Bolshevik Party and became a Marxist philosopher.[27] In 1926 he published a book, *Russia, Before and Now* (*Rossiia prezhde i teper*), in which he confessed his fascination with Nietzsche, claiming that the bourgeoisie abuses Nietzscheanism. Meanwhile, "Superman, if one looks only at his internal meaning ... is a man of superior will and superior doubts ... in this internal meaning [the image of Superman] is glorious to a proletarian, not at all so to a bourgeois."[28]

The Nietzschean fascination with Bolshevik power entered the mainstream of the new Soviet literature. The prominent Russian writer Aleksei Tolstoi (1883–1945), who became an outspoken National Bolshevik,[29] expressed Nietzschean ideas from the very start of his political conversion in 1922. In his science-fiction novel *Aelita*, published in that year, he contrasts the Bolshevik superman Gusev with emasculated Martians who are afraid to use power. Anticipating a Martian holocaust, the Martian leader Gor (actually a Western liberal in disguise) says, "Ay, we've let our chance slip by. We should have loved life furiously and ardently – ardently."[30]

Tolstoi later became close to Stalin and suggested Peter the Great to him as a supra-historical model worthy of imitation.[31] Tolstoi died in 1945, having survived all the purges, like the majority of Russian Nietzscheans. They all turned out to be well fitted for survival under critical conditions, theoretically encouraged in this ability by their Nietzscheanism.

A prominent place in early Soviet Nietzscheanism certainly belonged to Yuri Olesha (1899–1960). In his novel *Envy* (1927) he compares the Bolshevik superman Andrei Babichev, a high-ranking Soviet food industry official, with the degraded intellectual Kavalerov. Babichev's attempts to help Kavalerov only increase the latter's inferiority complex and make him violently envious of Babichev. The message is that people like Kavalerov cannot be helped to survive: their fate is to perish, and they should be helped to do so.

The Nietzschean influence on Olesha is immediately obvious, and he himself admitted to it much later. Olesha recounts that the poet Mayakovsky, whom he adored, had suddenly remarked: "Olesha is writing a novel, *Nietzsche*." Olesha corrected him: "*Nishchii* [*Beggar*], Vladimir Vladimirovich, the novel *Nishchii*." "It's all the same," Mayakovsky replied with a flash of genius. "Indeed," Olesha commented, "a writer writing a novel about a beggar – taking into consideration the times and my peculiarity as a writer – should have read much of Nietzsche."[32] Olesha's reference to Mayakovsky in this context was by no means accidental. Mayakovsky, no less than Gorky, was an important transmitter of Nietzsche to Soviet society. His Nietzscheanism is discussed in Bengt Jangfeldt's chapter in this volume.

Some Russian Nietzscheans had a rather ambivalent attitude to Nietzscheanism, due to their fear of its influence on potential foreign enemies. In 1924 the young writer Konstantin Fedin (1892–1977), then a Bolshevik fellow-traveler and later – after Stalin – Secretary-General of the Soviet Union of Writers, published a novel, *Cities and Years*, with a strong Nietzschean subtext. His hero, Andrei Startsev, confronts his old German friend, Kurt, who has become a fully-fledged German Bolshevik-Nietzschean. Kurt says:

"Blood, blood, that's what frightens you. And this eternal fear that evil gives birth to evil. And what can you offer me in exchange for evil? My veins are being drawn out of me, a thread at a time, endlessly, for the whole of my life. And it is suggested I build my life on good, because evil breeds evil. Where can I find good if there's evil all around me? Prove to me that it's impossible to attain good from evil ...

"That means the greatest thing in your life during these years was love!"

Andrei said, "Yes."

And again waiting several minutes, in the cold night, in the darkness, he said, "And in mine it was – hate."[33]

Eventually Kurt shoots and kills Andrei when he realizes that Andrei did not arrest another German prisoner of war in Russia, a monarchist officer who once had helped him in Germany. In *Cities and Years* a German Nietzschean dominates a Russian, but later, in his novel *The Rape of Europe* (1933–35), Fedin makes Russians dictate their will to Germans and other Europeans.[34] Apparently Fedin was frightened by Nietzscheanism only when it could be used against Russians.

Ambivalence towards Nietzsche can be seen in the works of another prominent Bolshevik fellow-traveler – Leonid Leonov. He distinguished between two kinds of Nietzscheanism. His novel *Soviet River (Sot)* (1930) glorifies the gigantic Bolshevik assault on the traditional Russian, whom he presents as merely fertile soil for the future. The individual is doomed, nobody escapes suffering and deprivations, but it is all for the sake of the future. This was creative, progressive, Bolshevik Nietzscheanism. But there was also a reactionary Nietzscheanism, which Leonov condemned. One of the negative characters in *Soviet River* is Vissarion Baulin, a former Tsarist officer who becomes a monk in order to hide from the authorities. In purely

Nietzschean terms, but in a negative context, Baulin dreams of a new suprahuman Attila who would save humanity from degradation:

I say that the world is now on a hitherto unprecedented wane, its basis hatred and vengeance, its laws are for knaves and its mechanical invention for the weak, its art for the insane ... Civilization – that is the path: degeneration – that is the fulfillment ... Helladas, the balance of the beginning – is left behind, alone ... Listen, I say: back to the Thesis ... Back to the foremother of all, the Helladas ... The weak will die in a year, but [Attila] shall seat the strong on horseback and lead them back once more to the Thesis.[35]

(2) Bolshevism beyond good and evil

Other pro-Bolshevik Nietzscheans emphasized a different aspect of Bolshevism: its militant amorality, which became a main instrument in the Bolshevik struggle for power. For these Nietzscheans, evil was no less instrumental than good. Some of them even claimed that good may be achieved only through evil.

Mikhail Prishvin (1873–1954) was regarded, in the late Soviet period, as one of the principal Russian writers.[36] He also survived the purges, his literary prominence constantly increasing. He openly admitted his fascination with Nietzsche. In his book *The Chain of Kashchei* (*Kashcheeva Tsep*), published in 1923, he remarked on *Zarathustra*, "In this book philosophy joined poetry in a miraculous way and what crawled in Kant and others, here soared like a meteor, lighting the world for one unique moment."[37] His recently published notebooks from the 1930s are even more revealing of his deep Nietzscheanism, beyond good and evil in the best Nietzschean tradition:

What is creativity? The struggle against evil in the first place, but a struggle, not a negation, a switch changing the direction of the acting power of evil. As a result, evil becomes good ... Not good but evil always wins, since evil has all the means for the struggle. But victorious evil inevitably decomposes. Creative works (good ones) imperceptibly dominate destruction, which is a faceless force.[38]

The case of Isai Lezhnev (Altshuler) (1891–1955) is politically more important. Both before and after the October Revolution he was a left-wing radical and a philosophical disciple of Shestov, Bogdanov, and Lunacharsky, and certainly was an admirer of Nietzsche. Lezhnev accepted the October Revolution as a national revolution which would help Russia to unite humanity.[39] In 1922 he launched a non-Party journal which became a rallying-point for national-minded Bolshevik fellow-travelers, the majority of whom were Nietzscheans. In its first issue Lezhnev made an explicitly Nietzschean statement in which he declared a sacred war on all principles. One can easily recognize Shestov's interpretation of Nietzsche in Lezhnev's declaration. Lezhnev said:

Principles taken as they are, if they are intelligible, self-contained realities, do not fit life, do not cover it properly, they are not adequate for life in all its complicated peculiarity ... A new man has reached the path, with no heavy chains of traditions, spontaneous and integral, free of the cobweb prison of ideological prejudices and outmoded principles. It is high time to liberate ourselves from this verbal prison and to stop regarding legal categories as self-contained absolute realities in a vacuum of pure speculation.[40]

Ilia Ehrenburg (1891–1967) was also a committed Nietzschean, which probably helped him not only to survive in Stalin's time, but even to become one of the main Soviet political spokesmen. In 1922 he published his book *Julio Jurenito*, a variation of *Zarathustra*. Jurenito is a man without convictions, without a religious or ethical code, without even a simple philosophical system, who breaks all the prohibitions of all existing ethical codes, but who does not justify this by creating a "new" religion. He dreams of the time when all cathedrals will be destroyed and all prayers forgotten: one should defile the sacred, one should break the commandments, one should laugh more and more loudly, and if it is forbidden to laugh from laughter one should laugh from torment, from fire, in order to clear a space for him who is to come. Jurenito regrets that he will die and not see the wild fields where free people will dance, crying with mindless, childlike laughter. He sends his last kiss to all those who are without a god, without a program, without an idea.[41]

Ehrenburg was widely regarded in the 1920s as a moral nihilist and a Nietzschean.[42] Marietta Shaginian (1888–1982), a disciple of Merezhkovsky's circle and later a prominent Soviet writer, said approvingly in her 1923 review of *Julio Jurenito* that Ehrenburg loved the Bolshevik Revolution as Nietzsche's bridge to the future.[43] (Another most interesting confirmation of Lenin's tacit Nietzscheanism is that, according to his wife, Lenin admired *Julio Jurenito*).[44]

A sympathetic though ambivalent description of a Nietzschean can be found in the novel *Feodosiia* by Ivan Novikov (1877–1959), a religious intellectual who joined Soviet literature and later became quite prominent because of his books on Pushkin and Turgenev. One of the novel's main characters, Tatiana Ganeizer, comes in 1905 from St. Petersburg to the Crimea, where she meets the Nietzschean painter Piskarenko. His catchphrase is, "I know nothing of justice. I know and see only the struggle and it is the movement which is beauty in its turn." For Piskarenko class war is only the conjunction of two sets of justice, and therefore there is no point in anyone's complaining. Reflecting on his words, Tatiana concludes that although they are cruel, perhaps even cynical, nonetheless they are impossible to ignore.[45]

When Piskarenko remarks, "Losses and sacrifices should be disregarded. They are mere sentiment," he is told, "You only repeat Nietzsche."[46] He replies, "I am my own Nietzsche. But Friedrich had good ideas. He has an aphorism, 'It is good to step from peak to peak,' and this aphorism has an apt comment, 'But one needs long legs for it.'"[47]

Piskarenko is a rebel. "I became a revolutionary too. I don't want to endure the *ancien régime*. I am leaving. I have become a fisherman in my own way."[48] In fact, he commits suicide by jumping from a mountain into the sea, thus accomplishing Nietzsche's aphorism, "Die at the right time!"

(3) The Dionysian revolution

Revolution and revolutionary violence were seen through the Nietzschean prism by many pro-Bolshevik intellectuals as a manifestation of Dionysian ecstasy which could also continue after the Revolution. John Maynard has stressed Nietzsche's influence on a group known as the Scythians, who became the backbone of early Soviet culture. It included writers and poets such as Blok, Bely, Briusov, Esenin, Kliuev, and others who welcomed the October Revolution as a "Dionysian escape from common sense."[49] Maynard believed that the Scythians' revolutionary messianism was entirely foreign to Nietzsche. He was right, but one can see how Nietzscheanism in Russia soon became a corollary of Russian nationalism and messianism, since it promised the remaking of man not only into *homo novus*, but first and foremost into the Dionysian Russian *homo novus*, in contrast with the typical man of the old West.

Most Scythians were soon disappointed, but Olga Forsh (1873–1961) maintained her Dionysian intoxication. Forsh, then a minor Scythian, was a graduate of Merezhkovsky's circle, like her friend Shaginian. She later became prominent for her historical novel *Dressed in Stone*. In *Hot Shop* (*Goriachii tsekh*), a novel published in 1926, she contrasts the Apollonian and Dionysian dimensions of the October Revolution. The revolutionary worker Kuzma meets Serafima, a young woman who explains the October Revolution as an outbreak of love, an abundance of happiness and Spirit. Serafima cites Dostoevsky, but not Nietzsche. Her idea of the Dionysian October Revolution is contested by the Jew Abram, a proponent of a rationalistic, Apollonian revolution. There is another fully-fledged Nietzschean in the book, the Jew Wüste,[50] presented as a kind of Zarathustra:

It happens that a very kind man should burn, rob, under the pressure of a fatal, inexorable force ... [Wüste] took away faith, hope. He pushed people out into the cold from their long-occupied sinecures. He infected them with his pain, his depth, his disgust for cheap hosannas. Man has nothing. He should create everything for himself. But during this creation, it is better to perish than to take a stone instead of bread, the categorical imperative instead of living God, a transient, pitiful human "love" instead of glorious heaven, or progress and chicken-soup for the next generation instead of a personal resurrection.[51]

Serafima says:

To be possessed with a rage of love means to reforge one's own wicked nature into a bright one and to enter into the easy, confiding, joyful relations with people that exist only in childhood ... not at the snail's pace of evolution but through a revolution, here and now, not waiting for the fulfillment of some historical era ... Inequality, scarcity, any evil, should be eliminated not only by a political revolution but by the strength of purest will which liberates elementary life enchained by dark passions. It is high time for everyone to arise from squalor, it is necessary to understand that the miracle of the Sistine Madonna is not a possession of the clergy but of living and vitally necessary Life.[52]

Kuzma tells Abram about the marvelous life he led during the Revolution of 1905: abundance, he says, is the solution to any dualism – of soul, of society, of theory and practice. Abram responds, "It is only for a few days, since [Abram], as a practical man, knows that this revolutionary idyll is no more than a beautiful ephemeral butterfly, while the state needs modest ants."[53]

A very important example of a pro-Bolshevik Nietzschean who became a prominent writer was Vikenty Veresaev (1867–1945), the brother of the Bolshevik leader Petr Smidovich. His major work on Nietzsche, first published in 1915, was reprinted in the USSR in 1928 and in 1930. In this book, *Apollo and Dionysus*, Veresaev adopts many of Nietzsche's ideas, although not without reservations.[54] He calls Zarathustra's way "Living Life," a term taken from Dostoevsky.[55] Veresaev accepts the Nietzschean definition of truth, calling it a priceless pearl and even a talisman.[56] He also supports another very central Nietzschean idea, namely that modern man is only a bridge, not a goal in himself. The only thing that should be loved in man today is that he is in transition. According to Veresaev,

Superman is this very individual, a perfect personality who grows on the soil of human decomposition like a bright flower on fertile manure. The height of human happiness and human vocation is to strive to serve as the fertilizer for the creation of the coming Superman.[57]

Veresaev encourages man to set foot on the road of Living Life, the road that should lead to the future and that, he claims, is the main metaphysical and religious meaning of humanity and also the meaning of its social liberation.[58]

For Veresaev, the lack of "social order" is frightening, but not only because of its injustice and the suffering and deprivation to which it dooms the majority. Most frightening is that it drains people, depriving them of what is most valuable and necessary – of life itself.[59]

The juxtaposition of Apollo and Dionysus is central to Veresaev's book. His Apollo, however, is not a symbol of rationality alone, but a symbol of life, of the will to live.[60] Veresaev also accepts Nietzsche's interpretation of Dionysian ecstasy, attempting only to stress, as did others, that Dionysus is actually the foundation of authentic collectivism.

FOREIGN INFLUENCE

The picture of early Bolshevik Nietzscheanism will not be complete if we ignore a secondary branch of Western Nietzscheanism which, unlike its source, was always accepted in Soviet Russia and exercised enormous impact there. Several Western Nietzscheans, among them Bernard Shaw, H. G. Wells, and Upton Sinclair, were never censored in the USSR. Knut Hamsun should also be added to this list, since he became *persona non grata* in the USSR only during World War II, when he collaborated with the Nazis.

However, no one had more of a Nietzschean influence on Soviet readers than Jack London. His collected works were published in the Soviet Union in 1928–29. In his novels *The Iron Heel* and *Martin Eden*, London expresses his outspoken brand of Nietzscheanism, the first appeal of which is that people should not be slaves. Ernest Everhard, the hero of *The Iron Heel*, is presented by the author as:

... Simple, direct, afraid of nothing, and he refused to waste time on conventional mannerisms ... He was a natural aristocrat – and this in spite of the fact that he was in the camp of the non-aristocrats. He was a superman, a blond beast such as Nietzsche has described, and in addition he was aflame with democracy.[61]

Martin Eden, similarly, is told by a friend, "You are antediluvian anyway, with your Nietzsche ideas."[62]

London was extremely popular in Russia. One can safely assume that Soviet leaders, not only the general public, liked London in his entirety. One of his short stories, "Love of Life," whose hero, lost in Alaska, succeeds in surviving and finding his way back to safety thanks to his enormous will, was a favorite of Lenin himself, according to his wife.[63]

STALINIST NIETZSCHEANISM

In speaking of Stalinist Nietzscheanism we should identify at least two stages. The first lasted roughly from 1928 until 1933, when Nietzsche was adopted officially by Nazi propaganda after the Nazi victory in Germany. After that year, no positive direct reference to Nietzsche was possible in the USSR: officially, he was totally rejected.[64] Actually, however, Nietzsche was not rejected but was internalized, and this unacknowledged internalization comprises the second stage of Stalinist Nietzscheanism.

One of the best expositions of the first stage is Moris Leiteisen's book *Nietzsche and Finance Capital*. Though noting that Nietzsche was a spokesman for finance capital and even for imperialism, Leiteisen did not hesitate to stress a certain affinity between Nietzsche and Bolshevism:

Nietzsche is the most distant thinker for us but at the same time he is close to us. Reading his works, one breathes pure and sharp mountain air. There is a clarity and lucidity of concept, there is nothing hiding behind a beautiful sentence. There is the same nakedness and unambiguity of class relations, the same struggle against all illusions and ideals, the Nietzschean struggle against petty gods and first of all against the most haughty and deceptive one of them – democracy ...

What brings us together is Nietzsche's struggle against the individualism and anarchy of capitalist society, his passionate dream of world unification, his struggle against nationalism ... We will find in Nietzsche gleams of historical materialism and some thoughts, some conclusions which we can accept completely. Everything of his that is sunny and joyful, his "Yes" to Life, his superhuman happiness, his triumph and pride of the masters of the earth and the rulers of the world will be close and comprehensible to us when the rulers of the world will not be those who were pointed out by Nietzsche, and when all that was destined for a small group will be shared by millions.[65]

During the second stage of Stalinist Nietzscheanism, Nietzsche's continuing, if concealed, impact can be observed. One can, for example, find ambivalent remarks on Nietzsche in literature: for example, Aleksandr Malyshkin (1892–1938), then a leading Soviet writer, described in a book published in 1937 a negative character, the journalist Kalabukh, who is very fond of Western philosophy, especially Bergson. A positive character, Soustin, another journalist, while not admitting to Nietzsche's influence, confesses that in his youth he was an avid reader of Hamsun, who was also influenced by Nietzsche. Characteristically, Soustin tries to stress Nietzsche's superiority over Bergson in a conversation with Kalabukh which seems out of place in the book. When Kalabukh praises Bergson, Soustin cannot help intervening, saying that Nietzsche expressed Bergson's ideas earlier. Soustin does not criticize Nietzsche at all:

[KALABUKH:] A philosopher should talk all his life, constantly approaching the objective though never reaching it. Indeed, Bergson claims that even the age when this or that philosophical system was created, plays only a secondary role. He says (only listen!) that if Spinoza had lived before Descartes he would certainly have written differently, but nevertheless it would be Spinozism ... [SOUSTIN:] But this is somehow reminiscent of Nietzsche. He said that the creation of an artistic image is always initiated by a vague musical excitement.[66]

It is obvious that this remark, a positive comment on Nietzsche in contradiction to the official Soviet image of Nietzsche as a precursor of Nazism, is totally unrelated to its context. It is possible that Malyshkin simply wanted an opportunity to mention Nietzsche.

Nietzsche played a considerable role in the formation of Stalinism; his adherents were extremely helpful to Stalin in his quest for power and in his struggle for its consolidation in the late 1920s and early 1930s. On the one hand, Nietzsche enabled many Russian radicals to accept Stalin as an outspoken manifestation of certain Nietzschean concepts. What indeed did Stalinism claim that was incompatible with Nietzsche? Terror, the cult of personality, militant atheism – all tallied. On the other hand, Nietzscheans could not have taken Stalin's ostensible Marxism seriously. Nietzsche's principled relativization of truth allowed them to interpret the ideological aspects of Stalinism as purely instrumental for the sake of power. Nietzscheans could see Stalin's cynical use of socialism to achieve power as totally legitimate, even though socialism itself was abhorrent to Nietzsche. It was thus that very many Nietzscheans of the prerevolutionary Russian intelligentsia were sincerely capable of supporting not only the Bolshevik Revolution but also, and even more enthusiastically, Stalin himself. They could even be Party members.

Lezhnev serves as a conspicuous example. After arrest and exile from the USSR for almost five years, Lezhnev confessed his old sins and joined the Bolshevik Party on Stalin's personal recommendation. In 1934 he was nominated to a key position as head of *Pravda*'s art and literature department, and actually was one of those who directed the Soviet cultural purge until 1939. After that Lezhnev was the main Soviet interpreter of Sholokhov until his death.

An attentive look at Lezhnev's confession, which was published in book format, reveals a new variation of Nietzschean amorality. The sincere recantation fits very neatly into this fundamental amorality which permitted any and every ideological volte-face for the sake of personal or collective survival. Lezhnev publicly criticized all his past idols, including Shestov and Nietzsche, but his criticism itself remained purely Nietzschean. "If one is sincerely and seriously attached to morality [i.e., proletarian morality] and regards it as the only worthwhile objective on earth, he should eliminate empty talk about good and evil as defined by Tolstoi, Dostoevsky, Kant, and Nietzsche."[67]

But in making his disclaimer, Lezhnev could not hide his fundamental dependence on Nietzsche. An example of his inherent Nietzscheanism is his vicious attack on the Old Bolshevik leaders, who were already doomed but who were still at liberty when Lezhnev's book was published. "What boundless banality," he wrote, "lies in the fact that people maintain their physical being when their age has gone, never to return."[68] Certainly, this is a repetition of Nietzsche, who advocated death "at the right time," but it is more likely that the direct inspiration here was not Nietzsche but Bogdanov, who in his science-fiction book *Engineer Menni*, published in 1919, compared old people to vampires. An old man, according to Bogdanov, is not merely a parasite but an active enemy of life.

He is not really a man, because the human and socially creative being in him has already died. He is but the body of such a being. An ordinary, physical corpse is also harmful – it must be removed and destroyed lest it contaminate the air and spread disease. But a vampire, a living corpse, is much more harmful and dangerous if he was a strong man during his lifetime.[69]

Aleksandr Fadeev became the main Party watchdog of the Union of Soviet Writers, and *The Nineteen* (*The Rout*) became a standard Soviet school textbook. Old Nietzscheans such as Forsh, Shaginian, Ehrenburg, Aleksei Tolstoi, Leonov, Fedin, and Novikov became pillars of Soviet literature. Gladkov claims an important place here as well. His novel *Energy* (1932–38) is full of Nietzschean pathos. Baikalov, a Bolshevik Superman who is about to die,[70] thinks in typical Nietzschean terms of the processes of human reconstruction. He is not concerned with the cost of these processes:

When new life is in the act of being smelted, dross is inevitable. But there is no tragedy in this. Tragedy lies in the fact that man leaves life while he is still alive, and stops being a creative force. One should cultivate in oneself life-long youth.[71]

The new generation to whom Nietzsche might have appealed could not rely directly on the source but depended on various secondary Nietzschean figures in Russian and world culture. Thus Nietzscheanism indirectly became the weapon of a new social group, the Stalinists who wished to legitimize their quest for power against the old revolutionary elite which was already doomed. Most of them came from the shattered peasantry, still an absolute majority of the population, who had flooded the cities and towns, eventually to be used by Stalin as his main power base in the struggle against the old revolutionaries. Among them were also to be found members of the old privileged classes who, since they now had a new identity, wittingly or unwittingly looked for revenge against those who had devastated their class, or who perhaps survived by being "more Catholic than the Pope."

Certainly, Stalinist Nietzscheans made a revaluation of Nietzscheanism, selecting those ideas which best suited the new time. If, for example, the old elite had regarded the peasantry only as fertile soil for the future society, the new peasant Nietzscheans regarded the old intellectual elite as Bogdanovian vampires who should be eliminated. The new Nietzscheans must surely have been supported by the old ones, such as Lezhnev: almost all of them happily survived the purges.

A most outspoken new Nietzschean was Fedor Panferov (1896–1960), a peasant writer who made a name for himself with his four-volume novel *Bruski* (1928–37). He became a central spokesman for Stalinist culture up till and after Stalin's death. The main character in *Bruski*, Kiril Zhdarkin, is a peasant who participated in the Civil War, a model Superman from the new ascending elite which eliminated the old one. The old elite is represented in the novel mostly by people with non-Russian names – Lemm, Bakh, and so on. Zhdarkin, however, is a Dionysian blond beast who knows no restraints in his quest for power and in his passions. In his capacity as a member of the Supreme Soviet, he permits a four-day orgy, with violent fighting and drinking, in his native village. During the Rabelaisian affair Zhdarkin also drinks, makes love with women who passionately desire his strong embrace, and fights happily.[72] His local critics complain to Moscow and he is summoned there. The above-mentioned Lemm, a senior Party official, wants to punish Zhdarkin, but Central Party Committee intervention saves him.[73]

Zhdarkin retains his Dionysian features from one volume of the novel to the next. Upset by a lovers' quarrel, he carries out almost unbelievable deeds: he jumps his horse from a hill down to the Volga and crosses the river half-conscious, the horse dying because its back is broken.[74] (The Volga is about a kilometer wide at this particular point.) At the very end of the novel Zhdarkin breaks his rifle in half with his hands in a moment of exaltation.[75]

A central place in Stalinist Nietzscheanism also belongs to the playwright Vsevolod Vishnevsky (1900–51) who, unlike Panferov, came from the Petersburg Russian nobility.[76] Vishnevsky made his name with the play *An Optimistic Tragedy* (*Optimisticheskaia tragediia*, 1933) which was an imitation of Greek tragedy complete with a chorus of two Baltic sailors. The play treats the Civil War and the Baltic fleet; almost all the characters perish, some as a result of the struggle's internal logic, some meaninglessly. However, the chorus justifies the deaths in typically Nietzschean fashion: those who perished during the Civil War are only a bridge to, or fertile soil for, the future society. At the play's very beginning one member of the chorus says, "Life doesn't die. People can laugh and eat on their neighbors' graves, and it is marvelous."[77]

The author's remarks for the theatrical production are even more significant. In his preface, Vishnevsky described "a roar, the power and grief of which are overwhelming. Spontaneous combustion of mighty ecstasies which stop the breath and burn."[78] At the end the author comments:

Everything lives. Dust motes dance in the sunlight. There are numberless living creatures. Everywhere movement, the rustling, pulsating, and trembling of inexhaustible life. Ecstasy springs up in the heart when one looks at the world which gave birth to those who spit at the inveterate lie, the fear of death. Arteries pulse. Like great rivers, flooded with light, like titanic natural forces, frightening in their swell, sounds come which are already cleansed of melody – raw, crude, colossal – the roaring of cataclysms and streams of life.[79]

Vishnevsky's dependence on Veresaev's conception of "Living Life" is obvious. Indeed, Veresaev's book *Apollo and Dionysus* had been reprinted in the USSR in 1932. In it, Veresaev discusses extensively the reasons why Greek tragedy is so profoundly pessimistic and cannot be otherwise.[80] By the very title of his play Vishnevsky challenges this notion of eternally pessimistic tragedy. His concept of an "optimistic tragedy" with a new interpretation of death was integrated into Stalinist culture. In the Bolshevik age tragedy finds its optimistic solution. A most important pursuit of Stalinist culture was its attempt to create an image of a Soviet Nietzsche – actually an anti-Nietzsche. This role unwittingly fell on Nikolai Ostrovsky (1904–36), a young Bolshevik who participated in the Civil War. Later he became fatally ill and lost his sight. Totally incapacitated, Ostrovsky wrote *How the Steel Was Tempered* (1932–34; English translation is titled *The Making of a Hero*). The Russian name (*Kak zakalialas stal*) sounds structurally similar to the Russian translation of *Zarathustra* (*Tak govoril Zaratustra*) – in Russian *tak* and *kak* (*thus* and *how* respectively) may be interchangeable. This autobiographical novel by a half-educated author combines the story of a disabled man of iron will (like Nietzsche) and the plot of *Martin Eden*. Like Martin before his intellectual conversion to Marxism, the novel's hero, Pavel Korchagin, is a troublemaker. Ruth, in the earlier novel, is paralleled by the bourgeoise Tonia, with whom Korchagin falls in love, who tries to educate him as Ruth educated Martin. Korchagin, following Martin, becomes disappointed with Tonia, but he finds a solution in revolutionary struggle rather than in suicide. Korchagin's fight for literary recognition is also strongly reminiscent of Martin's, but unlike the latter, Korchagin does not seek money.

At the critical moment, the superman in Korchagin also saves him from suicide:

Who would condemn a warrior who did not wish to drag out the misery of it? And his hand went to his pocket and fingered the smooth metal of his Browning, and his fingers made practiced movements – taking the butt in their grip. Slowly he drew the revolver out of his pocket. He said to himself out loud, "Who would ever have thought that you would come to this?"

The muzzle was staring him scornfully in the face. Then he put the revolver on his knees and swore savagely. He said to himself, "Paper heroics, my boy! Any fool at any time can kill himself. That is the most cowardly and the easiest way out. Put that revolver away and never let anybody know you thought of it. Find out how to live even when life has become unbearable. Make your life useful."[81]

In his novel Ostrovsky mentions important books he has read, *The Iron Heel* among them.[82] It is unlikely that he left unread the more popular *Martin Eden*. Mikhail Koltsov, who published the first article on Ostrovsky in *Pravda*, cited Gorky and London as two basic influences on him.[83]

Another source of inspiration for Ostrovsky was a novel by an obscure Anglo-American writer, Ethel Lilian Voinich, which had won great popularity in Russia since its publication in Russian in 1898. A romantic novel, *The Gadfly* tells of a lone warrior who sacrifices his life for the sake of the Italian Revolution. Ostrovsky interpreted the novel in the following terms: "Books depicting characters of a masculine type, strong-minded and strong in revolutionary spirit, fearless and irrevocably consecrated to our task, had made a lasting impression on me and left me with a desire to be just like them."[84]

It is understandable that the new Nietzscheanism met stiff resistance from Gorky. His old Nietzscheanism was that of a new proletarian master race which would integrate the best of world culture, a collective cultural Nietzscheanism. Such people as Panferov, Ostrovsky, Vishnevsky, or Gladkov had nothing in common with genuine culture. They were the shock brigade of a new stratum with their quest for power, a threat to everything that the new revolutionary elite had achieved after the October Revolution. Most of them came from the peasantry or the *Lumpen* and brought with them their own values: cruelty, contempt for culture, a leaning towards Dionysian anti-cultural outbursts. Gorky declared war on them. In February, 1934, he published an open letter which betrayed his deep anxiety. He said that "muzhik" power was a socially unhealthy force, the nature of which was animal, and that cultural-political Party work must be directed at uprooting it from the conscience of the muzhik.[85]

Gorky did not conceal that it was not only Panferov who worried him. At almost the same time he attacked Vishnevsky. "What does [his] play have in common with optimism?" he asked. "It is not enemies who perish here."[86] This remark betrays Gorky's concern that the play could be used in a philosophy justifying the elimination of the old revolutionary elite. Gorky also stubbornly resisted awarding literary legitimacy to Ostrovsky. He said not a word about him, in spite of pressure to do so.[87] In his letter to Gladkov, moreover, he referred to *Energy* in a very negative way.[88]

Gorky was defiant but helpless: his position had greatly deteriorated after Kirov's assassination in December, 1934, due to his defense of his friend, the Old Bolshevik Lev Kamanev. In January, 1935, *Pravda* published an open letter from Panferov complaining about Gorky's arrogance toward writers and comparing it to Stalin's "gentle and tolerant" attitude.[89] Actually, Panferov called on Stalin to take over the overseeing of literature from Gorky.

This marked the end of Gorky's supervision of Soviet literature. A few months later, Ostrovsky was declared an outstanding writer, and his book a model. All Gorky's efforts to stop Panferov, Vishnevsky, and others were futile. His death in June of 1936 was a great relief, not only to Stalin, who probably accelerated it with the wrong medical treatment. It was also a relief for those aspiring Nietzscheans for whom Gorky had been one of Bogdanov's vampires who did not want to die at the right time.

The Stalinist Nietzscheans were also busy creating the image of the absolute Superman: Stalin. Panferov, Vishnevsky, Gladkov, Aleksei Tolstoi, and others started to build his image as an omnipotent, omniscient, benevolent Superman, a model for the master race. Gladkov even suggested that the leader's mistakes were non-mistakes. One of the characters in *Energy* says, "The leader cannot and should not blush. The leader should be just and sinless even in his mistakes."[90] The leader should exhibit a total lack of compassion toward those, even relatives or close friends, who have become obstacles to him for any reason. Historical examples were suggested, such as Peter the Great, who mercilessly tortured and executed his own son when he became a threat. This episode was dramatically stressed in the movie *Peter the First* (1937–39), directed by Vladimir Petrov, who also wrote the script together with Aleksei Tolstoi.

It would, of course, be misleading to regard Stalin's cult only in Nietzschean terms. History knew numerous glorifications of tyrants long before Nietzsche. Still, the participation in the formation of Stalin's cult by writers such as Aleksei Tolstoi, Panferov, Vishnevsky, and Gladkov served to emphasize that the Nietzschean concept of the Superman was closely compatible with tyranny and that no tyrant could afford to ignore such an opportunity for philosophic legitimization.

The central problem here is whether Stalin himself was influenced by Nietzsche and if so, whether the influence was conscious or unconscious. Stalin must have been aware of Nietzsche, if only through popularizations, and could not have been ignorant of the Nietzschean concepts of Superman, fascination with power, and militant amorality. But it is impossible to pinpoint any formal dependence on Nietzsche in Stalin's works, especially in his speeches after his full accession to power, since these were most certainly the work of ghostwriters.

However, circumstantial evidence exists in favor of Stalin's Nietzscheanism. Firstly, Stalin's behavior can easily be described in Nietzschean terms, in spite of his declared ideology, which might have been relativized. To the end of his life, Stalin's Marxism was almost totally devoid of content and could have been jettisoned at any moment.[91] Secondly, Stalin's thought can also be judged from the statements of his mouthpieces. In the esoteric political culture of his time, he made extensive use of expendable spokesmen to voice those of his most intimate political and philosophical ideas which could seem controversial and which could not be used within official statements. Important information can be garnered from Stalin's personal choice of writers and publicists.

Stronger evidence in favor of Stalin's Nietzscheanism can also be suggested: his staunch support of Lamarckism at the expense of Darwinism, which was manifested in the notorious campaign against genetics of Trofim Lysenko (1898–1976). The campaign, although it was in force only from 1948, had been prepared much earlier.[92] Lysenko not only rejected genetics, but claimed that it was possible to transform one species into another by human will, thus directing evolution. To a large extent he relied on the obscure experimenter Ivan Michurin (d. 1935), who was publicized as a national hero and great scientist. Michurin's famous motto was: "We cannot wait for the mercy of nature. Our task is to take steps ourselves." The frenetic story of Lysenko, who caused enormous harm to Soviet science, is a good monument to the Nietzscheanism of the early Bolsheviks, who hated the very idea of incremental evolution.

Nietzscheanism remained triumphant until Stalin's death. The official encouragement of Jack London's enormous popularity is evidence of this. Soon after World War II, at the height of Stalin's cultural campaign against the West, when almost all of Western culture was vilified, London was one of the few exempted, and his works were reprinted. The Soviet writer Boris Polevoi (1908–81) even attempted to adapt Lenin's favorite story by London, "Love of Life," in his novel *A Story about a Real Man* (1946), which became a model Soviet book. The hero is a Soviet combat pilot who was downed by the Germans during a mission to help Soviet partisans. Wounded in the legs, he nevertheless succeeds in crossing the front lines, crawling through forests while subsisting on plants and berries. His legs are amputated and he receives prostheses. But thanks to his outstanding will-power, he returns to the air force and his combat pilot duties.[93] The difference between this novel and London's story is that the latter's hero is an individual who struggles for his own life, while Polevoi's hero wants to survive in order to serve his country, a difference of motivation rather than of action.

CONCLUSION

By the end of Stalin's time a political culture had emerged in which the metaphysical Superman, Stalin, served as a model for numerous minor supermen. This new master race regarded its own population and the rest of the world as a herd which must obey it. Nietzscheanism, simplified and vulgarized, was an important component of Soviet society's actual political culture. Together with Russian nationalism and other components, it was no less important than that society's overt Marxist ideology, whose implementation it helped to shape.

NOTES

* Because of the author's untimely death in 1991, some of the notes to this chapter are incomplete.

1 Nikolai Trifonov, "Lunacharskii i Gorkii," in *Gorkii i ego sovremenniki*, ed. Klavdia Muratova (Leningrad, 1968), p. 114.

2 Moris G. Leiteisen, *Nitsshe i finansovyi kapital* (Moscow, 1928), pp. 17, 20. For Nietzsche's influence on the young Lunacharsky see A. L. Tait, "Lunacharsky: A 'Nietzschean Marxist'?" *Nietzsche in Russia*, ed. Bernice Glatzer Rosenthal (Princeton, 1986).

3 Stefan Zweig, *SS* (Leningrad, 1928–32), X, p. 27.

4 *Entsiklopedicheskii slovar' Granat* (Moscow, 1910–48), XLI:3, p. 222.

5 Stanislav Zarnitskii and Anatoli Sergeev, *Chicherin* (Moscow, 1966), p. 17.

6 Larisa Reisner, "Avtobiograficheskii roman," *LN* 93 (Moscow, 1983), p. 218.

7 Cf. Mary Louise Loe, "Gorky and Nietzsche," *Nietzsche in Russia*.

8 Cf. Mikhail Agursky, "The Bolshevik Abaddon: Gorky as Theomachian," *Christianity, the State and Society in Contemporary Russia*, ed. Nikolai Petro (Boulder, CO, 1989).

9 Cf. his letters to Vasili Rozanov, in *Kontekst* (Moscow, 1978), p. 307.

10 Cf. Maksim Gorkii, Editorial, *Novaia Zhizn'*, December 24, 1917.

11 Vladimir Lenin, *Collected Works* (Moscow, 1960–71), XXXVIII, pp. 58, 454; XXXIX, p. 205.

12 Ibid., XXXI, pp. 173–74; XXX, p. 223; XXVII, p. 259.

13 Maksim Gorky, "On the Russian Peasantry," *Journal of Peasant Studies* 4 (October, 1976), p. 26.

14 Alexander Fadayev, *The Nineteen*, trans. R. D. Chargues (London, 1928), p. 206.

15 Peter Scheibert, "Der Übermensch in der russischen Revolution," *Der Übermensch* (Stuttgart, 1961), p. 189. In the original, "Die Beseitigung des Untermensches als revolutionäre Aufgabe."

16 Cf. Maksim Gorkii, "Storozh," *M. Gorkii. Sobranie sochinenii* (Moscow, 1962), X, pp. 15–36.

17 Fedor Gladkov, *Cement*, trans. A. S. Arthur and C. Ashleigh (New York, 1929), p. 296. This attitude can be compared with those expressed in Zamiatin's *We*.

18 Fedor Gladkov, "Kroviu serdtsa," *ZIF* 1 (1928), pp. 409–10.

19 Iuda Grossman-Roshchin, *Iskusstvo izmeniat' mir* (Moscow, 1929), p. 245.

20 Vera Aleksandrova, *Literatura i zhizn'* (New York, 1969), p. 46.

21 His first literary work (now lost) contained a criticism of Darwinism. See Maksim Gorkii, "O tom kak ia uchilsia pisat'," *SS*, XXIV, p. 489.

22 Gorkii, "Storozh," p. 30.

23 Maksim Gorkii, "O beloemigrantskoi literature," *SS*, XXIV, p. 350.

24 Maksim Gorkii, *Letopis' zhizni i tvorchestva Gorkogo* (Moscow, 1958–60), III, p. 242.

25 Ivan Skvortsov-Stepanov, *Istoricheskii materializm i sovremennoe estestvoznanie* (Moscow, 1926).

26 Ieronim Iasinskii, "O Bol'shevikakh, o sverkhcheloveke i o zhabakh," *Petrogradskaia vecherniaia gazeta*, November 27, 1917; Anatoli Lunacharskii, "Sretenie," *Izvestia*, November 17, 1917.

27 Mikhail Agursky, *The Third Rome* (Boulder, 1987), p. 258; Nikolai Gredeskul, "Byt li estestvoznaniu mekhanicheskim ili stat' dialekticheskim?" *Pod znamenem marksizma* 1 (1928).

28 Nikolai Gredeskul, *Rossiia prezhde i teper'* (Moscow/Leningrad, 1926), p. 225.

29 Agursky, *The Third Rome*.

30 Aleksei Tolstoi, *Aelita* (Moscow, 1958), p. 235.

31 Alexei Tolstoi, *Peter the First*, trans. Tatiana Shebunina (New York, 1959).

32 Yuri Olesha, *Povesti i rasskazy* (Moscow, 1965), p. 500.

33 Konstantin Fedin, *Cities and Years*, trans. Michael Scammell (New York, 1962), pp. 285, 288.

34 Konstantin Fedin, "Pokhishchenie Evropy," *SS* (Moscow, 1959–62), IV.

35 Leonid Leonov, *Soviet River*, trans. Ivor Montagu and Sergei Nolbandov (New York, 1932), pp. 243–44, 251.

36 *Prishvin i sovremennost'* (Moscow, 1978).

37 Mikhail Prishvin, "Kashcheeva tsep'," *SS* (Moscow, 1956–57), I, p. 393.

38 Mikhail Prishvin, "Zapiski o tvorchestve," *Kontekst* (October 1930), pp. 273 (December 1931), p. 279.

39 Agursky, *The Third Rome*, p. 282.

40 Isai Lezhnev, "O Bismarke i o zhenshchine," *Rossiia* 1 (1992), p. 10.

41 Il'ia Ehrenburg, *Julio Jurenito*, trans. Anna Bostock (Philadelphia, 1963), pp. 37, 49, 316–17.

42 Nikolai Tereshchenko, *Sovremennyi nigilist* (Leningrad, 1928).
43 Agursky, *The Third Rome*, p. 275; Marietta Shaginian, "Il'ia Ehrenburg," *SS* (Moscow, 1971–73), I, pp. 769–70.
44 Victor Erlich, "The Metamorphosis of Ilia Ehrenburg," *Problems of Communism* 12:4 (1963), p. 22.
45 Ivan Novikov, *Feodosiia, SS* (Moscow, 1967), III, p. 404.
46 Ibid., p. 442.
47 Ibid., p. 444.
48 Ibid., p. 469.
49 John Maynard, *Russia in Flux* (New York, 1951), pp. 107–8.
50 "Wüste" means "desert" in German [ed.].
51 Ol'ga Forsh, *Goriachii tsekh, SS* (Moscow, 1962–64), II, p. 350.
52 Ibid., p. 425.
53 Ibid., p. 459.
54 Vikenty Veresaev, *Apollon i Dionis Polnaia Sobranie Sochineniia* (Moscow, 1928–30), VIII.
55 Fedor Dostoevsky, *A Raw Youth*, trans. Constance Garnett (New York, 1947), p. 236.
56 Veresaev, *Apollon i Dionis*, p. 122.
57 Ibid., p. 122.
58 Ibid., p. 124.
59 Ibid., p. 125.
60 Ibid., p. 29.
61 Jack London, *Novels and Social Writings* (New York, 1982), p. 326.
62 Ibid., p. 853.
63 *Lenin o literature i iskusstve* (Moscow, 1967), p. 556.
64 B. Bernadiner, *Filosofia Nitsshe i fashizm* (Moscow, 1934).
65 Leiteisen, *Nitsshe i finansovyi kapital*, p. 144.
66 Aleksandr Malyshkin, *Liudi iz zakholustia* (Moscow, 1950), pp. 228, 262.
67 Isai Lezhnev, *Zapiski sovremennika* (Moscow, 1936), pp. 62, 114, 216, 279.
68 Isai Lezhnev, *Zapiski sovremennika* (Moscow, 1934), p. 7.
69 Aleksandr Bogdanov, "Engineer Menni," *Red Star*, trans. Charles Rougle (Bloomington, IN, 1984), p. 213.
70 Fedor Gladkov, *Energiia* (Moscow, 1934), p. 305.
71 Ibid., p. 310.
72 Fedor Panferov, *Bruski* (Moscow, 1949), II, p. 9.
73 Ibid., p. 33.
74 Ibid., pp. 581–82.
75 Ibid., p. 652.
76 Viktor Khelemendik, *Vsevolod Vishnevskii* (Moscow, 1980).

77 Vsevolod Vishnevskii, "Optimisticheskaia tragediia," *Izbrannoe* (Moscow, 1954), p. 159.

78 Ibid., p. 158.

79 Ibid., p. 211.

80 Veresaev, *Apollon i Dionis.*

81 Nikolai Ostrovsky, *The Making of a Hero*, trans. Alec Brown (New York, 1937), p. 418.

82 Ibid., p. 299.

83 Mikhail Kol'tsov, "Muzhestvo," *Pravda*, March, 17 1935.

84 Ostrovsky, *Making of a Hero*, p. 373.

85 Maksim Gorkii, "Otkrytoe pismo Serafimovichu," *SS*, XXVII, p. 148.

86 Maksim Gorkii, "O boikosti," *SS*, XXVII, p. 159.

87 Raisa Ostrovskaia, *Nikolai Ostrovskii* (Moscow, 1974); Semen Tregub, "Iz vospominanii," *Vospominania o Nikolae Ostrovskom* (Moscow, 1974), p. 353; Nikolai Ostrovskii, "Pisma," *SS* (Moscow, 1969), XXX.

88 Maksim Gorkii, "Pismo Gladkovu," *LN* 70 (Moscow, 1963), p. 124.

89 Fedor Panferov, "Otkrytoe pismo Gorkomu," *Pravda*, January 28, 1935.

90 Gladkov, *Energiia*, p. 54.

91 Cf. Klaus Mehnert, *Stalin versus Marx* (London, 1952).

92 Cf. Zhores Medvedev, *The Rise and Fall of T. Lysenko*, trans. I. Michael Lerner (New York, 1978).

93 Boris Polevoi, *A Story about a Real Man* (Moscow, 1946).

CHAPTER II

Superman imagery in Soviet photography and photomontage

Margarita Tupitsyn

> If the forces within man compose a form only by entering
> into a relation with forms from the outside, with what new
> forms do they now risk entering into a relation, and what
> new form will emerge that is neither God nor man? This is
> the correct place for the problem that Nietzsche called
> "the superman."
>
> Gilles Deleuze, "Man and Overman"

Nietzsche's influence in the visual arts, unlike the case with literature and philosophy, has not been well documented. Even though one finds little actual reference to the German philosopher in the writings of twentieth-century Russian/ Soviet artists, their well-publicized slogans, ideals, and visual production indicate the presence of Nietzsche's ideas. One of the prime sources for the artists' familiarity with Nietzsche lies in their close friendship and collaboration with poets, writers, and thinkers, many of whom, as the chapters in this book show, read the philosopher or were familiar with his ideas. The unmistakable overtones of Nietzsche's teachings are present in the Symbolist painting of Michael Vrubel who "responded to Nietzsche's call for a fierce individualism."[1] The Futurists, who called themselves *budetliane*, proposed to suspend all differentiation between past, present, and future.[2] They rejected the concept of "eternal novelty" to which the Italian Futurists adhered and instead advocated "the will to repetition" and "the eternal recurrence" which made "the nihilistic will [of the Futurists] whole and complete."[3] After the Revolution, Suprematists and Constructivists who acquired substantial influence in the defining and structuring of the State's various cultural practices strongly believed in the ability of esthetics in general, and of artists in particular, to create a new world. Attempting to bring "art into life" (one of their slogans), they went beyond the medium of painting into the applied arts, design, and architecture. Although, unlike the Russian Symbolists, Suprematists and Constructivists (the avant-garde) did not directly compare themselves with a god, their idea of endowing an artist with limitless possibilities in the transformation of the world carried a large load of Superman overtones that in this case echo Nietzsche's linkage of the death of God and the birth of the Superman.

Stalin's First Five-Year Plan, launched in 1928, shifted avant-garde artists' attention from the idea of "the artist as Superman" to that of the masses as super-humanity prepared to fulfill this colossal project. Accordingly, artistic forms such as easel painting which required the artist's attention and craftsmanship were relegated to a supplementary position, while mechanically-reproduced media, such as photography and photomontage, advanced to the forefront of cultural life. These less conventional media attracted a number of avant-garde artists who during the First Five-Year Plan abandoned non-objective painting as an ineffective form for agit-art. It is in this context that Superman imagery emerged in their work. Images of giant workers and soldiers appear in many posters and paintings of the revolutionary and Civil-War period. But these were done by different artists who were linked to past models, specifically to folkloristic traditions which represent a popular hero as a giant. The practitioners of photomontage aimed at applying that newly-invented radical art form to glorify socio-political reality. This approach distinguished them from radical German artists, such as John Heartfield, who used the media to criticize German politics, particularly those of Hitler.

In 1932, when the Plan was declared complete a year ahead of time, and all separate artists' organizations were ordered to dissolve, a distinctly new era in Soviet art began. At this point Nietzsche's belief in the culture-forming power of myth strongly manifested itself in a new way. Instead of extolling their own esthetic doctrines or submitting to the collective, avant-garde artists submerged themselves in creating myths for the power structure. In this chapter I will trace models of Superman imagery which developed over the course of the First Five-Year Plan in photography and photomontage; I will also discuss the transition from Superman imagery to the falsification of documentary material and the mythologization of Soviet reality that occurred in the mid-1930s, through the formation of Socialist Realism.

Whether or not the leading avant-garde artists actually read Nietzsche is difficult to determine, but the cultural climate was saturated with his ideas, by way of Anatoly Lunacharsky, Maksim Gorky, and other ideologues of early Soviet culture. As early as 1904 Lunacharsky, the future Commissar of Enlightenment, wrote: "We have to support the growth of trust of the people in its strength, in a better future, look for rational paths to that future ... draw pictures of the future glowing with happiness ... develop the feeling for tragedy and joy for struggle and victory, for Promethean aspirations, stubborn pride, and unite hearts in a common striving towards a Superman – this is an artist's task."[4] When Lunacharksy expressed these utopian instructions to artists, their realization was only his private dream. After the Revolution, however, as an influential cultural and educational functionary, he began to fulfill that dream by granting a great deal of freedom to artists who through images rather than words could appeal more effectively to a largely illiterate population. As a result, Lunacharsky's cause became a common task.

Until the start of the First Five-Year Plan no particular iconographic arsenal was mandated by the government. Rather, various styles were offered (from realism to abstraction) and association with Bolshevism and use of Bolshevik rhetoric validated the work of art politically. Unlike the Futurists, who could only theorize about changing the world, Constructivists and Suprematists who acquired the most influence were directly participating in shaping the socio-cultural environment of postrevolutionary Russia. At this period the Nietzschean conception, earlier promoted by literary Symbolists, "of the artist as the superman par excellence – the destroyer of old worlds and creator of new worlds,"[5] had the most perfect circumstances for realization. By the mid-1920s, however, it became clear that abstract painting did not adequately serve the needs of the masses, because despite all the artists' solidarity with Bolshevik political aspirations, abstract forms failed to convey a revolutionary message that was immediately obvious to the viewer. With the First Five-Year Plan what was represented mattered even more, because the government expected specific actions from the people in response to the Plan, such as hard work and enthusiasm. At the beginning of the Five-Year Plan, therefore, avant-garde artists who practiced photography gave up the idea of "the artist as Superman," and shifted from belief in the power of the individual creator to exaltation of the collective creativity of the workers.

An effective introduction to the series of representations dealing with superman imagery of the period is El Lissitzky's (1890–1941) poster *USSR Russische Ausstellung* (1929) (Illustration 11.1) and Gustav Klutsis's (1895–1938) poster *Speed Up the Rate of Industrialization* (1930). Produced by artists with a Constructivist background, both posters offer oversized and powerful female and male faces partially merging into each other and sharing one eye. The resulting neither male nor female representation illustrates Michel Foucault's belief that "the superman ... is the advent of a new form that is neither God nor man and which, it is hoped, will not prove worse than its two previous forms."[6] Produced for an international audience, Lissitzky's poster dispersed the idea of the Soviet masses as super humanity "at work on their own new world," one of the slogans of the time. Klutsis's double image, looming over a smoky industrial landscape, was intended more for a local Soviet audience, nameless men and women, whom it inspired to all kinds of superhuman deeds. These two examples of a new humanity, like many others which glorify both the Soviet Union and the Plan's unfolding, are executed with photomontage technique. The latter allowed artists easily to manipulate the scale of every image and object, which in painting, by

11.1 El Lissitzky, *USSR Russische Ausstellung*, 1929, lithograph. Courtesy Barry Friedman Ltd, New York.

11.2 Anonymous, *Everyone to the Election of Women Delegates*, 1930, lithograph.

11.3 Valentina Kulagina, *International Women Workers' Day*, 1930, lithograph.

contrast, would acquire a grotesque structure or surreal overtones.[7]

Commissioned from artists and photographers and produced by IZOGIZ ("Izobrazitelny otdel gosudarstvennogo izdatel-stva," the Visual Art Department of the State Publishing House) during the First Five-Year Plan, many of these posters show a single or a group image of giant workers, coal miners, and farmers descending toward the industrial landscape, strolling in the background or working at modernized factories and plants. Significantly, in this mass-distributed production the image of a superhuman transgresses gender; female representations appear in heroic roles as often as male ones. Women were usually depicted operating speedy assembly lines or agitating the public to participate in important social activities such as elections. In the poster *Everyone to the Election of Women Delegates* (1930) (Illustration 11.2), a large figure of a woman dominates the space; below her other females much smaller in scale work on tractors or appear as nurses ready to protect the country from a potential imperialist attack. In Valentina Kulagina's *International Women Workers' Day* (1930) (Illustration 11.3) a giant female factory worker operates a hefty textile machine. In the foreground and much smaller in size, packed-together women workers commemorate the holiday, mindful that their present position was made possible by the Bolshevik liberation of women. Klutsis's poster *The Struggle for Heat and Metal* (1933) (Illustration 11.4) profoundly demonstrates the artist's complete identification with the deeds of collective labor rather than with the glory of a creative ego. This poster was conceived as a result of Klutsis's trip to Donbass, during which he actually dressed as a coal miner and descended into the mines. In a letter to his wife Kulagina, he wrote: "Only now I understand all the seriousness and hardship of the coal miner's labor."[8] Here, Klutsis chose to include his self-portrait in a coal miner's outfit with a lantern. For this poster the artist made preliminary photographs of himself, which he then combined with a photograph of a miner, and with an intricate industrial landscape, stretching out at the giant figures of the two men. Klutsis creates a new authorial paradigm, authentic-

11.4 Gustav Klutsis, *The Struggle for Heat and Metal*, 1933, lithograph. Fuel/

ating the worker above the artist. All these posters may be characterized by Lunacharsky's definition of "monumental realism," which according to him "has a right to build gigantic images which although they are non-existent in reality function as personification of the collective forces."[9]

By the end of the First Five-Year Plan mass-produced representations of collective unanimity still predominated, but we can see the first signs of a shift toward images which express the power of one voice. For such an iconographic change one finds an analogue in Nietzsche's *The Birth of Tragedy*. Nietzsche asserts that tragedy has its origin in the satyr chorus, that primitive form of tragedy in which the voice of Dionysus was hidden. And this is exactly how the images in First Five-Year Plan posters and photomontages were structured. Gargantuan, collective labor was performed in response to Stalin's call for a vast industrialization, but Stalin's presence was always submerged amidst the Dionysian enthusiasm of an unanimous workforce. In Attic tragedy, however, Dionysus (for us, Stalin or any other Soviet hero) steps out of the chorus and puts on the mask of Apollo, realizing that to manifest himself he must invest his ambitions in "the other," in this case – the God of illusion. This results in a culture which is based on fiction, and as such it breaks with the traditions of avant-gardism which Clement Greenberg defined in 1947 as art "which comes closest to nonfiction, has least to do with illusions."[10]

This shift from the depiction of an anonymous worker as a kind of Nietzschean "Higher Man," able to overcome any hardship, to the glorification of a specific leader, the Superman, as a major force in socialist construction and as an incarnation of the will to power, brought with it a number of dilemmas. First, artists such as Lissitzky and Klutsis had to resolve the issue of the relation between the images of Lenin and Stalin. Well before Lenin's death, Klutsis produced a photomontage, *The Electrification of the Entire Country* (1920), in which the leader was depicted as the Superman, the earliest known example of such an interpretation before the First Five-Year Plan period and at a time when other avant-garde artists still shunned representational forms. Then the choice was unquestionably to magnify Lenin, whose huge figure is carrying with him a structure of metal scaffolding and architectural sections – a symbol of the technological modernization promised by the Bolshevik government. By 1930, however, Stalin, the mastermind of the Five-Year Plans, was ready to compete with Lenin for a sovereign position in propaganda images. The first new relationship between the two leaders is reflected in another Klutsis poster, *Under the Banner of Lenin for Socialist Construction* (1930), where Lenin's large head, in the foreground, obscures much of Stalin's face, from which a dark eye stares enigmatically at the viewer. Here Stalin is presented still in the shadow of his former superior, but in the next few years he assumes an overwhelming presence, as in Klutsis's poster *The Victory of Socialism is Guaranteed in Our Country* (1932) (Illustration 11.5), or in Lissitzky's photomontage *The Current is Switched On* (1932) for the magazine *USSR in Construction*, or in Klutsis's montages for the first color *Pravdas*, published in 1935 (Illustration 11.6). In all these examples Stalin has moved to the central dominating position, gazing out over vast industrial sites, glowing industrial cities, and rural fields cultivated by tractors.

The second dilemma, namely to find the right relation between the leader and the masses, is identifiable in various photographic representations of the period. Arkady Shishkin's photograph *Voting Unanimously for the Kolkhoz* (1930) (Illustration 11.7) shows a collective of male and female peasants grouped closely together around a table and voting.[11] But unlike scenes dedicated to the theme of voting, which presented the masses as active participants in the process, here we see a rather passive group of peasants cautiously raising their hands as if intimidated by Stalin's image, which although severely cropped can be discerned on the right side of the photograph. Similarly, in many photographs of sport parades produced by Aleksandr Rodchenko (Illustration 11.8), Georgy Zelma (Illustration 11.9), Georgy Petrusov, and many other photographers, the crowds of male and female athletes demonstrate their physical perfection and appear to be a kind of super-humanity competing with the idea of an individual

11.5 Gustav Klutsis, *The Victory of Socialism is Guaranteed in Our Country*, 1932, lithograph.

11.6 Gustav Klutsis, *Design for Pravda*, 1935, photomontage.

Superman. As in posters and photomontages glorifying the First Five-Year-Plan, in these sport scenes one finds no differentiation of gender as far as the presentation of the superhuman is concerned. As in *Voting Unanimously for the Kolkhoz*, where Stalin's portrait is imposed on the collective, here portraits of

11.7 Arkady Shishkin, *Voting Unanimously for the Kolkhoz*, 1930, photograph.

11.8 Aleksandr Rodchenko, *Sport Parade*, 1936, photograph.

11.9 Georgy Zelma, *Sport Parade*, 1936, photograph.

various leaders creep into the frame of representation and serve as metaphor for the authoritative, Zarathustrian voice. Also in these photographs Red Square usually serves as the background for the parades and thus becomes the main point of signification. Together they function in accord with Roland Barthes's description of the message power of a photograph in which one may find a specific way of "the posing of objects, where the meaning comes from the objects photographed;" they can be artificially arranged or chosen for inclusion.[12] Barthes further points out that "Such objects constitute excellent elements of signification," which for him is synonymous with the mythological[13] and for us, in the case of the photographs discussed, presents important signs of the mythologizing machine at work.

In photomontage production the changing relationship between the representation of masses and leaders is much more dramatically illustrated. In it the metaphor of scale began to be equated with the hierarchy of power, and the masses increasingly play a subordinate role vis-à-vis the gigantic leader. In Klutsis's montage and poster *The Reality of Our Program is Real People, It's You and Me* (1931), by means of montage, Stalin suddenly appears in the ranks of marching coal miners; structurally, at least, the image remains "democratic," or perhaps one can say "anti-Superman," since no distinction of scale is made between the leader and workers. However, in subsequent montages such as *October to the World* (*c.* 1933) (Illustration 11.10), two gigantic figures of Lenin and Stalin (equal in size) are positioned on top of the tiny crowds, with Stalin literally stepping on some of them with his boots. Unintentionally, this compositional choice allegorizes the ongoing purges and arrests of people to provide labor force at the construction sites. *October to the World* also reflects a growing cult of Stalin's personality that at this point replaces or rather merges with a simplified and literal version of the Nietzschean notion of the Superman. Here we witness the return of the God-form, and with this return, in Gilles Deleuze's words, "man does not exist."[14]

Lunacharsky's support of the concept of a tyrant before his

11.10 Gustav Klutsis, *October to the World*, c. 1933, photomontage.

death in 1933 is especially significant in the context of increasing artistic attention to a single power image. He stated that a tyrant "works on history, and thus he is *a priori* higher than the 'shaded' individual, the average person 'who raises the nature of man not a jot ...'"[15] This support of a tyrant, together with Lunacharsky's earlier call for a "leaning towards the Superman, towards the beautiful and powerful creature, towards the complete organism in which life and rationality will celebrate victory over the elements,"[16] creates an ideologically and philosophically unprecedented vision of the overman. This new version, based on the cult of personality sustained by means of oppressing the masses is sharply distinct from the idea of a Superman as "the formal compound of the forces within man" and as "the form that results from a new relation between forces"[17] – the version that was allegorized by a hero/heroine tirelessly executing the superhuman projects of the First Five-Year Plan.

By the mid-1930s, photography and photomontage were recognized by the Soviet establishment as effective weapons in a growing process of fictionalization and creation of illusions about Soviet reality in general, and about the figure of Stalin in particular. Many archival photographs and photomontages demonstrate how the course of mythologizing was undertaken by "correction" and/or fabrication of existing photographic images of purged party members or military personnel. Klutsis's self-altered (most likely out of fear) photomontages of Stalin and his *apparatchiks*, some of whose portraits were literally torn off or effaced, are among the striking examples of this process.[18] Vasily Elkin's poster *Glory to the Red Army* (1933) shows generals and *apparatchiks* standing on or near Lenin's Mausoleum, observing the parade of the numerous Lilliputians (workers and soldiers) who densely cover the rest of the poster. Sometime in the late 1930s, the artist, haunted by fear, "edited" the poster, crossing out the "de-crowned" supermen, purged members of the military elite. To these dramatic manifestations of the terror evoked by Stalin's growing cult of personality, one may add hundreds of altered photographs with some people removed. Together these images present powerful examples of Soviet ideologues' will to falsification.

Parallel to this process of falsification of documentary material, Socialist Realism, whose doctrine was officially in place by 1934, aimed at estheticizing political myths. The latter objective echoed Nietzsche's belief that: "Without myth every culture loses the healthy power of its creativity: only a horizon defined by myths completes and unifies a whole cultural movement. Even the State knows no more powerful unwritten laws than the mythical foundation that guarantees its connection with religion and its growth from mythical notions" (*BT*, p. 135). What was developing in the visual arts, as well as elsewhere, may be designated, in Allan Megill's words, as an "aesthetic will to falsification,"[19] which relates to Nietzsche's connection of the "will to art" to the will "to lie, to flight from 'truth', to negation of 'truth'."[20] Lunacharsky's report on Socialist Realism (1933) betrays clear signs of such Nietzscheanism when he asserts that "...truth does not look like itself, it does not stay in one place, it is flying ... and we must see it like that. Those who do not see it like that are bourgeois realists and thus pessimists, whimperers ..."[21] In the same report Lunacharsky concluded that even "useful truth but objectionable from the point of view of Socialist Realism is a lie."[22] In accordance with this ideological background, Socialist Realism's creators (or rather fabricators) began to build the collection of ready-made myths that over time crystallized into a huge metalinguistic structure constantly reiterating itself in worn clichés, endless representations of labor, great leaders, war and revolutionary heroes and heroines – and thus exhibiting the eternal recurrence of the same. This status of Socialist Realism's development may be supported by yet another statement of Nietzsche; in "On Truth and Lie in an Extra-Moral Sense," Nietzsche writes: "A mobile host of metaphors, metonymies, anthropomorphisms: in short a sum of human relations which have been poetically and rhetorically intensified, transferred, and embellished and after long usage seem to a nation fixed, canonical and binding."[23]

Based on such recycling of the same myths, Socialist Realism must be distinguished from various other forms of realism, especially from American Social Realism with whose name it is often designated.[24] In order to understand the prime elements of difference between these styles, both of which operate with realist forms, one may turn to a group of artists called AKhRR ("Assotsiatsiia khudozhnikov revoliutsionnoi Rossii," the Association of Artists of Revolutionary Russia), among whose members were Evgeny Katsman, Isaak Brodsky, and Mitrofan Grekov. Because in 1928 AKhRR's production received an ultimate stamp of official approval when the entire Politburo made a visit to one of the group's exhibitions, and because many of AKhRR's artists subsequently became major protagonists of Socialist Realism's doctrine, the convention has been to see this group as proto-Socialist Realists. In reality, however, they demonstrate how the change from Social to Socialist Realism occurred. Throughout the 1920s these and other AKhRR artists traveled to factories and collective farms and painted scenes and people at the moment of their maximal connection with actual reality. Such an application of realism as a means of documenting historical events (thus competing with photographers of the same period) is distinct from the quest of Socialist Realism for mythical scenarios played out in painting and other media, as if protecting people from the harsh realities and "useful truth." This dichotomy between the objectives of Socialist Realism and those of the AKhRR group may be viewed within the framework of an Apollonian–Dionysian confrontation. Apollo wraps man in the veil of *maya* and thereby protects him from the harsh realities of his altogether frightening and pitiful existence. Dionysus "annihilates" the veil of *maya* and thus opens the way for a direct and unmediated participation in reality. This shift from Dionysian "participation in reality" to Apollonian illusionism (*simulacrum*) was performed through a careful introduction into what one may designate as "true realism," an authoritative, Zarathustrian voice manifested through the constantly repeated master-narratives and the master-image of Stalin. As such, Socialist Realism serves the Nietzschean notion that, in Megill's words, art is "completely out of contact with reality and only conveys the illusion of such a contact by inventing a self-contained world of its own."[25] This strategy allowed official culture to serve the ideological project of the eternal recurrence of the same myths, which in turn kept people from seeing the truth of everyday reality, remaining in a perpetual flight from it.

As this chapter illustrates, the notion of a Superman manifested itself in varied guises, ranging from representations of enormous workers with Dionysian joy in labor on the one hand, to Stalin as Superman on the other. Thus an attempt to apply one idea to different socio-cultural epochs resulted in an exposure of a crucial gap between them and outlined three distinct periods in Russian avant-garde history associated with the notion of Superman. The first phase developed under the slogan "the artist as Superman," which began at the birth of Russian avant-garde in the early twentieth century and reached its peak shortly after the Revolution, when Constructivists and Suprematists dominated the cultural life of the newly formed society. It was replaced in the late 1920s by artists submitting to a collective anonymity which overshadowed all signs of personality cults, whether manifested through esthetics or politics. With Stalin's successful disposal of his rivals and his boundless lust for power, however, the presence of a single personality manifested itself again, only this time it was not an artist who wanted to transform the world through his or her utopian esthetic aspirations, but a tyrant ready to achieve his goal through cruelty and falsification. These three moments of Nietzscheanism in Soviet visual culture attest that there is no one and final version of Nietzsche's idea of a Superman. Instead the idea can enter different historical contexts and result in an immense variety of cultural formations and ideological manifestations. As Jacques Derrida correctly points out about Nietzsche: "a thousand possibilities will always remain open."[26]

NOTES

1 For a discussion of Vrubel's art in relation to Nietzsche's ideas see Aline Isdebsky-Pitchard's "Art for Philosophy's Sake: Vrubel Against 'the Herd,'" *Nietzsche in Russia*, ed. Bernice Glatzer Rosenthal (Princeton, 1986), p. 219.

2 For a further discussion of *budetliane* see my "Collaboration on the Paradigm of the Future," *Art Journal* 52:4 (Winter 1993), pp. 18–24. On the connection between Russian Futurism and Nietzsche in general see Bernice Glatzer Rosenthal, "A New Word for a New Myth: Nietzsche and Russian Futurism," *The European Foundations of Russian Modernism*, ed. Peter I. Barta (Lewiston, NY, 1991), pp. 219–50, and the chapters on Mayakovsky and Khlebnikov in this volume.

3 *The Deleuze Reader*, ed. Constantin V. Boundas (New York, 1993), p. 91.

4 Anatolii Lunacharskii, "Osnovy positivnoi estetiki," *SS*, VII (Moscow, 1967), p. 99. For discussion of Lunacharskii's esthetics see Aleksandr Gangus's essay, "Na ruinakh pozitivnoi estetiki," *Novyi Mir* 9 (1988), pp. 147–63.

5 Ann M. Lane, "Bal'mont and Skriabin: The Artist as Superman," *Nietzsche in Russia*, p. 195.

6 Discussed in Gilles Deleuze, "Man and Overman," *The Deleuze Reader*, p. 102.

7 On the development of the photomontage technique in the Soviet Union see my "From the Politics of Montage to the Montage of Politics," *Montage and Modern Life: 1919–1942* (Cambridge, MA, 1992), pp. 82–127.

8 Letter, September 7, 1931, Don River Basin Industrial Complex, Klutsis Family Archive, Moscow.

9 Anatolii Lunacharskii, "Sotsialisticheskii realism (Doklad)," *SS*, VIII, p. 498.

10 See Greenberg, "The Present Prospects of American Painting and Sculpture," in *Clement Greenberg: The Collected Essays and Criticism*, II, ed. John O'Brian (Chicago, 1986), pp. 169–70.

11 This photo may reflect Stalin's "Dizzy with Success" speech (March, 1930) in which he stated that *kolkhozi* were to be formed on the voluntary principle, not by force.

12 Roland Barthes, "The Photographic Message," *Image, Music and Text*, trans. Stephen Heath (New York, 1977), p. 22.

13 Barthes, "The Photographic Message," ibid.

14 *The Deleuze Reader*, p. 100.

15 Lunacharskii, as quoted by Gangnus, p. 151.

16 Lunacharskii, "Osnovy pozitivnoi estetiki," *SS*, VII, p. 99.

17 *The Deleuze Reader*, p. 102.

18 Because Klutsis was arrested in 1938 it is also possible that it was his wife Valentina Kulagina who removed *apparatchiks'* faces from his late montages. For a further discussion of Klutsis's late work see my "Gustav Klutsis: Scenarios of Authorial Pursuits," *The Print Collector's Newsletter* 22:5 (November–December, 1991), pp. 161–66.

19 Allan Megill, *Prophets of Extremity: Nietzsche, Heidegger, Foucault, Derrida* (Berkeley, 1985), p. 37.

20 Megill, *Prophets of Extremity*, ibid.

21 Lunacharskii, "Sotsialisticheskii realism (Doklad)," *SS*, VIII, p. 497.

22 Lunacharskii, "Sotsialisticheskii realism (Doklad)," ibid.

23 *Philosophy and Truth: Selections from Nietzsche's Notebooks of the Early 1870s*, ed. and trans. Daniel Breazeale (New Jersey, 1990), p. 84.

24 To call Socialist Realism Social Realism has been a common mistake for many Western writers on the subject.

25 Megill, *Prophets of Extremity*, p. 50.

26 Jonathan Culler, *On Deconstruction: Theory and Criticism After Structuralism* (Ithaca, 1982), p. 131.

PART IV

Nietzsche Among Disaffected Writers and Thinkers

From beyond the abyss: Nietzschean myth in Zamiatin's "We" and Pasternak's "Doctor Zhivago"

Edith Clowes

When the Revolutions of 1917 burst upon the Russian literary intelligentsia, as if fulfilling apocalyptic hopes of personal or political transfiguration, the philosophy of Friedrich Nietzsche had long since become entwined in literary culture. This chapter will treat latter-day revaluations of two Silver Age myths of transfiguration, both strongly influenced by Nietzsche's thought. These are the confrontation with Nietzschean–Marxist "God-building" ideology in the novel *We* (*My*, 1920) by Evgeny Zamiatin (1884–1937), and the much later reconsideration by Boris Pasternak (1890–1960) of mystical Symbolist "God-seeking" in his novel *Doctor Zhivago* (*Doktor Zhivago*, 1957). While Zamiatin certainly read Nietzsche and Pasternak very probably did so – and we will be concerned with these historical receptions – our primary concern will be to show how both writers deliberately rethought two Russian myths in which Nietzsche's thought was appropriated, transformed, and, thus, "buried." So, after reminding ourselves of central Nietzschean characteristics of the two myths, we will examine Zamiatin's and Pasternak's responses precisely to these features.

In the prerevolutionary era Nietzsche's literary reception had passed through two major cycles.[1] The first was the popular cult of the Superman which insisted on the unconditional, anarchic rights of self-will in both personal and public life. It is to this simple and vulgar reading that Soviet detractors of Nietzsche have returned time and time again. The next stage in Nietzsche's reception involved a thorough discreditation of this rampant egotism in two very deep and culturally productive responses to Nietzsche's philosophy, mystical Symbolist God-seeking and revolutionary romantic God-building.[2] This essay will address yet a third stage which responded to God-seeking and God-building and offered a fresh engagement with Nietzschean motifs. Embedded in the God-seeking of Merezhkovsky and Ivanov was a myth of the "Dionysian Christ." Rejecting traditional asceticism, this figure embraced the "earth," understood as human passion and creative will, and embarked upon a quest for a life-transfiguring spirituality. In contrast, the radical God-building movement of Gorky, Lunacharsky, and Bogdanov crystallized in opposition to God-seeking and generated a Promethean myth of the masses as a source of life-transforming energy. This movement took its central idea from Feuerbach's religious anthropology, Marxist Prometheanism, and Nietzsche's voluntarism and emphasis on creative psychology.[3]

Both of these myths were oriented towards the future when the anticipated transfiguration of human consciousness would occur. In the God-building myth, as to a lesser degree in God-seeking, spiritual apocalypse was closely associated with social revolution. Zamiatin and Pasternak, both of whom flourished as writers during and shortly after the Revolution, shared a sense of being already beyond the apocalyptic cataclysm. From a vantage point beyond the revolutionary abyss, each writer in his own way would polemicize with and reevaluate the very myths that, at least to their believers, had made revolution such an urgent and compelling necessity.

Zamiatin probably discovered Nietzsche just before that most productive period of his career, during the Civil-War years from 1918 to 1921. Victoria Rooney speculates that he read Nietzsche while working in England in 1917.[4] Upon his return to Petrograd he became a close associate of the Scythian group of writers who counted in their numbers such erstwhile admirers of Nietzsche as Bely, Blok, and Ivanov-Razumnik. His reading of Nietzsche shared some central points with theirs. Since Zamiatin's critical writing of the following years was saturated with a Nietzschean "presence," it seems very likely that 1917 was indeed the time of his discovery. One could even argue that this discovery helped to propel him to the much higher level of creative innovation and critical insight that he subsequently attained. Relying strongly on Nietzsche, he forged a bold esthetic view well beyond his early Andreev-inspired "neo-realism." Incidentally, Andreev's own brand of Nietzscheanism, which had helped to fuel the popular cult of Nietzsche fifteen years before, had no real impact on Zamiatin.[5]

An important challenge to Zamiatin's personal appropriation of Nietzsche was the Nietzschean-Marxist God-building myth. Zamiatin was active in Civil-War Petrograd, where the cultural "bosses" were Gorky and Lunacharsky, the very authors of God-building, and Bogdanov, the organizer of Proletkult with its Promethean concept of the working masses. Zamiatin worked most closely with Gorky on a variety of editing, translating, and publishing ventures.[6] Important for Zamiatin's encounter with God-building was his participation in Gorky's monumental project for the theater: the production of a series of plays written by leading literary talents of the day about the development of the world's great religions and scientific theories.[7] Gorky wished to inspire worker audiences, to instill pride in them by bringing them to the Nietzschean insight that had sparked his own literary-political career: that these phenomena were not bestowed from above by an omnipotent God but conceived and created by the human spirit, the strongest value-giving force in the universe. Zamiatin's contribution to this project was the play, *Fires of St. Dominic (Ogni sviatogo Dominika*, 1919). Here, instead of following the God-building program of Gorky's enterprise, Zamiatin wrote in a generally ironic, anti-religious tone, criticizing all fanatics, both religious and political. He compared Russian Bolshevism to the Catholic Church, the Civil War to the Spanish Inquisition.[8] Already in this work his scepticism set him at odds with the quasi-mystical ardor of Gorky's God-building.

Despite the clear differences in view, Zamiatin's interpretation of Nietzsche did coincide at some points with that implicit in God-building. With the God-builders Zamiatin shared a strong impatience with present life and rich expectations of the future. However, if the God-builders awaited one future event, namely revolution, that would once and for all fuse the Apollonian self-consciousness of the artistic "I" with the vital Dionysian energy of the masses' "we," Zamiatin saw the future as a never-ending series of revolutions, each of which would in some way help to transform human consciousness from the "we" of primitive society and allow the emergence of the complex and creative "I." To support his faith in the future, Zamiatin in "On Literature, Revolution, and Entropy" (1924) relied in part on a Nietzschean epistemology:

all truths [*istiny*] are faulty: the dialectical process resides precisely in the fact that today's truths become mistakes tomorrow; there is no final number.

This (sole) truth is only for the strong [*dlia krepkikh*]: weak-nerved brains certainly need the limitedness of the universe, a final number, "the crutches of certainty" [*dostovernost'*] – in the words of Nietzsche. The weak-nerved do not have the strength to include themselves in the dialectical syllogism.[9]

With Nietzsche and the Scythians, and against the God-builders, who valued the masses' life-giving "enthusiasm," Zamiatin stressed the provocative, rebellious individual or "heretic," as he called him, who bore humanity into the future. Zamiatin chose neither the masses nor even the God-builders' "mass-man" (a single character who embodied the creative energy of the masses) as the highest form of humanity. He took as his model of the heretic Albert Einstein, hardly Gorky's monumental archetype of the artist and social leader. In Einstein, Zamiatin found an actual, historical figure, and a great contemporary scientist who, significantly, was an outcast, socially as a Jew and intellectually as a scientific thinker whose theories challenged the accepted Newtonian world-view. Only a person possessed of such inner fortitude, Zamiatin argued, could understand the human predicament because he could dare to imagine earthly life *sub specie aeternitatis*. As if following the Nietzschean dictum, "in order to see a city whole, one must go beyond its walls" (*GS*, p. 342), Zamiatin's heretic is able disinterestedly to examine and criticize the longstanding political, moral, and metaphysical assumptions by which we evaluate existence.

Very much in opposition to the anti-philosophical tenor of his time, Zamiatin called for a "philosophical" literature written in an appropriately innovative language that would open to the imagination the possibilities of the future. Stylistic innovation, he wrote, was essential to the creation of new consciousness. Again he was implicitly going beyond the God-builders, who, while committed to an ideologically inspirational kind of art, stayed with a tediously conservative "realistic" style. In "On Synthetism" ("O sintetizme," 1922), he suggested as the best possible style for the near future a fusion of classical realism and Symbolist mysticism. Zamiatin saw the essence of the new art in a synthesis of "irony," the negation of simple, concrete reality, and the heightened, ecstatic perception of the moment, its passions, colors, lines and forms.[10] The new synthesis of art and philosophy Zamiatin found in some combination of Nietzsche, Whitman, Gauguin, Seurat, and Picasso.

Despite his "individualist" stance, Zamiatin did not totally reject the God-building concept of the masses [*narod*]. In 1924, in "On Literature, Revolution, and Entropy," he reappropriated in his concept of philosophical art the God-builders' hostility to civilization (which the Scythians also shared) and their claim to the masses as a force of renewal – and once again he deliberately inserted Nietzsche, now in his own "heretical" image, into the equation. Now, he said, "literature needs huge, lofty, winged, philosophical perspectives, it needs the latest, most terrible, most fearless 'why?' and 'what next?'"[11] Zamiatin noted that along with children and philosophers, such as Schopenhauer, Dostoevsky, and Nietzsche, only the people have the freshness and courage to ask the difficult questions. The masses, he noted, were producing the "new people" just coming into cultural and scientific life, who would grasp new "truths" and "realities."[12] What made Zamiatin's idea of the people different from that of Gorky or Lunacharsky was that he saw in the masses a group of potential individuals. If the God-builders (and Bogdanov's protégés, the proletarian poets, as well) looked for the fusion of the individual "I" with the collective "we," Zamiatin proceeded in the opposite direction, expecting new heretics to emerge from the primordial collective consciousness.[13] As he put it in his article, "Tomorrow" (1919–20), history would move from oppression to freedom and from mass consciousness to individual consciousness. Recalling Nietzsche's thought that the herd instinct is much older than the "I" ("The 'You' is older than the 'I'," *GS*, p. 175; *Z*, p. 86), he wrote, "we have experienced the epoch of the suppression of the masses; we are experiencing the epoch of the suppression of the individual self in the name of the masses; tomorrow will bring the liberation of the self – in the name of man."[14]

In his theoretical essays, Zamiatin altered several aspects of the God-building view of Nietzsche. He undermined the simplistic, somewhat dogmatic thrust of this sort of thinking and restored to Nietzsche the "modernist" tension between irony and mythopoetry. He redefined the God-builders' vision of the future, which anticipated a monolithic utopian order, instead seeing the future as the eternal recurrence of revolution. He denied the God-builders' romantic notion of a *narod* as a life-nurturing mass consciousness, now seeing the people rather as a constellation of potential individual selves. All of these aspects of Zamiatin's "modernist" reappropriation of Nietzsche are reenforced in the parody of God-building that is central to his novel, *We*.

A number of articles have been written about *We* as a parodic response to literary currents of Civil-War Petrograd, in particular Proletkult, its organizer Bogdanov, and a writer-labor-organizer related to it, Aleksei Gastev.[15] Such discussions address several traits of the ideology of the One State, for example, the Promethean heroization of labor, the harmonization and rationalization of all aspects of human life, both public and private, and the exclusively collective mentality that insists on the primacy of the group, the "we," over the individual self.[16] Other aspects, such as the permitted survival of religious feeling and the emergence of a concept of monumental, semi-divine selfhood embodied in the Benefactor, have not received adequate attention. These "religious" traits of D-503's mentality, in my view, are best explained as a response to the myth of God-building which, while it certainly informed Bogdanov's Proletkult, was best formulated (and, indeed, the term "God-building" coined) by Gorky in works from his prerevolutionary exile, the novel, *Confession* (*Ispoved'*, 1908), and the article, "The Destruction of Personality" ("Razrushenie lichnosti," 1909).

The title of Zamiatin's novel places it in close relation to the collectivist vocabulary of God-building and its heirs, Proletkult and Gorky's World Literature projects. Right away the protagonist, D-503, establishes himself as an "unreliable" narrator whose God-building mentality the reader is meant to treat skeptically. An engineer (Bogdanov's ideal of future man), D-503 affirms the God-builders' preference for "we" over "I."[17] The God-building idea of the masses as a blind, God-like, creative whole is suggested early and repeated frequently. In the second entry, we find the masses during their prescribed daily walk, striding four abreast. The four people in the narrator's row, who turn out to be the main characters in the book, are: D-503; O-90, D's registered companion; I-330, another woman; and S-4711, a strange man with pink wing-like ears. Taking the letters alone, we find that they spell: D-I-O-S. Here we have the genitive form of the Greek god, "Zeus," implying that each individual is part "of the god." Although several other meanings have been suggested for Zamiatin's use of letter-names, this combination could hardly be coincidence: the "people," in the prevalent ideology as D-503 propounds it, are "god."[18] This Promethean theme is reiterated throughout the novel. D-503, who is even called a "Builder," has a strong sense of having aided in the creation of the world in its present utopian form. He writes: "And I felt: it was not the generations before me, but I – yes, I – who have conquered the old God and the old life. It was I who created all this" (*We*, p. 5). Still later, he makes the point clear that the masses are God-like: "the gods have become like us. Ergo, we have become as gods" (*We*, p. 69).

Gorky's God-building idea of monumental selfhood resonates in Zamiatin's figure of the Benefactor. Links have been established between the Benefactor and Dostoevsky's Grand

Inquisitor, particularly in each leader's cynical rationalization of unfreedom for the sake of happiness and the willingness of each to execute those that challenge the status quo.[19] Heller suggests a parallel between the Benefactor and the new cult of Lenin that spread in the later years of the Civil War.[20] Another important subtext is provided in the works of Zamiatin's chief protector in the early Soviet years, Gorky. Throughout his early and middle periods, in programmatic works such as "Man" ("Chelovek," 1904) and "The Destruction of Personality" ("Razrushenie lichnosti," 1909), Gorky unfolded a Feuerbachian-Nietzschean theory of periodic rebirth, creation, and legitimization of values. In "Destruction of Personality" and his God-building novel, *Confession*, Gorky argued that deities were the apotheosis of the highest virtues of a people, personified and immortalized in the figure of a hero who has survived in the collective memory. Gorky picked the period of the German Reformation and emergence of the Faust myth as the best example of God-building: "In this period of social storms, selfhood [*lichnost'*] becomes a focal point for thousands of wills that have chosen it as their representative organ, and it arises ... in the wonderful light of beauty and strength, in the bright flame of the yearnings of its nation."[21] Eventually, according to Gorky, the people relinquish their greatest virtue, their deep value-creating power, investing their god with it, and they gradually become enslaved, viewing themselves as helpless and imperfect servants, the very opposite of their ideal. The god, now become a tyrannical figure, is seen as a harsh but fair judge who enforces his absolute will.

The literary-cultural process of the last century, Gorky continues, has completed this process of alienation from the ideal: writers and thinkers have overthrown the absolute Christian God, reinvesting themselves with value-creating power. Such self-assigned "creativity," Gorky argues, is barren unless it is coupled with the true value-creating will of the people. Now, in the early twentieth century, Gorky believes that the masses are again entering a God-building phase and are asserting their value-assigning energy. What Gorky yearns for in both

"Man" and *Confession* is the emergence of a new social leader who will enact the popular creative will.

Zamiatin's Benefactor, as D-503 envisions him, is just such a social leader. The all-powerful ruler of the One State has received his power from the masses. D-503 exclaims proudly: "What a fiery gust of exaltation one must feel to be the instrument, the resultant of a hundred thousand wills! What a great destiny!" (*We*, p. 48). Although, to start with, the Benefactor seems the apotheosis of deep creative energy of thousands of wills, he is revealed eventually as the opposite. With his heavy iron hands, he becomes a symbol of heaviness and oppression (*We*, p. 212). His face is inscrutable, hidden high up in the haze: he has become ineffable, much like the old Christian god. He does not represent the will of the people which, as Zamiatin shows, is rebellious, anarchic, and in continual flux, but exists to perpetuate the power of the One State, a false order bridling the people's will.

From the very start Zamiatin deflates the utopianism inherent in God-building. As Richard Stites has remarked, it is clear that Zamiatin's work is an "emphatic repudiation of Bogdanov's [collectivist, technocratic] utopia" and, it might be added, of the collectivist voluntarism of Gorky.[22] Rationalism and collectivism, in Zamiatin's view, bring not innovation and freedom, but ossification and conformism. Rather, in agreement with Nietzsche's and the Scythians' "regressive-progressive" thinking, he points to atavistic qualities, such as the sexual instinct and the savage, anarchistic power of the ego, as the source of the deep creative force needed to change life.[23] We soon learn that the individuals that comprise the God-building collective, symbolically D-I-O-S, are not only disparate but very much at odds in acting out their separate wills. D-503 is a thinking, creative person who, until he starts his diary, is devoted blindly to the oppressive One State; I-330 is a revolutionary dedicated to overturning the society, O-90 is interested only in domestic tranquility, S-4711 is a "Guardian," a police agent concerned with controlling the others. D-503, the ultimately rational mind, arrives at contradictions which can only be resolved at the end by having a futuristic kind of lobotomy in a high-tech machine that surgically removes the human fantasy. By keeping a diary in praise of "we," D-503 has stumbled unwillingly upon individual consciousness (*We*, p. 111). The reader learns, although D-503 never quite fully acknowledges it, that over the 200 years since the last revolution the collectivist "we" has ossified into the One State, an oppressive force that, far from enacting the will of the many, strives for total control over the populace.

Despite its Futuristic technology, in this "Eden" very old values still hold sway. Much as in ancient Christian society, here too, "humility is a virtue, and pride a vice; 'we' is from God, and 'I' from the devil" (*We*, p. 128). Even now, a "herd" mentality, an anaesthesia of the spirit, much as Nietzsche might present it, represses individual will. Relying very much on Nietzschean thinking, D-503 comes to the conclusion that the utopian state is nothing more than the "crutches of certainty," yet another version of an absolute truth erected to comfort the weak of heart. He is strong enough to understand that there can be no "final number" and realizes that this insight means that he must support I-330's plans for rebellion. Nonetheless, unlike I-330, who at the end resists the operation that is to deprive her of her imagination, D-503 sounds relieved to have the "splinter" of doubt taken out of his brain. The Nietzschean "truth" that all truths are finite is too much to bear.

It is significant that Gorky, who otherwise admired Zamiatin greatly, criticized *We* very harshly. In a letter of 1929 to his biographer, I. A. Gruzdev, Gorky noted that "Zamiatin is too intelligent for an artist and should not allow his reason to direct his talent to satire. *We* is hopelessly bad, a completely sterile thing. Its anger is cold and dry; it is the anger of an old maid."[24] Here Gorky attacked those aspects of Zamiatin's literary personality that led the younger writer to make fun of his elder's quasi-religious God-building ideology and merged into a distinct literary-philosophical view, one inspired in part by a rereading of Nietzsche. Zamiatin, a skeptic, was incapable of giving credence to the prevalent religion of the people that was at least in some of its elements endorsed by Gorky. That he publicly parodied it during Gorky's "reign" in Petrograd cultural life must have incensed the older man. The best Gorky could do was to counterattack using imagery hinting at Zamiatin's sexual (read: artistic) impotence. Although there is no proof that he tried to hinder the publication of *We*, Gorky may have hoped that Zamiatin's innovation could not be productive in Russian literary life. And indeed, until April, 1988, when *We* was finally published in its native country and language, it was not.

How does Zamiatin's appropriation of Nietzsche figure in the Russian reception process? We can say that it embodied the typical (that is, rivalrous) course of reception among "strong" writers in the modern era and the stifling effect of Soviet censorship on this process (see Rosenthal's Introduction). Certainly the Russian "heretic" arrived at his own concept of Nietzsche's philosophy very much in an ambience of polemic. Through the usual process of discreditation and reconstruction, he diminished the religious, myth-building, mass-Dionysian character of god-building and asserted an anarchistic, skeptical, individualist reading of Nietzsche akin to the Scythian one. The reception process, however, even at this early stage in Soviet history, was already being affected by political forces. Although Zamiatin's articles were published (but only once, never reissued until the 1980s), the novel, as is well known, was announced but did not appear until April, 1988, almost seventy years later. Thus, already by the end of the Civil War, through the publishing limitations placed on a leading Russian Nietzschean of the day, the skeptical spirit of modernism and one of its guiding philosophical lights, Nietzsche, were being removed as influential forces in the cultural life of the new society.

The other writer of Zamiatin's generation who inadvertently kept alive the reception of Nietzsche was Pasternak, who wrote his Dionysian novel, *Doctor Zhivago*, under the vastly different cultural atmosphere of the years around Stalin's death. His assimilation of the other major prerevolutionary Nietzschean myth, Symbolist God-seeking, reveals a somewhat different problem in Nietzsche's Soviet reception. By the 1940s and

1950s, when Pasternak wrote *Doctor Zhivago*, Nietzsche had long since been disallowed in official culture. What is more, in contrast to Zamiatin, Pasternak as a younger man had never felt an affinity for the German philosopher, preferring the neo-Kantian thinking current in leading literary-philosophical circles of the 1910s. Pasternak was concerned in this final work to bear witness to the prerevolutionary Russian cultural tradition, which, as it happened, included a strong response to Nietzsche. If Pasternak's ultimate hope was resurrection of this culture, his immediate purpose was its mere survival.

Pasternak first learned of Nietzsche in 1903 through a family friendship with the composer Aleksandr Skriabin who, to use Pasternak's phrase, "proselytized the Superman."[25] Pasternak's autobiographical sketch from the 1950s, "People and Situations" ("Liudi i polozheniia"), suggests that the young poet was captivated by people with aggressive, dominant personalities. His infatuation with Skriabin anticipated his later and more famous fascination with Mayakovsky. In both men he was drawn to a personality which in its artistic self-expression strove for creative realization far beyond the bounds of the created artifact. While writing of Mayakovsky in his early autobiography, *Safe Conduct (Okhrannaia gramota*, 1930), Pasternak linked this idea to the generally romantic view of the poetic personality as the "measure of life." In "People and Situations," he used specifically Nietzschean terms to define Skriabin and more generally the Russian creative mentality:

Skriabin's thoughts on the Superman showed an age-old Russian taste for the extreme. Really, not only did music need to be supermusic in order to mean something, but everything in the world had to overcome itself in order to be itself. A person [and] the activities of that person had to contain an element of infinity which gave the phenomenon a definition, a character.[26]

Like so many writers before him, Pasternak acknowledged Nietzsche's importance for Russian art by russifying him, identifying his impact as yet another expression of a native Russian tradition.[27]

Despite his admiration for the strong artistic personality, there is no evidence that Pasternak himself strove to emulate this poetic archetype.[28] Indeed, in his autobiographical works he pursues a subtle but persistent critique of this kind of person and evolves an opposing view of the artist as a spontaneous and ecstatic consciousness, not unlike Viacheslav Ivanov's concept of the creative self that strives to fuse the "small self" with the larger spiritual communality. In his sketch of Skriabin in "People and Situations," Pasternak notes his father's philosophical opposition to Skriabin and disdains his own admiration for Skriabin's "freshness of spirit" by saying that he was still too young really to have understood the composer's worldview.[29] About Mayakovsky Pasternak writes in *Safe Conduct* of his disappointment at his towering contemporary's inability to enter into other people's experience.[30] For example, Mayakovsky was oblivious to the spiritual renewal that Pasternak underwent in 1918 following the composition of his great lyric cycle, *My Sister, Life*. As Pasternak put it, there was never real "intimacy" between Mayakovsky and him.[31] Such was the shortcoming of the dominant personality that made itself the measure of all things.

Pasternak uses Nietzsche to extend his subtle polemic against the idea of the creative self as the measure of life. The Nietzschean image of the Superman becomes a vulgarized emblem of this type. For example, in his narrative poem, "Spektorsky" (1924–30), about a young poet and his experience of the Revolution, a main theme is the failure of "individualism." One of Spektorsky's acquaintances, Sasha Balts, is just the sort of self-deluded, egotistical follower of the cult of the Superman that took root in the popular imagination before the Bolshevik Revolution.[32] Much later, in *Doctor Zhivago*, the Superman is equated with an egotistic mentality that demanded for itself "special rights and privileges."[33]

Despite Pasternak's complex feeling toward Nietzsche and Russian Nietzscheans, he came of age in the prerevolutionary years when many leading writers and thinkers were stimulated by Nietzsche's anti-Christian challenge, were finding links between his Dionysian thought and the Christian tradition, and were synthesizing aspects of his philosophy in an image of the earthly Christ.[34] Since Pasternak was close to Bely, worshiped Blok, was friendly with Ivanov, especially around 1917, and was acquainted with Berdiaev, it was unavoidable that he should be aware of their ideas.[35] If his "People and Situations" reveals a serious consideration and even admiration for aspects of the Nietzschean creative personality, his final novel, *Doctor Zhivago*, shows a strong affinity for the Dionysian-Christian mysticism that was so strong in Symbolist and neo-Christian circles. In both works, finished in the final years of Pasternak's life, the poet struggled to revive a creative tradition which, acknowledged or not, Nietzsche had strongly influenced.

One important source for Pasternak's concept of the earthly Christ put forth in his novel was Berdiaev's treatment of the archetype in his book, *The Meaning of the Creative Act (Smysl tvorchestva*, 1916). Drawing on the experience of the mystical Symbolists, particularly Merezhkovsky and Ivanov, Berdiaev created in this work his own theory of the historical evolution of Christianity and Christian values. Significantly, Pasternak heard Berdiaev lecture on religious philosophy during the Civil War years following the publication of *The Meaning of the Creative Act*.[36] It is fair to suppose that the archetype of the earthly Christ figured in some way in Berdiaev's lectures.

A philosophy close to Berdiaev's neo-Christianity is espoused by two characters, Yury Zhivago and his uncle, Nikolai Vedeniapin. Although several other historical figures have been discussed as possible historical prototypes for Vedeniapin, there are several reasons to put Berdiaev among them. "Uncle Nikolai" suggestively bears the same first name as Berdiaev.[37] His surname "Vedeniapin" shares the sounds, "v," "e," "d," and "ia" with "Berdiaev," thus bringing the latter name to mind. The intellectual tastes of both men can be loosely compared. Berdiaev started his intellectual career as a Marxist, became a Kantian, and evolved as one of the most original Russian Christian thinkers of the early twentieth century. Vedeniapin similarly combined an interest in all the leading philosophers of the day, Marx, Kant, Tolstoi and Soloviev. Nietzsche is another thinker who belonged in this pantheon but who, because of his official image as "bourgeois decadent" and precursor to Nazism, could not be mentioned publicly in the Stalin era.

Vedeniapin's personal biography develops along the lines of the three historical stages of Christianity outlined in *The Meaning of the Creative Act*. Borrowing the neo-Christian historiographical convention started in Russia in the 1890s by Merezhkovsky, Berdiaev divides moral-religious history into: pre-Christian, Christian, and modern periods that enforce three corresponding moral psychologies: law, redemption, and self-creation. Nietzsche is Berdiaev's greatest inspiration for the third period.[38] Vedeniapin's spiritual development runs parallel to these historical stages: he starts his adult life as a priest, thus submitting to a strict dogma, but at his own request has been defrocked. Still, as we learn in the first pages of the novel, he keeps close ties with the ecclesiastical establishment. Since then he has devoted himself to the ritual of social redemption so common to the intelligentsia of the second half of the nineteenth century: he has helped to serve the people by editing a progressive newspaper in the Volga region. And as an adherent of Tolstoian teaching, he has converted to a simplified, socially committed revision of Christianity. Vedeniapin grows beyond Berdiaev's first two historical periods of Christianity – law and redemption – and, building on them, goes on to the third stage, in which he liberates himself from dogma and ritual and develops his own philosophy.[39]

Vedeniapin conceives of history with much the same periodization as the neo-Christians had. He discredits the pre-Christian period of "law" more decisively than Berdiaev does. He pictures the period before Christ as a time of enslavement of whole nations to the tyranny of perverted individuals, the "pockmarked Caligulas" (*DZ*, p. 10). Vedeniapin emphasized personal ideals of compassion and creativity over social values of discipline and obedience. He defends the striving, creative individual against the conformist pressures exerted by groups and collectives when he remarks, "there are gifted men ... but the fashion nowadays is all for groups and societies of every sort. Gregariousness is always the refuge of mediocrities" (*DZ*, p. 9).

Vedeniapin's moral vision incorporates aspects of Berdiaev's second and third historical stages, redemption, self-sacrifice, and then self-creation:

You can't make discoveries without spiritual equipment. And the basic elements of this equipment are the Gospels. What are they? To begin with, love of one's neighbor, which is the supreme form of vital energy ... And then the two basic ideals of modern man – without them he is unthinkable – the idea of free personality and the idea of life as sacrifice. Mind you, all this is extraordinarily new. (*DZ*, p. 10)

Vedeniapin's outright dismissal of the pre-Christian period as an era of slavery, of "blood and beastliness and cruelty," may be interpreted as Pasternak's own comment on social and cultural conditions in Russia of the 1940s and 1950s when he was working on his novel (*DZ*, p. 10). Vedeniapin's views, idiosyncratic and seemingly outdated in the 1950s, bear unmistakable undertones of protest against repressions that Pasternak himself and his contemporaries had experienced at the heavy hand of the "pockmarked Caligula" of the day, the pockmarked tyrant, Joseph Stalin. Thus, Pasternak reshaped Berdiaevian, or more generally neo-Christian, views to fit the cultural context of a later day.

Yury's Uncle Nikolai is the spiritual mentor of the politically uncommitted intellectuals in the novel – Misha Gordon, Sima Tuntseva, and Yury himself. These people reiterate Vedeniapin's preference for the individual over groups of all kinds – nations, societies, and even intellectual circles. For Yury it is the "mystery of the individual" that makes life meaningful. He encapsulates his neo-Christian idea in a conversation with his friend, Gordon: "In that new way of living and new form of society, which is born of the heart, and which is called the Kingdom of Heaven, there are no nations, there are only individuals" (*DZ*, p. 122).

In his own development Yury experiences the neo-Christian three stages of spiritual development. It is he who fulfills the ideal of Christian self-creativity first suggested by his Uncle Nikolai. Yury goes through his own period of "law" when he conforms in every way to the social norms of his milieu. He is educated, he gets married, has a family, serves his nation in war. In his professional life as a doctor, Yury lives through the second stages of "redemption." He serves other people, actively helping to alleviate misery. However, neither his conformity to social standards nor his service to nation and society satisfies a deeper creative urge. Gradually, this impulse which has lain dormant for years takes over. Just as Zarathustra goes to the mountain, abandoning the "level plain" of "humanism," as Berdiaev called it, Yury leaves the plains of central Russia, where he served society as a doctor and a family man, for the Ural Mountains where he will fulfill his deepest personal creativity.

Yury's inner quest now resembles the God-seeking rite conceived by Ivanov that became around 1905 a shortlived cult among mystical Symbolists, for example, Blok and Bely.[40] Pasternak, who became friendly with Ivanov in 1917, was almost certainly familiar with his Dionysian-Christian mysticism. It is important to note that in this period Ivanov was expanding his own earlier study of ancient Dionysian rites, seeing in them precursors to the Christian rite of sacrifice. He would publish his research in the early 1920s as a doctoral dissertation.[41] In his first probings from 1903 and 1904, Ivanov posited that a persona could realize the deepest form of spirituality, which he called "being-in-love" [*vliublennost'*], as well as his fullest creative energy, by invoking the god Dionysus and entering into a struggle with him. Outwardly the poetic self enters a love relationship with a female Dionysian persona in which both selves would transcend the bounds of narrow selfhood and be merged together. Inwardly the poet searches for and challenges the Dionysian daemon, a quest which closely follows Christ's three-day transfiguration: his ascent to Golgotha, his burial, his descent to hell, and his resurrection. The ascent of the self as *bogoborets* (wrestler with the god) parallels Christ's ascent to Golgotha. Now ego and self-will are predominant: the self ascends to a divine level and challenges the god. Just as Christ after the crucifixion returns to earth, is buried, so the poetic self now returns to the earth, sacrificing personal ego to the deity and shedding the narrow confines of personal desire and self-will. At this stage the self becomes *bogonosets* (bearer of the god). Now the self descends to the limitless "hell" of orgiastic passion, much as Christ descends to hell. It loses all self-consciousness and merges in "blind conception" with the god.[42] Christ is transfigured after his ordeal. Similarly, the poetic self emerges anew, resurrected, creatively renewed, and ecstatic in the consciousness of "being-in-love."

Yury becomes *bogoborets* when he abandons his familial duty and starts an affair with Lara, clearly a Dionysian type (Ivanovian, certainly not adhering to Nietzsche's concept of women), with a profound intuitive sense and strong, if anarchic, life-giving passion. Yury betrays Tonia, all the while tormenting himself with feelings of guilt. Interestingly, the Nietzschean subtext for this experience is suggested to the reader in the form of a disclaimer. Yury rejects, as most scrupulous Russian intellectuals of the early twentieth century would have, the image of himself as a kind of vulgar "superman," exercising the "special rights and privileges" of free love (*DZ*, p. 305).

During his captivity among the partisan guerillas of the Forest Brotherhood, Yury becomes *bogonosets* or bearer of the god. In the Siberian woods he has a vision of an ethereal female figure, very much like a larger-than-life icon of the Virgin: "there hung before him in the air, from one side of the forest glade to the other, a blurred, greatly magnified image of a single, astonishing, idolized head. The apparition wept, and the rain, now more intense, kissed and watered it" (*DZ*, pp. 369–70). He is filled with a powerful consciousness of Lara, now transfigured as the Dionysian god within him, which propels him to risk being shot by the partisans and to escape the guerilla camp. He makes his way through a wasteland filled with ruined, hungry, savage people, back to Yuriatin to Lara. With her help he survives a mortal bout of typhoid fever. Having shed all the outer characteristics that defined his former social, political, and professional self, isolated from the outer world, together with Lara and a local follower of Vedeniapin, Sima Tuntseva, he spends long winter evenings meditating about their lives and the national events around them.

Yury's and Lara's escape to Varykino is the beginning of Yury's mythic descent into hell. Sexual passion is made quite explicit here as we learn that the two lovers forget entirely about duty, even about Lara's daughter, Katia, and lose themselves to hours of oblivious love-making. It is through this blind Dionysian orgy that both lovers arrive at the final stage of creative renewal and the ecstatic consciousness of "being-in-love." Lara becomes physically pregnant, and Yury becomes spiritually pregnant, realizing his deep artistic energy. However, Yury's poetic achievement comes only at great cost: the destruction of his moral fiber. Deceiving himself into thinking that he can save Lara from the ravages of the Civil War, Yury unwittingly sacrifices his beloved by sending her away with her lifelong tormentor, the self-serving lawyer, Viktor Komarovsky. Now Yury completely gives himself over to Dionysian frenzy. Totally isolated, having sacrificed everyone close to him, he now sacrifices his reason and his physical health to vodka and sleepless delirium. Paradoxically, as he ruins his earthly self, he also "overcomes" himself, finding higher self-expression in a cycle of religious verse that is itself an enactment of personal, spiritual resurrection. Here in Yury's tragedy is the last Russian embodiment of the Dionysian Christ.

One important way in which Pasternak departs from neo-Christian God-seeking myths is in the final outcome. If Ivanov and Berdiaev optimistically anticipate new spiritual consciousness. Pasternak, who stands beyond the revolutionary abyss, is more ironic. We are allowed to see the very real suffering of Lara, who perishes in a labor camp and their child, Tania, who is abandoned and abused, one of the Civil War's millions of homeless children. Yury really does go partly mad. But unlike the divine madness of Nietzsche's archetype of the tragic hero in *Birth of Tragedy* or of Ivanov's transfigured poetic self, Yury's half-madness does not reaffirm life. He returns to Moscow a morally spent and wasted man. He cannot really even be dignified with the title that the narrator gives him, a "Seeker after Truth." Yury has lost his will to strive. He is unable to make decisions, and has become quite irresponsible. He has paid for his creative ecstasy with his rationality, his strength of will, his moral vitality. In this world beyond the abyss of revolution there is no Nietzschean balance between Dionysus and Apollo, no Apollonian veiling of the dark aspect of Dionysus: tyranny, madness, and self-destruction. An exile in his own land, Yury escapes his new family and friends and dies of a heart attack. Even the optimism of the epilogue, of Gordon's and Dudorov's final conversation, seems contrived. The dark, violent side of the Dionysian has overwhelmed Yury, the old order he symbolizes, and, indeed, the whole Russian land.

Pasternak also departs from Nietzschean precursors in the religious valuations made in Yury's actual poetry. It is true that he focuses on the religious experience of the individual. However, the poems, particularly "Magdalene," reaffirm the un-Nietzschean ideas of love and redemption. There is no mention of creativity as a virtue or a life goal. The final poem, "Garden of Gethsemane," asserts an older kind of "pantocrator" image of Christ, the arbiter of law and justice. Berdiaev's and Nietzsche's affirmation of personal will and creative genius is lacking. For Pasternak, the Christian experience is ultimately concerned with transcending narrow human will and achieving higher unity with other people and with nature. In this final view, the only individual of lasting worth is Christ, the sufferer, the resurrected god-man, the judge of rulers and nations – not the human creator.

Doctor Zhivago may be seen as a kind of latterday God-seeking saint's life in which traditional Christian values are fused with modern ideals. Here in the anti-philosophical, anti-religious desert of the Soviet 1950s, Nietzsche's reception is resurrected along with the whole dialogue of early Russian neo-idealism and Symbolism. Nietzsche's work, the source of the idea of human creative will, had been forgotten. The idea itself had been absorbed into the culture of the Russian Renaissance, synthesized into a modern Christian ideal, and now was revitalized in a later period.

Since Pasternak there has been very little new evidence of vitality in this or any other thread of Nietzsche's reception. Until the mid-1980s no officially-sanctioned author would permit himself to write about "reactionary" themes, for example about religion or the irrational, or write in any faintly "modernist" style. The beginning of a new interest in Nietzsche seemed possible with the appearance in the 1960s of the talented Russian critic, Andrei Siniavsky, and his underground pseudonymous self, Abram Tertz. As Max Hayward noted, Siniavsky-Tertz was very concerned at least to preserve and at best to reopen the prerevolutionary heritage.[43] This writer has been compared to Zamiatin. Certainly the prescription that Tertz gives in his essay, "On Socialist Realism" (1959), for a phantasmagoric literature of the future bears more than a chance resemblance to Zamiatin's idea of a literature of the fantastic in his two articles, "On Synthetism" and "On Literature, Revolution, and Entropy," with their call for a fusion of realism and Symbolist mysticism, of Whitman, Nietzsche, and Picasso.

In his role as officially-permitted critic, Siniavsky did more than anyone of his time to revive Pasternak's legacy in Russian poetry with his rich introduction to the "Biblioteka poeta" edition of the poet's verse. In his notes to the section, "Poetry from a Novel," he reminded his readers that Pasternak had written a novel, *Doctor Zhivago*, that had not yet appeared in the Soviet Union. Very little can be said about Siniavsky-Tertz's knowledge or response to Nietzsche. In a personal conversation following a lecture at the University of Illinois in Urbana in September, 1981, Siniavsky and his wife mentioned that they liked Nietzsche but found his philosophy "strident" [*kriklivyi*]. At the very most, it is possible to detect in some work, for example, Tertz's notes from prison, *A Voice from the Chorus* (*Golos iz khora*, 1974), a distant affinity with Nietzsche's aphoristic style and esthetic views. The perceived relationship between religious culture and art, Tertz's psychology of creativity that links deep suffering and cultural creativity – all bring to mind Nietzsche.[44]

From the Revolution to the late 1980s, the vital Nietzschean strain in Russian literature, like everything connected with "modernism," has lived a peripheral existence in the no-man's-land between official Soviet and exile Russian cultures. Only early in 1988, during glasnost, did works such as *We* and *Doctor Zhivago* appear openly, published by officially-sanctioned Soviet houses. Recovery of these two works has had significance so far only for the reassessment of Soviet political history. Only time will tell whether they will play a role in the further development of Russian literary history. Although both God-building and God-seeking themes have re-emerged in works published in the late 1980s, they betray none of their Nietzschean heritage. God-building, which was a key to the development of high Stalinist culture, is suggested obliquely in Anatoly Rybakov's treatment of Stalin in *Children of the Arbat* (*Deti Arbata*, 1987).[45] Here the monumentalism that had been part of God-building is unmasked as powermongering, the Prometheanism – as mere demagoguery. God-seeking is a prominent concept in Chingiz Aitmatov's *The Executioner's Block* (*Plakha*, 1986), where the central character Avdy Kallistratov, a drop-out from theological seminary, proselytizes a Christianity founded on seeking the god within one's self.[46] Interestingly, one of Avdy's teachers at seminary slightingly calls his thinking *bogoiskatel'stvo* (God-seeking). And Avdy, who is bested by a group of teenaged drug-dealers, in turn refers to them as "supermanizing [*supermenstvuiushchii*] youths."[47] Despite the very ambiguous attitude to Nietzsche, all these events bode well for the revival of that rich merger between *belles lettres* and speculative thought that has been the unique achievement of Russian literature.

NOTES

1 For detailed accounts of Nietzsche's prerevolutionary literary reception, see *Nietzsche in Russia*, ed. Bernice Glatzer Rosenthal (Princeton, 1986); Edith W. Clowes, *The Revolution of Moral Consciousness: Nietzsche in Russian Literature, 1890–1914* (DeKalb, 1988).

2 D. S. Merezhkovsky called this cult a "childhood disease fatal to adults." See Merezhkovsky, *Polnoe sobranie sochinenii* (St. Petersburg, 1911), XII, p. 257.

3 For more on God-building and God-seeking, see George L. Kline, *Religious and Anti-Religious Thought in Russia* (Chicago, 1968); Christopher Read, *Religion, Revolution and the Russian Intelligentsia, 1900–1912: The "Vekhi" Debate and its Intellectual Background* (New York, 1980); Raimund Sesterhenn, *Das Bogostroitel'stvo bei Gor'kii und Lunacharskij, bis 1909* (Munich, 1982).

4 Victoria Rooney, "Nietzschean Elements in Zamyatin's Ideology: A Study of His Essays," *Modern Language Review* 81:3 (July, 1986), pp. 675–86.

5 For more on Andreev's reception, see E. Clowes, "Literary Reception as Vulgarization: Nietzsche's Idea of the Superman in Neo-Realist Fiction," *Nietzsche in Russia*, pp. 315–31.

6 Alex M. Shane, *The Life and Works of Evgenij Zamjatin* (Berkeley, 1968), p. 32. For a quite detailed account of Zamiatin's and Gorky's literary relations, see N. N. Primochkina, "M. Gork'ii i E. Zamiatin (k istorii literaturnykh vzaimootnoshenii)," *Russkaia literatura* 4 (1987), pp. 148–60.

7 Shane, *Zamjatin*, p. 32.

8 Ibid., pp. 32, 137–39.

9 Evgenii Zamiatin, "O literature, revoliutsii, i entropii," *Litsa* (New York, 1967), p. 253. For an English translation of Zamiatin's essay, see Yevgeny Zamyatin, *A Soviet Heretic*, ed. and trans. Mirra Ginsburg (Chicago, 1970).

10 Zamiatin, *Litsa*, p. 234.

11 Ibid., p. 252.

12 Ibid., p. 252.

13 Kathleen Lewis and Harry Weber, "Zamyatin's *We*, the Proletarian Poets, and Bogdanov's *Red Star*," *Russian Literature Triquarterly* 12 (1975), pp. 253–78.

14 "Zavtra," *Litsa*, p. 174.

15 Beside Lewis and Weber, see Edward J. Brown, *Brave New World, 1984, and We: An Essay on Anti-Utopia* (Ann Arbor, 1976); Leonid Heller, "Zamjatin: Prophète ou temoin? *Nous Autres* et les Realités de son Epoque," *Cahiers du monde russe et sovietique* 2–3 (1981), pp. 137–65; Patricia Carden, "Utopia and Anti-Utopia: Aleksei Gastev and Evgeny Zamiatin," *Russian Review* 46 (Winter, 1987), pp. 1–18.

16 Carden suggests that Zamiatin may have taken his title from Proletkult poetry, particularly the work of Aleksei Gastev, a writer, teacher-turned-worker and labor-organizer, particularly lauded by Bogdanov. In this poetry the pronoun "we" is pervasive. See Carden, "Utopia," p. 15.

17 *My* (New York, 1967), pp. 8–9. *We*, trans. Mirra Ginsburg (New York, 1972). Citations are taken from the English edition and will be noted in the text with "*We*" and the appropriate page number.

18 Lewis and Weber, for example, find in the names an allusion to characters in Bogdanov's *Red Star*: Lewis and Weber, "Zamyatin's *We*," p. 270.

19 Shane, *Zamjatin*, pp. 139–40. See also Robert Louis Jackson,

Dostoevsky's Underground Man in Russian Literature (The Hague, 1958), pp. 150–57.

20 Heller, "Zamjatin," pp. 157–58. See also Nina Tumarkin, *Lenin Lives!* (Cambridge, 1983).

21 A. M. Gor'kii, *Sobranie sochinenii v 30-i tomakh*, XXIII (Moscow, 1953), p. 34.

22 Richard Stites, "Fantasy and Revolution: Aleksandr Bogdanov and the Origin of Bolshevik Science Fiction," Introduction to: Aleksandr Bogdanov, *Red Star* (Bloomington, IN, 1984), p. 14. See, also, Zenovia Sochor, "A. A. Bogdanov: In Search of Cultural Liberation," *Nietzsche in Russia*, pp. 293–311; Sochor, *Revolution and Culture: The Bogdanov-Lenin Controversy* (Ithaca, 1988).

23 I have borrowed the term "progressive-regressive" from Ophelia Schutte, *Beyond Nihilism* (Chicago, 1984), p. 8.

24 Shane, *Zamjatin*, p. 87.

25 Boris Pasternak, *Vozdushnye puti* (Moscow, 1982), p. 422. For more on Scriabin and Nietzsche, see Ann M. Lane, "Bal'mont and Scriabin: The Artist as Superman," *Nietzsche in Russia*, pp. 195–218.

26 Pasternak, *Vozdushnye puti*, pp. 272, 425.

27 For another example of the russification of Nietzsche, see Clowes, "Dmitry Merezhkovsky's New Christ: The Synthesis of Spirit and Flesh," *Revolution of Moral Consciousness*, pp. 115–34.

28 See Guy de Mallac, *Boris Pasternak: His Life and Art* (Norman, OK, 1981), pp. 33–35. See also *Pasternak on Art and Creativity*, ed. Angela Livingstone (Cambridge, 1985), pp. 8–9; Boris Pasternak, *Perepiska s Ol'goi Freidenberg* (New York, 1981), p. 87. Here Pasternak's cousin, Freidenberg, and not Pasternak himself, turns out to be the Nietzsche enthusiast. For more about Pasternak's concept of selfhood [*lichnost'*], see my article, "Characterization in Doktor Zhivago: Lara and Tonja," *Slavic and East European Journal* (Fall, 1990), pp. 322–31.

29 *Vozdushnye puti*, p. 422.

30 Ibid., p. 274.

31 Ibid., p. 451

32 Boris Pasternak, *Stikhotvoreniia* (Moscow-Leningrad, 1965), p. 322.

33 Boris Pasternak, *Doktor Zhivago* (Milan, 1957), p. 312. *Doctor Zhivago*, trans. Max Hayward and Harari (New York, 1958), p. 304. Citations are taken from the English edition and will henceforth be given in the text with "*DZ*" and the appropriate page number.

34 See Clowes, *Revolution of Moral Consciousness*, pp. 115–74.

35 *Vozdushnye puti*, p. 447.
36 de Mallac, *Boris Pasternak*, pp. 105–5.
37 Mary F. and Paul Rowland, *Pasternak's "Doctor Zhivago"* (Carbondale, IL, 1967), p. 22. The Rowlands suggest that Berdiaev is one of several "leaders of religious-philosophical societies" whom Vedeniapin resembles.
38 Nikolai Berdiaev, *The Meaning of the Creative Act* (New York, 1955), p. 170.
39 Ibid., p. 90.
40 See, especially, V. I. Ivanov, "Simvolika esteticheskikh nachal," *SS*, 4 vols. to date (Brussels, 1971), I, pp. 824–29.
41 Ivanov, *Dionis i pradionisiistvo* (Baku, 1923).
42 Ivanov, "Simvolika," p. 829.
43 Max Hayward, *Russian Writers, 1917–1978* (New York, 1983), pp. 273–75.
44 See, for just a few examples, Abram Tertz, *A Voice from the Chorus* (New York, 1978), pp. 6–7, 12–13, 16–17.
45 See Katerina Clark, *The Soviet Novel: History as Ritual* (Chicago, 1985), pp. 152–55; Anatolii Rybakov, "Deti Arbata," *Druzhba narodov* 4–6 (1987): for example, 4 (1987), pp. 10, 108; 5 (1987), pp. 73–74; 6 (1987), p. 126.
46 Chingiz Aitmatov, *Plakha* (Riga, 1986), pp. 58, 75–76, 82, 190.
47 Ibid., pp. 75, 190.

CHAPTER 13

Mandelstam, Nietzsche, and the conscious creation of history

Clare Cavanagh

One often hears: that is good but it belongs to yesterday.
But I say: yesterday has not yet been born. It has not yet
really existed.
> Osip Mandelstam, "The Word and Culture" (1921)

Perhaps the past is still essentially undiscovered.
> Friedrich Nietzsche, *The Gay Science* (1882)

"History is a nightmare from which I am trying to awake,"
James Joyce's would-be artist Stephen Daedalus proclaims in a
famous phrase. Most of the writers and thinkers of Joyce's
generation, however, saw themselves as faced not with history's
nightmarish, inescapable presence, but with its – perhaps
equally nightmarish – absence. The Modernist artist felt
himself to be "excommunicated from history," in Mandelstam's phrase. Cut loose, for better or for worse, from his
moorings in the past, he was awash in a boundless sea of
contemporaneity, and he could read his exile from the past in
one of two ways, or so Charles Feidelson and Richard Ellmann
suggest. It might be either a "liberation from inherited patterns," or "deprivation and disinheritance." The Modernist
must, in other words, cast his lot either among the "Futurists"
or the "Passéists." He must either celebrate his release from the
dead weight of tradition or forever mourn the loss of an
infinitely precious, infinitely distant past.[1]

This schema is far too narrow to encompass the range of
responses to the pervasive modern "sense of an ending," as
Ellmann and Feidelson readily admit. It is used, however, with
monotonous regularity when we come to the Russian post-
Symbolists and their perceptions of history. Osip Mandelstam

and his Acmeist colleagues are the committed Passéists, determined to protect the remnants of "world culture" from the
ravages of a hostile age, while their poetic siblings and rivals
the Futurists are equally set on jettisoning this culture from the
"steamship of modernity." The truth, at least in Mandelstam's
case, is more complex. "Classical poetry is the poetry of revolution," he exults in "The Word and Culture" (1921), and this
is where Mandelstam, the practitioner of what one astute early
critic calls "classical transsense,"[2] meets with Friedrich
Nietzsche, the revolutionary classicist and self-proclaimed
herald of a philosophy of the future (*CCPL*, p. 116).

This pairing might at first seem most unlikely. It is
Nietzsche, after all, who calls in his *Zarathustra* for "bold
adventurers" to shatter the old values, and who warns that "he
who has to be a creator always destroys" (*Z*, pp. 176, 85).
Mandelstam the Acmeist yearning for "world culture" insists,
on the other hand, that "affirmation and justification of the
real values of the past is just as revolutionary an act as the
creation of new values" ("Storm and Stress," 1923; *CCPL*,
p. 176).[3] Their true positions on the values, and the burdens,
of the past are, however, far more complex and far closer than
these quotes would indicate. Mandelstam was acutely aware
that a resurrection of past values is, by necessity, a revaluation
of values, and that the past is brought to life again within the
present only by way of an intense, intentional creative act.
"Remembrance and invention go hand and hand in poetry,"
he proclaims in "Literary Moscow" (1922). "To remember
also means to invent, and the one who remembers is also an
inventor" (*CCPL*, p. 146). His words evoke the Nietzsche of
Beyond Good and Evil who notes that "we make up the major
part of [all] experience and can scarcely be forced not to
contemplate some event as its 'inventors'" (*BGE*, p. 105). The
genuine historian is also, as Nietzsche reminds us, an artist; and
he must have the courage, he insists, "to recast the well known
into something never heard before" and to "refashion what has
happened into history."[4] Mandelstam echoes Nietzsche's challenge when he summons us in "Government and Rhythm"
(1920) to what he calls "the conscious creation of history"

(*CCPL*, p. 110). For Mandelstam, as for Nietzsche, the strong creative will must endlessly battle a recalcitrant past in order to master it, and make it serve his ends. Mandelstam and Nietzsche meet in their efforts to discover ways to convert the past to new energy, in their struggle to take possession of history and make it serve the needs of what both perceived as a radically disrupted age.

Nietzsche's influence was ubiquitous in early twentieth-century Russian culture, and, like any self-respecting Silver-Age poet, Mandelstam had read his Nietzsche. In an early letter, he speaks of the charm of Nietzsche's *Zarathustra* (*CCPL*, p. 478); and his later writings testify to his knowledge of key Nietzschean images and notions: "eternal recurrence," "the creation of new values," "the birth of tragedy from the spirit of music." He could scarcely have avoided them: they were the cultural currency of the age. Moreover, the classical culture he cherished came to him by way of two self-proclaimed Nietzscheans: Viacheslav Ivanov (1866–1949), the high priest of the second-generation Russian Symbolists; and Tadeusz Zielinski (1859–1944), whose lectures on ancient Greece and Rome he attended at St. Petersburg University. Mandelstam's own writings indicate a far greater familiarity with Nietzsche than his scattered, frequently indirect references might indicate. Indeed, the striking affinities between his vision of history and Nietzsche's suggest that Mandelstam was likely drawn to Ivanov and Zielinski precisely because of the Nietzschean legacy they offered him, a legacy that was to prove invaluable in his efforts to recuperate a vital, usable past for an age and a poetry badly in need of new history. This Nietzschean heritage, much like the French philosopher Henri Bergson's more overtly acknowledged influence, permeates Mandelstam's poetry and prose, and in this essay, I propose to explore Mandelstam's own creative reworking of Nietzsche's lessons on "the advantage and disadvantage of history for life" (*H*, *passim*).

Perhaps the Nietzschean strains in Mandelstam's work have been overlooked, at least in part, due to Nadezhda Mandelstam's determined efforts to preserve Mandelstam from any taint of unwelcome outside influence. "Lack of outside influence," she asserts, "may be organic to a poet's work." The poet whose work she has in mind here is, of course, Mandelstam himself, and yet Nadezhda Mandelstam's own memoirs testify to an acute, pervasive anxiety of influence, if not on Mandelstam's part, then on the part of his widow. She works assiduously throughout her writings to defend Mandelstam against any hint of influence by Futurists, Formalists, and other avantgarde undesirables. Her greatest efforts are reserved, though, for Mandelstam's immediate poetic forebears, the Symbolists, and, in particular, for his early mentor, Viacheslav Ivanov and what she calls his "blasphemous" theories. Ivanov's only service to his rebellious offspring was, she insists, "the impetus provided by repulsion from his doctrines."[5]

Such repulsion can itself constitute a – peculiarly Nietzschean – form of influence, and elsewhere in the memoirs, Ivanov and his dubious doctrines do indeed take on a highly suggestive, hybrid identity: Mandelstam conducts his polemical battle, so Nadezhda Mandelstam claims, with a poet she names "Viacheslav Ivanov-Nietzsche" and "his Dionysian interpretation of art." The Symbolists, she notes, were in thrall to Nietzsche's teachings "to a man," and his influence forms part of the insidious legacy the Acmeists were to reject – although Mandelstam himself was presumably "organically" immune to its effects.[6] Mandelstam's own writings tell, however, a very different story. "Your seeds have been implanted deep in my soul, and I am frightened looking at their enormous sprouts," the eighteen-year-old poet confides to Ivanov (*CCPL*, p. 447). Significantly, Mandelstam himself associates his favorite's "magnificence" with that of the philosopher whose influence his widow so deplores. In another letter of 1909, he praises the charm of Ivanov's latest collection, *Po zvezdam*, which "it shares with *Zarathustra*." He continues: "Your book has something else in common with *Zarathustra*: each word in it fulfills its destiny with ardent hatred and each sincerely hates its place and its neighbors" (*CCPL*, p. 478).[7]

Mandelstam here strikes at the heart of the affinity that he himself shares with Nietzsche and his *Zarathustra*, an affinity

based on creative opposition, on fruitful enmity and productive
strife; and he hints at the operations of this kind of creative
antagonism in an early letter to another mentor, the minor
Symbolist V. V. Gippius. "Lately," Mandelstam confesses, "I
have felt a special attraction to you and at the same time I have
sensed a special kind of distance separating me from you ...
You will forgive my boldness if I say that for me you were what
some people call a 'friendly enemy [*drugo-vrag*].' ... I always
regarded you as the representative of some dear yet hostile
principle [*dorogoe i vmeste vrazhdebnoe nachalo*], and the charm of
that principle lay in its duality" (*CCPL*, p. 475; *SS*, II, p. 483).
Mandelstam might be paraphrasing the Nietzsche of *Thus
Spoke Zarathustra* who insists that "in a friend one should have
one's best enemy" (*Z*, p. 168). Mandelstam the committed
Acmeist was quick to repudiate the influence of Ivanov and his
Symbolist colleagues in his later works. The seeds that
"Ivanov-Nietzsche" had sown early on in the eager soul of the
future Acmeist were not easily uprooted, though, and their
offshoots are visible even in the early writings in which Mandelstam makes his first and most fervent Acmeist declarations
of faith.

Acmeism would seem to have been born to serve as a
counterweight to the "Dionysian" Symbolism that Nadezhda
Mandelstam disdains. The movement made its 1913 début,
fortuitously enough, in the St. Petersburg journal named for
Dionysus' antipode, *Apollon*; and it set out to subdue the Dionysian excess of the Symbolist era by means of what could be seen
in Nietzschean terms as its Apollonian devotion to lucidity and
precision, its Apollonian reverence for form, for balance, for
"boundaries and partitions" (*CCPL*, p. 65).[8] Dionysus and his
disruptive energies, however, lie hidden within the very structures that Mandelstam erects as tributes to the new Acmeist
esthetic. In both his manifesto "The Morning of Acmeism"
(1913) and his programmatic poem "Notre Dame" (1912), the
Gothic cathedral stands as emblem and essence of the new
movement. Gothic architecture, with its "rational abyss," its
intricate, subtle, carefully crafted structures which give reign
to the human imagination while containing it within the

bounds of reason, logic and measure, is the Acmeists' answer to what they perceived as the formless excess of Symbolist poetics (no. 39). The society that creates these structures bears in its Acmeist incarnation a clear resemblance to Nietzsche's Apollonian culture, with its guiding rule of the "individual, i.e. the delimiting of the boundaries of the individual, measure in the Hellenic sense" (*BT*, p. 46). Mandelstam celebrates in his Middle Ages "the free play of weights and measures, a human society conceived as a complex and dense architectural forest wherein everything is efficient and individual, and there every detail answers to the conception of the whole" (*CCPL*, p. 181).

The cathedral that embodies this social structure bears within it, though, the seeds of its own destruction. In the same essay in which he celebrates Gothic order, Gothic reason and restraint, Mandelstam warns us that "the modest exterior of a work of art often deceives us with regard to the monstrously condensed reality contained within" (*CCPL*, p. 60). The monster hidden within Mandelstam's Notre Dame is the arch-enemy of the Acmeist, and Apollonian, reverence for balance and measure. His Notre Dame is not simply a pinnacle of human "organization"; it is also an "organism." More than that – it is, Mandelstam insists, a "festival of physiology, its *Dionysian* orgy" (*CCPL*, p. 63; my italics). "Ivanov-Nietzsche"'s dangerous art has penetrated to the very heart of the new Acmeist esthetic, as Mandelstam sees it, and its presence there is no accident. Mandelstam's phrase evokes not only his tutelage at the hands of his early mentor, whose vision of culture has its roots in "ancient, brutal Dionysian orgy."[9] It also takes us back to Nietzsche himself, for whom the creative energies of human nature were first unleashed in "the Dionysian orgies of the Greeks" (*BT*, p. 39). It alerts us to the presence of warring forces – chaos and order, building and disruption, formlessness and form – at work within the very structures that exemplify Mandelstam's culture, and the nature of these forces, which shape Mandelstam's vision of history and tradition throughout his writings, leads us, in turn, to Nietzsche and to his vision of a culture and a history given life by fruitful enmity and endless strife.

"Only the day after tomorrow belongs to me. Some are born posthumously," Nietzsche proclaims in *The Antichrist* (*A*, p. 114). For all his self-celebration as "a future and a bridge to the future," though, Nietzsche was acutely concerned throughout his work with the burden of the past, and with the properly "life-promoting" use of history (*Z*, p. 161; *BGE*, p. 11). He was, like Mandelstam, a classicist and a philologist (although his scholarly credentials were far more impressive than Mandelstam's), whose measure of all culture was the civilization of Greek antiquity, the Hellas that Mandelstam celebrates throughout his poetry and prose. "We have given things a new color; we go on painting them continually. But what do all our efforts to date avail when we hold them against the colored splendor of that old master – ancient humanity," Nietzsche laments in *The Gay Science* (*GS*, p. 197). "One no longer is at home anywhere," he mourns elsewhere, and the home he seeks has its roots, like Mandelstam's world culture, in "hospitable Hellas": "At last one longs back for that place in which alone one can be at home, because it is the only place in which one would want to be at home: the Greek world!" (*WP*, p. 225).[10] In *The Birth of Tragedy*, Nietzsche anticipates the "yet-impending rebirth of Hellenic antiquity" that will revitalize "the desolation and exhaustion of contemporary culture" (*BT*, p. 123). Mandelstam likewise turns to ancient Greece as he seeks refuge from a restless, orphaned present. "Hellenism," he observes in "On the Nature of the Word" (1922), "is the warmth of the hearth [*ochag*] experienced as something sacred," "it is the humanizing and warming of the surrounding world with the most delicate teleological warmth" (*CCPL*, pp. 127–8). For Mandelstam as for Nietzsche, the universe of ancient Hellas is a human-centered cosmos, "with man as the master of his own home" (*CCPL*, p. 131). The task of the latter-day Hellene, for both writers, is to hellenize a hostile cosmos, to humanize the world, and so "feel ourselves more and more master within it" (*WP*, p. 329). The true classicist must assist at the rebirth of the Greek antiquity that will regenerate a barren age.

The resemblance between these Hellenistic homes, these

shelters from a troubled modern age, is not simply coincidence. Mandelstam's Nietzsche came to him chiefly from two sources, as I've mentioned: Ivanov and Tadeusz Zielinski. Zielinski, a classics professor for many years at St. Petersburg University, was one of the first European classicists to embrace Nietzsche's teachings, and he tutored an entire generation of Russian artists and thinkers in his own version of Nietzschean antiquity.[11] In ancient Greece, Zielinski proclaims, Hellas "was an extended community" built around a "common hearth [*ochag*]." For Zielinski, as for Mandelstam and Nietzsche, ancient Greece is an antidote for the ailments of the modern era. It provides a model for a less fortunate age, an age whose "centrifugal tendencies," Zielinski complains, "divide us from one another," and "introduce isolation and coldness where once there was shelter and warmth."[12]

Mandelstam would, in fact, have found Zielinski's version of Hellas more congenial than Nietzsche's in crucial ways. "A Christian who is at the same time an artist *does not exist*," Nietzsche announces in a late essay (*TI*, p. 72). The self-proclaimed "anti-Christian," whose philosophy grows in large part from his struggle to overturn two millenia of what he sees as a lethally anti-Hellenistic Christian legacy – "Christianity has robbed us of the harvest of the culture of the ancient world," he charges (*AC*, 183) – would hardly have appealed to Mandelstam, who sought to find his way back to antiquity by way of Western Christianity. Mandelstam might be answering Nietzsche in "Pushkin and Skriabin" (1915) where he claims that true art is always "imitation of Christ" and finds "the legitimate heir of the myths of antiquity" in "the myth of long-forgotten Christianity" (*CCPL*, pp. 91, 93). Zielinski likewise revises Nietzsche's version of Judeo-Christian history in his study of ancient Greek religion (*Drevne-grecheskaia religiia*, 1918; trans. as *The Religion of Ancient Greece*, 1929). The Christianity that is for Nietzsche a fatal "revaluation of all the values of antiquity" (*BGE*, p. 61) becomes for Zielinski, as for Mandelstam, a source of Hellenic spiritual wealth in an impoverished age. For Zielinski and his student, modern Christians are "Hellenism's heirs," not its enemies.[13]

Mandelstam's response to Christian culture is complex, shifting, and ambivalent, and I will not discuss it in depth here. Rather I wish to return to the Hellenistic home that Mandelstam shares with Nietzsche, and to explore the ways in which their visions of ancient Greece exemplify and shape the kind of culture they work to create for the modern age. Both writers are alike in their perception of a present cast adrift from its moorings in history. "The chaotic world has burst in," Mandelstam announces in "Humanism and the Present" (1923): "No laws concerning the rights of man, no principles of property and inviolability any longer protect the human dwelling, no laws preserve the house from catastrophe, provide it with any assurance or security" (*CCPL*, p. 182). "For some time now," Nietzsche remarks in *The Will to Power*, "our whole European culture has been moving as toward a catastrophe," and he foresees an "age of tremendous wars, upheavals, explosions" in the coming century (*WP*, pp. 3, 79). He was acutely aware, one critic notes, "of living at a time when whatever stability tradition has provided is crumbling dangerously."[14] In such an uncertain, profoundly unstable age, a warm and welcoming Hellenic hearth lit by antiquity would seem attractive indeed. Yet neither Mandelstam nor Nietzsche seeks refuge from the present within the closed and cozy walls of this mythical past. Alike in their perceptions of a modernity rife with crises, they are alike, too, in their views on how the past is best put to use in this new, disruptive age.

Zielinski's Hellenism represents an effort to forge a new order, a "new social cosmos," from a world in flux. The Hellenistic era, in his reading, resembles the turmoil faced by Mandelstam, Nietzsche and other troubled children of modernity; in it "the old lines separating nations, classes, families, races and even sexes" had vanished, leaving chaos in their wake.[15] Zielinski's new cosmos, however, does not seek to contain this chaos by creating a static, unchanging, relentlessly rigid order that would combat its anarchic energies. His Hellenism draws upon these energies, and uses them to shape a vibrant new culture that derives its vitality precisely from its continuous clashes with chaos. This antiquity, this history, which draws its strength from strife and opposition, is the past that Mandelstam and Nietzsche seek to revive in their writing.

"One must still have chaos in one, to give birth to a dancing star," Nietzsche exclaims in one of *Zarathustra*'s most memorable aphorisms (*Z*, p. 46). Mandelstam, heir to what he perceived as the "Judaic chaos" of his family past as well as to the turmoil of the modern age, would surely have agreed.[16] "Poetic culture," Mandelstam writes in "Badger's Hole" (1922), "arises from the attempt to avert catastrophe" (*CCPL*, p. 137). This culture, however, contains within itself the very forces that it works to forestall. In the same essay, Mandelstam celebrates culture's "catastrophic essence;" elsewhere such disruption becomes the core of what he calls the "accidental, personal, and catastrophic" domain of lyric poetry. Russia's "classical repertory," Mandelstam remarks in "Iakhontov" (1927), "resembles a powder keg on the verge of exploding" (*CCPL*, p. 267). Nietzsche likewise exhorts us to create just such an explosive culture: "The secret for harvesting from existence the greatest fruitfulness and the greatest enjoyment is – to live dangerously! Build your cities on the slopes of Vesuvius!" (*GS*, p. 228). Nietzsche's exemplary ancient city is not Athens or Rome, but Pompeii, which courts catastrophe by its very existence, and which, paradoxically, has been preserved for modernity precisely because it dared to rise on a volcano's slopes. "Classical poetry," Mandelstam proclaims in "The Word and Culture," "is the poetry of revolution" (*CCPL*, p. 116). Nietzsche would have agreed. Only classical taste, he claims, enables an artist or nation to translate chaos into form; and yet, he warns us, "to be classical, one must possess all the strong, seemingly contradictory gifts" (*WP*, pp. 465, 446). Among these gifts is the vital force of anarchic formlessness, for, as he observes, "we are ourselves a kind of chaos" (*BGE*, p. 151).

Nietzsche's antiquity is endowed from the start with just such a wealth of contradictory powers. Its cultural energies are generated by the battle of Apollo's form-giving force and the "immoderate, disorderly," ecstatic powers unleashed by Dionysus (*WP*, p. 540). "Apollo could not live without Dionysus!"

Nietzsche exclaims in *The Birth of Tragedy*, and all culture, all history derive in his view from the "creative tension and fruitful struggle" that endlessly engage these warring forces (*BT*, p. 46).[17] In the passage from which I have just quoted, Nietzsche glosses his "Dionysus" as "the 'titanic,' the 'barbaric;' " and his definition takes us back to Mandelstam and the monstrous Dionysian forces he implants within his Notre Dame. Though Dionysus himself does not appear in the poem which Mandelstam constructs in honor of the medieval church, the energies he represents are present nonetheless, and they work with, and against, the forces of Acmeist order to create the kind of history and culture that Mandelstam calls elsewhere "active, forceful, thoroughly dialectical, a living battle of different forces which fertilize each other" (*CCPL*, p. 141).

The disruptive powers of the flesh make themselves felt in "Notre Dame" from the start. The Gothic cathedral of the poem's opening stanza is a tenuous amalgam of Acmeist (or Apollonian) building and Adamist (or Dionysian) body:

> Where a Roman judge had judged a foreign nation
> A basilica stands, and joyful and first
> As Adam once was, a light groined arch,
> Spreading out its nerves, plays with its muscles.

"One should inaugurate culture in the *right place*," Nietzsche notes, and the right place, he insists, "is the body" (*TI*, p. 552). This creative body, "if it is a living and not a dying body," "will have to be an incarnate will to power, it will strive to grow, spread, seize, become predominant" (*Z*, p. 62; *BGE*, p. 203).[18] In "Notre Dame," Mandelstam orchestrates an uneasy stand-off between Adam's expansive, growing shape and the fixed, containing constructs of the church as building. The historical structure of the first line – the basilica built where Rome had once ruled France – is infected midway through the second line by the body's primal vitality, by the Notre Dame that is a "festival of physiology." This festival threatens literally to raise the roof off Notre Dame, to lift its light vault right off the church. It threatens to disrupt, in other words, the already unstable balance of building and body at work in the first stanza.

"Wherever the great architecture of culture developed," Nietzsche observes, "it was its task to force opposing forces into harmony without suppressing or shackling them" (*HH*, p. 168). Mandelstam's culture is built upon just such antinomies, and the range and richness of these opposing powers can be inferred from "Notre Dame"'s opening stanza. I have suggested the church as an Acmeist, or Apollonian, order which struggles to contain the body's expansive, anarchic Dionysian force. This opposition can be read in other ways as well. Invention and remembrance go hand in hand in poetry, as Mandelstam reminds us. Nietzsche employs a related dialectic to make the same point on a grander scale: "the unhistorical and the historical are equally necessary for the health of an individual, a people and a culture" (*H*, p. 10). The church as *akme* resides inside of the European history ("where a Roman judge had judged a foreign nation") of which it is a crowning achievement, a pinnacle, a peak. The church as Adamist body, though, is "joyful and first;" its exuberant energies thrive in defiance of history's confines. Indeed, Acmeism's double christening – it was first conceived as both "Acmeism" and "Adamism" – calls attention to its ambitious, contradictory, very Nietzschean intentions. Acmeism, as Gumilev instructs us, derives from the Greek Akme, "the highest degree of something, the flower, a flourishing time," "the prime of all powers, spiritual and physical." As Acmeists, the poets are rooted in history and represent the climax of a long and venerable tradition. As Adamists, however, they precede all history, and the enormous cultural debts they have contracted as Acmeists are balanced by their Adamist, historyless newness and primal force.[19]

"Where races are mixed, there is the source of great cultures."[20] Mandelstam's poem – indeed, all his poetry – might have been written to illustrate Nietzsche's maxim; it takes place at the juncture of histories, cultures, and nations. The warring forces of which his poetry is formed are not only order and chaos, history and newness. His work derives just as crucially from the conflict of foreign and native. "The Russian language, just like the Russian national spirit is formed through ceaseless hybridization, cross-breeding, grafting and foreign-born [*chuzherodnykh*] influences," Mandelstam announces in "On the Nature of the Word" (*CCPL*, p. 120). The same could be said of his "Notre Dame," which rises up where Rome had judged a foreign nation, and which holds within its hybrid form, a later stanza tells us, "Egyptian might and Christian modesty" as well as a "Gothic soul." The poem itself begins in foreignness. Its title is borrowed from another culture and another speech, and the Latin letters that head a Russian text seem themselves to enact the confrontation of Rome and a foreign nation that the poem's first line describes. This juxtaposition, in turn, alerts us to the presence of another foreign body concealed within the medieval church, that of Mandelstam himself, the Central European Jew (he was born in Warsaw) come from Russia in quest of Western European culture. This Notre Dame, late-born and foreign, arises, we are reminded, as the result of a very particular set of foreign influences gone to work upon a culture not its own.

"Where for happy generations the epic speaks in hexameters and chronicles, I have merely the sign of the hiatus, and between me and the age there lies a pit, a moat, filled with clamorous time" Mandelstam laments in his autobiography *The Noise of Time* (1925) (*POM*, pp. 122–3). As Central European Jew, adoptive Russian, child of the modern age, Mandelstam was barred several times over from the cultural continuity he craved. Small wonder, then, that he was drawn from the start to a vision of history and culture that values disruption as much as order, that thrives upon incursions of chaos, and that requires the contributions of newcomers, foreigners and outsiders for its continued existence. "Notre Dame" was written, however, before world war, revolution and civil war had put this vision to the test. It is not surprising that so many of the essays I have drawn upon thus far in discussing Mandelstam's invented and remembered culture date from the early twenties. These essays – "The Word and Culture" (1921), "On the Nature of the Word" (1922), "The Nineteenth Century"

(1922), "Humanism and the Present" (1923), and others – mark his most sustained, intensive effort to map out a relation between his particular brand of tradition and the individual talent, on the one hand, and the radical break with the Russian and European past that was the Revolution, on the other. Whether it is named outright or hides behind the catastrophes and crises that haunt the essays, the Revolution is the cataclysmic, endlessly cunning enemy that Mandelstam and his culture confront continuously in his post-revolutionary critical prose.

For Nietzsche, Paul de Man remarks, "modernity exists in the form of a desire to wipe out whatever came earlier, in the hope of reaching at last a point that could be called a true present, a point of origin that marks a new departure." In *On The Advantage and Disadvantage of History for Life*, Nietzsche challenges the "critical" historian, who must, he argues, "possess the strength, and must at times apply this strength, to the destruction and dissolution of the past in order to be able to live" (*H*, p. 21).[21] Translated from the sphere of historical study into the realm of political action, Nietzsche's comments might read like a call to the kind of revolution that uprooted Mandelstam. Yet, as we have seen, Nietzsche relies no less than Mandelstam on a complex dialectic of past and present to bring his cultural vision into being. "The unhistorical and the historical are equally necessary for the health of an individual, a people and a culture," he insists in *On The Advantage and Disadvantage of History*, and the essay's title itself assures us that Nietzsche seeks not to cast off the past entirely, but to find its proper place and applications in the present (p. 10). He seeks not to abandon history, but to transform its dead weight into a present "pregnant with the future" (*GS*, p. 329). This quest for present energy derived from past experience preoccupies Nietzsche throughout his writing, and the terms in which he presents this quest provide useful parameters for discussing Mandelstam's postrevolutionary prose.

In *The Birth of Tragedy*, Nietzsche speaks of "the tremendous historical needs of our unsatisfied modern culture." The culture he describes, however, suffers not from too little history, but too much: "Mythless [modern] man stands eternally hungry, surrounded by all past ages, and digs and grubs for roots, even if he has to dig for them among the remotest antiquities" (*BT*, p. 136). He describes this condition still more vividly in *On The Advantage and Disadvantage of History*: "Historical knowledge floods in ever anew from the inexhaustible springs, the alien and disconnected throngs about, memory opens all its gates" (p. 23). Modern humanity, as Nietzsche sees it, is the victim of this ubiquitous history. We are, he laments, mere "latter-day men, the children of a fragmentary, multifarious, sick, strange age" (*WP*, p. 541).

In Mandelstam's vision, the artist likewise dwells in what Nietzsche calls the "disorderly, stormy, belligerent household" of modernity (*H*, p. 23). With the "frail chronology of our age" shattered once and for all by war and revolution, humanity is adrift in a chaos of history (*CCPL*, p. 91): "As the room of a dying man is open to everyone, so the door of the old world is flung wide before the crowd. Suddenly everything becomes public property. Come and take your pick" ("The Word and Culture"; *CCPL*, p. 116). The task of the modern poet, or poet-philosopher, is to translate this chaos into a new and usable culture of the future. "We appear as colonizers to this new age, so vast and so cruelly determined," Mandelstam proclaims in "The Nineteenth Century": "To Europeanize and humanize the twentieth century, to provide it with teleological warmth – this is the task of those emigrants who survived the shipwreck of the nineteenth century and were cast by the will of fate upon the shores of a new historical continent" (*CCPL*, p. 144).

Nietzsche did not live to see the new century whose coming he both heralded and feared (he died in 1900), while Mandelstam experienced all the sufferings and upheavals of this new era in its peculiarly harsh and unforgiving Russian variant. They were alike, though, in their recognition that the new age demanded a new brand of history, and in their condemnation of the kind of history practiced by their nineteenth-century precursors. The shipwreck of the nineteenth century is, both writers seem to say, due in large part to the faulty navigation of the historians entrusted with charting its course.

"Only the builder of the future has a right to judge the past," Nietzsche proclaims in *On The Advantage and Disadvantage of History* (p. 38). The nineteenth-century historian, however, "looks backwards," not forward (*TI*, p. 25). He is not an artist, a creator, but a "grave-digger" or a "costume-maker," who seeks in history not a way to shape the future, but a release from the rigors of the present (*H*, p. 46). This historian, and his pupil, "the historico-aesthetic cultural Philistine," are "parodists of world history," and such parodists, Nietzsche charges, require history only "as a storage room for costumes" (*H*, p. 46; *BGE*, p. 150). And these parodists, along with their passive public, have been "brought to a condition which can hardly be altered for a moment even by great wars and great revolutions," by the very forces, in other words, that drive true history and culture in Nietzsche's vision (*H*, p. 28).

Mandelstam's nineteenth century is likewise paralyzed by its misuse of a history it consumes without reflection: "Being nothing but vision, empty and rapacious, it greedily and impartially devoured any object, any epoch" (*CCPL*, p. 139). It shares the taste of Nietzsche's Philistine for quick changes and fancy dress – it is gifted, he notes, with a "monstrous capacity for reincarnation" (*CCPL*, p. 143). Its approach to the past is abstract, impersonal, and omnivorous. "The bygone age did not like to refer to itself in the first person," Mandelstam observes in "The Nineteenth Century": "It enjoyed projecting itself onto the screen of some distant epoch; in that flowed its life, its dynamism ... It would pluck something out of the darkness, burn it up with the blinding glitter of its historical laws and then apathetically allow it to plunge back into nothingness, as if nothing had happened" (*CCPL*, p. 139). Mandelstam's nineteenth century, like Nietzsche's, rummages indiscriminately among pasts in its search for diversion or distraction; it lacks a creative engagement with the history it consumes. The name that Mandelstam gives to this misguided historicism betrays the Nietzschean genealogy of his nineteenth century. This age, he claims, is "Buddhist" in science, religion, and art (*CCPL*, p. 142). It is a "cradle of Nirvana," the "conduit of Buddhist influence in European culture," and this influence leads in turn to inertia and sterility, to stasis, to "nonbeing" (*CCPL*, p. 143). It is recognizably the same age that Nietzsche labels a "Buddhist epoch for Europe," an era whose "Buddhistic" tendencies translate into "cultural pessimism" and a "yearning for nothing" (*GS*, p. 155; *BGE*, pp. 51, 7). For both Mandelstam and Nietzsche, Buddhism signifies the nineteenth century's impotence in the presence of cultural abundance, its failure to redeem the weight of history.

Mandelstam and Nietzsche share their scorn for what Nietzsche calls "our present cultured historiography," for the unfortunate "culture worship," which, according to Mandelstam, "overwhelmed the schools and universities of Europe during the nineteenth century," and thus embalmed the vital history that "might have been alive, concrete, brilliant and knowledge-bearing in both the past and future" (*BT*, p. 122; *CCPL*, p. 445). In *The Birth of Tragedy*, Nietzsche mocks the antiquarian, the "dependable corrector of texts" or "linguistic microscopist" who leaves the letter of the ancient text intact while annihilating its spirit (*BT*, p. 122). "I do not know what meaning classical philology would have for our age," he observes in *On The Advantage and Disadvantage of History*, "if not to have an untimely effect within it, that is, to act against the age and so have an effect on the age to the advantage, it is to be hoped, of a coming age" (p. 8). Mandelstam is equally vehement in his "Conversation About Dante" (1933), in which he puts Nietzsche's theories energetically into practice. He calls for "joint international endeavors" to create "an original anti-commentary" to Dante's work that will disrupt "the work of generations of scholastics, creeping philologists and pseudo-biographers, and restore to life the Dante whose "contemporaneity is continuous, incalculable and inexhaustible," and whose cantos "are missiles for capturing the future" (*CCPL*, p. 444, 420).

"The historian looks backwards; at last he also *believes* backwards," Nietzsche charges in *Twilight of the Idols* (p. 25). Mandelstam and Nietzsche, who refuse to traffic in the "manufactured nails known as images of cultural history" that the nineteenth century had used to seal the coffin of the past, must believe forwards if they are to propel a changed and rea-wakened past into the future (*CCPL*, p. 398). Both writers are acutely aware of the dangers and difficulties of this mission. Mandelstam mourns the fate of the poet who cannot meet the monumental challenge of transforming past into future in *The Noise of Time*: "To remember not living people but the plaster casts struck from their voices. To go blind. To feel and recognize by hearing. Sad fate! Thus does one penetrate into the present, into the modern age, as via the bed of a dried-up river" (*POM*, p. 127).

Nietzsche also fears the treacherous power of the past he seeks to master. "It is dangerous to be an heir," he warns (*Z*, p. 102). We must learn to resist the pressures of history, he insists, if we "latecomers" are to recast ourselves as "conquerers even if we look like heirs and prodigals" (*H*, p. 43; *BGE*, p. 55). "A conquerer? Or an inheritor? A harvest? Or a ploughshare?" (*Z*, p. 161). These questions plague Nietzsche throughout his writings as he struggles to master a recalcitrant past whose existence is a continuous challenge to the potency of his vision. "To redeem those who lived in the past and to recreate all 'it was' into a 'thus I willed it'" – this is how he perceives his task in *Zarathustra*: "'It was': that is what the will's teeth gnashing and most lonely affliction is called ... All 'It was' is a fragment, a riddle, a dreadful chance – until the creative will says to it: 'But I willed it thus.' Until the creative will says to it: 'But I will it thus! Thus shall I will it'" (pp. 161, 163). This creative will, which imposes its own shape upon the past that it would master and projects this past, recast in its own image, into the future ("thus *shall* I will it"), takes us back to Mandelstam's strategy of invention and remembrance, to the strategy that allows him to recreate the past as he recalls it in the present, and so permits him to outwit history's terrible weight. "We are free of the burden of memories," the inventive rememberer exults in "The Word and Culture" (*CCPL*, p. 114).

Nietzsche anticipates in this passage other tactics that Mandelstam, following his lead, will employ in his battle to turn the past to new purposes. Nietzsche's creative revision of the past involves three grammatical transformations: as the passive "it" becomes the willing "I," the past tense ("it was") becomes a present ("I will") and a future ("I shall will"). Past becomes future, in other words, through the agency of the creative will. Mandelstam was possessed early on by what Nietzsche calls "the pathos of distance"; he is drawn as strongly to the future as the past (*BGE*, p. 201). "No, I was never anyone's contemporary," he proclaims in a poem of 1924 (no. 141). The true poet, he announces in "On the Interlocutor" (1913), refuses to content himself with a mundane, comfortable present or the incomprehending, ill-chosen audience that fate has chosen for him. He ignores his "boring neighbors" (no. 67), and aims instead at an unknown "reader in posterity," at a "distant friend," at "future contemporaries" (*CCPL*, pp. 69, 73, 71). He thus assures his poetry's unfettered flight into the future. Nietzsche likewise directs his writings to a reader in posterity, to his true peers of the future, though his brashness in claiming his place in the coming age far exceeds Mandelstam's. His real audience is, he asserts, the "Europeans of the day after tomorrow," the "first-born of the twentieth century" – appropriate company for a philosopher himself "born posthumously" (*BGE*, p. 145; *AC*, 114). He is, he exults, a "Caesarian cultivator and cultural dynamo," and his own writings take their meaning from works as yet unwritten and readers still unborn: they are, as the subtitle to *Beyond Good and Evil* proclaims, a "prelude to the philosophy of the future" (*BGE*, p. 128).

"We will prove our rightness in such a way that in answer to us the entire chain of cause and effect, from alpha to omega, will shudder," Mandelstam boasts in an early essay ("The Morning of Acmeism"; *CCPL*, p. 65). The mature poet of the twenties is still more audacious as he disrupts the chain of cause and effect and subverts the relation of present to past: "I say: yesterday has not yet been born. It has not yet really existed. I want Ovid, Pushkin, and Catullus to live once more, and I am not satisfied with the historical Ovid, Pushkin and Catullus ("The Word and Culture;" *CCPL*, p. 113). He outlines the means by which he proposes to father his poetic precursors in the passage that follows: "The silver trumpet of Catullus – *Ad claras Asiae volemus urbes* – alarms and excites us more forcefully than any Futurist riddle. Such poetry does not exist in Russian. Yet it must exist in Russian. I chose a Latin line because it is clearly perceived by the Russian reader as a category of obligation: the imperative rings more vividly in it. Such an imperative is perceived as that which must be, not as that which has already been" (*CCPL*, p. 114). The past is transformed by means of a grammatical operation that will be familiar to the reader of Nietzsche, as a past declarative ("what was") becomes a future imperative ("what must be"). History is no longer fixed and finished, a burden beneath which the lateborn poet must struggle. It is unfulfilled potential, whose fruition in the future lies entirely in the hands of the living poet who may or may not choose to answer its commands. In this drastic inversion of cause and effect, the past becomes dependent on its offspring for its continued future existence, for it is only through the good offices of the present that the past may be reborn as future. "Not a single poet has yet appeared," Mandelstam exults in "The Word and Culture" (*CCPL*, p. 114).

Nietzsche's doctrine of "eternal recurrence," the endless repetition of the past within the present, lies at the heart of Mandelstam's vision of culture, as other scholars have noted. For Mandelstam, all history is, ideally, synchronic. The past is continuously reborn as present, and the task of the poet is to capture this convergence of ages in his work. Mandelstam himself movingly describes this "profound joy of recurrence" in his poem "Tristia" (1918): "All once was, all will come again/And the moment of recognition alone is sweet to us" (*CCPL*, p. 114; no. 104). For Mandelstam as for Nietzsche, though, the artist of history does not confine his response to recognition alone. He is actively engaged in reshaping the past as it recurs within the present. In fact, if he does not intervene, if he does not serve as midwife at the rebirth of past ages within the present moment, these ages may be stillborn, or unborn. Their energies will be lost to the present. History exists, in other words, only through the efforts of inventive latter-day interpreters. "I want to live in the imperative of the future passive participle – in the 'what ought to be,'" Mandelstam announces in his "Journey to Armenia" (1933); and he echoes the Nietzsche who commands his fellow "fighters against history" to transform the past into what he calls the "so it ought to be" (*CCPL*, p. 114; *H*, p. 49). "What has been" becomes "what must be" in the hands of the poet, or philosopher, of the future who reinvents all history for the sake of a culture that has not yet come to pass.[22]

The shape that this culture of the future takes in Nietzsche's writings must have been in crucial ways deeply congenial to Mandelstam. "The value and meaning of contemporary culture lie," Nietzsche proclaims, "in mutual blending and fertilization," and he anticipates in his work the birth of what he calls a new, "hybrid Europe" (*WP*, p. 395; *BGE*, p. 130). Mandelstam, like Nietzsche, envisions "a powerful, synthetic European culture created by the union of disparate and warring elements."[23] They are alike, too, in their perception of a modernity that offers peculiar possibilities to the poet or philosopher willing to take on the task of shaping new cultures from old. In the disrupted modern era, all ages, all nations, all histories are equally close at hand: as Mandelstam bids us, "Come and take your pick" (*CCPL*, p. 116). The "Caesarian cultivator" or modern poet-synthesist has ample material to choose from as he sets to work upon the hybrid Europe that will emerge from his labors.

In an early essay, Mandelstam contrives to create a new kind of national identity, one that is based not on birthplace or passport, but on the active, willing fusion of disparate cultures into a new, synthetic whole: "Synthetic nationality does not bow down before national self-consciousness, but rises above it as sovereign individuality, independent and therefore national ... What a striking contrast to 'Nationalism,' that poverty of the spirit with its persistent appeals to the tribunal of the rabble!" ("Petr Chaadaev," 1915; *CCPL*, p. 88). Mandelstam's synthetic nationality betrays its Nietzschean origins not only in its aristocratic disdain for the unenlightened rabble. Nietzsche, like Mandelstam, looks to a new culture that will emerge from the efforts of self-created, hybrid men, the "good

Europeans" who stand beyond the bounds of nationality narrowly construed (*HH*, p. 228). "An essentially supra-national and nomadic type of man is coming up," he announces: "In an age of disintegration that mixes races indiscriminately, human beings have in their bodies the heritage of multiple origins, that is opposite and often not merely opposite, drives and value standards," and it is from such natures, "rich in contradictions," that we may expect the birth of the culture of the future (*BGE*, pp. 176, 111; *TI*, p. 44). Mandelstam's culture thrives on "inoculations of foreign blood" (*POM*, p. 81). Nietzsche's "good European" likewise derives his vitality from his capacity to meld foreign pasts into his very self – "Such a nature would draw its own as well as every alien past wholly into itself and transform it into blood, as it were" (*H*, p. 10) – and he encapsulates history in his own being. "Manifold and mixed racially," his "good Europeans" are the rightful "heirs of the thousands of years of European spirit." Yet such exemplary Europeans are at the same time the "children of the future," the "most modern of moderns," the heralds of a new, synthetic age (*GS*, pp. 340, 338, 341).

Nietzsche's new Europeans are, he insists, innately homeless, nomads and emigrants by their very nature (*GS*, p. 340; *BGE*, p. 188). As such, they bear a clear affinity not only to Mandelstam the Jewish émigré, stranded on the margins of his adoptive culture. They are also akin to Mandelstam the Modernist outcast, and to his fellow survivors of modernity's upheavals. Nietzsche is himself, he proclaims, the "Good European" par excellence. "Even by virtue of my descent," he boasts in his sui generis autobiography *Ecce Homo*, "I am granted an eye beyond all merely local, merely nationally conditioned perspectives; it is not difficult for me to be a 'good European.' . . . I am perhaps more German than present-day Germans could possibly be . . . And yet my ancestors were Polish noblemen: I have many racial instincts in my body from that source" (p. 225). This exalted Polish ancestry is, Ronald Hayman assures us, a fiction.[24] It is Nietzsche's attempt to create for himself the kind of identity that would insure his place among the true Europeans who will be first to reach the coming age;

or perhaps it is a reminder to his fellow Europeans that the culture one works to invent and remember for the future must have its beginnings in one's own imaginatively recreated past.

Mandelstam had no need to invent such a hybrid history. It was his by rights, as his autobiography, *The Noise of Time*, demonstrates. He gives, however, an object lesson in self-invention in a prose sketch, "Theodosia" (1925), that was originally intended to form part of *The Noise of Time*. The hero of one segment is a self-christened Jewish artist, Mazesa da Vinci. "He chose his name himself," Mandelstam relates: "In the first half of his sobriquet – Mazesa – he retained a blood link with his family ... And thus Mazesa, with the addition of the feminine ending, turned his family name into his first name." Through his adopted surname, though, he lays claim to a grander genealogy: "Mazesa inherited from his involuntary godfather [the Renaissance's] fruitful uproar of the three dimensions, and his bedroom resembled a Renaissance vessel under sail" (*POM*, p. 146). Such inventive ransackers of the past are destined to become, for Mandelstam as for Nietzsche, first among the conquerers of a hellenized, hybrid future.

"Man must become harder," Mandelstam declares in "On the Nature of the World." "He must be the hardest thing on earth: he must be to the earth what the diamond is to glass" (*CCPL*, p. 132). His command might be taken from Nietzsche, who declares that the central precept for all creative spirits is "the imperative, 'become hard!'" (*GM*, p. 309). In the essays of the early twenties Mandelstam insists on the necessity for such mastery in a disrupted cosmos. He returns again and again to the need for the "indomitable will" that would create not just "a human-centered poetry and poetics," but a human-centered universe as well (*CCPL*, p. 131). In these essays, moreover, he seems convinced of his capacity to achieve just such a transformation. The new age will be colonized by strong poets; a new culture will be synthesized from the rubble of the past; yesterday will be reborn in tomorrow; classical poetry will be the poetry of revolution; and determined Acmeists will reign in a brave new postrevolutionary world.

The poetry of this period tells, however, a very different

story. Mandelstam claims in "The World and Culture" that "yesterday had not yet been born." In "January 1, 1923" (no. 140), though, he fears that yesterday is dying, and that he, the scion of a bygone age, is dying with it:

> Who has kissed time on its tired temple
> With a son's affection, afterwards
> He will remember, how time lay down to sleep
> In a wheaten snowdrift outside the window.
> Who has lifted time's aching eyelids –
> Two large sleepy orbs –
> He always hears the noise of when the rivers roared,
> The rivers of fraudulent and god-forsaken times . . .
> Oh, clay life! Oh, dying age!
> I am afraid that only he will understand you
> Who has the helpless smile of a man
> Who has lost himself.

The Mandelstam of the postrevolutionary essays is the "modern poet-synthesizer" who possesses what Nietzsche calls "the power distinctively to grow out of [himself], transforming and assimilating everything past and alien, to heal wounds, replace what is lost and reshape broken forms out of [himself]": "Such a nature would draw its own as well as every alien past wholly into itself and transform it into blood" (*H*, p. 10). The grieving poet of "The Age" (1923; no. 135) or "The Horseshoe Finder" (1923; no. 136) is worlds apart from this miracle-worker, this artist-alchemist. He is lost himself ("I no longer have enough of me for me"), and losing blood himself ("blood the builder gushes from the throats of earthly things"). He cannot heal his ailing age or make it whole again:

> Where to begin?
> Everything cracks and sways
> The air quivers with comparisons
> No one word is better than any other (no. 136)

> My age, my animal, who will dare
> To look into your pupils
> And mend with his own blood
> The backbone of two centuries? (no. 135)

He dwells helplessly among the broken forms he had meant to renew.

"Only strong personalities can endure history," Nietzsche warns. "The weak are extinguished by it."[25] The history that Nietzsche had to endure was, however, far different, and far less terrible, than the history experienced by Mandelstam. Nietzsche died at the dawn of the new age his writings herald: he did not live to see the upheavals and explosions that he prophesies in his work. His revolutions are revolutions of the spirit alone. His battleground is the printed page, and on it only metaphoric blood is shed. Nietzsche's enemies do not carry arms. They are the "historico-esthetic Philistines" of late nineteenth-century Europe whose comfortable bourgeois existence his works were intended to disrupt. Nietzsche's struggle with these philistines, and indeed his struggle with history itself, takes place within the relatively safe domain of art. "The existence of the world is justified only as an *esthetic* phenomenon," he announces in *The Birth of Tragedy* (*BT*, p. 22; my italics). Nietzsche's vision of history, like his vision of the cosmos itself, is finally esthetic. The past for Nietzsche is raw material for the strong creative will who wrestles it into submission, who gives it new shape, who turns it to new purposes in his work.

Mandelstam did not have the luxury of conceiving a purely esthetic history subject to the poet's will alone. When asked about the "apparent incoherence between [his] verse and [his] critical prose," T. S. Eliot replied that "in one's prose reflexions one may be legitimately occupied with ideals, whereas in the writing of verse one can only deal with actuality."[26] The actuality Mandelstam faced in the early twenties did not permit him to imagine only crises of the spirit catalyzed by the visions of poet-philosophers. The abuses of history he witnessed were not at the hands of professors and pedants alone; he saw, and felt, history misused by generals and politicians, demagogues and dictators. Mandelstam, living in postrevolutionary Russia, was forced to recognize that the artist does not always rewrite history. History may rewrite the artist instead. It may place him in the margins or the footnotes of its text. It may erase him from its pages entirely. In his essays, Mandelstam could envision, like Nietzsche, the creation of a dynamic, disruptive *œuvre* that would become a prelude to the culture of the future. In his poetry, however, he must reluctantly admit that what he writes might be instead a postscript to the culture of the past.

"Human lips which have no more to say preserve the shape of the last word they have said," Mandelstam mourns in "The Horseshoe Finder." This was not, however, Mandelstam's last word, poetic or otherwise, on his quest for culture, for a renewable, vital past, that he had begun with his first writings early in the century. He wrote no poems at all for a number of years, from the mid-twenties until 1930. By the late twenties and "Fourth Prose" (1930), though, he had learned to define himself not in terms of his age, but against it, and his new, fruitful enmity inspired him, in turn, in his quest to take possession of the past and force it to serve the aims of the poet-pariah.[27] Like Nietzsche, he had come, once again, to operate in opposition to the present for the sake of past and future as he works to create his world culture. "In poetry," Mandelstam proclaims in an early essay, "the boundaries of the national are destroyed and the elements of one language exchange greetings with those of another over the heads of space and time" ("Remarks on Chénier," 1914; *CCPL*, p. 81). He envisions a similar conquest of time some two decades later in "Conversation About Dante" (1933): "Time is the content of history understood as a simple synchronic act; and vice-versa: the contents of history are the joint containing of time by colleagues, competitors, and co-discoverers" (*CCPL*, p. 420). Nietzsche not only proved to be one of Mandelstam's most challenging competitors and co-discoverers in his efforts to master the past; it was in large part from Nietzsche himself that Mandelstam imbibed this "life-enhancing," energetic, and imaginative vision and revision of history (*BGE*, p. 11).

NOTES

1 James Joyce, *Ulysses* (New York, 1961), p. 34. Osip Mandelstam, *The Complete Critical Prose and Letters*, ed. Gary Harris, trans. Jane Gary Harris and Constance Link (Ann Arbor, 1979), p. 84. Further references to this edition will appear in the text, abbre-

viated as "*CCPL*." Richard Ellman and Charles Feidelson, *The Modern Tradition: Backgrounds of Modern Literature* (New York, 1965), p. vi.

2 Boris Bukhshtab, "Poeziia Mandel'shtama," *Voprosy literatury* 1 (1989), p. 136. The essay was written in 1929, but was first published in Russia only sixty years later.

3 The phrase "world culture" is Mandelstam's, from his famous description of Acmeism as a "yearning for world culture." See Nadezhda Mandelstam, *Vospominaniia*, I, 3rd edn. (Paris, 1970), p. 264. In further references to this and to the second volume of Nadezhda Mandelstam's memoirs (*Vospominaniia*, II, 3rd edn. [Paris, 1982]), I will cite Max Hayward's English translations (Nadezhda Mandelstam, *Hope Against Hope* [New York, 1970], *Hope Abandoned* [New York, 1974]).

4 Friedrich Nietzsche, "On the Advantage and Disadvantage of History for Life," trans. Peter Preuss (Indianapolis, 1980), pp. 37, 11. Further references to this essay will be abbreviated in the text as *H*.

5 *Hope Abandoned*, pp. 30, 40–44, 408. Mandelstam contradicts his widow's testimony in "On the Nature of the Word," where he comments that Ivanov "was a great help in the formulation of Acmeist theory" (*CCPL*, pp. 130–31). This and many other such discrepancies indicate the dangers of using Nadezhda Mandelstam's splendid memoirs uncritically. On Mandelstam and Ivanov, see John Malmstad, "Mandelshtam's 'Silentium': A Poet's Response to Ivanov," *Vyacheslav Ivanov: Poet, Critic and Philosopher*, ed. Robert Louis Jackson and Lowry Nelson, Jr. (New Haven, 1986), pp. 236–52.

6 *Hope Abandoned*, pp. 109, 43–44.

7 Osip Mandelstam, *SS*, 4 vols., ed. G. P. Struve, H. Struve and B. Filipoff (Washington, 1967–71; Paris, 1981), II, p. 487. Poems will be identified by their number in this edition. This is the only explicit reference to Nietzsche that I have located in Mandelstam's writings. For Ivanov's reading of Nietzsche, see Bernice Glatzer Rosenthal, "Introduction," in *Nietzsche in Russia*, ed. Bernice Glatzer Rosenthal (Princeton, 1986), esp. pp. 20–24; and Edith Clowes, *The Revolution of Moral Consciousness: Nietzsche in Russian Literature 1890–1914* (DeKalb, IL, 1988), pp. 116–72.

8 For a more detailed discussion of Nietzsche and the Acmeists, see Elaine Rusinko's essay in this volume.

9 Clowes, *Revolution of Moral Consciousness*, p. 139.

10 The phrase "hospitable Hellas" is taken from Zielinski. F. (Faddei) F. Zielinski *Drevne-grecheskaia religiia* (Petrograd, 1918), p. 82. Translation taken, with modifications, from Thaddeus

Zielinski, *The Religion of Ancient Greece*, trans. George Rapall Noyes (London, 1926), p. 113.

11 On Zielinski and Nietzsche, see James M. Curtis, "Michael Bakhtin, Nietzsche, and Russian Pre-Revolutionary Thought," *Nietzsche in Russia*, pp. 331, 344–48.

12 *The Religion of Ancient Greece*, pp. 113, 117, 100.

13 Ibid., p. 16. Mandelstam in fact takes Zielinski as the basis for a complex revision of the Judeo-Christian tradition in several poems from the period of *Tristia* (1922). This revision represents, among other things, Mandelstam's attempt to overcome his own Jewish origins. As such it reveals, like Zielinski's overtly anti-semitic reading of Judeo-Christian history, disturbing biases against what Zielinski calls "the negative source of Christianity" (p. 86). See Clare Cavanagh, "Judaic Chaos," *Osip Mandelstam and the Modernist Creation of Tradition* (Princeton, NJ, forthcoming).

14 John Burt Foster, Jr., *Heirs to Dionysus: A Nietzschean Current in Literary Modernism* (Princeton, 1981), p. 114.

15 Katerina Clark and Michael Holquist, *Mikhail Bakhtin* (Cambridge, MA, 1984), p. 32.

16 Mandelstam describes the "Judaic chaos" of his childhood in his autobiography *The Noise of Time* (1925), translated in *The Prose of Osip Mandelstam*, ed. and trans. Clarence Brown (Princeton, 1965), pp. 88–94. Further references to this edition will be abbreviated in the text as "*POM*."

17 This is Foster's phrase, *Heirs to Dionysus*, p. 51.

18 Throughout his work, Nietzsche rejects the Christian culture which suppressed, so he claims, the living body that was sacred to the Greeks: "Christianity, which despised the body, has been the greatest misfortune of humanity so far" (*TI*, p. 552). Mandelstam, by bringing Nietzsche's Dionysian body within the walls of the Christian church, is challenging not only Acmeist esthetics, but Nietzsche's version of Christianity as well.

19 Nikolai Gumilev, *SS*, 4 vols. (Washington, 1968), IV, pp. 171, 309. On Acmeism's second name and its significance, see Elaine Rusinko, "Adamism and Acmeist Primitivism," *Slavic and East European Journal* 32:1 (1988), pp. 84–97.

20 Quoted in Walter Kaufmann, *Nietzsche: Philosopher, Psychologist, Antichrist* (Princeton, 1974), p. 10.

21 Paul de Man, "Literary History and Literary Modernity," *Blindness and Insight: Essays in the Rhetoric of Contemporary Criticism* (Minneapolis, 1983), p. 148. I have borrowed de Man's translation of Nietzsche's phrase here, p. 149.

22 On Mandelstam and "eternal recurrence" see: Iu. I. Levin,

D. M. Segal, P. D. Timenchik, V. N. Toporov, T. V. Tsiv'ian, "Russkaia semanticheskaia poetika kak potentsial'naia kul'turnaia paradigma," *Russian Literature* 7:8 (1974), pp. 47–82; Omry Ronen, *An Approach to Mandelstam* (Jerusalem, 1983), pp. xii, 87–88; Gregory Freidin, *A Coat of Many Colors: Osip Mandelstam and His Mythologies of Self-Presentation* (Berkeley, 1987), p. 108.

23 The quote is Stephen Donadio's, from his *Nietzsche, Henry James and the Artistic Will* (New York, 1978), pp. 104–5.

24 Ronald Hayman, *Nietzsche: A Critical Life* (Middlesex, 1983), p. 273.

25 Quoted in Stephen Donadio, *Nietzsche*, p. 99.

26 T. S. Eliot, *After Strange Gods* (New York, 1934), p. 30.

27 On Mandelstam's poetics of opposition in "Fourth Prose," see Clare Cavanagh, "The Poetics of Jewishness: Mandelstam, Dante and the 'Honorable Calling of Jew,'" *Slavic and East European Journal* 35:3 (1991), pp. 317–38.

CHAPTER 14

Nietzsche's influence on the non-official culture of the 1930s

Boris Groys*

This essay will discuss several thinkers, few in number but historically significant, who remained independent of official ideology: Gustav Shpet (1878–1940?), A. A. Meier (1875–1939), Mikhail Bakhtin (1895–1975), and the writer Mikhail Bulgakov (1891–1940). During the thirties, these authors strove to continue the tradition of Russian non-Marxist thought and to examine the cultural situation from that point of view. While one cannot really speak of a consensus among them, all of them still, to a greater or lesser degree, based their thought on the ideological heritage of the Silver Age, which was based primarily on a combination of Nietzscheanism and the Russian Sophiological tradition (the latter derived primarily from the philosophy of Vladimir Soloviev). The influence of Nietzsche in their texts can be established by the continuity of a specifically Russian religious reading of Nietzsche and the characteristic philosophical language connected with it, a language which continued to provide a fundamental lexicon for describing the world, as late as the thirties.

This circumstance makes these above-mentioned authors especially interesting for the history of ideas, in as much as they continue the Nietzschean tradition in the circumstances of Soviet socialism of the Stalin period, which is radically different from the context of the bourgeois culture of the nineteenth century in which Nietzsche himself formulated his theory and critique of culture. In the West, this context subsequently underwent significantly fewer radical changes than in Russia, so that Western followers of Nietzsche could identify relatively

367

easily with cultural positions taken by him. Russian authors in the thirties, on the contrary, found it necessary to redefine, in terms of the Nietzschean tradition, their own proper point of departure in a cultural situation that was entirely new for them personally and also historically unprecedented. It is exactly to an investigation of these attempts at self-definition in the culture of Stalin's time, that this chapter is dedicated.

Stalinism and the contemporary totalitarian structure of power associated with it constituted the essential reality to which all writers of the thirties constantly had to relate, whatever their actual theme at any given moment, even if necessity demanded that they do so in a more or less veiled manner. A major determining factor in the relationship between Stalinistic ideology and the heirs of the Russian Religious Renaissance is specifically the Nietzschean component, which contributed to both the official culture and to the non-Marxist world-view. This Nietzschean component did not allow these non-Marxist thinkers to assume a position in radical opposition to official culture; at the same time, by belonging to the other tradition of Nietzschean reception, they could not identify with official culture. More importantly, they used the terminology of Russian Nietzscheanism to comprehend and theoretically to resolve this conflict.

The "atheistic" line of Russian Nietzscheanism, which was thus mainly absorbed into official Soviet culture, was complemented by a second, considerably more philosophically-developed, line. As a result of postrevolutionary repression, however, this second, "religious" reception of Nietzsche had become almost extinct by the 1930s. The very possibility of such a reception, despite the genuinely inimical attitude of Nietzsche himself toward Christianity, arose as the result of a particular philosophical situation which had taken form in Russia at the very moment when interest in Nietzsche's work first began.[1]

In the 1870s and 1880s the philosophical pessimism of Arthur Schopenhauer (1788–1860) made a lasting impression on a series of Russian thinkers. In his relatively early work, "The Crisis of Western Philosophy" (1984), Vladimir Soloviev

(1853–1900) interpreted the Schopenhauerian self-negation of the World Will as an extreme radicalization of the one-sided rationalism of Western European thought, with its emphasis on abstract reason to the detriment of the world and matter.[2] Following the old Slavophile tradition, Soloviev saw the sources of Western philosophic rationalism and Schopenhauer's nihilism in the abstract rationalized theology of Western Christianity (Catholicism and Protestantism). According to Soloviev, this onesidedness corresponds to the onesidedness of Schopenhauer's understanding of the World Will as "unconscious" and, consequently, purely destructive. Soloviev saw the only way out of this situation in a return to the principles of true Christianity, preserved but insufficiently articulated philosophically in the tradition of Russian Orthodoxy. In Soloviev's reading of Orthodoxy the spirit is not opposed to matter; its aim becomes the deification of matter, the world, and mankind. Soloviev wrote elsewhere about the necessity of the union of the free human spirit (endowed in Soloviev's interpretation with a fair portion of materialism, militarism, eroticism, and estheticism) with the Church, or Sophia, as the eternally feminine "divine matter," an "enlightened" variant of the Schopenhauerian World Will, understood as the World Soul.[3]

The philosophical and esthetic teachings of Nikolai Fedorov (1828–1903) and Lev Tolstoi (1828–1910) also constitute an original response to Schopenhauer's philosophy. While both Fedorov and Tolstoi saw in Schopenhauer's thought the self-negation of Western culture, Tolstoi turned for salvation to a deindividualized, elementary life, understood positively, not negatively as in Schopenhauer, while Fedorov demanded the restoration of all individual life and its reintegration into universal life. Both Fedorov and Tolstoi pinned their hopes on Russia.

Nietzsche's teachings came to Russia at the very moment when Russian thought had already made an optimistic "positive" reinterpretation of Schopenhauer's World Will, which in its own unique way represents the philosophical essence of Nietzscheanism. In this context, Nietzsche's *The Birth of*

Tragedy from the Spirit of Music was his first work to become especially popular in Russia. In the Russian philosophy of the Symbolist period Nietzsche's "Dionysian impulse" merged with Slavophile "unity in love and freedom" (*sobornost'*) and Solovievian "Sophia-ness;" in fact, it became a codeword for an image of a Russia that carried within itself both the destruction of Western culture and the possibility of its renewal. Furthermore, although Nietzsche's Dionysian impulse met with complete acceptance in Russia, his idea of the "Superman" (or, in the terminology of the Russian Religious Renaissance, the "Man-God") was basically rejected, or at the very least understood as a dangerous deviation from the path that led to the Solovievian integrity of the "God-man," a deviation dictated by Western rationalism and individualism, reaffirmed and perpetuated by the theory of the Superman and thereby depriving Russia of her eschatological victory.

This approach to the particular configuration of the thought of Russian non-Marxists at the beginning of the twentieth century does much to explain the way in which they comprehended the Russian Revolution and Stalinism. In the Revolution they welcomed the Dionysian impulse that was destroying the old world of European culture; at the same time they feared the threat of the deification of man, "the Man-God" (as opposed to Soloviev's "God-man"), which they perceived as a new victory for Western rationalism and individualism in an even more radical form. This Man-Godhood, however, which was becoming more definitely established, could not be completely rejected as long as there was hope for its "transfiguration into God-manhood." As long as this hope continued, the force of Man-Godhood kept its hidden attraction even for those who more or less openly opposed it.[4]

Educated primarily on the "Russian" Nietzsche, the heirs of Russian Silver Age thought could not speak out in the 1930s against the new Stalinist regime from the position of individualism, the rights of man, moralism, democratism, etc., as would seem natural to us from today's perspective. On the contrary, they saw the source of the rationalism, utilitarianism, alienation, coldness, and hierarchic tendency that char-

acterized the new regime specifically in this Western individualistic tradition, and they strove to counteract it with an
ever greater Dionysian dissolution of the individual, an ever
greater loss of the boundaries, privileges, and security of the
individual. The protest of this group of thinkers against Stalinist culture can most accurately be described as favoring early
Nietzsche and rejecting the later Nietzsche.

Let us see how this was reflected in the writings of four major
figures of the unofficial culture on the eve of Stalin, beginning
with A. A. Meier, whose late philosophical essays represent a
transformation in his own view of Nietzsche. A writer of the
Symbolist period and an active member of the Petersburg
Religious-Philosophical Society, Meier published his work in
various places, including the almanac *Fakely* ("Torches,"
1906–8); he played a substantial role in the formulation of the
program of "mystical anarchism." After the Revolution Meier
took part in the work of the last officially-tolerated center of
non-Marxist Russian thought, the "Free Philosophical Association" ("Vol'fila," 1919–24). Late in 1917, Meier and G. P.
Fedotov organized an unofficial religious-philosophical circle
in Petrograd. This circle, striving to continue the work of the
Petersburg Religious-Philosophical Society under the new
political conditions, played an important role in the intellectual life of the old capital in the twenties. In 1928, Meier
and other members of the circle were arrested. Meier was freed
in 1935 and before his death in 1939 wrote a large number of
works on philosophy and culture, in which he attempted to
reflect the new historical experience he had gained.[5]

The basic tenets of Meier's world-view were delineated in his
early article, "Religion and Culture" (1909).[6] Its main thrust
lies in its discussion of the conflict between relative cultural
values and absolute religious claims, expressed through the
rejection of culture in the name of a higher Divine impulse.
This conflict in the Russian thought of that time is usually
associated with the opposition between the "Hellenistic" line
in Christianity, the major representative of which was considered Viacheslav Ivanov (1866–1949), who tried to unite
Christianity and Dionysianism, and the "Judaic" line, repre-

sented by Lev Shestov (1866–1938), who urged that God be sought beyond the limits of all rational, ethical, esthetic, and other cultural criteria. Both Ivanov and Shestov proceeded from their own experience of Nietzsche: the difference between them lay only in the fact that Ivanov, rejecting rational science and ethics, preserved esthetics and "myth," while Shestov rejected the sphere of culture in its entirety. Although Meier's point of view is close to Viacheslav Ivanov's in many of his other works, in "Religion and Culture" he essentially shares Shestov's position.

Meier begins his article with a reference to Nietzsche: "'It has become cold,' as Nietzsche's wise man, seeking God, said. In places an awareness that the 'murder of God' created this cold, that life is becoming an ever emptier and pettier game, is beginning to take hold."[7] Here Nietzsche appears as the initiator of a new search for God and for a new religious consciousness. And this is not the only role Nietzsche plays in "Religion and Culture." Just as important for Meier is the Nietzschean analysis of culture as the sphere of the will to power; Meier uses this as a basis for the rejection of culture as a whole. For Meier, culture is fundamentally oriented toward the satisfaction of the demands of the individual, isolated man, but:

having bowed down to himself, man bowed before the worst of gods – the man of the future – We are people, and bowing down before the man of the future, we bow before the oppressor of the future. The God of the future is the great Solitary One, standing on the corpses of millions, he is the Powerful One, loving no one, but subordinating all ... Power is not an empty word. Power is beautiful and vital, and the ideal of power can be an inspiration. The Superman is not a dead impulse, and serving him is a whole religion in itself, but it is the inverse of the religion of overcoming, the religion of freedom, the true religion.[8]

Meier thus sees the Nietzschean analysis of culture in Shestovian terms as a total critique of culture, necessitating a search for a transcendent God, i.e. he sees it as the direct opposite of the position explicitly advocated by Nietzsche himself.[9]

Meier subsequently connects this search with Communism, which he sees as a secularized version of the chiliastic, religious impulse leading to the "Kingdom of God on Earth." Within this religious perspective Meier criticizes the actual socialist movements of his time for their inability to achieve true collectivism and for reducing it to the demand for the collectivization of property; this leaves the personality relatively autonomous and does not completely abolish its legal and cultural basis. He writes: "The sin of the collectivists possibly lies in their postponement of the freedom which contemporary humanists prize into their kingdom of the future."[10] Meier contrasts this limited socialist ideal with the religious communist ideal, based on love, and the community of life as a "wedding feast," a holiday, the beginning of all creativity. He exclaims: "How could it [such Communism – B.G.] do otherwise than forget all about the guarantees of freedom and about the autonomy of the personality, if it was born from faith in the liberating power of love?"[11] Meier sees the basic threat to this chiliastic hope once again in culture, understood as the power of man over nature and consequently over other men. And so in our time, writes Meier, with another reference to Nietzsche as "the last great European thinker," culture appears to be of necessity syncretic and cold, i.e. a symptom of the waning of life.[12]

The strategy behind Meier's handling of Nietzschean thought, generally representative of Russian thought of that period, becomes clear in this article. Meier seems to subject all of European culture, including all of its scientific, moral, and legal values, to Nietzschean criticism. He agrees with the later Nietzschean diagnosis of culture as the expression of the will to power, having as its *telos* the birth of the Superman, but he understands this diagnosis not as a new foundation for culture, but as its final negation. He opposes to it the Dionysian ecstasy of the early Nietzsche, purified of all cultural–mythological deposits, i.e., from all things "hellenic," and in such form taking on a Judaeo-Christian chiliastic orientation.

Within the context of Meier's early chiliastic expectations, which persisted during the 1920s in the ideology of his circle (it was dedicated to "making the Bolsheviks listen to reason"), Meier's writings of the 1930s are particularly interesting when viewed as a reaction to the development of actual cultural processes of the time.[13] In articles such as "Revelation (On the

'Revelation [of St. John the Divine]')," written between 1931 and 1934, Meier re-examines the very concept of "Life," which earlier, under the influence of Nietzschean *Lebensphilosophie*, stood at the center of his philosophical interests and aspirations. Meier now views "Life" not as an alternative to culture, but as an abstraction which has meaning only within the framework of general cultural and, concretely, philosophical discourse; consequently, it is unable to be its foundation.[14] Further on he emphasizes the personal source of culture, founded in the idea of a personal God. The personality receives its basis in the "glorification" of God, in prayer, in "personal song."

Correspondingly, Meier also re-evaluates the choral source of Greek tragedy. He now sees Dionysian dithyrambs as "unenlightened" and juxtaposes them to individualized psalmody.[15] Culture no longer appears to Meier exclusively as the expression of the will to power. Meier now uses this description basically to describe the culture of the New Time. The religiously-oriented and enlightened Dionysian ecstasy, directed toward the transcendent, is consolidated in the Word, in the transcendently-oriented culture of the Middle Ages. Accordingly, the opposition to culture as a whole loses its Nietzschean character of unconscious vital force or unarticulated Dionysian "other," and acquires the character of an articulated, but demonic, cultural impulse for Meier. Hence Meier directly criticizes Nietzsche on the very point on which earlier he had agreed with him.

In his extensive study, "Thoughts on Reading *Faust*" (1935), which is basically a critique of the Faustian orientation on "the deed" (Meier prefers the Christian orientation on "the word"), Meier specifically writes about the "doubling of Faust," seeing in Mephistopheles Faust's inevitable companion:

In the antique tragedy, if you will, there were also two heroes, not one: the second and no less important character was the chorus, the carrier of consciousness, always standing beside the consciousness of the hero ... After Nietzsche we also know that the chorus provided the hero with the opportunity to "see himself surrounded by a crowd of spirits and feel his inner unity" with them ... Still, in antique tragedy this second "major" character was more closely tied to the first, being the expression of a single truth, binding for all and affirmed by all; on the other hand, this second character was somehow separate from the hero himself, stood outside him, and, on occasion, was even opposed to him. In the modern tragedy, the situation is different. On the one hand, the second person should be completely and distinctly an "other," a separate, almost independent personality, with a different attitude toward life and with a different will (because here the hero's "I" is doubled); on the other hand, this is not really another person, but the very same hero, his other "I," his *Doppelgänger*, his shadow, his demon. There is no wholeness of the antique hero, but there still is no opposition of the communal choral consciousness to the individual consciousness of the hero. True, the double sometimes plays the role of the chorus – but he plays this role weakly because the chorus and one of the two souls of Faustian man are two different things. In *Faust* choruses of good and evil spirits frequently appear instead of the traditional chorus, but they are already far removed from the people.[16]

In this passage, which is highly reminiscent of Bakhtin (Mikhail Bakhtin was connected with Meier's circle and arrested for virtually the same "crimes" as Meier)[17], the place which Nietzsche's Dionysian impulse occupies is clearly visible: it loses its impersonality and authority and becomes the individualized voice of the philosopher's own *alter ego*, or even that of many different *alter egos* – the different "good and evil spirits," no longer comprising a unity. Meier's thought develops through constant dialogue with Nietzsche, but this dialogue itself is now placed in a cultural context. The individualization of the voice of the "other" is undoubtedly connected above all with the reification of Communism and the revolutionary impulse in Russia during the Stalinist regime. In other words, the single, ambivalent Dionysian impulse – as destructive as it is creative – becomes individualized and as a result divides into the "good" religious element and the "evil" Superman element, and to unite these is just as impossible as it is to simply separate and juxtapose them. Just as the religious philosopher is aware of his demonic double, this double is innerly connected to the philosopher and needs him. (The idea is that Satan needs God for his self-definition and self-assertion). Thus Meier continued to find religious content in the socialist idea even in the 1930s and anticipates its internal religious transfiguration.

At the same time, probably under the influence of the rise of German fascism, Meier writes a political critique of "naturalism" and its claims to the superiority of the Aryan race, even though in this case, too, he finds a hidden religious perspective.[18] For Meier the criticism of modern totalitarian movements, which he designates "sociologism" and "naturalism," does not imply a turn instead to a third force – "humanism." Meier writes: "Indifferent humanism is in the religious sense a blank space, and, if you like, most distant from Christianity."[19] Meier further proclaims that Buddhism, as a religion of universal indifference, is the fundamental opponent of Christianity. The acme of religious consciousness for Meier becomes the sacred sacrifice to the highest Divine "I," in which he sees an enlightened and individualized variant of the Dionysian mystery.[20]

Here Meier's Nietzschean training becomes apparent: for him there can be no moral, legal, and individualistic censure of the "tragedy of life," including the tragedy of the Russian Revolution and the Stalinist terror, because he comprehends such censure as being based on irreligious, vile *ressentiment*, as described by Nietzsche, and as being Buddhistic and nihilistic. On the contrary, he strives to give meaning to his own experience of suffering by understanding it as a sacrifice in a sacred mystery drama.[21] In such a sacrifice, everything individual and separate, as well as the internal dichotomy of consciousness, becomes irrelevant; in this sense one can speak here of the Nietzschean Dionysian impulse. But Meier integrates this impulse within ritual, so that this impulse becomes subject to "the word" and is given the goal of glorifying the transcendent God, i.e., he loses his "vitality" and spontaneity, and becomes rooted in culture and tradition. In his doctrine of sacrifice Meier continues to adhere in essence to the original program of the Russian Religious Renaissance, to integrate Nietzscheanism into the Christian perspective, but with a corresponding correction of this perspective.

Meier is not alone in describing the cultural situation of the 1930s as the dualism between public life as Stalinist, Apollonian (Superman) supremacy, and personal life as Dionysian sacrifice. Another example is found in Mikhail Bakhtin's theory of carnivalization, outlined in his book on Rabelais, written in the late 1930s and early 1940s, but published only in 1965.[22] In this work Bakhtin interprets the European carnival as a form of ritual lowering of all existing social hierarchies and the temporary conquest of individual isolation in favor of collective ecstasy and equality before the face of "popular laughter." The carnival tradition is examined further by Bakhtin as a source of a definite line of "carnivalized literature," or more broadly, carnivalized culture within the structure of the general culture of the New Time. Bakhtin claims that the "impulse toward laughter" and the use of "low" genres, usually excluded from "official culture," are characteristic of carnival culture. Bakhtin's theory is arguably an attempt to comprehend Stalinist culture;[23] we will discuss only those aspects that touch upon the topic under discussion.[24]

Like both the theoreticians of Russian Formalism and the theoreticians of official Stalinist culture, Bakhtin derives his general theory of culture from the Nietzschean model, according to which culture is the arena of struggle between different ideologies, deeply ingrained in the very life experience of its bearers. For example, the culturally-oriented Russian Formalist school, which was close to the avant-garde and still influential in the thirties, interpreted the entire history of culture as a struggle between different tendencies, different artistic wills, a struggle in which young, new artistic movements win because of their vitality, while old movements become "automatized," lose their vital impulse and thus their attraction. Viktor Shklovsky's work in particular, because of its excessive use of vitalist and erotic metaphors, reveals the degree to which the external formalism of analysis is subordinated to the logic of the artistic will and force: the new artistic device is primarily understood as an instrument employed "in order to return the sensation of life, to feel things," to intensify desire.[25] Drawing on Nietzsche, this teaching about the purely vital struggle of artistic tendencies, in which the new and the young must be victorious, marks that point at which Russian Formalism intersects with Stalinist culture, which insists that the struggle between progressive and "vital" ideologies and reactionary and "decadent" ideologies is the fundamental content of the cultural process.

Bakhtin considers such "dialogism" of ideologies to be the basic characteristic of culture, most completely expressed in the "polyphonic novel."[26] According to him, this dialogism is not the means of a theoretical search for truth (as we find in the classical Platonic model of philosophical dialogue), but a form of living conflict in which the struggling ideologies are never questioned by its bearers, since those ideologies play only an instrumental, utilitarian role. The Bakhtinian dialogue is oriented not toward the achievement of truth or consensus, but toward the vital victory of one side or the other. Unlike the Formalist and Stalinist critics, however, Bakhtin maintains that historically the struggle of ideologies never ends with the ultimate victory of one of them. The Formalists postulated such a victory as the result of the exhaustion of vital energy (or "automatization") of the obsolete ideology; the idea of a victory by means of a superior argument is irrelevant here, for if the ideology preserves its vitality, then it always finds counter-arguments that will be perceived as more convincing. For Bakhtin, however, any ideology is capable of revitalization, in its own way, in the ideal, eschatological space beyond life and death. For this reason the dialogue between ideologies, in which, according to Bakhtin, both the living and the dead participate equally, potentially stretches into infinity.

To the extent that Bakhtin sees ideologies as vital convictions determined by the specific inner-worldly, "corporeal" position of its bearers (Nietzschean perspectivism), different ideologies can find their own kind of inner merging beyond any rational consensus only on the level of life, or pure corporeality, itself. This kind of unification in the "grotesque body" is the essence of Bakhtinian carnival. During the time of carnival any particular ideology's claim to truth, and consequently to superiority, becomes the object of derision (for Bakhtin, following

Nietzsche, the claims to truth and superiority coincide). Bakhtin's carnival corresponds to Nietzsche's Dionysian mystery, conquering all that is individual; unlike Nietzsche's mystery, however, this conquest takes place within defined, culturally-coded forms: carnival is the game of masks in which Dionysian intoxication does not happen in fact, but is only staged or simulated within a particular framework. Thus, although bodies are mixed, a single consciousness, or a chorus (as in Nietzsche) does not result (this is reminiscent of Meier's argument, *vide supra*). Carnival as a new variant of Nietzsche's Dionysian impulse subsequently becomes in Bakhtin the source of the "carnivalesque," or "polyphonic" novel; it has a specific author who is able, from within his own consciousness, to stage a carnival of ideologies. Nietzsche himself viewed the novel as an extension of the Dionysian musical impulse; he considered it a continuation of the Platonic dialogue containing within itself all esthetic forms and subordinating poetry to itself (*BT*, pp. 89–93). Nietzsche's arguments were later incorporated by Bakhtin into his literary analyses.

Bakhtin opposes the carnivalesque unity of the world to another unity, which he calls "monologic," i.e. a unity arising from the establishment in fact of the superiority of one ideology that then determines "serious" reality. In Bakhtin these two unities form not a dichotomy, but a dualism similar to Nietzsche's dualism of Apollonian and Dionysian impulses, beneath which lies an inner interdependency. In his book on Rabelais, Bakhtin describes carnival in severe enough colors: the esthetics of carnival generate a constant alternation of "enthronings and dethronings" acccompanied by "mirthful" tortures, murders, insults, defamation, pelting with excrement, and so on. At the center of Bakhtin's carnival stands the cult of "'pregnant death,' active during the 'mirthful time,' which in killing gives birth; it does not allow anything old to be perpetuated, but never ceases to give birth to the new and the young."[27]

If it is justifiable to see a metaphor for official Stalinist culture in Bakhtin's monologism, then carnival is not a "democratic alternative" to this culture, but its irrational, destructive

side. The Bakhtinian description of carnival more than anything else is reminiscent of the atmosphere of Stalinist show
trials, with their unexpected "enthronings and dethronings."
But Bakhtin sees this irrational side of Stalinism (from the point
of view now of a victim of repressive Stalinist policies; Bakhtin
was himself such a victim) in a Nietzschean way as a Dionysian
or sacred sacrifice, and thereby gives a higher religious
meaning to his own life as well.

At the same time Bakhtin has a negative attitude toward any
form of isolation of the individuum and, correspondingly, to
the guarantee of his rights liberally understood, insisting on the
destruction of any such self-isolation in the "Great Time" and
on the participation of everyone in the single space of carnival.
The question naturally arises here of how Bakhtin combines his
emphasis on individual ideology with joy on the occasion of the
destruction of the individuum. The individuality of ideology,
however, is not identical with the individuality of the concrete,
human "I" as its bearer for Bakhtin. Ideology marks a particular place in the world, a place which anyone can occupy in
principle; in other words, ideology is a mask which anyone can
put on. From this point of view the figure of "pregnant death"
becomes comprehensible: the annihilation of one "obsolete"
bearer of ideology puts another in his place, and this sacrificial
victim provides every concrete ideology (and, consequently,
every dialogic process as a whole) with eternal youth. Bakhtin
understands concrete individuality as a particular corporeality, doomed to die: only "ideology," and not the "I" or the
soul, can achieve cultural immortality.

The impersonal, or extra-personal, status of Bakhtinian
"ideologies" as culturally encoded states of consciousness, or
types of the authorial word not rooted in a particular individual consciousness, has its most likely source in a variant of
Russian phenomenology developed by Gustav Shpet. Influenced by Nietzsche and Soloviev, Shpet refuses to assign different phenomenological states of consciousness to their concrete
"I," even if it be transcendental, as Shpet's teacher Edmund
Husserl does.[28] In his relatively early work, "Consciousness
and Its Proprietor,"[29] Shpet, following Soloviev's "Theoretical

Philosophy,"[30] affirms the fundamental impersonality of consciousness; he considered the concept of the subject as an abstraction and a metaphysical illusion, recognizing only the corporeal dimension of subjectivity.

In his later work, *Esthetic Fragments* (1922–23), Shpet wrote a commentary on Tiutchev's famous poem, "Silentium":

> Truly, truly SILENTIUM is the subject of the last vision, super-intellectual and super-intelligible, completely real *ens realissimum*. "Silentium" is the highest limit of cognition and existence. Their merging is not the metaphysical toy identity (with a German mainspring inside) of being and consciousness, not a mystery, an open Christian secret, but a radiant joy, a triumph of light, a "divine death" [*vseblasaia smert'*], divine, in that one that will never show mercy to that which must die without any, consequently, hope for its resurrection, the glad incineration of panhuman vulgarity, a mystery, revealed like the azure and gold of the sky.[31]

Shpet may be alluding to Tiutchev's poem "Cicero" (which is usually published near "Silentium" in collections of his poetry because it was written the same year), in particular to the famous verses:

> Blessed is he who sojourned in this world
> In its most fateful and portentious moments!
> He was a guest of the immortal gods [*vseblagie*]
> An interlocutor bid to the feast;
> A witness to their lofty spectacles,
> He was admitted to their august council –
> And living still, resided in the heavens,
> And immortality imbibed he from their cup.

This poem was very popular at the time. Its allusion to Plato's "Feast" (Symposium) might have been important to Shpet.

In this passage Shpet cleverly unites the Nietzschean polemic with Christianity and German Idealism and a reference to Nietzschean themes in Russian poetry (Viacheslav Ivanov's *ens realissimum*[32] and Andrei Bely's *Gold in Azure*[33]) with an apologia for death phrased in such a way that death is deprived of its "nihilistic" or "pessimistic" pathos. This is because consciousness is impersonal in principle, and so the disintegration of concrete individual consciousness does not mean for Shpet its negation by the forces of the unconscious, as is the case, for example, in Schopenhauer. In this way death loses its "sting": it coincides with a philosophical reflection that reveals that the subject is fundamentally nonsubjective. In an anti-Christian form and with the use of Hesserlian phenomenology Shpet repeats the basic device of Russian religious philosophy. In this way he prepares the way for Bakhtinian neo-Christian and neo-Nietzschean syncretism and even for discrete Bakhtinian images: Shpet's "glad death" is reminiscent of Bakhtin's "pregnant death." On the other hand, Shpet, proceeding from the Nietzschean proximity of the impersonal and the musical, emphasizes the priority of the poetic word, a position Bakhtin would oppose; Bakhtin comes from the individualized understanding of "the other" as "the other ideology," the *alter ego*.[34] [Translator's note: *vseblagaia smert'* echoes *Blagaia vest'* a reference to the Gospels (commonly translated as "Good News" or "Glad Tidings"). Shpet may also imply a death that is good, or positive, in that it is natural, useful, meaningful, proper, and in the natural and *right* order of things; in this respect, the concept is akin to Nietzsche's dictum "die at the right time!"]

Mikhail Bulgakov's novel, *The Master and Margarita*, can be regarded as a highly original literary illustration of Bakhtin's theory of the carnivalesque novel. There is no explicit evidence that Bulgakov was acquainted with Bakhtin's theories, but he could have read Bakhtin's book on Dostoevsky, which appeared in 1929. Written in the thirties but not published until much later, *The Master and Margarita* develops further many of the themes of the Russian Religious Renaissance in novel form. The immediate source for Bulgakov's novel is Goethe's *Faust*. The action takes place in two "spaces": in the Moscow of the 1930s, where Mephistopheles-Woland and his retinue stage a series of provocations, saturated with the symbolism of carnival; and in scriptural Jerusalem, where Christ and Pilate engage in a potentially eternal dialogue. The appearance of Woland in Moscow and the subsequent immersion of the Soviet capital in "mirthful time and space" evoke death, injury, madness and destruction on a scale unknown in Goethe, but these events are meant to be perceived comically, since the victims, as Shpet would have said, are the representatives of human banality and vulgarity. In *The Master and Margarita* this terror of carnival surpasses and paralyzes the usual and "monologic" terror of the NKVD (security police), which in the novel is treated ironically and thus estheticized. Instead of issuing a moral judgment from the point of view of the victim of this terror (which Bulgakov certainly was during his lifetime), the novel generates a purely Nietzschean sense of superiority, abetted by the moral support of superhuman forces over which the NKVD has no power and which provide not only metaphysical consolation, but also very real revenge in this world, not the next.

Even more distinctly Nietzschean motives appear in Bulgakov's interpretation of Christ in the Jerusalem chapters of *The Master and Margarita*. If, in the literary–esthetic treatment of these scenes, there is reference to Ernst Renan's *Life of Christ*, then in their philosophical–ideological content they turn out to be in exclusive proximity to the interpretation of the Scriptures and the image of Christ suggested by Nietzsche in *The Antichrist* (there can be little doubt that Bulgakov read this book, since it was rather well known in Russia at that time). Nietzsche contrasts his own conception of Christ with Renan's, maintaining that concepts like "genius" and "hero," used by Renan, are not applicable to Christ (*AC*, p. 141) Nietzsche himself characterizes Christ, according to his "psychological type," as an "idiot" (*ibid*). This description undoubtedly refers to the image of Prince Myshkin ("the Russian Christ") in Fedor Dostoevsky's novel, *The Idiot*, especially since this description is surrounded in *The Antichrist* with numerous allusions to Dostoevsky. Nietzsche mentions epilepsy, and Siberia, and finally writes:

That queer and sick world into which the Gospels introduce us – as in a Russian novel, a world in which the scum of society, nervous disorders, and "childlike" idiocy seem to be having a rendezvous ... It is regrettable that a Dostoevsky did not live near this most interesting of all decadents – I mean someone who would have known how to sense the very stirring charm of such a mixture of the sublime, the sickly, and the childlike (*AC*, p. 142)

Bulgakov, or rather Bulgakov's fictional *alter ego*, the Master, realizes Nietzsche's desire and writes the "Russian Gospel," following Nietzsche's recipe, given in *The Antichrist*, almost literally. He frees the scriptural Christ from all elements of *ressentiment*, discipleship, protest, morality, orientation on the traditional type of the "prophet," etc., and avoids making Christ a hero. Bulgakov's "evangelist" type (in the novel he appears under the name of Levi Matthew) is ignorant, vengeful, lower-class, and infinitely distant from any understanding of Christ's actual intentions; he is inclined to attribute a fictional "teaching" and fictional acts to Christ. Bulgakov's Levi Matthew corresponds fully to Nietzsche's understanding of the "psychological type of the evangelist." Through the text of the Gospel, Bulgakov's Master "guesses" (both Nietzsche and Bulgakov use the same term here) the "psychological type" of Christ; according to Nietzsche, one must be a combination of a doctor and a philologist to do this (Bulgakov, by the way, was trained as a doctor; his father was a theologian[35]). Nietzsche understood the "psychological type of the Redeemer" as the result of a decadent weakening of life at the peak of its refinement and aristocratism: the Christian "passive resistance to evil" and the "search for the Kingdom of God within you" are presented here not as the external demands of morality, but as an internal necessity of life for natures too overrefined, vulnerable, and morbid, to be capable of active, vital struggle (*AC*, pp. 117–29, 126–28, 141, 159–60).

Bulgakov describes just such an over-refined nature in his novel, where his Christ appears under the emphatically Judaicized name of Yeshua Ha-Notsri (which possible also refers to Nietzsche's idea of the inner unity of Judaism and Christianity). In *The Master and Margarita* Yeshua-Christ is shown basically through his "fictional" (i.e. non-scriptural) dialogues with Pilate, whom Nietzsche characterized in *The Antichrist* as the worthiest figure in the Gospels (*AC*, p. 162). In other words, Bulgakov's Christ is first and foremost the interlocutor of authority, infinitely distant from the people and from their false, "base" consciousness. Bulgakov's Christ does not speak in parables and does not instruct; he appears, rather, as a doctor and a psychologist.

Pilate also corresponds completely to the Nietzschean description of the refined and decadent nature of the ruler: he suffers from nervous headaches and wants only peace and quiet. To Pilate's famous question, "What is truth?" Bulgakov's Christ gives a fully Nietzschean, "physiological" answer: "The truth is, first of all, that your head aches."[36] Thus Christ appears in the novel as a character in collusion with authority and in eternal dialogue with it; he is internally bound to authority by the general experience of elitism and suffering. But since authority in the person of Pilate is subject to a false "scriptural" interpretation of Christianity as directed against earthly power, Christ perishes. Pilate in *The Master and Margarita* is Christ's double, although he is incapable of admitting it to himself.

The Jerusalem chapters of *The Master and Margarita* appear as the fragments of a novel within a novel, written by the Master, and at the same time as Dionysian visions, or carnivalesque mysteries, evoked from non-being into the carnival atmosphere of Moscow by Woland's narration. Again there is an obvious parallel to Bakhtin: the carnivalesque, Dionysian mystery turns out to be "guessed" by the lonely author, who in Bulgakov's novel is the nameless, i.e., impersonal, or more accurately, the supra-personal Master. The Master forms a new pairing with Woland, and Woland is, among other things, analogous to Stalin.[37] At the same time, Woland acts essentially "as one" with Christ. Only he realizes the will to power of which Christ is deprived. Thus Christ and Woland jointly arrange the fate of the Master, while Margarita (the Master's ideal helpmate) is transformed into a witch in Woland's service. In Bulgakov's novel there exists a unique circle of the chosen, entry to which is given "beyond good and evil," and to which belong both rulers of reality, like Stalin, and rulers of the imagination, like the Master; this elite circle is opposed to the moralistic proletarian "class consciousness." The theme of the

intimate dialogue of the artist with authority (concretely Bulgakov's dialogue with Stalin) is characteristic not only of Bulgakov's work, but also of the work of other Russian authors of
that period.[38]

All of the authors discussed above, irrespective of the degree
of their personal acquaintance, belonged essentially to one and
the same circle of the Russian intelligentsia and were all
formed by the influence of the religious–Nietzschean theme of
the conquest of rationalism, rational morality, nihilism,
pessimism, and Schopenhauerian "Buddhism" of which we
have already spoken. By the 1930s these writers could no
longer support the appeal of the Russian Religious Renaissance to dissolve the individuum in the impersonal Dionysian
element and the corresponding desire to combine Christianity
and socialism into a single chiliastic utopia. They perceived the
Stalinist regime either as the victory of the will to power, the
coming of the Superman, or the one-sided victory of the Apollonian impulse. As early as the 1920s, literary works showed this
Apollonian–Dionysian dualism divided between two characters, one a representative of the Communist "iron will" and
the other a representative of the musical–poetic impulse; these
characters frequently appeared as brothers, or even twins.[39]
We can say that, if the dichotomy of conscious and unconscious
components in official Soviet literature identified by Katerina
Clark can be understood as a variant of Apollonian–Dionysian
dualism, then that dualism, taken from the Dionysian and not
the Apollonian side, also determines the thought of the non-
official cultural opposition of that period.

From this arises the characteristic dualism of these authors in
regard to Stalinist culture: they perceive it as the one-sided
development of the principle of the will to power, ignoring the
esthetic, poetic, Dionysian and dialogic–polyphonic basis of
culture. But this onesidedness does not evoke in them a morally
motivated negation, that "accusation to the world" against
which Nietzsche warned and which he considered to be an
indicator of a base frame of mind. On the contrary, they saw
their own creativity either as being in a dualistic relationship
with authority (as the Dionysian impulse is to the Apollonian

or as the focus of the God-man is to the focus on the Superman, etc.) so that authority appears to them as their own *alter ego*, and/or as the sacred Dionysian sacrifice. Especially character-istic in this respect is the extraordinary identity of the historical material with which the official and alternative cultures of the thirties worked: characteristic of both is the typically Nietzschean interest first of all in antiquity, in the European Renaissance, in early German Romanticism (especially in Goethe), and in the particular problems, arising in this context, of the heroic, the mythological, the popular, and so on. Although Aleksandr Meier, Mikhail Bakhtin, Gustav Shpet, and Mikhail Bulgakov were edged out and crushed by the official culture, it would be a mistake to view them in terms of any moral-political opposition to that culture. It is more productive to view the situation as a case of actual Nietzschean dualism, in which cultural–political repression by itself, realized as an instrument of the will to power, appears as an unavoidable part of a general tragic vision of culture and the world as a whole.

NOTES

* Translated by Maria Carlson.

1 For more detail on the religious reception of Nietzsche in Russia, see Ann Lane, "Nietzsche Comes to Russia," and Bernice G. Rosenthal, "Stages of Nietzscheanism: Merezhkovsky's Intel-lectual Evolution," both in *Nietzsche in Russia*, ed. Rosenthal, pp. 51–68 and 69–94, resp.

2 Vladimir Solov'ev, "Krizis zapadnoi filosofii; protiv pozitivis-tov," *SS*, I (rpt. Brussels, 1966), pp. 27–151.

3 Vladimir Solov'ev, "Chteniia o Bogochelovechestve," *SS*, III, pp. 179f.

4 Typical in this respect is the work of Nikolai Berdiaev, *Istoki i smysl russkogo kommunizma* (Paris, 1955).

5 For A. A. Meier's biography and a history of his circle, see N. P. Antsiferov, "Tri glavy iz vospominanii," *Pamiat'*; *istoricheskii sbornik* 4 (Paris, 1981); see also foreword and addendum in A. A. Meier, *Filosofskie sochineniia* (Paris, 1982).

6 Meier, *Filosofskie sochineniia*, pp. 31–95.

7 Ibid., p. 31.

8 Ibid., pp. 39–42.

9 Lev Shestov considered Nietzsche's teaching about the Superman to be the rejection of a philosophical position proper and a transition to traditional moralizing, always having as its aim the maintenance of the *status quo*. See Lev Shestov, *Dobro v uchenii gr. Tolstogo i F. Nietzsche* (St. Petersburg, 1900), pp. 200ff.

10 Shestov, *Dobro v uchenii*, p. 89.

11 Ibid., p. 94.

12 Ibid., p. 74.

13 See E. N. Fedotova, "Vospominaniia," Meier, p. 454.

14 Meier, *Filosofskie sochineniia*, pp. 178ff.

15 Ibid., p. 148.

16 Ibid., pp. 305–6.

17 On Bakhtin's ties to the religious-philosophical circles of the twenties, see Katerina Clark and Michael Holquist, *Mikhail Bakhtin* (Cambridge, MA, 1984), pp. 125–41. The philosopher S. A. Askol'dov, a member of Meier's circle, also wrote on the problem of "the other" in the context of Dostoevsky's novels; see S. A. Askol'dov, "Psikhologiia kharakterov u Dostoevskogo," *F. M. Dostoevskii; Stat'i i materialy* (Moscow/Leningrad, 1924), book 2.

18 See Meier, "Mysli pro sebia" (1937), in his *Filosofskie sochineniia*, pp. 445–46.

19 Meier, *Filosofskie sochineniia*, pp. 444.

20 Ibid., p. 447.

21 See Meier, "Zametki o smysle misterii (Zhertva)" (1933) in his *Filosofskie sochineniia*, pp. 105–65.

22 Mikhail Bakhtin, *Tvorchestvo Fransua Rable i narodnaia kul'tura Srednevekov'ia i Renessansa* (Moscow, 1965).

23 Clark and Holquist, *Bakhtin*, pp. 305ff.

24 For more information on Bakhtin and Nietzsche, see James M. Curtis, "Michael Bakhtin, Nietzsche and Russian Pre-Revolutionary Thought," *Nietzsche in Russia*, 331–54.

25 Victor Shklovskii, "Iskusstvo kak priem" (1917), in *Poetika. Trudy russkikh i sovetskikh poeticheskikh shkol* ed. D. Kirai and A. Kovach, (Budapest, 1982), pp. 82, 84ff. For more on the role of Vitalism in the system of Stalinist culture, see V. Papernyi, *Kul'tura 2* (Ann Arbor, 1985), pp. 132ff.; see also Alexandar Flaker, "'Gesunde' oder 'kranke' Kunst," *Die Axt hat geblueht ... Europäische Konflikte der 30er jahre Erinnerung an die frühe Avantgarde* (Düsseldorf, 1987), pp. 115–21, in which the author traces the genealogy of anti-formalist criticism of the Stalinist period from Nietzsche through Gorky and Lunacharsky to the 1930s.

26 The theory of the "polyphonic novel" was developed by Bakhtin

in his book *Problemy tvorchestva Dostoevskogo* (1929), then expanded
in his *Problemy poetiki Dostoevskogo* (Moscow, 1963).

27 Bakhtin, *Tvorchestvo Fransua Rable*, p. 22.

28 In Gustav Shpet's brief foreword to *Iavlenie i smysl* (Moscow,
1914) (in which he appears to still be a true disciple of Edmund
Husserl while objecting to Husserl's basing of phenomenology on
transcendental subjectivity), he maintains that while writing *Iavlenie*, he was constantly haunted by Wagner's music. In this
manner Shpet wants to realize in himself the Nietzschean type of
"the Socrates who practices music," in whom the impersonal
Dionysian impulse manifests itself on the philosophical level.

29 Gustav Shpet, "Soznanie i ego sobstvennik," *Sbornik statei po
filosofii, posviashchennyi G. Chelpanovu* (Moscow, 1916),
pp. 156–210.

30 Vladimir Solov'ev, "Teoreticheskaia filosofiia," *SS*, IX,
pp. 89–166.

31 Gustav Shpet, *Esteticheskie fragmenty*, II (Petrograd, 1923), pp.
76–77.

32 See also Viacheslav Ivanov, "Dve stikhii v sovremennom simvo-
lizme," *SS*, II (Brussels, 1974), pp. 537–61, in which Ivanov
likewise makes the correlation between the Dionysian mystery
and individual creativity.

33 Andrei Belyi, *Zoloto v lazure* (Moscow, 1904).

34 Mikhail Bakhtin, *Voprosy literatury i estetiki* (Moscow, 1975), p. 81.

35 Marietta Chudakova, *Zhizneopisanie Mikhaila Bulgakova* (Moscow,
1988), pp. 12–13, 50.

36 Mikhail Bulgakov, *Master i Margarita*, in his *Romany* (Moscow,
1973), p. 441.

37 Marietta Chudakova, "Soblazn klassiki," *Atti del convegno
"Michail Bulgakov,"* ed. E. Bazzarelli and J. Kresalkova (Milan,
1986). There is another reference to Stalin in the scene at
Woland's ball in *Master i Margarita*. A nameless villain who has
sprayed his enemy's office walls with poison in order to kill him is
a new guest at the ball; the author may have had in mind the
ex-head of the NKVD Genrikh Yagoda (1891–1938), who was
accused of just this crime during the Stalinist show trials of the
thirties.

38 For more information on Pasternak's "dialogue with Stalin" in
the thirties, see Marietta Chudakova, "Bez gneva i pristrastiia,"
Novyi mir 9 (1988), pp. 256ff.

39 Typical examples include Iurii Olesha's *Zavist'* (1927) and Boris
Pilniak's "Dvoiniki" (1933).

PART V

Nietzsche and the Nationalities: A Case Study

CHAPTER 15

Nietzsche's influence on Hebrew writers of the Russian Empire

Menahem Brinker

The last two decades of the nineteenth century and the first two decades of the twentieth century were an epoch of crisis and transition in Russian Jewish life. The wave of pogroms in 1881 and 1882, the beginning of the Industrial Revolution that impoverished hundreds of thousands of Jewish families, and the "May Laws" of 1882, which made life in the Pale of Settlement unbearable, combined to create a new self-consciousness among the Jews. The period in which large sectors of the Jewish intelligentsia preached Russification had ended, although integration into general Russian society did not cease; in fact, it expanded beyond the limits of the upper classes and reached the masses. Educated Jews witnessed the collapse of traditional forms of life and modes of cultural creation. Hebrew and Yiddish writers came to be regarded by young and secularized elements of the Jewish people as a new spiritual and intellectual leadership to replace traditional rabbinic authority. Many of the teachings of these new authorities were greatly influenced by the works of Friedrich Nietzsche.

By the early twenties, most of these writers had died or emigrated to Palestine, but their books and ideas continued to circulate openly in Soviet Jewish society. After Stalin's death, *samizdat* versions of their works helped to inspire the Jewish national revival. Under Gorbachev their publication became legal and translations of the Hebrew poetry of this period appear in the Russian press.

Between the 1880s and 1920 secular Hebrew literature indeed flourished. Books of poetry, novels, and essays were sold in thousands and sometimes in tens of thousands, a phenomenon which would not repeat itself until the establishment of the state of Israel with its millions of readers of Hebrew. This unprecedented burst in the consumption of Hebrew literature was rooted in the fact that young Jews were leaving the traditional *yeshivot* (rabbinic academies) and becoming secularized in their tens – perhaps hundreds – of thousands without knowledge of any European language such as Russian or German. Naturally, they were totally dependent upon Hebrew and Yiddish in the formation of their new cultural identity.

This audience was simultaneously a symptom of and a major factor in what is now called the "period of national revival." The granting of political emancipation to Jews in Western Europe aroused hopes for a similar development in Eastern Europe. Despite pogroms, persecution, and the impoverishment of large sections of the Jewish population, especially small merchants and artisans, Jews entertained hopes for a better future. Various political solutions were offered. Zionists insisted upon the need to create a new homeland for the Jews in Palestine. Others advocated the collective colonization of Jews in Argentina or emigration to other parts of the New World. Still others formulated political programs for solving Jewish problems within Eastern Europe. The autonomists envisaged emancipation (i.e. equal rights) accompanied by educational, linguistic, and cultural autonomy. Socialists recommended that Jews join the Revolution which, among other things, would solve the "Jewish Question." Many of them joined the Bund, a very popular Marxist organization (at its peak it included hundreds of thousands of Jewish workers), which advocated the maintenance of a distinctive linguistic and cultural Jewish identity during and after the Revolution. Others joined Russian socialist parties directly, becoming Social Revolutionaries, Bolsheviks, or Mensheviks. These Jews accepted the idea that Jewish national existence would evaporate together with other national identities after the Revolution. They thus opted for assimilation.

Yet despite the obvious allure which auto-emancipation, a socialist revolution, or emigration had for many Eastern European Jews, some perceived a threat to Jewish national existence as long as Jewish cultural problems were not resolved. The writers and thinkers who were becoming the new leaders of the nation's younger generation agreed that Jewish culture must not be abandoned to orthodox rabbis. To do so would leave Jews with only two options: traditional religious culture, which for many meant stagnation as well as intellectual and emotional repression; or assimilation, seeking their humanity outside the Jewish people. This tragic choice was repeatedly described by Micha Yosef Berdichevsky as "the rent in the heart."

The call for national renewal was, therefore, at least in part, a call for the Europeanization of Jewish culture. Hebrew writers recommended the introduction of European tastes, styles, views, and values into Hebrew literature and Jewish culture. They idealized the new generation of Jews as "European Hebrews" and engaged in vehement disputes concerning the ways of achieving a harmonious synthesis of the spirit of Judaism with the spirit of modern Western Europe.

It is against this background of acute awareness of cultural crisis, on the one hand, and an appeal for cultural renewal, on the other hand, that Nietzsche's extreme impact on Hebrew letters in the years 1885 to 1920 should be understood. No other single European thinker had the same influence on Hebrew literature during this period. Nietzsche's name, the titles of some of his works, and some of his most renowned battle cries ("the revaluation of all values," "the death of God," "beyond good and evil," and others) recur repeatedly in Hebrew essays and novels. The Nietzsche known to the authors of this time was, generally, the early and middle one: the author of *The Birth of Tragedy*, *On the Use and Abuse of History for Life*, and *Human, All Too Human*. Of his later works only *The Genealogy of Morals* and *Beyond Good and Evil* had some influence. *Zarathustra* influenced several poets (especially Yaacov Cohen and Zalman Schneor) with its style and Symbolism, but the ideas of eternal recurrence and the meaninglessness of history were either ignored or totally rejected by Hebrew writers.

Some Hebrew writers, notably Micha Yosef Berdichevsky, Yosef Hayyim Brenner, Hillel Zeitlin, and David Frishman, read Nietzsche himself in German. Others came to know his ideas through commentaries, especially those of George Brandes and George Simmel, whose German books on Nietzsche were translated into Russian a few years after their original publication.[1] It is difficult to assess how many of Nietzsche's own writings were known to most Hebrew authors and how much their knowledge of his ideas was derived from secondary sources.

Yet the Hebrew writers' focus on the early Nietzsche and on his commentators is understandable. Nietzsche appealed to them because of his trenchant criticism of exaggerated spirituality, asceticism, and all forms of faith in the supernatural. It was these that Hebrew secularists identified as the historical limitations of traditional Judaism, sometimes using Nietzsche's own words in describing "sins against life" and "against nature."

The poet Shaul Tchernichovsky (1885–1943), who along with Hayyim Nahman Bialik was considered one of the two greatest poets of the period, wrote an ode to Hellenism, "Facing the Statue of Apollo," which celebrates the vitality of Greek culture and protests the narrowness of Jewish religious life:

> I bow to life and courage and beauty;
> To all the precious things of which we were robbed
> By men degenerate, dessicated and hollow
> Rebels against life, from my rock and my redeemer
> God of gods, of the wonders of the desert,
> The god of those who stormed Canaan in conquest –
> They have tied him up with the straps of phylacteries . . .[2]

Tchernichovsky and another poet, Zalman Schneor (1886–1959), each wrote several series of poems imagining pagan rites in ancient Israel. These series comprise a considerable part of Schneor's and Tchernichovsky's poetic attempts to rewrite Jewish history.[3] The monotheistic prophets who are ranked so highly in almost all historical or philosophical writings on Judaism, who are usually viewed as the clearest expression of the Jewish spirit, are represented in these poems as censors and spiritual despots. Monotheistic faith is viewed as a repression of the vibrant Dionysian drives of the ancient Hebrews. At the same time the Biblical false prophets, worshipers of pagan deities, regarded by the entire Jewish tradition as the worst representatives of the deadly sin of idolatry, are presented as the authentic spokesmen of life and of life's most natural and healthiest drives.

Two oppositions, the demands of life/the yoke of tradition and nature/the book, had been familiar concepts to readers of Hebrew literature since the 1860s due to the mixed influence of *Haskala* (Enlightenment) and German Romanticism. The Jewish Enlightenment, in which many rabbis participated, spoke of the need for reforms in Judaism to reconcile *Halakha* (religious law) with modern realities in order to avoid a clash between religion and life. Nietzsche's influence radicalized these already existing conflicts to the point of an open rejection of the past. This rejection sometimes also implied a repudiation of the yoke of collective tradition in the name of the instinctual and cultural needs of the modern Jewish individual.

Earlier generations had used the opposition between life and the book to stress the need for *Halakhic* reform. They wished to achieve a compromise between the harsh demands of orthodox life and modernity. *Haskala* thinkers criticized frozen *Halakha* but never questioned the morality of religion itself. They tried to demonstrate, albeit naively, that no basic contradiction between the religion of reason and the essence of Judaism exists.

By the end of the nineteenth century, the younger generation felt differently. It recognized the incompatibility of a historic view of Judaism with a religious one. This sharpening of older oppositions was the focus of the work of Micha Yosef Berdichevsky, a novelist and critic, and of Ahad Ha'am, who, together with Berdichevsky, was one of the two most influential essayists of the period. Berdichevsky, perhaps the most profound thinker in modern Hebrew literature, titled a collection of his essays *Shinui Arakhim (A Revaluation of Values)*, an explicit allusion to Nietzsche's "revaluation of all values."[4] His views initiated an ongoing debate with Ahad Ha'am, joined by twenty other writers, which continued for nearly two decades.

The novelist and critic Yosef Hayyim Brenner (1881–1921), the most important commentator on the life of the Russian–Jewish intelligentsia at the beginning of the century, frequently referred to Nietzsche and his ideas, and not only in his critical work. In all Brenner's novels, characters discuss Nietzsche's ideas with varying degrees of originality and depth. Other novelists of the time had their characters discuss Nietzsche, but in Brenner's novels Nietzsche's ideas are one of the basic motifs. The novels depict fashionable Nietzscheans who boast of their amoral attitude to life and support their easy-going, often cynical, behavior towards women with quotations from Nietzsche.[5] Their depiction fuses a superficial Nietzschean pose with imitation of other literary characters such as Lermontov's Pechorin.

Other characters in Brenner's novels are described as profoundly influenced by Nietzsche's writings, as well as by Schopenhauer and Tolstoi. These characters often suffer from an inner struggle caused by the conflict between Nietzsche's ideas and the values by which they were educated. One of them, Uriel Davidovsky in the novel *Mi-Savid la-Nekudah* (*Around the Point*), who is obviously immersed in the study of *The Birth of Tragedy*, kills himself at the end of the novel. Davidovsky is modeled on Brenner's friend Sender Baum, leader of the Homel study group of young Jewish intellectuals, devoted to contemporary philosophers. Nietzsche's writings were the focus of their studies.

The Homel study group also included the Hebrew and Yiddish essayist Hillel Zeitlin (1877–1942), one of three Hebrew essayists whose work often refers explicitly to Nietzsche's personality and ideas. The second, Aharon David Gordon (1856–1922), was the spiritual teacher and mentor of the Second Aliyah, when between 1903 and 1914 hundreds of Jewish youths left their homes and occupations in Eastern Europe and journeyed to Palestine to devote themselves to the cultivation of the land. The third was David Frishman (1859–1922), the best-known Hebrew literary critic and editor of his time.

The works of these essayists exemplified one typical attitude towards Nietzsche in modern Hebrew literature. All three regarded Nietzsche himself with reverence. Zeitlin, who was the first Hebrew author to write a book-length essay on Nietzsche,[6] refers to his thought as the "inner holy experience of a great man;" Gordon speaks favorably about his "inner struggles," while Frishman admires his originality, his audacity, and his style.

All three, however, used Nietzsche's inspiration to arrive at conclusions which were very far from Nietzsche's own. Zeitlin's intellectual evolution is very similar to that of some Russian interpreters of Nietzsche, and he was influenced directly by at least one of them, Lev Shestov, whose work he knew very well. Zeitlin accepted Nietzsche's trenchant critique of idealism and utilitarianism as substitutes for lost religious faith. After a period of spiritual wandering Zeitlin returned to an austerely orthodox mode of life and became an active and popular religious revivalist in Poland until he was murdered by the Nazis in 1942.

Gordon, who lived in Palestine as a manual laborer from 1905 until his death in 1922, considered Nietzsche the most sincere European rebel against the emotional entropy of modern man and a severe critic of the subjugation of man's inner being to the cold pragmatic and commercial dictates of urban society. Gordon appealed to Jewish youth to follow his own example in leaving urban life for physical labor on the land in Palestine, to redeem both their own alienated humanity and the alienation of the whole Jewish nation. His appeal combined Tolstoian motifs with the economic teachings of Russian populists, seeing agriculture as the primary occupation and source of life. Gordon, who remained a traditional Jew to the end of his life, rejected Nietzsche's ideas almost totally, but he continued to use Nietzsche's personality to show both the need for and the possibility of spiritual renewal.

Frishman's central aim was to achieve national revival by opening the eyes and ears of the repressed Jewish soul to the beauties of art and imagination. Frishman was clearly influenced by Nietzsche's ideas on sickness, recovery, and the therapeutic value of artistic creativity. His views on style and the artistic personality were influenced by the same Nietzschean sources; his disdain for the spirit of objectivity in literary criticism derived from Nietzsche's writing style. Frishman appealed for criticism that did not shy away from polemics based on personal taste or subjective preferences. His own translation of *Zarathustra*, often quoted by Hebrew writers, was in a high Biblical style that unwittingly bordered on parody.[7]

By the second decade of this century a clear Nietzschean note could be heard in official and semi-official Zionist tracts and proclamations, as well as in poems, stories, and essays inspired by Zionism. All of them preached the need to create "a new Jew," "a new Hebrew," or a new human being "out of the Jew." Max Nordau spoke of a "Jewry of muscle;"[8] Hayyim Nahman Bialik's mythological poem "The Dead of the Desert" articulated what became the very popular Zionist slogan, "last of the enslaved / first to be free."[9]

The case of Bialik (1873–1934) is a very interesting one. He was torn by the contradictory appeals of what he called the "two magnets": the spiritual and historical depth of tradition on the one hand, and the spirit of modern Europe on the other. The lion was the most common symbol in his poetry, taking on a very high degree of complexity. It represented, with different and changing emphasis, natural and instinctual repressed drives (especially the sexual drive), unrestrained physical power, and even the non-Jewish world. In an early poem Bialik used the symbol to renounce what he understood (under the influence of his teacher Ahad Ha'am) as the spirit of Nietzscheanism.

> I'm stripped and vanquished by the enemy,
> And yet I save my God, and God saved me . .
> Than be with lions, with lambs I'd rather perish.
> Nor jaws nor claws have I to rend my prey;
> My strength is God, a God who lives for aye! . . .
> Thus lions' whelps with golden manes and bright
> My eyes beheld on reindeer's hillocks slain.
> All flesh is grass, its strength is withered,
> God's spirit blows upon it and it's dead.[10]

Yet in a longer and much more important later poem Bialik's attitude is more ambivalent. The dead of the desert (an allusion

to the generation of ancient Hebrews that did not reach the
land of Israel and was buried in the desert) are compared to
dormant lions. Their fierce power is hidden as long as their
eternal sleep is unbroken. Yet periodically their sleep *is* dis-
turbed. The poem describes one such episode of rebellion
against heaven. The dead of the desert declare:

> We are the brave!
> Last of the enslaved!
> First to be free!
> With our own strong hand,
> Our hand alone,
> We tore from our necks
> The heavy yoke.
> Raised our heads to the skies,
> Narrowed them with our eyes.
> Renegades of the waste,
> We called barrenness mother.
> On the topmost crags,
> Among leveling clouds,
> We drank from the fount
> Of the eagle's freedom
> And who shall command us?
> To arms, comrades!
> Seize sword and lance,
> Spear and javelin – advance!
> Heaven's rage defy
> And in storm reply.
> Since God denies us,
> His ark refused us,
> We will ascend alone.[11]

The rebellion fails and the dead of the desert go back to their
former state. Various interpretations were given to this enig-
matic poem. The rebels against heaven were seen as secular
Zionists, as repressed anti-cultural instincts, or as modern
atheists in general. Some critics noticed Nietzschean symbols
and expressions. Very clearly the poem manifests a basic ambivalence towards the rebellion and the rebels. Yet it was the
linguistic formulae Bialik used in the episode and not the sad
fate of the rebels that penetrated Zionist education.

Hebrew writers praised the virility and valor of the fighting man, and recommended these qualities as virtues for the new Hebrew. The very appeal of the epithet "Hebrew" in contrast to "Jew" signified a conception of the Diaspora period as decadent in comparison to the virile and brave Biblical period. Several Nietzschean polarities (denial/affirmation of life, sickness/health) were employed to proclaim a new era that would witness the dominance of the new Jewish values and virtues and the emergence of a new Hebrew man.

At the same time, among some of the more thoughtful writers, an ambivalence towards Nietzsche emerged. The philosopher of *amor fati* and the eternal recurrence was much less attractive to Hebrew authors than the critic of ascetic ideals who opposed the repression of sensuality and the denial of life.

When the poet Yaacov Cohen, a militant Hebraist and Zionist, used the metaphors and phraseology of Frishman's translation of *Zarathustra* to predict the coming of a new heroic generation, the novelist and critic Brenner responded sarcastically. He asked:

Is it indeed with this pathetic weapon, some misquoted phrases of Zarathustra, on marching to the future, that you few and proud ones are going to conquer the future ... create the Hebrew revolution, destroy the spirit of the Diaspora and everything derived from it?[12]

Brenner's acute awareness of the more profound and problematic Nietzsche is further evident in his response to the poet Schneor, who had written a long poem in praise of the glories of war, mocking the prophetic apotheosis of peace. Brenner, after equating Schneor with a servant girl enjoying herself while pursuing a battalion of soldiers on their way to their deaths, also calls him "a militarist journalist who saw the back of Nietzsche but did not see his face."[13]

Perhaps the best way to understand both the enormous importance of the discovery of Nietzsche for modern Hebrew literature and the inability of his most ardent admirers to adopt a full Nietzschean attitude towards the problems they faced is through analysis of the thought of Micha Yosef Berdichevsky (1865–1921). Within the confines of this essay we can do no more than follow the main outline of his thought and the main counter-argument raised against him by Ahad Ha'am (the pen-name of Asher Ginsburg). The original polemic took place between 1896 and 1910. After the deaths of these two leaders of the Hebrew literary intelligentsia (Ahad Ha'am's in Tel Aviv; Berdichevsky's in Germany), their followers continued the dispute. In fact, its echoes are still heard in the Jewish intellectual world.

During the last decade of the nineteenth century many of Berdichevsky's essays used slogans and long quotations from Nietzsche's writings.[14] "To construct one temple another must be destroyed" is quoted at the beginning of a collection of his essays, and he quotes Nietzsche's discussions of the priests' forgery of Jewish history (paragraphs 25–26 of the *Antichrist*) almost fully on two separate occasions.[15] Berdichevsky used Nietzsche's ideas on *The Use and Abuse of History for Life* to warn his readers against the paralyzing power of the Jewish past, insisting on the absolute right of every modern Jew to revalue Jewish tradition from the standpoint of his own cultural needs. Berdichevsky claimed that "the yoke of the book" maimed the Jew. By "the book" he meant the whole edifice of legal literature from the Bible through the Mishnah, Talmud, and all later layers of exegetical literature heaped one on top of the other. In Berdichevsky's eyes this structure blocked Jews from direct contact with the nature around them as well as with the natural in themselves. In his view Jewish culture had been frozen around the book. It could not evolve because it failed to acknowledge the creative powers of negation, rejection, free selection, and innovation. Jewish culture could accept new ideas only when they were presented as interpretations of old and established ones.

Berdichevsky's appeal for renewal was a double protest. First, it was a protest against the subjugation of the present to the past; second, it was a protest against the sacrifice of the individual and his needs to the collective spirit. Berdichevsky had no fear that the liberation of the individual would end in the annihilation of the Jewish collectivity. On the contrary, he insisted that assimilation was so attractive to many Jews only because of the narrowness and monolithic character of Jewish culture.

Ahad Ha'am, Berdichevsky's opponent, viewed lack of cultural unity as a danger to national survival during an era of rapid secularization. As a remedy for the inner pluralism of modern Judaism, Ahad Ha'am attempted to construct a minimal national philosophy acceptable to both religious and secular Jews. His cultural Zionism derived from the same source. He saw in the creation of a cultural center in the land of Israel a unifying force which would counter the factors of dispersion.

Berdichevsky's stand was quite the opposite: only pluralism and even cultural individualism, meaning the free introduction into Jewish culture of any European idea, style, value, or taste which modern Jews found attractive, could save Jewish culture from inner stagnation and prevent the desertion of the finest Jewish youth. Berdichevsky claimed that only when individual Jews were fully Europeanized could they possibly create, together with their co-nationals, a veritable modern Jewish, or rather Hebrew, nation. The Zionist idea, therefore, appealed to Berdichevsky on cultural grounds. He thought that the conditions of exile were responsible for the overly spiritual and repressive character of orthodox Jewish culture. In the long run only the normalization of the Jews, which would come with political-territorial existence, would permit the renewal of Jewish culture.

It is possible to identify, even from this very schematic presentation, those areas of Nietzsche's thought which were of great importance to Berdichevsky. His choice of *Shinui Arakhim* ("A Revaluation of Values") as the name of his most important collection of essays is especially significant. Berdichevsky did not simply condemn the attenuation and stifling of natural tendencies by repressive morality. He defined new values, and in Nietzschean language praised the need of the strong individual to wage war, castigating the spirit that at any price seeks peace and compromise with itself, its master, or its neighbor.[16]

Berdichevsky viewed the era of exile as the era of Jewish decline. He called the spirit of meekness dominant among Jews during this era "the spirit of Yavneh."[17] Orthodox tradition praised the first-century scholar Yohanan ben-Zakkai for accepting political domination as the price of religious autonomy centered on Yavneh, while denouncing the rebels who had fought against Rome for Jewish political sovereignty. Modern historians like Graetz regarded Yavneh as a demonstration of the idealistic nature of Judaism which prefers spiritual values and inner freedom to political freedom. Berdichevsky was the first Jewish thinker to condemn the spirit of Yavneh and to praise unambiguously the courage and determination of the rebels. Many followed him in this dramatic act of revaluation. Indeed, this constituted Berdichevsky's single most significant contribution to the new monumental histories of the Jews written by Zionist historians, which transformed the anti-Roman rebels into inspiring monuments of Jewish courage.

For Berdichevsky, however, this specific revaluation was just one detail in the total genealogy of traditional Jewish religious culture which he was engaged in describing. He considered the monolithic past ascribed to this culture to be a façade created by rabbinic interpretive narration. Rabbinic authority had done its best to conceal not only antinomian tendencies but also all other non-Halachic vital trends, whether mystical or philosophical.

Following the Spanish expulsion of the Jews in 1492, Berdichevsky believed, unity and conformity were indeed genuine, but were the result of repression. Thus the finest Jewish minds and creators, people like Spinoza or Heine, were compelled by the narrowness of ghetto culture to leave the Jewish people. According to Berdichevsky, it was rabbinic authority that had succeeded in imposing a unified structure on Jewish history and on the psychology of the individual Jew. Therefore, the liberation of the spirit of individualism through free contact with Europe was a precondition for national cultural renewal.

In contrast, the cultural Zionist Ahad Ha'am treated the Yavneh story favorably. He regarded Yohanan's request as a manifestation of the cunning of the Jewish instinct for survival. The edifice of Talmudic culture constructed by rabbinic sages sustained Jewish national existence after the loss of political freedom in 70 AD and the exile that followed it.

Ahad Ha'am was well aware of Nietzsche's attractiveness to the younger generation of writers and readers. He was sensitive to the powerful note of liberation that Berdichevsky had drawn from Nietzsche's revaluation of all values and transferred to the discussion of the situation of the modern Jew. Yet his own idea of the way in which a modernization of Jewish culture should be achieved was diametrically opposed to that of Berdichevsky. Ahad Ha'am believed in evolutionary processes and in the organic, unique character of all national cultures. He advocated openness to Europe, but predicted that the spirit of the nation would select from European (i.e. universal) culture only those elements which it could assimilate to its own patterns.

Influenced by the philosophy of language of the British Empiricists (especially John Stuart Mill), Ahad Ha'am believed that the content of human experience (that is, the prelinguistic images or ideas that words denote) is universal. Yet its form, the expression of this experience in specific languages, is shaped by the history of specific nations, and so is national. Thus to him Europeanization meant absorbing those European ideas and values which could assume a specifically Jewish form.

Ahad Ha'am distinguished between the universal content of Nietzsche's philosophy and its peculiar historical and national form. He claimed that the universal core of Nietzsche's thought was the idea that human progress should be measured by the successes of great individuals, rather than by the conditions and status of the multitude. He believed that this idea could be absorbed within Jewish culture if the individual achievements occurred in pursuit of truth and justice.[18] Jews, he thought, would always ascribe the highest value to rational cognition and strict morality rather than to artistic or physical excellence.

It is clear that Ahad Ha'am's conception of national culture cannot be contained within the opposition of universal content and national form. It is not the form of Nietzsche's thought but some of his most central ideas which Ahad Ha'am could not tolerate. Yet the very fact that he chose Nietzsche for a demonstration of his peculiar view of cultural assimilation points to the unique role of Nietzsche for the Hebrew writers of the Russian Empire.

Both the teacher Ahad Ha'am and disciple Bialik received their images of Nietzsche from secondary sources. In contrast, Berdichevsky and Brenner read Nietzsche directly and knew him better. Thus they never considered him a simple-minded enemy of the spirit and advocate of brute force. Brenner radicalized Berdichevsky's and Nietzsche's genealogical suspicion of traditional Jewish values when he advocated armed self-defense in Palestine in 1920 and quarreled with a Tolstoian pioneer who proposed a non-violent response to the Arab raids of the time: "Of course there is a level which is *above* militarism. But there is also a level which is *below* militarism."[19] Thus Brenner sarcastically asserted that Jews' well-known hatred of bloodshed might derive from customary cowardice rather than from moral choice. But at the same time he condemned sheer militarism with a positive gesture towards a level of culture which is above it, where armed force may no longer be necessary.

Berdichevsky and Brenner articulated clearly, albeit often in highly provocative militant language, the suspicion shared by other modern Jews that the origin of the traditional Jewish denigration of physical labor and military values was actual impotence in both spheres. They charged Jewish ideologists with making powerlessness a virtue. Berdichevsky and Brenner used Nietzschean language to urge Jews to become once again a national entity capable both of doing good and committing evil.[20]

It is here that the strength of Nietzsche's impact is felt not only in Hebrew literature but also in Zionism and modern Jewish history generally. Yet it is at this same point that we witness the limits of Nietzsche's influence. Both Berdichevsky and Brenner believed deeply that a modern Jewish nation, once created, would display in its political behavior and general culture certain qualities traditionally ascribed to the Jewish spirit. Neither of them could accept Nietzsche's revaluation of all values as an answer to ultimate moral problems.

This rejection of Nietzsche's positive philosophy is easy to understand when we recall that Nietzsche's revolutionary values were meant to guide the lives of lonely philosophers who raise themselves above general needs and concerns. The *fin-de-siècle* Hebrew writers, however, were seeking new values for their entire public, values intended to edify and enlighten the younger generation of a whole nation. They could hardly treat this public derisively as the blind, ignorant masses or the herd.

Therefore, Nietzsche's critique of ascetic ideals, his opposition to the repression of sensuality and to the denial of life could attract them, while with the exception of Brenner they were not engaged by his celebration of fatalism. The Superman's triumph over the purposelessness of being and eternal recurrence of the same in the spirit of *amor fati* could hardly impress a generation which had high expectations for the near future, not only for themselves but for the entire Jewish people.

For the same reason, Nietzsche's general influence tended to merge with romantic appeals to nature and naturalness which entered Hebrew literature at more or less the same time. In Hebrew poetry, for example, it is particularly difficult to separate Nietzsche's influence from that of Schelling's nature-mysticism. The new Hebrew man envisioned by Jewish critics and writers, and later by political Zionists, was Nietzschean to the extent that courage, physical well-being, and virility were valued and all forms of otherworldliness rejected. Yet the new Hebrew was far from being a Nietzschean Superman. Determined to believe in progress, he did not disdain the masses or cultivate aristocratic tastes and styles, nor did he accept the meaninglessness of all human history with stoic magnanimity.

Berdichevsky's work is full of this mingling of Nietzschean and Romantic motifs. Despite the fact that he protested against the "yoke of [religious] tradition" and recommended that all past values be reassessed in light of their relevance to the "needs of life and the present," Berdichevsky's approach is far from fully Nietzschean. He was not content with Nietzsche's description of Jewish history. Berdichevsky did agree with Nietzsche that the turn Jewish religion had taken, first with the prophets and later with the destruction of the Second Commonwealth, from a national God of war and conquest, to a moral and personal God, signified a decline in Jewish vitality. But in very un-Nietzschean fashion Berdichevsky believed that the earlier tribal God also indicated a decline in vital power when compared to the ancient gods of the valleys and of the mountains who were worshiped by the Israelites before the revelation at Mount Sinai. This apotheosis of precultural and extra-cultural nature reflects the influence of Romantic ideas on Berdichevsky's thought. So too does his prediction that the soul of contemporary man will always be torn between the attractions of modernity and the charms of the past. In Berdichevsky's view there could never be a full and absolute overcoming of traditional values.

Berdichevsky's disciple Brenner was even more aware of the difficulties facing the modern Jew who wished both to absorb as much as he could of Nietzsche's moral heritage, and to participate in the national Jewish revival. Brenner demonstrated a profound understanding of the tragic aspects of Nietzsche's philosophy – perspectivism, cognitive and moral relativism, the fictionality of all ultimate interpretations of man's destiny – not shared by any other Jewish intellectual. Brenner fully accepted these aspects of modern philosophy. In one of his essays he called Nietzsche "the genius of Aryan culture."[21] He admired the daring way in which Nietzsche dealt with the death of God and his willingness to recognize its consistent and pitiless consequences.

Yet the manner in which Nietzschean themes are treated in some of Brenner's novels demonstrates a basic ambivalence towards them. At least four of his novels,[22] all of which are devoted to the depiction of the Russian–Jewish intelligentsia at the turn of the century, repeat the same pattern. The protagonist and his antagonist are attracted to the same woman. The hero, who is actually an anti-hero, lacks confidence in his power to attract the young heroine's attention. He suspects that his own attraction to her is not serious enough, and doubts whether his attitude to her will remain stable. Meanwhile the antagonist finds it easy to flirt with the heroine and steal her heart. The over-reflective and inhibited hero is obviously jealous of the other's success, especially of his spontaneity and almost absolute lack of reflection.

The protagonist conducts imaginary discussions in which the antagonist preaches to him about the right of strong natures, condemns his slave morality, and advocates uninhibited surrender to the demands of all ruling instincts. The protagonist responds to these claims in the same ideological language, recognizing the need to act according to dominating instincts. Yet for him the only candidate for domination is the moral instinct. There is no point in blaming the protagonist since both the strong and the weak characters have only partial views of reality. Each views life within the inherent limitations of his own perspective. Therefore neither can claim superiority for himself or for his values; each must accept his fate. The judgment of the strong is no more valid than that of the weak; in fact it may well be that the strong are only superficially stronger than others.[23] This paradoxical reversal of "strong" and "weak" marks Nietzsche's discussion of these terms as well, most notably in *The Genealogy of Morals*.

True, these characters preach vulgarized versions of Nietzsche. Theirs is the fashionably shallow Nietzscheanism of their day. But it is clear that in rejecting the imaginary preaching of the strong, Brenner's Jewish anti-hero defines the limits of the Nietzschean elements which he can absorb. The conflict can easily be interpreted as a conflict of cultural ideals: the protagonist is always a prototypical Jew (e.g. in the novel *Mi-Saviv la-Nekudah* ["Around the Point"] he is named Jacob, the son of Isaac Abramsohn) while the antagonist is an assimilated Jew or a Russian.

The fact that the Nietzschean characters are always assimilationists is very significant. They embody Brenner's view that an extreme individualist, who is seriously interested only in the cultivation of his own personality and is totally pessimistic or nihilistic concerning the improvement of the fate of the masses, will assimilate. Why should such a person remain loyal to his sick and poor brothers? What positive value can he attach to Jewish solidarity? In the final analysis Brenner apparently joins Ahad Ha'am in the belief that no matter how much a Jew may admire Nietzsche, ultimately he can not consider Nietzsche's new values as those by which he actually lives.

The most important factor to bear in mind when discussing Nietzsche's impact is that the writers discussed above indeed experimented with a good number of his ideas – ideas concerning the origins and function of ascetic ideals, the Dionysian origin of tragedy, the illusionistic nature of Apollonian art, the instinctual anarchy of modern sensibility, and the consequent need for a style, form, and ruling instinct. These ideas helped the writers develop a better understanding of themselves and of their art. It also helped them in shaping a critical relation to Jewish tradition.

Nietzsche sharpened these writers' sensitivity to the miserable external situation of the Jew and to the tension between the theoretically lofty Jewish pretense – the mission to the nations – and the reality of Jewish existence. His influence pressed them to destroy the pretense and to seek to reconstruct actual existence. They regarded such a reconstruction as the final test of whether or not vital and creative forces survived in the Jewish people.

Nietzsche's slogans and images perfectly fit their desire for a cultural revolution that would lead to national renovation. Yet the same Hebrew writers could not subscribe to his entire outlook. It was his compelling personality that occupied their minds much more than the systematic inner connection of his ideas. Concerning issues that went further than the general feeling of the necessity for cultural renewal, Nietzsche's greatest impact was in reinforcing an acute awareness of a profound crisis – the atrophying of all traditional values and aspirations – rather than in offering an answer to the problem.

NOTES

1 Concerning the speed with which Brandes and Simmel's works on Nietzsche were translated into Russian, see *International Nietzsche Bibliography*, comp. and ed. Herbert William Reichert and Karl Schlechta (Chapel Hill, North Carolina, [1960]).

2 Shaul Tchernichovsky, *Shaul Tshernichovsky*, trans. David Kuselewitz (Tel Aviv, 1978), p. 91. The lines quoted are the final part of the poem. The Hebrew version is "Le-Nokhah Pessel Apollo,"

Mivhar Shaul Tshernikhovski ("Selected Works of Shaul Tcherni-chovsky", Tel Aviv), p. 167.

3 Zalman Schneor published a volume of poetry called *Luhot Genuzim* ("Hidden Tablets," Tel Aviv, 1952). The book is devoted to fictional pagan poems purportedly written by the ancient Hebrews and censored by the priests and the prophets. Among his "pagan poems" Tchernichovsky wrote a sonnet cycle called *La-Shemesh* ("To the Sun"). It combines motifs from Nietzsche and Schelling. The cycle is translated in Shaul Tchernichovsky, *Shaul Tshernichovsky*, pp. 9–23.

4 Micha Yosef Berdichevsky, "Shinui Arakhim," *Collected Essays of Berdichevsky* (Tel Aviv, 1960). The essays in this collection were written between 1890 and 1896.

5 This is true for at least four of Brenner's novels: *Ba-Horef* ("In Winter," 1902); *Mi-Saviv la-Nekudah* ("Around the Point," 1905); *Bein Mayim le-Mayim* ("Between Water and Water," 1909); and *Shekhol ve-Khishalon* ("Breakdown and Bereavement," 1918). Only the last novel has been translated into English (see note 23 below).

6 The essay was first published in *Ha-Zman* ("Time"), a Hebrew monthly "for life, literature, art, and science," no. 1 (Vilna, 1905). Zeitlin opens with the declaration that Nietzsche's significance derives in the main not from his philosophical "findings" but from the passion with which he sought truth. This assessment was quite common. Another Hebrew critic, Reuven Brainin, praises Nietzsche's writings for the "confessions of a soul" which they present, in *Sifrut* ("Literature," Warsaw, 1908).

7 David Frishman, *Targumim* ("Translations," Israel, n.d.). The translation was first published in Warsaw in 1910. The Biblical, sometimes prophetic, style fits many parts of Nietzsche's *Zarathustra* well; yet there are certain parts where a parodic effect is created. For example, because of its style and despite its content, the section on the compassionate (in part II of *Zarathustra*) sounds as if it were one of the sermons of Jesus.

8 Max Nordau, "Muskeljudentum," *Jüdische Turnzeitung*, June, 1903; English translation in *The Jew in the Modern World*, ed. Paul Mendes-Flohr and Jehuda Reinharz (London, 1980), pp. 434–35.

9 Hayyim Nahman Bialik, *Selected Poems*, bilingual edn., trans. Ruth Nevo (n.p., 1981), p. 113.

10 Bialik, "Al-Saf Beit ha-Midrash" ("On the Threshold of the House of Prayer," *Selected Poems of Hayyim Nahman Bialik*, trans. and ed. Israel Efros (New York, 1965).

11 Bialik, *Selected Poems*, p. 113.

12 Yosef Hayyim Brenner, *Ktavim* ("Writings," Tel Aviv, 1985), III, p. 795.

13 Ibid., IV, p. 1646. The essay was written in 1920.

14 Berdichevsky, "Old Age and Youth," *Collected Essays* (Tel Aviv, 1960), p. 32. The essay was written in 1896.

15 Ibid., p. 48.

16 Ibid., p. 20: "We were told: a man should love peace and always seek peace. He should be at peace with heaven and with other people ... and I tell you: you should never go half way. Never compromise ... a man should remove from his way every obstacle and every inhibition."

17 The "spirit of Yavneh" is a reference to a Talmudic legend about the beginning of Rabbinic Judaism. Yavneh was one of several academies where the authors of the Mishnah and later of the Talmud occupied themselves in the exegesis of Biblical law. Rabbi Yohanan ben-Zakkai, the leading figure among the sages who opposed the anti-Roman rebellion of the first century, was to be granted one request by the emperor Vespasian following the destruction of the Second Temple. Yohanan's request, "Give me Yavneh and its sages," became the symbol of Jewish willingness to accept political slavery as long as spiritual and religious autonomy were guaranteed.

18 Ahad Ha'am [Asher Ginsburg], "The Revaluation of Values," *Selected Essays*, trans., ed., and introd. Leon Simon (Philadelphia, 1962), pp. 217–41. The essay was written in 1898. The Hebrew version is in Ahad Ha'am, *Collected Works* (Tel Aviv, 1959), pp. 154–58.

19 Brenner, *Ktavim*, IV, p. 1639. The essay was written in 1920, when the Jewish pioneers were considering the organization of national professional defense forces for the first time.

20 Berdichevsky had various formulae to express this idea. One of them was: "We are told to be a holy nation ... but a beaten, tortured, persecuted people cannot be holy ... A holy nation must also be an existing nation," *Collected Essays*, p. 21.

21 Brenner, *Ktavim*, III, p. 657. The essay was written in 1912.

22 See note 5 above.

23 See Brenner, *Breakdown and Bereavement*, trans. Hillel Halkin (Philadelphia, 1971), pp. 159–65. The novel was written between 1914 and 1916, and was published in 1918.

Index

414

CAMBRIDGE STUDIES IN RUSSIAN LITERATURE

General Editor MALCOLM JONES

Editorial Board: ANTHONY CROSS, CARYL EMERSON,
HENRY GIFFORD, BARBARA HELDT, G. S. SMITH,
VICTOR TERRAS

Dostoyevsky and the Process of Literary Creation
JACQUES CATTEAU
translated by Audrey Littlewood

The Poetic Imagination of Vyacheslav Ivanov
PAMELA DAVIDSON

Joseph Brodsky
VALENTINA POLUKHINA

Petrushka – The Russian Carnival Puppet Theatre
CATRIONA KELLY

Turgenev
FRANK FRIEDEBERG SEELEY

From the Idyll to the Novel: Karamzin's Sentimentalist Prose
GITTA HAMMARBERG

The Brothers Karamazov *and the Poetics of Memory*
DIANE OENNING THOMPSON

Andrei Platonov
THOMAS SEIFRED

Nabokov's Early Fiction
JULIAN W. CONNOLLY

Iurii Trifonov
DAVID GILLESPIE

Mikhail Zoshchenko
LINDA HART SCATTON

Andrei Bitov
ELLEN CHANCES

Nikolai Zabolotsky
DARRA GOLDSTEIN